TINÁ7 CHT
TI TEMÍXW

A Walk Through the History of the Squamish People

TINÁ7 CHT TI TEMÍXW

WE COME FROM THIS LAND

THE SQUAMISH NATION

PAGE TWO

CONTENTS

FOREWORD

ONCE, WHEN my granddaughter came home from high school some time ago—maybe fifteen years ago or so—she was kind of sad. We were having a barbecue. I asked her what the problem was.

"You know, Papa," she said, "we're learning history and social studies in school."

"Yes?"

"Well, why aren't they talking about our history? Where are our stories? Where's our history?"

And at that point, I didn't have an answer.

I thought about it. I was on council at the time, and we had done research into our history. I said, "A whole lot of research has been done, and it's probably sitting on a shelf somewhere in our offices, gathering dust."

So, I thought about a book that could begin to share some of this history. It is a way to teach the people who we are and where we come from—which should never be forgotten. All our successes come back to who we are and where we come from. We need to be able to teach our children and grandchildren. These stories come from our hearts, our mouths, and our minds. We must always remember the old people, and we must tell the young people who they are. A lot of our own people, young and old, still don't know our history because of residential schools.

We did research when we filed a court action against the federal government in the early 1970s for the return of the Kitsilano reserve. I was involved right from the outset. About ten years before I was elected to council in 1965, the law had been changed to allow us to hire a lawyer or advisor for the Squamish (for decades, First Nations were not allowed legal representation). So, we hired a lawyer, Paul Reecke. Paul called a meeting at his place in West Vancouver just after our election—so, Joe Mathias, Glen Newman . . . and there were about five of us who were new in the council. We sat down, and Louis Miranda was there. We sat and talked. Louis talked about old times, a lot of things. Louis had lived at Seṅáḵw, and he said there was a fishy deal that took place. It sounded like the land had been wrongfully taken.

We asked Paul, "Can you have a look at this?" So, he did. He came back to us in a few weeks and he said, "I think there's something here."

Paul suggested a lawsuit against the federal government, so we had an assembly with the people. Of course, their question were: What chance have we got? How much is this going to cost? We said, "Well, it is going to cost a good sum of money."

I was sitting there thinking, Here is Squamish, little Squamish, with one lawyer, and the justice department has six hundred lawyers in Ottawa. We'll be fighting them with this one lawyer against all the resources they have. I thought, That's pretty scary.

But our people said, "If it's an injustice, let's do it." We took the case to court and won.

That's just one of our stories. For every village, there's a story; there's a history.

When we talk about history, to me, it means: What's the *name* of this place? I say "Eslha7áṅ" and Pierre Scott comes to mind. I say "Ch'ích'elxwi7ḵw," and the first thing that comes to my mind is Big George; he was the *siỷáṁ* (headman) there. You say a place name—families come from that village. They now say "Vancouver." Our people say "Ḵ'emḵ'emel̓áỷ," a place where there are a lot of big-leaf maple trees.

It's important we look at the villages, and from there comes the history, the stories. There are so many different families who will tell the stories. Our people understand these stories because they bring them to a place—"This is where my great-great-great-grandfather was. That's where I come from. That's where my origin is—*here*."

I have wondered about putting our history in a book. We can write our history, we can put it in good words, but it's tough. We can't fit all our history and teachings in a book. We need a place where we can sit, and the oral history has to come up. You have to get up and talk to others. The way I learned. When you walk into a longhouse, there are no books, no tape recorders. They tell you the stories. There is so much to talk about. How can we tell a ten-thousand-year story?

But I hope this book can offer a snapshot of our history and encourage young ones to ask questions. Younger generations—they're not asking the questions. When young people sit and listen to the old people when they talk, that's where we learn. The stories, the history: we have to do it right. We need an education that teaches storytellers. We need urgency now to sit down and plan the best way to do this and get these stories out to our people. I'd like to see a program designed to give our kids scholarships to study the history of Squamish.

Not long ago, we had no running water and no electricity, and sanitary conditions were not good. Our people were very poor; jobs were scarce. We didn't have money to build houses; we didn't have money for education. The changes we've made over the years—how did we do it? That's a story.

From my first days on council in 1965 to my first budget, the chair of council at that time was an Indian agent. Here comes this white man walking by—the coat on, and the briefcase. And I said, "Who is that white man?!"

He took the meeting minutes. He did everything. The first budget I saw at that time was $200,000, and our revenue was in Ottawa. It's gone from that to over $100 million. How did that happen? That in itself is a story.

It took us a while to get here. In my lifetime, it took fifty years of planning. It wasn't done overnight. We battled the federal government, the province, and the cities. That's another story. How did we get control of social development from Indian Affairs? That's a huge story. The sports stories—the lacrosse, the canoe—all of these parts of our history... We live in one of the largest cities in Canada: Vancouver. We survived. We're still here. It's been difficult.

There's so much to tell.

We were at the Elders Luncheon recently, and all the tots came from the Little Ones School. They came marching in—it was just heartwarming. The little ones. I talked to my wife, Andrea; I said, "Remember the marching?" She looked at me. "St. Paul's school," she said. When we were in residential school, we marched everywhere, and we sang. Do you realize we were singing those hymns in Latin?

These little ones at the Elders Luncheon—right away, they say hello in Squamish. They sang and danced. Oh, it felt so good to hear.

I was that age when I first sang for my mom. When they passed the law outlawing potlatching, you couldn't use the longhouse. No more potlatch. You couldn't gather to sing. It stopped. We had to get it going again. My grandfather built a house in West Vancouver, where Park Royal is today. He called it a church, and he put up a cross. My grandfather said, "You fool them." That's where people used to gather to put their paint on and practise the ways of the *tl'áḵtax̱anaw̓txw*, the longhouse. The ban was in effect until 1951. That's how we got along with it. The blanket is sacred to us, always wrapping people. The old people hid the blanket. When the law changed, we picked up the blanket and shook it off. It's still with us. We still have the song. We still have the dance. They shake the blanket—it's still here yet. I teach my children as much as I can, and they're listening. They all wanted to go in the longhouse, because the teachings in there are life. It's life, from birth to death, the celebrations in the longhouse.

The little tots now—they'll learn them songs and dances. They also need the history of the Squamish. We've been through a lot, and there's a lot more to do. We've got to try to get the old stories to the young people.

In the traditions of our people, they were so helpful with each other. Any time there was illness in the community, they all helped with medicines. If any of the Elders needed some help, they all helped. If they wanted to talk, they'd bring some food and they'd sit at a table and talk, tell the stories. And the children would sit and listen. They listened to the names, and the people; they remembered the faces.

That's the way of our people. It has changed so much. In my lifetime, we never knew this stuff. The Squamish survived all of the residential schools, all of the rules and regulations and the Indian Act and city regulations and everything against our people. But we survived and we're moving that narrative. That's one of our stories.

Over time they've called us Indians, Aboriginals, First Nations, Indigenous. I tell them, "You don't call me First Nations. I'm not Indigenous. I'm *Squamish*. I'm Squamish."

This book is Squamish history.

PAÍTSMUK̲ (David Jacobs) · *Elder*

A NOTE ABOUT THE SḴWX̱WÚ7MESH SNÍCHIM

SḴWX̱WÚ7MESH SNÍCHIM (Squamish Language) words are included throughout this text. There are challenges to incorporating the Sḵwx̱wú7mesh Sníchim and English into the same book. Here are some important notes to keep in mind.

You will see some instances of incorrect spellings in this book, within direct quotes from historical documents. Many historical texts were written before our language had a written alphabet—it existed only as an oral language. People were trying to capture sounds that could not be expressed with the Roman alphabet. When quoting a historical text, we have often left the spellings how they originally appeared.

This book relies on spelling and grammar recorded in the *Sḵwx̱wú7-mesh Sníchim–Xwelíten Sníchim Sḵexwts* (*Squamish–English Dictionary*) and was checked by fluent speakers.

A glossary at the end of the book includes people's names, place names, and words used in this book. We hope this book can be an exercise for language learners, to remember words and names that pop up again and again and practise saying them out loud.

When someone has passed on, typically it is protocol to add "-t" to the end of their name. However, to avoid confusion of spelling and

pronunciation, we have not included the "-t" in the names of people who have passed on in this text.

A full pronunciation guide is available in the *Sḵwx̱wú7mesh Sníchim–Xwelíten Sníchim Sḵexwts*. Some audio and video pronouncers are easy to find online as well. Simply search something like "how to say words Sḵwx̱wú7mesh Sníchim." Community members can access more resources through the Nation.

CHET WA WANÁXWSW̓IT TA SWA7ÁM̓CHT: WE ARE HONOURING OUR ANCESTORS

This book affirms what our leadership proclaimed to the Canadian federal government when they signed an amalgamation agreement in 1923:

Sḵwx̱wú7mesh chat. We are Squamish.

Prior to the 1923 declaration, several *úxwumixw*—a term that means "people," generally or collectively, and also refers to a community with groups of houses and inhabitants—all recognized themselves by a common identity with the name Sḵwx̱wú7mesh. The Amalgamation was our declaration that, after being organized incorrectly by the Canadian government, we were one whole Nation. This book is a celebration of our journey affirming our shared existence as one people.

Our people have done tremendous work to record, protect, and share stories of who we are. This book is a small look into some of those stories. It is the cumulation of generations of knowledge. The contributions go beyond who is named in this book. It's every person who passed on stories and teachings, saved photos, and held on to our language. Our ancestors and our people today, through their tireless efforts and fierce love, made this book possible. And this introductory book only scratches the surface of the Squamish Nation's deep history.

Tiná7 Cht Ti Temíxw—We Come From This Land shares some of the interviews, books, historical documents, academic studies, and oral histories we have available—some public, some rare. We hope the endnotes are a launching point for each person to find out more about the different places, people, and stories we introduce here.

The Squamish Nation, and every person who worked on this book, respects the pluralities of our histories. This book does not include every fact or story. It may include a version of a story that is different from the oral history another family carries. We wanted to bring together the resources available to us, but it is not the be-all and end-all. This book is intended to be an introduction to the many stories and multifaceted histories of our people—a beginning, not an end.

In our oral tradition, our people reference where our information is coming from in our stories—we share who told us the story and whether they witnessed it directly or heard it from someone else. This book continues that tradition. We reference a wide variety of materials, who told what story, and where the information came from. The goal is to gather some of the rich historical documents we have, for our young people to access, and for others outside our community to understand the depth of our history.

By sharing some of the collective knowledge of our people, we are practising our cultural values. We're excited by how it can contribute to our ongoing legacy of telling our own history in many ways.

This book includes only a small selection of our stories, most of which have already been publicly shared or recorded. You will notice quotes from several non-Squamish sources, a result of the colonialism we have experienced. Anthropologists have been among our people for almost two hundred years now. Remember, our ancestors told them what they know about our past. The lives of our ancestors educated them. Sometimes, the anthropologists misunderstood or misrepresented what our people shared. We include these resources to

share the work our own people did to speak to our culture—the voices that are now important parts of the public record of who we are today.

Let's talk about ourselves. Let's share the wealth of knowledge and history left to us for safekeeping by our ancestors to hand down to our descendants. Hopefully this small part, a beginning, will help us celebrate what we each hold in our hearts and minds from our own families today.

We acknowledge here the strength of our ancestors, who held on to our traditional knowledge of our history, lands, resources, and technology.

We thank all of those who worked to collect information that informs what is written here.

PART ONE

SḴWX̱WÚ7MESH CHAT: WE ARE SQUAMISH

"We have the same connection to the land our ancestors had, for the land has always provided for us whether it be physically or spiritually."

CHEPX̱ÍMIYA SIY̓ÁM̓ (CHIEF JANICE GEORGE)

WHEN THE *world was created, everything was in darkness. All the daylight was kept in one little box. That one box was hidden in Seagull's house, and Seagull kept it all for himself.*

Now Raven, who was Seagull's brother, thought this wasn't fair. It was so dark, and so cold, too, without any daylight. If only he could get that box. But how? Raven sat down and thought and thought. "Aha." He had it—a plan, a great plan.

That night, when the tide was low, Raven went down to the beach and picked up some sea urchins. The sea urchins had shells with little sharp spines all over them. After he had eaten these sea urchins, he quietly tiptoed to Seagull's house. Noiselessly, he spread the sharp, spiney shells all around the doorstep. Then he crept back to his house.

Next morning, Raven strolled over to see his younger brother, Seagull. Seagull was in bed. His feet were all swollen. Poor Seagull.

"Oh my, what has happened to you?" cried Raven.

"Did you gather some sea urchins last night?" asked Seagull.

"Why, yes, I did," replied Raven, looking surprised. "Why?"

"Well, I guess those children of yours went and dropped their shells all around my front steps. I stepped on them, and now look at my feet, just full of thorns!"

"Let me have a look," said Raven helpfully. "Put your feet up here." Seagull lifted his feet.

"Now, how do you expect me to see in this darkness? Open your Daylight Box a little, Seagull." Seagull opened his box a tiny, tiny bit. Raven had a knife and he kept jabbing Seagull with it... in the wrong place.

"ow! ow! ouch!" yelled Seagull.

"Well, if you gave us a little more light, I could see what I was doing," complained Raven. "Give me more light!"

Seagull opened the box a bit more. Raven kept on pricking and jabbing Seagull's feet with his knife.

"Oh please, Raven, leave my feet alone. You can't get the thorns out, you're killing me." Seagull brought the box closer.

Quick as lightning, Raven threw off the lid, and the daylight escaped, and spread all over the room.

Then outside it went, spreading its lovely warm glow wider and wider until daylight spread all over the whole world.

Seagull saw his beautiful daylight escaping him, and he began to cry and cry. And he is still crying for his daylight today. Just listen sometimes: you can hear him too.

That is how Sx̱áaltxw Siy̓ám̓, the late Chief Louis Miranda, told the story of Seagull, Raven, and the Daylight Box. It is just one among many versions that have been told and retold through generations of our people. This story, like many others involving Sḵew̓ḵ—the trickster character depicted as a Raven—are often told to our children to teach them about important morals and values in our culture.

We are Sḵwx̱wú7mesh. Our oral literature and archaeological sites demonstrate our relationship with the lands and waters going back more than twelve thousand years. We have thrived and struggled in the face of a changing world, through melting ice, through the wealth of the cedar forests around us, and the onset of colonization.

We are over 4,100 people and growing, living within Sḵwx̱wú7meshulh Aysáy̓ch—the territory belonging to the Sḵwx̱wú7mesh—and beyond. Our 6,732-square-kilometre territory encompasses the watersheds of the Squamish River, Mamquam River, and Howe Sound in the north, and English Bay, False Creek, and Burrard Inlet in the south. Our territory encompasses saltwater and rushing rivers, old-growth forests at valley bottoms, and alpine forests high above the ocean. Mist and rain often hang low over the mountains; the fresh smell of

Detail from X̲álek̲'/Sek̲'yú Siỷam̓'s (Chief Ian Campbell's) Creation painting *Temíxw*.

dew greets us in the morning as the mist kisses our skin. The waters of Burrard Inlet and Howe Sound glisten, illuminated by the sun.

We have changed with these lands as they have changed. We have lived through volcanic eruptions and shifting ice. We lived here before old-growth cedar grew tall. We have lived here through profound societal change. We continue to rely on *sts'úk̲w'i7* (salmon) and respect the bonds we hold with the other beings in our territory, such as southern resident orcas, seals, deer, and eagles.

You will hear variations of stories within our history, and among other Indigenous Peoples you will hear about similar events and supernatural beings, like Iṅinyáx̲a7n, the name of a large supernatural bird depicted as having horns and causing thunder when it flapped

its wings, and lightning when it opened and closed its eyes, otherwise known as the Thunderbird; Sínulhk̲ay̓, the name of an enormous supernatural double-headed snake that caused convulsions in humans when in close proximity; and X̲aays, the name of brothers who travelled throughout the world causing transformations and becoming known as the Transformers. This book only includes a small selection of our stories that have already been publicly shared and recorded, and represents only a small part of the knowledge and history from our ancestors.

Ancient stories and place names are integral to beginning to understand who the Sk̲wx̲wú7mesh are. To the Sk̲wx̲wú7mesh, "landscape is not only physical, but also very spiritual and tied to a long distant past," said Sk̲wx̲wú7mesh archaeologist Yumk̲s, who is also known as Dr. Rudy Reimer, echoing our Elders, who tell us that as they travelled the land, parents, grandparents, and other family members shared the knowledge and history of our people with the young ones, pointing out landscapes and landmarks where crucial events occurred.

FACING: **X̲álek̲'/Sek̲'yú Siy̓am̓ (Chief Ian Campbell) painted *Temíxw* in residency at the Squamish Nation's Language & Cultural Affairs Department.**

The ancient materials that Yumk̲s studies demonstrate our relationship to place, our historical use, our travel and trade, and our kinship ties. Most of us know of historically important sites like Nch'k̲ay̓—the largest peak in Sk̲wx̲wú7meshulh Aysáy̓ch, known in English as Mount Garibaldi, where Sk̲wx̲wú7mesh canoes tied up after Sk̲w'ats' (the Great Flood); Siy̓ám̓ Smánit—the large "Chief Mountain," a rock formation, where the two-headed serpent passed and left a mark across the stone, near St'á7mes (Stawamus); or Ch'ich'iyúy—the Sisters, also known as the Lions, seen so clearly from Vancouver and North Vancouver.

We begin by introducing our ancient relationship with these lands, and the associated technologies, cultural practices, and traditional knowledge that have evolved alongside our shifting landscape.

1

WA P'I7K̲SÍM̓CHT ITTI: WE BEGIN HERE

Our story ranges in time and place from the areas of Howe Sound, where we travelled to and from winter villages along the Squamish River. In the summer, Sk̲wx̲wú7mesh families from up along the Squamish Valley spent time in our Burrard Inlet villages and campsites, harvesting foods that were essential for our economy and winter food stores. Some of us likely spent about six months of the year on the inlet, from when the herring came in March to the late summer or early fall.

We regularly traded up Sx̲wáymelh (the Fraser River) and over to Vancouver Island. Distinct stone materials from our territory have been found around the Salish Sea and as far as Puget Sound and alpine areas in the Olympic Peninsula in Washington State.

Today, Sk̲wx̲wú7meshulh (Squamish's People) are represented by their government called Sk̲wx̲wú7mesh Úxwumixw (Squamish Nation), which is composed of the elected body, called the council, and the administration. Sk̲wx̲wú7mesh Úxwumixw is one of many Indigenous governments in Canada. The Sk̲wx̲wú7mesh Sníchim (Squamish Language) is one of over thirty First Nations languages in modern-day BC. Before Canadian Confederation, there were even more individual tribes and dialects across the province. Sḵwx̱wú7mesh relationships with friends and former enemies are long-standing and widespread throughout our history.

Prior to contact, the Sḵwx̱wú7mesh lived in numerous villages across a vast territory.

Our Territory

Sḵwx̱wú7meshulh Aysáy̓ch is the *temíxw* (lands), *x̱echx̱áchu7* (lakes), *swelwá7lt* (streams), *sh'ḵweń* (ocean), and *staḵw* (freshwater) within the territory historically used and occupied by the Sḵwx̱wú7mesh, as defined by where we exercised our rights, including rights to ownership of areas that were governed according to systems of Sḵwx̱wú7mesh rules, customs, and ways.

Territory can be understood as the area of land under the jurisdiction of our people, and an area where our people carry rights and responsibilities to protect and steward the land.

This Sḵwx̱wú7mesh territory follows the height of land around the entire watershed draining into Howe Sound, False Creek, English Bay, Burrard Inlet, and Indian Arm; south along the height of land between Coquitlam River and Brunette River to Fraser River; across to the south or left bank of the Fraser River and proceeding downstream; taking in the left bank of the main stream and north arm to the sea. Our territory includes all those intervening lands, islands, and waters back along the seashore to Roberts Creek on the Sunshine Coast, and the sea, reefs, flats, tidal lands, and islands adjacent to our territory on the mainland, and out to the centre of Georgia Strait.

Tim Moody, a Squamish person born in 1910 and who died in 1978, prepared a manuscript titled "Early Squamish Indian History Prior to and During Governor Seymour's Regime at New Westminster," dated November 7, 1956. In his manuscript, he wrote: "Members of the Squamish tribes held and camped in several communities from the head of what is now called Burrard Inlet, along both shores, at New Westminster and Kitsilano, along the length of both shores of what is now known as Howe Sound to the head and 30 or 40 miles up the valley from the head; these were the territories and encampments held by the Squamish; prior, of course, to the entry of the Europeans."

Senlháliya, who was known as Lizzie Joseph (née Baker), who was born at X̱wáy̓x̱way ("mask," also known as Lumbermen's Arch), described the territory in a 1971 exhibit at the Museum of Vancouver:

Nilh swa7s ta Sḵwx̱wú7mesh tíwa.
Eyḵs ta S7elḵsen, ta swa7s ta Sḵwx̱wú7mesh
Ta7ḵswit kwi tiná7 ta shíchem ayḵs ta Shísha7lh.
Nam̓ ta Schen̓ḵ,
Nilh swa7s ta Sḵwx̱wú7mesh ḵ'aymin.
Hawḵ wa mi iniwílhem Xwmetskw'iyam
Iy
Hawḵ wa mi iniwílhem íytsi Sḵwx̱wú7mesh
Wa swa7swit ḵ'aswit wan am kwis wes yelx̱lhálemwit
Nilh wa lh7tim̓áswit, syetsm íytsi kwekwin selsi7l.

This belongs to the Squamish
From here (North Vancouver) to Point Grey
Belonged to the Squamish
Up to this side of Sechelt to Gibsons Landing.
These are the campsites of the Squamish.
None of the Musqueam crossed over
And
None of the Sechelt crossed over into
The area belonging to the Squamish
They had their own places to go food gathering.
That's the way the old people of long ago described this.

These two accounts are like other descriptions provided by other Squamish people at the same time.

A territory could also be understood to contain some fluidity, as resources in areas could be shared with external groups of people. Some resources were watched over by certain people and could be accessed through protocol. Those knowledgeable of the lands and resources protected important food and other resources in this way. Indigenous Peoples would enter one another's territories through marriage and kinship ties, for ceremony and celebration, and through permissions granted. Many villages and harvesting areas were occupied by different families from various areas for indefinite periods of time, so the dominant population may have fluctuated. Families were also likely to move between villages several times in their lives, perhaps because a village site had been washed away or an Elder moved to live with family at another village.

Point Grey, and generally the western end of the peninsula that terminates at Point Grey, was documented by multiple Squamish people by the names Elksn or S7elḵsn. X̱ats'alánexw Siy̓ám̓ (Chief August Jack Khatsahlano), Tim Moody, Sx̱áaltxw Siy̓ám̓ (Chief Louis Miranda), and Frank Charlie from Musqueam reported that Squamish came to the area in the summer and stayed there for several months, drying smelt they caught between Point Grey and False Creek. Several Squamish like Sx̱áaltxw Siy̓ám̓, Buffalo Mathias, Ted Band, and S7ápeleḵ Siy̓ám̓ (Chief Joe Capilano) referred to Point Grey as a "boundary" between Squamish and Musqueam territory. Jimmy Frank told a story of how the X̱aays (Transformer brothers) trained for power and started to enter Burrard Inlet on their journey through Squamish territory. In Sx̱áaltxw Siy̓ám̓'s telling of the epic story of the Squamish warrior Xwepelḵínem, Squamish people camped at Elksn drying smelt were attacked by warriors from a northern tribe.

Anthropologists Randy Bouchard and Dorothy Kennedy wrote that through intermarriage with other language groups, a village "would not necessarily be composed solely of speakers representing one linguistic group."

Anthropologists classify the Sḵwx̱wú7mesh as "Coast Salish," which refers to a family of languages that likely shared a linguistic genealogy to a type of proto-Salish language. The Coast Salish are a grouping of Indigenous Peoples with language similarities in the area around the Salish Sea down to Puget Sound. Through intermarriage, trade, and cultural ties, we share some similarities in language and traditional traits as a long trail of connections past and present, but each People is distinct, with their own society different from those of their neighbours.

FACING: Map by X̱áleḵ'/Seḵ'yú Siy̓am̓ (Chief Ian Campbell), showing places of historical significance in Sḵwx̱wú7meshulh Aysáy̓ch.

Another thing Coast Salish Peoples shared were our homes. The longhouses that our extended families inhabited were portable—people could take them apart and transport the large planks to rebuild at another site. Everything but the frames could be dismantled and would be lashed across the bows of two canoes for transport. We used mat shelters regularly, as evidenced by the place name Sosahlatch (place of woven mats), a well-known sheltered place on Gambier Island where these mats were left for the use of travellers. We used mat shelters as much lighter and smaller summer and emergency shelters.

Archaeological sites within our territory indicate at least ten thousand years of occupation in Howe Sound, and four thousand years of human occupation in Burrard Inlet. X̱ats'alánexw Siy̓ám̓ said the Sḵwx̱wú7mesh began to settle in permanent villages around Burrard Inlet and English Bay before white people arrived. With colonization and the wage economy, permanent settlement in the Burrard Inlet increased in the 1800s.

In Howe Sound, the Sḵwx̱wú7mesh could hunt marine life such as seals and sea lions, along with land animals such as deer and mountain goat, birds and small game. Burrard Inlet was rich with marine life including clams, mussels, and fish like sturgeon, eulachon, and herring. Squamish harvested the plentiful elk at Elksn and *stséḵi7* (sockeye salmon) was sourced from Sx̱wáymelh.

According to anthropologist Homer Barnett's work, three *úxwumixw* (communities) in the Squamish Valley were "just like one family": the people living at Yelhíxw (Ashlu Creek), Ch'éḵch'eḵts ("dirty mouth," Squamish River near Turbid Creek), and P'uy̓ám̓ ("blackened from smoke," an area near the Squamish River–Elaho River confluence). He said each family group would "own" a summer spot. Bouchard and Kennedy analyzed mid-1800s data that shows families from those three villages would move to reside at Sen̓áḵw ("inside the head of the bay," at False Creek, which also became known as Kitsilano Indian Reserve No. 6) and Iy̓al̓mexw (Jericho Beach) each year.

Barnett said people from T'e<u>k</u>w't'a<u>k</u>w'emaỷ ("place of thimbleberry bushes," near Evans Creek and the Squamish River–Cheakamus River confluence) went to Xwmélch'stn ("place of rolling waters," the village at the mouth of the Capilano River). He said people from Xwyekw'áyak̲'in ("farthest up the river," just north of T'ek̲w't'ak̲-w'emaỷ) went to English Bay.

X̲ats'alánexw Siỷám̓ said people would reside at Second Beach and Third Beach on English Bay. He said a man named Kwálk̲in from St'á7mes hosted a ceremonial potlatch at Iỷálshn, a former bay near the foot of Davie and Denman Streets.

As with present-day addresses, it seems our ancestors travelled and stayed at places where they were likely to be found when others were looking for them. We maintain these patterns with our modern get-togethers, like canoe races, sporting events, and cultural gatherings.

Many areas were happily shared between Indigenous Peoples, and families would have specific rights to and responsibilities for certain areas. Family ties would allow people access to different resources, and reciprocity came through trade and traditional ceremony.

Language and Culture

Our people have a language that is distinct from the language of our neighbours. We speak Sk̲wx̲wú7mesh Sníchim. It is known for its use of guttural sounds, glottal stops, and consonant clusters. It has some similarities to the Halkomelem language, but contains far more differences than similarities. In ceremony you can still hear each of our different Indigenous languages. There was a time when you could speak our language among any of our friends and neighbours and right away they would know you were Sk̲wx̲wú7mesh. Our language ties us to this place. There are fewer speakers today largely because of the impact of the Canadian Indian residential school system, which held a multi-generational policy to end the use of the Sk̲wx̲wú7mesh

Sníchim. Despite Canadian policy attempts to exterminate the use of our language, in recent years the number of learners, speakers, and users of Sk̲wx̲wú7mesh Sníchim has been constantly rising.

The Sk̲wx̲wú7mesh Sníchim was only written down recently, so you will occasionally see different spellings of the same words, a legacy of the range of European people who worked with our people to understand and document our language and various times when our Elders' words were recorded. The spelling for Squamish Language content in this Squamish history comes from the writing system developed with Sx̲áaltxw Siy̓ám̓ as a part of the BC Native Language Project, which began in the 1970s. The writing system was officially adopted by Squamish Nation council in the 1990s.

FACING: This figure, called *W'axayus*, once stood on the Sk̲wx̲wú7mesh reserve at Pukwayusem, near Brackendale. It welcomed the salmon run.

Our ancient stories inform our place names and our understanding of our territory. For example, Sk̲w'ats', the Squamish legend of the Great Flood, tells us of how places were named. We call Black Tusk in Whistler T'ak̲'t'ak̲'muy̓ín̓ tl'a in̓inyáx̲a7n ("landing place of the Thunderbird" or "Thunderbird's perch"). The Thunderbird is said to have brought *sts'úk̲w'i7* (salmon) to a lone survivor of Sk̲w'ats'. The Thunderbird also rested at Mount Cayley near the Cheakamus and Squamish River Valleys.

Living with the Seasons

X̲áp'ay̓ay (red cedar) is so central to our identity, culture, transportation, and ceremonies that it is hard to imagine the Sk̲wx̲wú7mesh lived on this territory for thousands of years before cedar forests as we know them today were established. Our growth to attaining extensive woodworking abilities was directly connected to the growth of *x̲áp'ay̓ay* on the land. Ten thousand to six thousand years ago, there

was little evidence of Western red cedar pollen, and the climate was likely too warm and dry. About six thousand years ago, *x̱áp'aỷay* began to increase in number, and it seems to have been truly well established by about five thousand ago. Since wood (and other materials we used, like wool) returns to the earth, relatively few archaeological remains are found. Stone tools are most common, along with many woodworking tools.

After a long winter, our people would be happy for March to come—it brought the season of the herring run and the first fresh harvest, after months of dried food. We'd then be able to harvest eulachon, as eulachon oil was an important trade item. Then the land and waters were teeming with life, and we would be busy gathering and preparing food.

The Sḵwx̱wú7mesh continued to rely on Burrard Inlet, Howe Sound, and the Fraser River to fish for *sts'úḵw'i7*, herring, cod, sturgeon, trout, halibut, and eulachon. We relied on shellfish like clams, oysters, prawns, mussels, and sea urchin. This is why Indigenous people in the region have often said, "When the tide goes out, the table is set."

FACING: ***Sts'úḵw'i7*** **(salmon) are often heralded as symbols of wealth and fortune. As such, salmon are celebrated with honour and featured prominently in Sḵwx̱wú7mesh heritage and art.**

The Sḵwx̱wú7mesh who travelled down from the Squamish River villages to First Narrows (the entrance of Burrard Inlet) and down to Indian Arm could hunt for larger game to keep up their stores while they were in the area. We called Burnaby Mountain Lheḵw'lhúḵw'aỷtn, which refers to the peeling bark of arbutus trees. Orcas and their calves would frequent the waters, returning for spring calving season and rubbing their bellies on gravel beaches, which was and still is very much looked forward to by Sḵwx̱wú7mesh. By canoe and traditional trails, the Sḵwx̱wú7mesh went to Sx̱wáymelh specifically for *stséḵi7*. Areas of what's now known as the metropolis of Vancouver were home to black bear, deer, small game such as rabbit, and the many types of plants and trees needed to replenish household items and tools when necessary.

Our people were busy every day. Everyone from young children to adults learned to trap small animals whenever we were out gathering food or plant materials. As boys grew older, they were trained as big-game hunters, saltwater hunters, or mountain goat hunters. Mountain goat hunters were well respected for having to travel over steep and dangerous mountain faces, and the wool was used for our famous weaving that provided warmth during cold winters.

Burrard Inlet's clam beds were crucial to Sk̲wx̲wú7mesh survival. Clams were steamed open, barbecued by a fire, and strung on cedar bark ropes to be stored. Smoked clams and oysters are still much loved, as are many types of small fish and *sts'úk̲w'i7*. Salmon was mostly smoke-dried. Other fish like flounder, sole, perch, and rockfish were available year-round, along with kelp, lingcod, and sea mammals.

Berries would also be dried on large, open-slatted drying racks built on a slant. Our lands are rich in berries: salmonberry, thimbleberry, blackcaps, huckleberries, and all kinds of blueberries, as well as currants. Usually, older brothers and sisters begin to teach the toddlers about berries. The children go out in April and May to get salmonberries, the first fresh berries of the season. The older children learn that they must give the first berries to a little one. This teaches respect for younger children, self-discipline, and the highly regarded ability to share.

We carried extensive knowledge about the lifeways and properties of the living plants and animals around us. Our use of plants as food and medicines was widespread. Andy Natrall, Syex̲wáltn (Dominic Charlie), and Sx̲áaltxw Siy̓ám̓ recorded some of our traditional uses. Ironwood flowers and hemlock helped with an upset stomach, and lung lichen (lungwort) mixed with water acted as a laxative. Fern rhizomes were a common plant food. Cottonwood seeds mixed with water were used to make hair grow. White fir was used in a bath to treat rheumatism (inflammation), and devil's club was also used to help with rheumatism as well as diabetes. Indian hellebore was numbing and could help with toothaches. Working with these plants required knowledge of their benefits and risks, as some are poisonous if ingested.

Our relationship with the earth, and the way we lived with the seasons, is exemplified in our words for each month:

Míṁna lhk̲aych’ (child month, January)
Tem wélhx̲s (frog time, February)
Temlháwt’ (herring time, March)
Tem tsá7tsk̲ay (plant-shoot time, April)
Tem yetwán (salmonberry time, May)
Temkw’eskw’ás (hot time, June)
Temk̲w’éleṁxw (blackberry time, July)
Tem t’ák̲a7 (salal berry time, August)
Temcháyilhn (fish time, September)
Temp’í7twáy (time of animals rutting, October)
Tem ek̲wáyanexw (time when animal hide changes, November)
Etl’íṁ lhk̲aych’ (short month, December)

Of course, our perception of time did not match perfectly with the Western Gregorian twelve-month calendar we know today. We have other phrases like *tem eshcháwm* (time for salmon to spawn, approximately mid-August to mid-November) and *tem kwu7s* (time of spring salmon, approximately July) that show our relationship with the earth and how the movements of the world around us helped us track the passage of time.

2

NA7 TKWI KWEKWÍṄ: IN THE LONG AGO

ORAL HISTORY is integral to our culture, and some oral literatures line up with geological data to reflect what the world around us looked like. For example, in one *sx̱wex̱wiy̓ám̓* (legend, mythical story), the Sḵwx̱wú7mesh experienced an event when the earth burned. Yumḵs (Dr. Rudy Reimer) suggested that this oral history references lava flow that emerged from the Opal Cone approximately ten thousand years ago.

The oral literature of Sḵwx̱wú7meshulh (Squamish's People) is passed down from generation to generation. Before we had a written language, this is how the next generation inherited knowledge. You may hear a *sx̱wex̱wiy̓ám̓*, or you may hear a *syets* (true story), an orally shared history that may include teachings, family trees, and significant events like war or peace-making.

Melḵws and the First Ancestors

In 1897, school teacher and amateur anthropologist Charles Hill-Tout sat down with a Sḵwx̱wú7mesh man named Melḵws. Hill-Tout spent time with Coast Salish Peoples from 1896 to 1906. He said he was connected with the Sḵwx̱wú7mesh by Roman Catholic bishop Pierre-Paul Durieu. This was Hill-Tout's first impression of Melḵws: "He was a decrepit creature, stone-blind from old age, whose existence till then had been unknown to the good bishop, who himself has this tribe in charge. I am disposed, therefore, to think that this account has not been put into English before."

Hill-Tout asked Melḵws his age. A tribe member who spoke English translated. Our ancestor could only share that his mother was "a girl on the verge of womanhood" when George Vancouver sailed up Howe Sound in 1792. Hill-Tout deduced Melḵws was about one hundred years old. Therefore, this is one of the oldest transcribed accounts of a Sḵwx̱wú7mesh historian, as translated by a member of the tribe and described by Hill-Tout. Hill-Tout also wrote that he felt he got only one-fifth of what was being related because it was beyond the interpreter's ability to translate it into English, or perhaps they did not want to relate the deep history to a white man.

*Before the old man could begin his recital, some preparations were deemed necessary by the other elderly men of the tribe. These consisted in [*sic*] making a bundle of short sticks, each about six inches long. These played the part of tallies, each stick representing to the reciter a particular paragraph or chapter in his story. They apologized for making these, and were at pains to explain to me that these were to them what books were to the white man. These sticks were now placed at intervals along a table round which we sat, and after some animated discussion between the interpreter, who acted as master of ceremonies, and the other old men as to the relative order and names of the tallies, we were ready to begin. The first tally was placed to [*sic*] the old man's hands and he began his recital in a loud, high-pitched key, as if he were addressing a large audience in the open air.*

This was the traditional way our historians kept track of each story in strict order as they were trained to do. By asking follow-up questions and hearing Melḵws recite tally by tally, Hill-Tout constructed a narrative in English:

In the beginning there was water everywhere and no land at all. When this state of things had lasted for a long while, the Great Spirit determined to make land appear. Soon the tops of the mountains showed above the water and they grew and grew till their heads reached the clouds. Then he made the lakes and rivers, and after that the trees and animals. Soon after this had been done, X̱i7lánexw [Hill-Tout wrote "Kalana"], the first man, was made. The Great Spirit bestowed upon him the three things an Indian cannot do without, viz., a wife, a chisel or adze, and a salmon trap. X̱i7lánexw was a good man and obeyed the Great Spirit's commands, and in course of time his wife bore him many sons and daughters, who spread out over the land and peopled it. When the land was full of people and X̱i7lánexw had grown very old, the Great Spirit took him away one day and the people saw him no more.

As X̱i7lánexw aged, the people grew "very wicked," according to the story, and after he was gone, they became worse. After a long time, the Great Spirit made waters rise to the top of the highest mountains.

All drowned except X̱i7lánexw's first-born, Chíyatmixw, and Chíyatmixw's wife.

These two escaped in their canoe, which floated about on the water for a long time, and at last, when they were nearly dead with hunger, settled on the top of a high mountain which was not quite covered with water. After this the water subsided, and Chíyatmixw and his wife descended from the mountain and built themselves a house, and in course of time repeopled the land again with their offspring. A long interval now went by and the people were happy and prosperous. Many salmon came up the Squamish every season, and there was food for everybody and to spare.

But the Great Spirit became angry with them again a second time after Chíyatmixw's death, and this time punished them by sending a great snowstorm upon the land. Day after day, and moon after moon, the snow fell in tiny flakes, covering everything and hiding all the land, and the streams, and the rivers, and the trees. The snow was remarkable for its extreme fineness, and it penetrated everywhere. It came into their houses and put out their fires, and into their clothes and made them wet and cold. (In this part of his

Tyee's (Floyd Joseph's) *Te Qoitcital the Serpent Slayer*, dedicated to his late father.

recital the old man was exceedingly interesting and graphic in his description, the very tones of his voice lending themselves to his story, and I gathered, long before the interpreter took up the story, that he had told of something that was very small and had penetrated everywhere.)

All the fish and firewood were consumed, and starvation set in. People began to die in hundreds: "Dead bodies lay around everywhere, dead and dying lying together.

"(Here the old man's voice was hushed to a plaintive wail, and the faces of his audience were an eloquent index of the tragic interest of this story of their ancestors' misfortunes.)

“Everything that could possibly afford sustenance was eagerly sought out and eaten. The hair was scraped from their store of skins, and the latter, soaked in the snow to make them soft, were then torn into pieces and devoured. But soon even this source of supply failed them, and their only hope now lay in the approaching salmon season.”

But when the *sts’úḵw’i7* (salmon) arrived there were few, and they were “skin and bones.” The hardier ones survived, but the sick and weak died until only a few were left. Snow continued to fall, and even *sts’úḵw’i7* skins and bones were eaten, and soon only a man and his daughter were left. They had survived by killing and eating their dog. They made soup from the slime of the *sts’úḵw’i7* and moss they acquired by burrowing deep through the snow. But the snow continued, their food was gone, and they lay down to die, “as the others had done,” Melḵws said in Hill-Tout’s transcript.

Then, the man saw a large bird (Hill-Tout wrote “fish-hawk” first, then “eagle”) swoop down to the ocean and rise with a large *sts’úḵw’i7* in its claws. The man launched his canoe, got within range, and shot down the bird, the fish still in its claws.

By means of this fish and bird they were enabled to sustain themselves for some time longer, and by the time this food was consumed a great change began to take place. The snow at last stopped falling and the sun appeared, and a great and rapid thaw set in. In a short space of time the great white covering of snow sank down, and the long-hidden trees, and streams, and rivers, and land were seen once more. The man now took his daughter to wife, and from those two the land was in course of time once more repeopled. Times of plenty came back, and the people learned to forget the terrible punishment the Great Spirit had sent upon their forefathers.

But misfortune returned—one season the salmon were “covered with running sores and blotches.” But the people depended on these salmon for winter. They preserved and stored them.

They put off eating them till no other food was available, and then began a terrible time of sickness and distress. A dreadful skin disease, loathsome to look upon, broke out upon all alike. None were spared. Men, women and children sickened, took the disease and died in agony by hundreds, so that when the spring arrived and fresh food was procurable, there was scarcely a person left of all their numbers to get it. Camp after camp, village after village, was left desolate. The remains of which, said the old man, in answer to my queries on this head, are found today in the old camp sites or midden-heaps over which the forest has been growing for so many generations. Little by little the remnant left by the disease grew into a nation once more, and then the first white men sailed up.

Other Creation Stories

In the 1900s, another amateur anthropologist, Oliver Wells, interviewed X̱ats'alánexw Siy̓ám̓ (Chief August Jack Khatsahlano) and Syex̱wáltn (Dominic Charlie), who were siblings with the same mother but different fathers. X̱ats'alánexw Siy̓ám̓ and Syex̱wáltn shared a lot of their knowledge, history, and oral stories with researchers throughout their lives. They were clearly committed to recording the knowledge they had at a time when our culture and language were being wiped out by colonization.

FACING: Syex̱wáltn (Dominic Charlie) of the Capilano Reserve watches the weather.

Syex̱wáltn and X̱ats'alánexw Siy̓ám̓ both told Wells that they knew Melḵws but had not heard that version of our creation story. Syex̱wáltn told Wells about Melḵws; he said he was his great-grandfather:

Wells: He was an old man when you were a boy?

Syex̱wáltn: He was very old. He used to paddle from here across there when it's low tide, to come down only when they are touching the ground with the paddle, they know it, you see. They follow the shore alone, to come to English Bay there. They were both blind, his wife and the old man.

Wells: They would make the trip alone, even though they were blind, eh?

Syex̱wáltn: Yeah, they were great people . . . I don't know how they get across here, and when they cross here. Well, they know. They know where they go.

Wells: Can they tell how strong the current is through the narrows?

Syexwáltn: They know. They're great old people.

X̱ats'alánexw Siỷám̓ said he did know about the big snow part of the story. After that deathly winter, he said, "the summer came too hot, and burned the whole Squamish, burned it from the mouth of Squamish up to the top."

X̱ats'alánexw Siỷám̓ also shared a similar version of the Great Flood story. In his account, there was only one man left. When he realized all his people were gone, he wanted to drown himself.

"This Thunderbird he come down and tapped him on his back, and he says, 'It's no use you going to die same as the others. You come up. I'll give you a woman after.' So he go in the curtain, grab the salmon, and give it to him. 'Now, this is good for you, the salmon.' And that Thunderbird's gone. Next day she was coming down with a big basket, everything all that what Indians can use, all packed up in that basket. And when she come to this fellow, he told her where to stay. So she come to this man; he looked and he said, 'Well sister, what have you got? You got anything good to eat?' So she opened up the basket and give him everything he wanted, and he's got food. That was the Ch'iyáḵmesh (Cheakamus) River people."

There are multiple creation stories of our first ancestors. There are several first ancestor stories each connected to individual villages. Sx̱áaltxw Siỷám̓ (Chief Louis Miranda) recorded and translated many stories between English and the Sḵwx̱wú7mesh Sníchim (Squamish Language). Sx̱áaltxw Siỷám̓ was born in 1892 and lived at Eslha7áṅ, the Mission Reserve, and dedicated much of his life to preserving the language and stories. He spent hours recording tapes and transcribing the language, and his efforts were integral to preserving our language. According to Sx̱áaltxw Siỷám̓, the first people were X̱í7nexwtṇ and his wife, who were created in the upper Elaho River region. The next couple was created at Chi'yáḵmesh and their descendants moved down the river, eventually reaching St'á7mes (Stawamus). In many of these stories, the first ancestors simply appear.

According to Sxwálh Siỷám̓ (Chief Jimmy Jimmy), the first man and woman came from the earth, and when they didn't behave, they were punished.

Anthropologists Dorothy Kennedy and Randy Bouchard's comprehensive *Squamish Indian Land Use and Occupancy* report, a significant body of work of over 760 pages, compiled data and information about how we have lived on and used our territory into our ancient history. They began their research with Sxáaltxw Siỷám̓ in the 1970s, and then the council of the day lent its support shortly after. They interviewed twenty Skwxwú7mesh Elders and pulled together many recordings, transcripts, and reports. They had unprecedented access to archival materials, accessible only with the Squamish Nation's consent.

The people who contributed to this important history are:

Chief Alvie Andrew
Sam Baker
Simon Baker
Ted Band
Adeline Billy
Bertha Billy
Arnold Guerin (Musqueam)
Lena Jacobs
Emma Joe
Norman Lewis
Buffalo Mathias
Chief Louis Miranda
Emily Moody
George Moody
Ed Nahanee
Andy Natrall
Ambrosine George Virag
David Williams
Louise Williams
Wilfred Williams
Rose Yelton

Bouchard and Kennedy stated that it seemed everyone agreed that the Skwxwú7mesh are descended from the survivors of a great flood. They noted the variety of stories for Chi'yákmesh: "Descending from the sky to the earth is a primary feature of 'first ancestor' stories. In the Gibsons story, the two brothers, Tsekánchtn and Sxeláltn descended at Schen̓k/Ch'kw'élhp. On the Squamish River, across from Ktin, Dominic Charlie [Syexwáltn] told of a man and his wife who descended to the top of a mountain. Their two daughters and a son

X̱álek̲'/Sek̲'yú Siỷám̓'s (Chief Ian Campbell's) painting of Nch'k̲aỷ and the Great Flood.

intermarried and became the ancestors of the Cheakamus people. Others, however, state that the Cheakamus people are descendants of a man who was raised by wolves near the Cheakamus River. George Moody and David Williams still know this story today. An interesting corroboration of this story is found in Franz Boas's 1886 list of Squamish villages where he identifies *stk̲áya* (wolf) as the 'mythical ancestor' for the village of Chi'yák̲mesh."

Syex̱wáltn talked about a man who appeared "up at Squamish" named Xí7nexwtn̓. Jimmy Frank said another first ancestor existed for people living on the Squamish River above its junction with the Cheakamus but did not remember a name.

According to anthropologists Homer Barnett and Oliver Wells, as well as Sx̱áaltxw Siỷám̓, Xwechtáal (the serpent-slayer) was the first ancestor at the village St'á7mes.

Ta S<u>k</u>w'ats': "Time of the Flood"

The story of S<u>k</u>w'ats' (the Great Flood), a *s<u>x</u>we<u>x</u>wiy̓ám̓*, is shared across many Indigenous Peoples around the world—it tells about the time water and ice covered the earth.

Here is how S<u>x</u>áaltxw Siy̓ám̓ told the story:

Long, long ago, when the Squamish Indians were first created, they were given three special helpers. These were: the Indian doctor, or sxw7úmten; *the medicine man or ritualist, or* kwtsi7ts; *and the prophet, or* esyéw. *The Indian doctor* [sxw7úmten] *had trained and fasted for many years until he had found the power of his spirit. He could help anyone who was sick, and that person would immediately become well again. This was because he was so powerful.*

An Indian medicine man [kwtsi7ts] *could also help a sick person if the Indian doctor* [sxw7úmten] *wasn't around. He didn't have the power of the doctor, but had learned certain magical chants and words, and knew the secret ways to use Indian paint on the sick person's body to heal him. The medicine man* [kwtsi7ts] *was also said to be able to cast evil spells as well as good.*

The prophet didn't have the power to heal, or special words or paint. What he did have was the gift to see into the future and predict what would happen to a person.

Well, in the early days, the old people gave the younger ones good advice on how to live and behave, such as how to be humble and kind. The young people followed this advice, and also learned to help anyone who was in trouble or need. They shared their food with one another and everyone was happy. There was always plenty to eat: deer, bear, and berries. When the fish were running, the rivers were full.

If anyone became sick, they called the Indian doctor [sxw7úmten], *who healed him. As time passed, however, the people began to forget the old ways. They didn't listen to the good advice of the old people. They didn't share their food; they didn't help those in need.*

One day a prophet [esyéw] *stood up in front of the people and said, "My friends, I have been told to warn you. Your way of life is not right. You do not help one another as the people used to do when they were first created. I am warning you—you must change your ways."*

He sat down, and the people were silent. Then an old man stood up and thanked the prophet [esyéw]. *"Listen to the words of the prophet. He knows what will happen if you do not change."*

After the prophet [esyéw] *finished speaking, he looked around to see what the people would do. Some of them laughed and others made fun of him. "Listen to that gloomy old man! What does he know?" "Why should we listen to what these old people say?" "We'll live our own ways. Nobody can tell us what to do!"*

Sadly the prophet [esyéw] *and the old people watched as they saw their words go unheeded. Everyone behaved as he pleased. No one helped his neighbour; none were humble and kind.*

Then—all the game on this land began to disappear: deer, bear, all land animals. The people weren't able to hunt, and they became hungry.

Again, the prophet [esyéw] *stood up. "You have received one of your punishments. Listen now, and return to the right ways, or something even more terrible will happen."*

Still the young turned aside and went their selfish ways. Soon the fish began to disappear from all the little streams and creeks. When the berry season came, no berries could be found. The people grew hungrier, and began to fight and quarrel among themselves.

Once more the prophet [esyéw] *stood up and he said, "This is the last time that I can warn you. Now you have received this severe punishment. Oh, change your ways now, for if you will not, a punishment so strong, I cannot speak of it, will happen!"*

The old people, as well, pleaded with the others, tried to get them to listen. But the people seemed to have become deaf to good advice. Now they were growing worse—fighting, quarreling. No one was happy; no one listened.

Then, one day it began to rain. The river started to rise. The Indian doctor [sxw7úmten] *seemed to lose his power. He could no longer cure the sick, and his patients died. The medicine man* [kwtsi7ts] *also lost his power. His special words and paints no longer worked.*

The rain continued and the river rose higher. The medicine man [kwtsi7ts] *used to be able to control the flooding of a heavy rain by taking a cedar stick, painting it, and chanting his words of power over it. Then he would place the stick on the riverbank. When the rising river reached the stick, the waters would stop. This time, though, the water wouldn't stop. The river kept rising higher and higher.*

When the water was about to come over the riverbanks, those people who had canoes put their families in them and rose up with the water. The others went into their houses with their families and animals. Gradually the water rose until it covered the houses and those inside all drowned. The people in canoes headed for the highest group to camp, and they had to go higher still.

Finally, all the land was covered and only the mountain tops were still showing. They floated to the highest peak in Squamish and anchored their canoes there. Day after day, the medicine man [kwtsi7ts] *continued to write on the side of the mountain to try to stop the flood waters. Day after day, the waters rose, until, when they looked around, all that could be seen above the water was the peak of Mt. Garibaldi* [Nch'k̲aỷ], *and another peak farther south downriver.*

The people headed their canoes for Mt. Garibaldi [Nch'k̲aỷ]. *The river was running very swiftly now, and after the canoes were anchored, some of them broke loose. The water was too swift to be able to paddle back, so some people from that group headed for the other mountain downriver. Those still anchored to Mt. Garibaldi* [Nch'k̲aỷ] *stayed there.*

Then the water started to go down. At first very quickly, then it slowed down until a large lake was formed. The people from Squamish went back to their old homesite. Others, from farther up the Squamish River, stayed there, and still others stayed at Cheakamus.

Those who survived were happy to be alive and back home, but they remembered with sadness their friends who had drowned. At last, the Squamish people did return to their senses. When the old people spoke, everyone listened. People helped one another and everyone was happy again. The Indian doctor [sxw7úmten] *and medicine man* [kwtsi7ts] *were powerful once more. The animals which the people used for food returned to the land.*

The creeks were once again filled with fish and there was an abundance of berries. Everyone remembered to be humble and kind.

Never again would the Squamish people suffer this terrible punishment. Never again would the flood cover the land.

It has been said that the medicine man's [kwtsi7ts] *paint can still be seen on the face of the mountain that some of the people were anchored to. The Squamish word for this mountain is S<u>x</u>el̓ts<u>k</u>wú7 [Ice Cap Peak on the Ashlu/Elaho divide] meaning "painted face."*

The mountain peak away to the south of the Squamish River, where some of the people landed, is called Mount Baker [Xwsa7<u>k</u>], *in Washington State, in the U.S.A.*

Archaeology shows that sea levels changed dramatically in our territory in this time. Over twelve thousand years ago, the sea level was eighty-five metres higher than it is today. It would take about seven thousand years for sea levels to stabilize at the levels we know today. As the sea level decreased and the land rebounded, the land changed. The climate became warmer—even warmer than it is today. Before cedar became widespread, around five thousand years ago, the land was mostly pine.

FACING: Mount Garibaldi, known as Nch'<u>k</u>aỷ, was one of the two mountains that remained above water during S<u>k</u>w'ats' (the Great Flood).

Some have wondered if Christianity influenced existing Indigenous stories, given the similarity of people becoming "very wicked" and being punished with a flood, and the story of Noah's Ark, in which "the Lord saw that the wickedness of man was great in the earth" and flooded the earth, sparing only Noah, his family, and several animals. We know pre-Contact spirituality included power through visions and prophecy, and giving thanks. Anthropologist Wayne Suttles theorized that there was little worship, and that some of our existing stories and practices were changed through "a series of compromises and reinterpretations" after Christianity was introduced.

Suttles pointed out that terms in different Salish languages typically vary widely. But multiple Coast Salish languages such as

Squamish, Lushootseed, Straits Salish, and Halkomelem all have terms that vaguely translate as "High Chief" or "Chief Above." This is very similar to the Chinook Jargon term "Saghalie Tyee," which means "God" or "High Chief." Chinook Jargon was a trade language, believed to be introduced to the Coast Salish with the arrival of fur traders and missionaries.

Suttles wrote, "It seems unlikely that if the concept of a supreme being had existed in pre-contact times he would have been everywhere designated by the same compound term 'Chief Above' or that this term should be identical with the Chinook Jargon term. It seems much more likely that this term was spread with Christianity." Of course, we do share some other similar stories and figures, like the X̲aays (Transformer brothers), with our neighbours. But they also took different shapes across cultures, and Suttles emphasized that the X̲aays were in our stories but not "worshiped" or addressed in prayer.

Either way, there is no doubt our people survived incredible sea-level changes and changes in temperature, and that the flood story is integral to our teachings.

The First Men at Ch'k̲w'élhp (Gibsons Landing)

Here is the story of the first men at Ch'k̲w'élhp/Schen̓k̲ (Gibsons Landing), as told by Syex̲wáltn in 1972, recorded by Sx̲áaltxw Siy̓ám̓. It's a good example of how a storyteller would also share who they heard the history from, and how they inherited it.

This story was told to us by our grandparents. My granduncle, Sxwcháltn, told me about the first people, who were created at Ch'k̲w'élhp. The first man appeared as an adult. His name was Tsek̲ánchtn. He had already built himself a house, when another man landed on his roof. The man started to dance on the roof. When he continued, Tsek̲ánchtn said, "You, my younger brother, come down from my roof, and come inside." The dancer got down and went inside. He then said to Tsek̲ánchtn, "I am the eldest!" Tsek̲ánchtn disagreed and his younger brother continued to dance. His name was Sx̲eláltn. When he went into the house, he had a sx̱wáy̓x̱wey *mask with him. Sx̱eláltn wouldn't stop dancing or take off the mask.*

Tseḵánchtn was bothered by his brother and suggested that he build himself a house on the other side of the bay. Sx̱eláltn, and the other people with him, built their home at Ch'ḵw'élhp. They never let Tseḵánchtn get any food; they were near the reef where the sea lions went ashore.

Tseḵánchtn had an idea [of] how he could get some food. He found a log and carved a likeness of a sea lion. The first, he made from a fir log, and it was too heavy. It appeared once on the surface of the water before it sank to the bottom. Next, he used red cedar, which worked very well. It bobbed up and down in the water and acted like a real sea lion. He carved it at a small lake above Gibsons Landing. He carried clam shells, mussels, and kelp up to the lake to give the log strength.

This was told to me by my granduncles, Sxwcháltn and Tiyáx̱altxw. My grandmother, Syex̱wáliya, came from Schen̓ḵ. X̱achá7lh, and S7átseltxw, my mother's cousins, come from there also. My mother's name was X̱way̓waat. My niece, who comes from Squamish and is the daughter of my brother, X̱ats'elánexw [X̱ats'alánexw], took my mother's name. X̱achá7lh used to launch his canoe and paddle down to Sen̓áḵw, False Creek, to visit us. My father also had a house at Iy̓álmexw [Jericho Beach], but it must have been torn down, as I can't remember it. I did see a ship, whose crew tore down a building owned by my father. They took the roof shakes, the support beams, the ridge pole, the walls, the rafters, and all the other parts of it. It is said that it was reconstructed in a museum in a place called Germany. They say that they found it, but really, they stole it.

When Tseḵánchtn finished the sea lion, he took it down to the salt water and said to it, "You will circle the bay, and when all of the people have hold of you, go across to Ts'x̱wém̓ḵsen [Gabriola Pass], the other side of Pná7lx̱ets' [Kuper Island]. Go along the route of the Cowichan people, to Lhemlhémelch' [Clemclemluts], which is near Cowichan Bay."

The people were taken across the gulf. Some of them let go at Ts'x̱wém̓ḵsen, others at Pná7lx̱ets', and the rest hung on until they came to the mouth of the Cowichan Bay. Sx̱eláltn went to Pná7lx̱ets'. When he arrived, he said

Slhx̱í7lsh (Siwash Rock), English Bay, c. 1890.

to his people, "I must go back, as there is something I left behind." He went back and got the sx̱wáy̓x̱wey *mask. That is how the mask reached the other side of the gulf.*

There are variations on this story as well.

Sx̱áaltxw Siy̓ám̓ said he heard this story from his granduncle Tiyáx̱eltx̱w (Howe Sound Jim), Tétemat (Josephine, Mrs. Chief Tom), and Lhéḵ'lhaḵ'elḵ (Doctor Jim). Sx̱áaltxw Siy̓ám̓ also said the one in the house was named Tseḵánchtn and the brother on the roof who wore the *sx̱wáy̓x̱wey* mask was named Sx̱eláltn. He said the brothers peacefully shared hunting at the reef for a while, but Sx̱eláltn's family became greedy and would not share. Sx̱áaltxw Siy̓ám̓ said Tseḵánchtn tried to approach the family multiple times, but "his relatives only laughed at him."

Tseḵánchtn was a powerful *kwtsi7ts* (ritualist) and it was said his relatives were not living according to their teaching "that they must love, respect and honour each and everyone [*sic*] of their relatives and that they should always be prepared to share whatever they had with their relatives and friends." He said Tsek̲ánchtn tried a green fir, which was too heavy, then a dry cedar, which was too light. He rubbed them with "seaweed, kelp, salt water grass, mussels and barnacles." Eventually, a partially dry fallen fir tree was the perfect weight. The hunters harpooned the sea lion. In this version, the hunters picked up their women and children first while they were moving slowly, and then the sea lion ramped up speed and brought them across the water. Sx̲áaltxw Siỷám̓ said the people drifted to Kuper Island and Nanoose Bay.

He said there were three couples total who appeared at Squamish and from whom the people descended: a couple at St'á7mes, a couple at Ch'iyák̲mesh with a man named Kw'ít'emk̲in, and a couple at the "extreme northwest end of our Squamish claimed land," with the man named X̲é7nex̲sten. He said they intermarried and spread.

X̲aays

X̲aays are central figures in Sk̲wx̲wú7mesh history. According to Sx̲áaltxw Siỷám̓, they appeared at Elksn (Point Grey). In some tellings, there are three brothers called X̲aays, and in some, there have been four brothers called X̲aays, and the youngest would change himself into a canoe for his three brothers. The youngest, "mischievous" brother used his slingshot to shoot a rock at a mountain, and shattered the mountain peak, leaving a flat surface—they called it Xwsa7k̲ (Mount Baker). The middle brother aimed a rock at Nch'k̲aỷ (Mount Garibaldi), but his younger brother hit his elbow, and the rock slipped from the sling and landed on a smaller mountain, "north of Point Atkinson and south of Eagle Harbour." Sx̲áaltxw Siỷám̓ continued the story:

The Transformers paddled along until they came to a man who was bathing. "Why are you bathing, grandfather?" asked the eldest Transformer. "I have good reason to bathe. My wife just gave birth to a baby boy. Therefore I am going to purify my body and soul so that I become worthy of such a child . . . When my wife is strong enough, she will do the same. I am going to stay here for two months or longer and then return to my wife and son. The first man that my son sees will be worthy of seeing. I want my son to grow up knowing honesty and cleanliness."

When he finished, the Transformer said to him, "Grandfather, you are a great man. Your wisdom will be followed by the future generations and respected." The Transformer cupped some water in the palm of his hand and sprinkled it on the man. Immediately he turned to stone. The rock was named Slhx̲í7lsh, which means "standing rock." The old people used to translate this as "standing with honour," because the man was an example of a true man. The white people call this "Siwash Rock." Further down is a smaller rock which was the man's wife. It is called S7ens.

There are many stories of the X̱aays transforming living beings. One of the most well known is about Siỷám̓ Smánit, known as "Chief Mountain" to locals. Thousands of people climb or hike this seven-hundred-metre rock every year and take pictures at the top. The ancient word *siỷám̓* signifies someone respected, an honoured leader or well-regarded person.

FACING: View of the Siỷám̓ Smánit—the Stawamus Chief. The ancient word *siỷám̓* signifies someone respected, an honoured leader or well-regarded person.

The rock was once a *tl'ák̲tax̲anaw̓txw* (longhouse). A *tl'e7énk̲* (big-time potlatch) took place, and all the Animal People were invited. The X̱aays immortalized the event by transforming the guests and longhouse into a mountain. The spirits are still within the rockface, revealing themselves at different times. The Sk̲wx̱wú7mesh are taught not to point at Siỷám̓ Smánit because pointing shows disrespect and brings rain and storms.

"They're hard to spot. All my life, I've looked and looked. Just recently, during an event at Totem Hall, I went and stood outside and I finally saw one, clear as day. It was the face of a man," language teacher Tsitsáyx̲emaat (Rebecca Duncan) said about the rock in an interview with the *Squamish Chief* local newspaper.

3

ÚXWUMIXW: SQUAMISH SOCIETY AND SOCIAL STRUCTURE

ACCORDING TO anthropologist Wayne Suttles, the Sḵwx̱wú7mesh society was defined by categories he deemed as nobles (upper class), commoners (lower class), and slaves. These classes were not "absolutely rigid," he said—through marriage, or through "long and severe training" that included daily bathing, one could rise in social standing. The upper class had important skills, special knowledge passed down from their ancestors, and could control access to valuable natural resources. The lower class was considered as the opposite—not having special skills, important knowledge, or authority over resources.

In Sḵwx̱wú7mesh Sníchim (Squamish Language), we have terms like *smanálh*, which means a high-class person or noble people. A person who is *smanálh* is considered like the opposite of a person who is *smáts'en* (proud; stuck up) or a person who is *esḵí7ḵel* (unskilled; ignorant; not knowing how to do something). A *st'ashem* was someone who was a child of a slave, someone considered a low-class person, or an illegitimate child. A slave was called *skw'iyúts*—but "slave" in this sense does not describe a situation such as when a person is considered property and forced to work for and obey another. A slave was someone who had been taken through a raid on an enemy tribe. The *skw'iyúts* would be considered part of the family in some ways and raised as a member of the community, thereby assisting in daily tasks and community life, but still understood to not possess great knowledge or skills like those who were *smańálh*.

Randy Bouchard and Dorothy Kennedy observed that behaviour was governed by "family pride." People adhered to a strict moral code, and acting inappropriately would "cast shame on an entire family."

Nch'áy̓uw̓am: Descendants of One Head (Headman)

The S<u>k</u>w<u>x</u>wú7mesh were exogamous, meaning spouses were selected outside of one's own village. Jimmy Frank said a marriage between cousins would be arranged only if a family was dying out. Marriage was often with neighbours like the Shishá7lh (Sechelt) and those who spoke S<u>k</u>'emíńem (Halkomelem).

The smallest social grouping was the single set of parents and their children, who would share one section of a *tl'á<u>k</u>ta<u>x</u>anaw̓txw* (longhouse). *Nch'áy̓uw̓am* (descendants of one head/headman) would live together in the *tl'á<u>k</u>ta<u>x</u>anaw̓txw*. Longhouses were large, sometimes two hundred feet long, and often had room for eight to ten fires, and people hung long *ta<u>x</u>ch* (cattail mats) as dividers. The longhouses were shed-roofed, meaning they were sloped to one side. Long planks were held in place by a frame of post and beams; the posts were often decorated, and sometimes the beams were as well.

People tracked their lineage from both their mother and father but lived patrilineally—so they would share the *tl'á<u>k</u>ta<u>x</u>anaw̓txw* with the families of their fathers, grandfathers, brothers, male cousins, and brothers-in-law. A wife would most often go to live with her husband's family, and less often a husband would go to live in his wife's village. If a man had more than one wife, each wife and her children would live in a separate section.

Each village was composed of several families. One of Charles Hill-Tout's more comical observations was that "their cousinships are endless and even perplexing to themselves."

An individual usually affirmed a bond with a particular line of descent, and their group of relatives that extended between villages would be their "kin-group," Bouchard and Kennedy wrote in anthropological terms. Therefore, each person's kin-group would be different. Some exceptions came about with marriages between sets of brothers to sets of sisters or even multi-generational marriages where a niece could be married to a man who was once married to her aunt, who had died.

Theoretically, treating both their parents' lines equally, which Bouchard and Kennedy call "bilateral" kinship, allowed a person to belong to many groups of kin. Especially if they were higher status, they could live in the village of either parent or grandparent. "Ties of marriage linked one village to another to form a social network that extended through Coast Salish society," Bouchard and Kennedy wrote.

But, they said, in practice, specific relationships would be stronger. A man would go to his wife's village if her family had higher status. And many couples lived in different villages for a time.

Speaking about Family

Our language itself lends understanding to our family relationships. "The Squamish terms for blood kin stress the equal balance between an individual's matrilateral (mother's relatives) and patrilateral (father's relatives) kin. Terms for siblings (brothers and sisters) are extended to cousins and distinguish older and younger siblings," reads the *Squamish Indian Land Use and Occupancy* report. "Squamish affinal (in-law) terms are quite unlike those in English—the term used by a Squamish man to refer to his sister-in-law is different from the term used by a woman to refer to her sister-in-law. Suttles has proposed that the Coast Salish affinal terms show the 'direction of the marriage, that is, the direction of the movement of women as wives.'" As well, in Squamish, the term *yáw̓ilh swáy̓wi7k̲a* means "bachelor"; but there is no term for an unmarried woman.

The language around family can also be very precise—for example, terms to refer to some family members change once your sibling is deceased, if they have children. So, *stáyalh*, a niece or nephew, becomes *swanimáylh* when the parents have died. There are corresponding term changes for other family members upon a death in the family. This stems from the kindness of our ancestors, who tried to lessen the pain of grief upon the demise of close family and so referred to them in specific terms to make it clear to any who heard who was in mourning or had lost family. When two people marry, both sets of parents are called *skw'ikw'íwas*, but if one of the married couple dies, the co-parents-in-law become *kw'enlh wa x̲aam,* which means "those who weep together." Understanding the Squamish Language terms for family members is of basic importance in comprehending Squamish social structure. Another example is *sch'á7mik̲w*: the name for great-grandchild and great-grandparent is the same. It works both ways. Think of being in a longhouse among a large extended family or at an event where multiple generations of a family are present. It is clear enough to say he or she is *sch'á7mik̲w* rather than describing the connection in detail.

FACING: Young Damien Joseph shows off some *sk̲'ay*—traditional smoked salmon.

Siy̓ám̓

Leadership in villages was usually centred when necessary, or created for a specific purpose. There was not always a single leader. The term *siy̓ám̓* is important to Sk̲wx̲wú7mesh social structure. *Siy̓ám̓* does not only refer to a chief, but more accurately means a highly

respected or honoured person, or a person so skilled in any way that they can provide and share generously with family and neighbours. A household could be led by a *siỷám̓*, but not necessarily every household was. A *siỷám̓* could be recognized as the leader of a whole village or across villages. A *siỷám̓* was highly respected and demonstrated generosity by distributing wealth. Jimmy Frank likened the word *siỷám̓* to "gentleman." X̱ats'alánexw Siỷám̓ (Chief August Jack Khatsahlano) said each community had a leader, but he would be "no king." He said, "Each man boss in his own family, but when they all get together—I don't know how you put it in English—but he's the best talker—not chairman, Indians have no chairman—but man who says most wise things." A *siỷám̓* was someone well respected and recognized as a leader, and so the term was not necessarily handed down generation to generation.

Missionaries and the Hudson's Bay Company would eventually name and recognize someone as chief as a way to negotiate with certain groups of people, but that did not always reflect the community's governance structure. But if one retained their traditional ways of life and went by *siỷám̓*, then missionaries and the company might not recognize them at all. Existing documents show that by 1880, each Sḵwx̱wú7mesh village recorded had a chief, and chieftainship was passed down in a loose hereditary structure. Those who were considered chiefs had to be approved by the federal government's Indian Office.

By the time Hill-Tout surveyed Squamish people, he noted that the "title of chief," a new concept, most often descended from father to son, though it may also go to a relative such as a brother if the chief married a lower-class wife. But even then, he could still pass on the chieftainship to his son, Hill-Tout wrote. The chief would give many potlatch feasts to secure "the good will of the tribe" toward his son. But after that, Hill-Tout said, it seemed that the son's children took their social rank from their mother rather than from their father, though in most cases, class was determined patrilineally.

But Suttles pointed out that it's clear from our stories that lower-class people could perform certain acts to rise above their social standing. This is demonstrated in the story told by Sx̱áaltxw Siy̓ám̓ (Chief Louis Miranda) of the deer who was a wolf slave, in which an enslaved deer tries to escape his wolf owners, and while he is ultimately caught and devoured, the story praises the deer for trying to better himself.

There were inaccuracies and imperfections in many early anthropological accounts of Squamish life, and while some errors are easily identifiable, a critical eye is always necessary with any source. Hill-Tout described there being a "supreme siam," a head chief, whom he identified as Te Kiapilanoq, who lived at Burrard Inlet. From around 1780 to 1870, there was a man famously known as Ḵiyáplánexw, and later recorded by the name "Old Man" Kiapilano. He was recognized as a highly respected leader across multiple villages. Hill-Tout said he was "head chief," and next in "rank" was a chief from the Squamish River area. But this was not correct. Archivist J.S. Matthews asked X̱ats'alánexw Siy̓ám̓ about this years later. He said Hill-Tout was wrong: "Not one big man chief; each head of a family."

Elders

At the centre of our communities are our Elders. This is the way it has always been. Elders hold family histories. Younger people are taught to respect the wisdom their Elders have. They are to be cared for and respected.

"Respect your elders, especially your mom and dad... as you grow older listen to mom and dad. They are not trying to deprive you of the privileges you think you are entitled [to]. No, their love for you is so great that they do not want you to be getting into the wrong ways of life," Sx̱áaltxw Siy̓ám̓ wrote. "As you grow up and start to earn your keep, remember to do something for mom and dad... do not wait my dear ones, until mom and dad are gone before you buy a bunch

Through the rain and mist stands the Siỷám̓ Smánit (Stawamus Chief).

of good clothes or a lovely big basket... always bear in mind, once you lose your dear parents that they are irreplaceable."

Xwechtáal (Andrew "Andy" Paull), a S<u>k</u>wx<u>w</u>ú7mesh political leader and activist, explained the importance of Elders as holders of wisdom and history: "It was the duty of the more responsible Indians to see that the history and traditions of our race were properly handed down to posterity. A knowledge of our history and legends was similar as an education is regarded among whitemen. Those who possessed it were regarded as aristocrats. Those who were indifferent, whether adults or children, were rascals. Being without means of transmitting it into writing, much time was spent by the aristocrats in imparting this knowledge to the youth. It was the responsible duty of responsible elders."

Life Cycles

What would the life of a Sḵwx̱wú7mesh person look like, birth to death, in the old days? First, they would be born protected by cedar—we had cedar carriers for our babies, and cradles for them to sleep in. And people would again be enveloped in cedar for their passage to the spirit world. In their life in between, they could take a number of paths within their community. These practices continue today.

Sx̱áaltxw Siy̓ám̓ described in great detail the lifeways of Sḵwx̱wú7meshulh (Squamish's People) before colonization.

Birth

If needed, a woman could get help from a *swx7úmten* (Indian doctor), who could use his *sná7em* (power) to help her through pregnancy and birth. If the *swx7úmten* helped the woman, he would then "look upon that child as his responsibility," Sx̱áaltxw Siy̓ám̓ said.

Children would be treated with the "fondest love and care." From a young age, they would begin to learn from their parents, he said. When a girl had her first period or "moon," she would be led through ceremony with a *kwtsi7ts* (ritualist).

Young boys would begin to learn how to use tools and be given a *ḵw'ḵiw'tl'us* (training arrow) to practise on first stationary, then moving, targets. "He is given the understanding that patience and faith is the solid foundation of all success," Sx̱áaltxw Siy̓ám̓ said. The boy would gradually learn to hunt, and eventually go through his own puberty ceremony. By his late teens, he would decide what path he wanted to follow—perhaps taking up his family's profession, such as canoe carver, or joining the highly respected mountain goat hunters. He could also choose the difficult path of becoming a *swx7úmten*, which would require going to spiritual places in the territory to gain healing powers. The journey could take many months or years to become "a full-fledged Indian doctor with the power to go out to seek and restore the ailing and lost soul of any sick person," Sx̱áaltxw Siy̓ám̓ said.

The boy would eventually be given a real bow, and arrows with a *sluxw*—the arrowhead attached so that when the arrow hit, the shaft fell loose but the arrowhead continued moving through the body—which always killed the game. They could choose to focus on saltwater hunting, such as for sea lions.

Another important role in the community that the young men could choose was the *kwtsi7ts* (ritualist). Or one may have the gift to see the future—the *esyéw* (prophet). The *esyéw* could provide advice, but if people did not listen, "sorrows such as famine could be placed upon the people," and the *esyéw* could not change the future, Sx̱áaltxw Siy̓ám̓ said.

Teachings

Children were taught how to take care while gathering plants and animals for food, and to show respect to the forests and waterways.

The forest was home to the *x̱áp'ay̓ay* (red cedar), known as the mother tree, which continued to nurture us as we entered adulthood. The tree would be cut in many ways to build homes, with planks used for seats and for sleeping platforms that would run along the walls of the home, and large pieces used for rafters and posts. People also used cedar to make dishes such as *x̱epiyúwelh* (shallow dishes for dry meat or fish) and *x̱wúḵwem* (deep dishes for soup). The outer rough part of the bark would be used for temporary shelters, while the inner bark was worked until it was soft, and used for baskets, clothing, capes, and baby blankets and diapers.

FACING: The traditional method of gathering cedar bark involves pulling the bark away in long strips while still preserving the tree.

As they grew up, children were given advice to not be selfish or dominating with their playmates, and to always be respectful, even during play. Sx̱áaltxw Siy̓ám̓ said children were always taught with "patience and kindness," and were told that any mistake "is an opportunity to learn to be in charge of their own change."

Marriage

Marriages were arranged. Parents would choose a woman they thought would make a good companion for their son, Sx̱áaltxw Siỷám̓ said. The young man would approach the woman's family's home and sit by the entrance. He might be splashed with water, or dust from the dirt floor, to test "how serious he [was] in his proposal." This could go on for up to four full days, and if he was accepted, he would be invited inside. They would marry right away, after gifts were exchanged between the families, and speeches and advice were shared. The bride's family then provided a meal. Upper-class men, like chiefs, often had multiple wives.

Marriage served as an economic union between families. According to Sx̱áaltxw Siỷám̓, if a couple had marriage problems, they could separate in a respectful way that maintained friendship but would no longer have economic obligations to each other.

For the duration of the marriage, parents of the married couple and other in-laws would take food to one another and receive items of wealth in return.

After the death of a spouse, the family of the deceased could provide another spouse, if possible, to maintain economic ties and for the well-being of the children. Occasionally, the reciprocal economic obligation ended, if the widowed mother and children returned to the home of her father or brother.

Suttles argued that exogamous marriage increased the chances of survival in the face of seasonal fluctuation of resources, as it often created access to non-local resources.

Everyday Life

We lived with the seasons, spending much of the summer harvesting and preparing food for the winter. Men hunted, and everyone caught fish to cure and store for winter. Mountain goat, deer, and bear meat could also be dried and cured for winter.

Some animals were never eaten—such as loons, which were associated with Indian doctors, and grizzly bears, which were considered sacred, Sx̱áaltxw Siy̓ám̓ said.

To fish, one might use fishing weirs, dip nets, harpoons, spears, fish traps built with stones, nettle lines with bone hooks, or several other methods. To cook the fish, one could boil it or barbecue it over a fire. In the old days, one would smoke their fish over the fire in their home, and later in quantity in a smokehouse.

If the fish, for example, *sts'úḵw'i7* (salmon), was barbecued, it could also subsequently be smoked. Several fish would be hung horizontally along a stick, first at the lower smoking rack, and gradually be moved higher until the fish were completely dry. Once dried, the *sts'úḵw'i7* was bundled in red cedar rope and stored in a cedar box.

Women oversaw cooking and drying fish. Smoked and dried salmon is called *sḵ'ay*. Another technique was *sḵw'élem*, which means barbecued salmon. A fish would be woven onto split horizontal sticks, which would face the fire so the fish could be broiled. The fish was stored in boxes and checked regularly for rodents, and was destroyed if it had been contaminated.

All slime, entrails, and the head had to be removed to smoke the fish, but the head would be cooked. The tail and bones had to be thrown in the river, as we were taught by the Salmon People. Two holes were pierced near the tail so the fish could be hung easily from a stick called a *ḵ'áwatshn*. A whole morning could be spent butchering and hanging, through the afternoon, before the fish was ready to go to the smokehouse or over the fire.

Salmon and steelhead eggs could also be smoke-dried and stored. To harvest herring eggs, people would anchor hemlock or red cedar boughs in a shallow bay and secure them to a float. These were left in the water for three days, and herring spawned on both sides of the boughs. The branches were then retrieved and spread out on a table or rack to dry in the sun, and flipped each day to ensure they dried evenly. The boughs were then placed in a cedar box. When the eggs

were ready to be eaten, the boughs were first submerged in water to soak overnight, and the softened eggs were eaten right off the branches or cooked until just boiled.

Women picked berries such as *t'áḵa7* (salal berries) and *sḵw'ḗlemxw* (blackberries). They had to go into the mountains and camp for a day or two to pick *iyálḵp* (Alaska blueberries). These would also be dried and stored.

When clams were gathered in Burrard Inlet, they could be eaten right away or smoked for later use. People would go to Iy̓ál̓mexw (Jericho Beach) in March for herring and P'ekwchá (Spanish Banks) in May for smelts. Before the arrival of colonizers, some Sḵwx̱wú7mesh people lived on Burrard Inlet to be closer to the saltwater, with homes at Xwmélch'stn ("place of rolling waters," Capilano), X̱wáy̓x̱way ("mask," also known as Lumbermen's Arch), and Ch'ích'elxwi7ḵw (Seymour Creek).

According to the Elders that Bouchard and Kennedy spoke to and their other research, winter was a time to stay indoors in the warmth, living on the food the people had gathered in the summer. Some ice fishing and waterfowl hunting could be done. It was a time for creativity—spinning wool and thread and repairing and building tools. Winters could be harsh, and food had to be carefully used.

In spring, people began harvesting green vegetables, and travelled for the herring spawn, herring run, smelt run, and *kwu7s* (spring salmon) run. April brought eulachon and steelhead in the Seymour, Lynn, Capilano, and Cheakamus Rivers. Summer brought deer, elk, and goat hunting, as well as smelt and sturgeon. Late summer into fall brought *stséḵi7* (sockeye salmon). People smoked and prepared food for storage.

In terms of how we expressed ourselves, people enjoyed beauty. Some people had some simple tattooing and used face paint. Crushed mica gave that paint a shimmery appearance. Hides, wool-woven clothes, and cedar-woven clothes could all be painted. Coast Salish

FACING: Sequailyah (Mrs. Chief George) cooking salmon over an open fire at No. 3 Reserve, c. 1940.

Peoples and other Indigenous groups practised forehead elongation by lightly binding the heads of infants to create a longer slope on the forehead, appreciating the aesthetic. According to Hill-Tout, Tim Moody was the last Squamish child this was performed on.

Travelling to the Spirit World

Our lives on Earth are full of richness. It's impossible to summarize all the details of a Sḵwx̱wú7mesh person's life cycle in this book. But Earth is a temporary resting place.

When people passed on, casket builders would make a box of red cedar, the final resting place for the physical body. Before the body met its resting place, the *kwtsi7ts* was called.

"Prior to contact with Europeans, the Squamish never buried the dead. They were put into an A-framed shed and made secure so that no animal could get at the corpse. The box is laid down then the shed is securely erected over it and covered with heavy boulders," Sx̱áaltxw Siy̓ám̓ said.

Islands near villages were often the final resting place of those who had passed on and were laid to rest in *x̱áp'ay̓ay* boxes. These were elevated off the ground, sometimes on planks or frames, as Sx̱áaltxw Siy̓ám̓ described, and sometimes in trees. There were also what X̱ats'alánexw Siy̓ám̓ translated as "deadhouses," as City of Vancouver archivist J.S. Matthews recorded: "[He] tells of how his father X̱ítelḵ was buried in a 'deadhouse,' a small wooden mausoleum, the body lying in a small canoe inside the 'deadhouse,' at the end of the Pipeline Road, First Narrows."

The passed on loved ones could be placed in a bentwood box, or in the case of a *siy̓ám̓*, in a canoe, then placed in a cedar slab shed. Immediate family followed the deceased to the burial ground, accompanied by other family, together with all their friends and a band of special mourners, who were engaged for the occasion. All those who followed painted the chest area of their garments with red paint. If this was not done, the next *sts'úḵw'i7* run would see a scarcity of fish. The mourners all cried aloud.

When a *siỷám̓* died, the whole community turned out to mourn. Hired mourners were paid for their services with blankets or skins. If a family was poor, no feast was had at that time, and the mourners' payment was deferred. When the family returned from the graveyard, they would burn cedar and salal berry and pat down the longhouse with boughs, particularly the part where the body lay.

Three or four days later, a ritualist might say the spirit was hungry. They would gather the best food, take it to the burial ground or the woods, and spread it on a wool blanket. A medicine man or woman invited the spirits to eat. The food was then burned in a fire, or sometimes distributed to the poor and old.

A widow would not eat in the presence of her children, and would bathe every day after. Spruce boughs were placed under her bed, and some hung at her head. Her head would be painted. A widower would also bathe and abstain from eating in front of his children for a month, and have boughs at the head of his bed. Three or four days after the death, all the relatives of the deceased (except the widow or widower) would cut their hair, collect it, and bury it.

After the haircutting ceremony, all those who attended the funeral went single file to the river or the inlet, and walked down into the water until it was up to their chests; then, at a word, they all dipped together once and came out again. The family would be reminded of the advice to be very careful with one another.

Throughout our lives, we bathed in the water, the children played, we made all we needed to live our daily lives, we did ceremony. We travelled to trade our goods with other Peoples and visit relatives. We survived wartime and tough winters and immense physical changes in the world around us.

4

WA LHTIM̓ÁCHT: LIFEWAYS

WEAVING WITH cedar and wool, creating natural dyes, carving, and dance and song were central in day-to-day life and ceremony in pre-Contact times. Hides and decorative items like beads were traded between the Squamish and our neighbours. Clothing was made mostly from wool and cedar bark. Goat hides were especially highly valued. Our stories were preserved in petroglyphs, painted on ancient stone.

By the time of Contact, Western red cedar was central to our way of living. Products fashioned from Western red cedar included large ocean-going canoes, large rectangular plank houses, house posts, ceremonial masks, complex latticework fishing weirs and fish traps, mats, intricate basketry, and various forms of clothing materials.

This was not the only tree valued. There were uses for so many other wood types: *k̲'emel̓áy̓* (broadleaf maple tree) was valued for making paddles; *t'ek̲t'k̲áy̓* (vine maple tree), for making bows (to hunt); and *k̲álx̲ay̓* (ironwood) was used to craft digging sticks and barbecue sticks, to name a few.

FACING: Woven garment using local resources by artist Sesémiya (Tracy Williams).

Ceremony

The onset of winter was a time of gatherings. Food and gifts were shared, with generosity displaying wealth and respectability. Winter was a time for ceremony, which brought people together in the *tl'áḵtax̱anaw̓txw* (longhouse).

"Our longhouse is very important for our Squamish people, as it is a house of celebration from birth to death, with ceremonies of baptism, blessings, puberty rights, namings, marriages, memorials, and receiving of *sx̱wáy̓x̱wey* [sacred] mask," said Sḵwx̱wú7mesh Elder Paítsmuḵ (David Jacobs). "In the winter months it is used for spiritual dancing and at this time, we learn the teachings of our ancestors, which will carry on for many generations to come."

Sx̱áaltxw Siy̓ám̓ (Chief Louis Miranda) recalled being told by his grandparents that when the snow disappeared and buds began to sprout with the beginning of spring, people would get together "for a huge ceremonial dance" performed by the entire group of adults and children. The purpose was to "offer thanks to whom it was who provided and protected them, for seeing them safely through the cold winter nights and begging and pleading for the new year to also be blessed with a bit of good luck," such as abundant *sts'úḵw'i7* (salmon) in the streams and plentiful berries and other foods. In the spring ceremony *ts'ets'iḵáy̓*, parents honoured the newborn babies and committed some to arranged marriages when they reached adulthood.

Blankets are still central to our ceremonies, as they were in the long ago. Goat hides and goat wool blankets were highly valued—as seen in one of the stories of Sx̱áaltxw Siy̓ám̓, in which Raven fooled a chief, disguising himself and offering a canoe full of mountain goat blankets for the chief's highly desired daughter. In the morning, the chief saw it was in fact only moss in the canoe, so Raven was kicked out of the longhouse and thrown into the water.

Music and dance are also central to our culture and ceremony. Traditional instruments included plank drums and drum boxes, rattles,

Sk̲wx̲wú7mesh dwellings on the shore of Coal Harbour, 1868.

hides, whistles, staffs with deer hoof rattlers—and, of course, the voices of singers.

Receiving our ancestral names has always been a significant ceremony and a signal of a new beginning in our lives. Children would go by nicknames until they received their ancestral name. You are expected to honour your name.

At ceremonies, witnesses are called and given thanks and expected to remember what they witnessed that day, to ensure it is known in the future.

Art as a Cultural Language

The style of traditional Coast Salish design, which may be carved on wood, bone, stone, or other materials, or painted, shares common characteristics across First Nations. It is typically two-dimensional and made up of three central shapes, as well as the negative space created

by integrating these shapes: circles, negative crescents, and trigons. The circle often represents unity, and the crescents often represent transition, like moon phases. Artwork portrays important figures and stories, and therefore the teachings within those histories and stories, along with places and resources important to our people. For a long time, the Northwest Coast style, known as formline, was more popularized and easily recognized by non-Indigenous people, and many Indigenous artists took on the style. Anthropologist Wayne Suttles theorized that this was partly because of more rapid degradation of Indigenous technologies in the south due to proximity to urbanization, but also because early settlers basically prioritized the northern style. He argued that early settlers "marginalized and misinterpreted" Coast Salish design.

FACING: Squamish Nation master carver Xwalacktun (Rick Harry) working in his studio. Xwalacktun is renown for his monumental carvings.

Much of Coast Salish art was carved but not painted. Everyday objects were carved into shapes. Bark shredder tools, bowls, house posts supporting the longhouse, pestles for crushing and grinding materials, and spindle whorls—any of these could be carved with abstract designs, or into human, animal, and supernatural figures. Mat creasers, used to crimp together cattail fibres to create sleeping mats, could also be carved. Adzes, clubs, combs, paddles—any of our everyday objects could be adorned with Coast Salish designs.

Weaving

The Coast Salish continue to be renown for their weaving. The blanket is a ceremonial object. "Wearing a woven blanket during ritual is transformative, moving the individual from the domain of the mundane to a sacred space," S<u>k</u>wx<u>x</u>wú7mesh weavers Chep<u>x</u>ímiya Siỷám̓ (Chief Janice George) and Skwetsímeltxw (Willard "Buddy" Joseph) wrote in a comprehensive book about Coast Salish weaving. "They are protective garments that at times of great changes in a person's life—celebrating a birth, participating in a marriage, mourning a death—offer emotional strength."

They also wrote that "people who are starting a new stage of their lives, perhaps receiving a new name, leaving childhood, or entering into a marriage, will stand on new blankets. These textiles symbolically separate them from their past and from the everyday world."

Weavers harvested plant fibres and animal fibres, which were usually spun in the winter. Mountain goat hair was used for ceremonial items, and cedar roots and bark were used for baskets and clothing. Nettle and hemp provided materials to make thread—more meticulous and painstaking work to separate the thin fibres from within the nettle stalk and spin them into thread. Twine was made from the bark of milkweed. Cattail was woven into sleeping mats, and bullrushes were woven into bags and matting.

Mountain goat hair was especially valued for blankets and clothing. The Squamish also raised woolly dogs for their fur (see chapter 10). The animal wool would be spun and wound down onto a *sél̓seltn* (spindle whorl), a disc-shaped tool used for creating yarn. Weavers would spin the wool and dye it different colours with natural dyes made from berries, plants, and clays.

Fern could act as a natural black dye; alder bark could make black, shades of brown, or orange-red. Beating diatomaceous earth into the fibres could clean and whiten the wool. Other dyes came from lichen, fungus, flowers, fruits, and charcoal. The Squamish used spindle whorls to spin yarn, and a simple rectangular frame with an upper and lower beam as a loom. Patterns are most often made up of squares, triangles, and straight and zigzagging lines that were shaped and sized differently to create unique patterns. Plants and roots brought white, brown, and green colours. According to Chepx̱ímiya Siy̓ám̓, red is used for protection and its healing power, while white symbolizes purity and new life or a new phase of life.

Cedar roots and bark were used for baskets, such as this woven basket with lid.

Spindle whorls were often carved with decorations, and the sides of a loom were sometimes also carved. Woven strips of fabric were used as headbands, pack straps, sashes, and belts. Today, weavers continue to carry responsibility in providing robes and blankets for ceremonies for significant stages of life, such as birth, namings, marriage, and funerals. Weavers create blankets for guests to sit on, for participants of the ceremony to stand on, and as the necessary regalia. At ceremonies, thanks will be given to those doing the work, such as greeters, speakers, witnesses, singers, and dancers, through gifts like blankets and headbands.

Along with wool clothing, we relied on cedar weaving for its water repellency, which is extremely effective in the warm and humid climate of our West Coast home. This skill has also been revived. For cedar weaving, the inner and outer bark had to be separated through drying or soaking, and the softer inner core was then beaten to further soften it. For apparel, cedar bark created skirts, capes, blankets, hats, and other items. Cedar bark and roots also were used to create baskets, often with intricate patterns. We also used some hides, which were sometimes painted and decorated.

Charles Hill-Tout said he was told "heraldic and totemic symbols... were never used in the old days," but posts and columns in the longhouses would be carved, and "the figure of a bird or some other animal would sometimes be placed on a pole in front of the homes or fastened to one of the gable ends."

Cedar Dugout Canoes

Though there were well-known trails to move about village sites and resource gathering sites, travel by canoe was the fastest way to get from one place to another. We relied on cedar dugout canoes, which could be up to eighteen metres long. The term "dugout" is deceptive: it is a carefully carried-out process to go from felling a giant cedar tree to travelling by canoe!

To get planks of wood to create these canoes, our ancestors would look for a cedar tree that was slightly leaning. They would cut into the tree, about halfway through the trunk. They would then drive wedges made of yew wood or elk antler into the cut. The weight of the leaning trunk, along with the force of the wedges, would cause the tree to split upward; the cut half of the trunk would break free and fall to the ground. The other half remained in the ground and could heal and continue to live.

The canoe carvers would then build the canoe right where the slab of cedar had fallen. They would work every day, dawn to dusk. After about a month, usually, the canoe would be complete, and they could carry it out of the woods to the water.

The X̱aays canoe is a large ocean-going canoe carved from a single cedar tree.

Canoeing continued to be the most common mode of transportation long after the colonizers arrived, and we still participate in canoe journeys and canoe races.

"We would travel by canoe from St'á7mes to the town of Newport (Squamish)... to go shopping. My sister Ch'átatult (Florence) and I would take the canoe. We would buck the tide but we made it. I was strong for a small woman," said the late Kwítelut (Lena Jacobs).

Our people's art as expression continues to be a language unto itself. We can share our stories and experiences. Songs capture emotion words can't. Artists interpret the world around us, bringing beauty to the everyday and preserving stories and skills for the future.

5

SWA7ÁM̓: ANCESTORS

THROUGH CONSIDERING oral history and the modern historical record, we can make more sense of the archaeological sites in Howe Sound and Burrard Inlet. Since boundaries were transient and permeable, it's not always possible to say definitively who lived at a village site or used a camp, especially in a shared area like Burrard Inlet, but these archaeological sites still give a valuable view into how people in these areas lived.

Around 2,200 to 3,500 years ago, a landslide at Nch'k̲aỷ (Mount Garibaldi) dammed the Squamish and Cheakamus Rivers, creating freshwater and brackish lakes. The rivers eventually broke through the sediment dams, connecting again with the Salish Sea. Glaciers shifted; the climate fluctuated. Around 1,500 to 2,000 years before the time of Contact with the Europeans, the physical world around us was much like we see today—the types of trees, the sea levels, the animals. The one exception was the "Little Ice Age," which created colder temperatures and advancing glaciers. Because of the colder temperatures, the tree lines in the mountains lowered, changing where we used land and resources at middle and high elevations.

We can find objects and places that represent everyday life during this time, such as settlements, camps, and areas we used to gather resources. One example of a resource gathering site is a culturally modified tree (CMT), which is a living tree we have selectively harvested from—for example, stripping bark. CMTs can be found throughout our territory, and may have been used hundreds of years ago or just the other day. CMTs have a notable ridge in the surface where someone harvested bark, a practice shared by many Indigenous Peoples in this part of the world. An incision is made close to the bottom of the trunk, parallel to the ground, and the bark is pulled outward, causing it to rip upward, often several metres up the trunk. The inner and outer bark is separated to use for things like weaving. But, as mentioned in the previous chapter, historically we also removed entire planks from cedar, leaving the old-growth tree alive, and in this way gathered the cedar we needed to build houses, canoes, and masks.

Porteau Cove Rock Shelter

At 8,600 years old, the Porteau Cove Rock Shelter (DjRt-12) is the oldest radiocarbon-dated site in Sḵwx̱wú7meshulh Aysáy̓ch (Squamish Territory) yet recorded. It is located on the east side of Howe Sound above Porteau Cove, close to present-day West Vancouver. Several massive boulders were used as cover for a hunting camp as far back as eight thousand years ago.

Archaeologists found several stone tools at the site, including a knife, a leaf-shaped projectile point, and a razor-sharp flake of volcanic glass (this is called obsidian, which is formed when lava rapidly solidifies without crystallizing). This piece of volcanic glass came from Nch'ḵay̓, where our ancestors sought refuge from the Great Flood. Archaeologists also found charcoal and signs of fire, along with pieces of shell and bones from birds and animals at the site.

Archaeologists surmise this was a temporary camp used for travelling along the bay. People using this camp would have hunted in the area and then returned to camp to butcher and cook what they caught.

There were also small shards of rock called debitage, which are a by-product of stone tool-making, suggesting that these hunters sharpened and made tools at the camp as well.

Tricouni Peak Lithics

"Lithics" refers to stone tools used by humans. By identifying where the stone was sourced, we can learn about ancient people's movement and trade. In his research, Yumks (Dr. Rudy Reimer) identified different sources of *smant* (rock) in our territory that our ancestors used. Some of those materials include rock sources that are found close to the present-day town of Squamish. Lithics from these sources have been found in Burrard Inlet, illustrating our seasonal movements. Analysis of these lithics in Burrard Inlet suggests that our seasonal movements north and south have been consistent for at least the past four thousand years.

A leaf-shaped projectile point recovered from Porteau-T1 in the DjRt-12 archaeological site in 2007.

The tools found at Tricouni Peak (DlRt-10) showed this was another temporary hunting site, situated high in the mountains between Squamish and Whistler. The site was identified by chance by a group of people on a weekend camping trip at Tricouni Peak. The tools matched rock found at the head of Howe Sound. A hearth was also found, which had been used in two separate events, approximately two thousand years ago and seven thousand years ago, illustrating regular use in the summer and fall for generations. The site's high elevation saved it from being worn away by changing sea levels. You can imagine our ancestors sitting around the hearth, telling stories. They traversed mountain peaks, looking at glaciers and lakes that are completely different today. Trees that would eventually grow ancient were still young.

K̲wek̲wu7úpay̓, Locarno Beach

The K̲wek̲wu7úpay̓ (DhRt-6) (Locarno Beach) archaeological site is located on the south shore of English Bay in present-day Vancouver. It spans over seven hundred metres along the shoreline, and as far as two hundred metres inland in some spots, and it is one of the largest and most significant archaeological sites in the area. "K̲wek̲wu7úpay̓" means "place with many wild crab apple trees." K̲wek̲wu7úpay̓ was first recorded in 1948 with a small cluster of evidence on the beach, but the area has been highly developed as Vancouver has grown, and construction has disturbed even more evidence of our presence there. The Locarno Archaeological Management Plan is an ongoing collaborative effort between local government and First Nations that have traditionally used the region to manage the area.

Archaeologists have found ornamental beads along with hundreds of stone tools at K̲wek̲wu7úpay̓: arrowheads for hunting, ground stone knives for fish butchering, scrapers and choppers, hammers and abraders, and all sorts of other objects for harvesting and processing goods. In fact, so many objects were found at K̲wek̲wu7úpay̓ that the types of artifacts found there are being looked to as representative of those used from 2,500 to 3,500 years ago. At K̲wek̲wu7úpay̓, archaeologists found *smekw'a7ál* (burial sites) and layers of shells, as well as hearths where people gathered and cooked together. They analyzed and dated the charcoal from two thousand to three thousand years ago. The sheer number of objects shows just how long we occupied K̲wek̲wu7úpay̓. This was a large and vibrant village where people came to live, fish, work, and harvest for thousands of years. Today at Locarno Beach, as you look out across the water, the wealthy Point

Grey neighbourhood is behind you, and across the bay you see the Vancouver skyline. The sun sets brilliantly to your left. Thousands of Vancouverites and tourists play games and use the beach throughout the year. Indigenous Peoples swam in those waters and watched the sunset from that spot.

St'á7mes, Squamish River

St'á7mes (DkRs-6) is an ancient village site and a current reserve at the mouth of the Squamish River under the shadow of Siỷám̓ Smánit (Chief Mountain, known as the Squamish Chief or Stawamus Chief in English). Although the site has been known to archaeologists since the early 1900s, the Sḵwx̱wú7mesh Úxwumixw (Squamish Nation) hired a company to do the first formal investigations into St'á7mes (Stawamus) in the 1990s. The excavations uncovered two distinct site types.

One was an older site type (dated to between 2,200 and 4,800 years ago) characterized by many stone tools and debris from the production of stone tools, showing they were made in that spot. These remains suggest a resource-specific area where people took advantage of the local stone, and perhaps also worked materials they brought to that spot.

More recent deposits (110 to 1,300 years old) include foundations and a layer of house floor. The oldest houses found here—wooden plank houses with communal living spaces that are typical in Coast Salish architecture—were determined to be more than one thousand years old. The house floor deposits contained many knives, as well as bone and antler tools, and fragmented fish bones and shells. The investigation uncovered intact and deliberate dog burials. These were likely household pets, some who may have gone hunting, and some were the long-haired woolly dog—a now extinct breed that was kept for its woolly coat to use for weaving.

Iṅinyáx̱a7n (Thunderbird) pictographs found at the EaRu-9 archaeological site.

St'á7mes was an ideal spot for our ancestors to settle. It is flat and dry, and sheltered from harsh sea winds. It is close to the Squamish River, where *sts'úḵw'i7* (salmon) and eulachon could be harvested, and close to other rivers and trails into alpine areas where we could hunt and collect other resources. It also was accessible to travel by land down south. Almost five thousand years later, Sḵwx̱wú7mesh continue to live at St'á7mes.

Nkwu'7say Smant, Squamish River

Nkwu'7say *smant* is another source of stone used to make lithics. These *smant* (rock) sources are important locations that Sḵwx̱wú7mesh used as rock quarries because they preferred the quality and accessibility of the stone there. Nkwu'7say, which translates as "place of the spring salmon," is close to Shovelnose Creek in Upper Squamish. The creek flows into the Squamish River from Mount Cayley in the northeast, and the streambed has easy access to many cobbles and boulders of good-quality dacite volcanic rock.

Oral history connects this site to the X̱aays, when the chief of the Spring Salmon People taught the Sḵwx̱wú7mesh how to fish, conduct a *sts'úḵw'i7* ceremony, and respect and treat the parts of *sts'úḵw'i7* to ensure they would return.

An archaeological site nearby that is likely a fishing camp (EaRu-2) includes stone flakes, cores, and fragments of tools from Nkwu'7say. This site, above the Squamish River, shows the process of manufacturing lithics. This site is close to the village P'uy̓ám̓, which means "blackened from smoke." People from P'uy̓ám̓ were considered of high status and renown for being great mountain goat hunters. Nkwu'7say *smant* is found far beyond P'uy̓ám̓ throughout our territory.

X̱wáy̓x̱way, Lumbermen's Arch

X̱wáy̓x̱way (DhRs-2) is a village that was once located on the north shore of what is now called Stanley Park in Vancouver, near the Lumbermen's Arch landmark. X̱wáy̓x̱way means "mask." There was a large village here, with a longhouse that was two hundred feet long. The highly spiritual and significant masks made here were constructed out of cedar trees in the area and used in ceremonial dances. Culturally modified trees still stand at X̱wáy̓x̱way.

The archaeological site has been severely damaged and over half of the site has been disturbed by the development of Stanley Park during the past century. Sections of shell deposits were used as road fill. They were removed from their original location, and there is no way to know the exact location they were taken from, which limits what we can learn from them now. Still, signs of our ancestors remain: shell deposits, hearths, stone artifacts, and a burial box. Our ancestors lived there until 1880, and it remained a hub of activity until we were forcibly removed so a road could be built around Stanley Park.

The Xwmétskwiyam, Sḵwx̱wú7mesh, and Sel̓íl̓witulh all claim connections to this ancient village before it was decimated by smallpox in the late 1700s and early 1800s. The Sḵwx̱wú7mesh lived there until the mid-1900s. In the past few years, there have been gatherings and mask dances at the site, showing that even though the physical history of the Sḵwx̱wú7mesh has been damaged, the culture remains alive.

Nepítl', Buck Mountain

This site is high in the mountains, with radiocarbon dates of activity as recent as 200 years ago and as far back as 1,400 years ago. Nepítl' (DlRt-9) is a rock shelter, where hunters would seek cover from the elements under an overhanging boulder.

Nepítl' has tool and bone remains that are characteristic of a hunting camp, as well as hearths and pictographs of humans and animals on the stone walls.

"Nepítl'" means "deer origin place," dating back to the X̱aays period. The Transformers met a man who was angered by all the changes they were making. He sharpened his spear, ready to act on his anger. The X̱aays took his spear, broke it into pieces, and placed the pieces on his head and legs, changing him into a deer, creating an animal for the Sḵwx̱wú7mesh people to hunt.

Ḵw'émḵw'em, Defence Islands

"Ḵw'émḵw'em" means "lots of kelp," referring to the presence of bull kelp in the area. Many Sḵwx̱wú7mesh people would harvest at these islands. Archaeologists have found lithic tools scattered on the pebbly peach, and have excavated hundreds of basalt, slate, and andesite stone artifacts. Four culturally modified trees stand nearby: three with bark removed and one cut down and partially carved into a canoe that was never finished.

Central panel view of pictographs found at the EaRu-9 archaeological site.

The only radiocarbon date from this site is from roughly nine hundred years ago, but oral history and stories place people using K̲w'émk̲w'em from time immemorial up until recent memory as a traditional burial ground and a place to hunt seal and fish, and harvest cedar.

In one *syets* (true story), warriors of the Sk̲wx̲wú7mesh and Yík̲wilhtax̲ ended their conflict and made peace by throwing their weapons overboard into the waters of Howe Sound close to K̲w'émk̲w'em.

We have many more oral stories. Our people tell the story of K̲ál̓k̲alilh, the Giant Cannibal Woman who stole children who stayed out too late at night. Our stories include giants, Wild People, and animals like the Salmon People. Our ancestors called on animals for help, like when a young man, Son of the Bright Day, called on the *techtechnís* (hummingbird), *sekém̓kem* (bumble bee), and *xwet* (Swainson's thrush) to help him ripen berries faster. Our oral stories tell us about our relations with our families, our surroundings, and our neighbours.

PART TWO

SÍIY̓AM̓, SÍIYAY̓, SÍIYUXWA7, MÉN̓MEN: CHIEFS, FRIENDS, ELDERS, CHILDREN

"For Squamish people of high status, marriage was primarily an economic union between families of different villages . . . [Homer] Barnett emphasized the value placed on 'many homes.'"

SQUAMISH INDIAN LAND USE AND OCCUPANCY REPORT

CULTIVATING GOOD relationships with other Indigenous Peoples was always essential to maintaining peace and accessing trade. We traded with our immediate neighbours to the north, to the interior, along the Fraser River, and over to Vancouver Island and into present-day Washington State. Distinct stone materials from our territory have been found around the Salish Sea and in Puget Sound and the Olympic Peninsula in Washington. Stone artifacts from as far as Oregon, as well as the Fraser River Canyon, have been found at archaeological sites near Gibsons, BC. Our neighbours are part of our oral histories, part of our families, and these relations are as important today as they have always been.

We travelled by land and sea to visit our neighbours. Interactions weren't always peaceful—Indigenous Peoples also travelled to raid other villages, often in retaliation for past raids. Multiple language groups would gather in some areas, like Burrard Inlet and the Fraser River. Certain resources, like fishing spots, could be under control of specific families. On the one hand, boundaries were "transparent and transient, and subject to the rise and fall of family fortunes," Randy Bouchard and Dorothy Kennedy described in the *Squamish Indian Land Use and Occupancy* report. But on the other hand, boundaries as they stood still had to be respected, and protocols had to be followed.

Part Two focuses on the Sḵwx̱wú7mesh perspective, drawing from oral histories and research, but there are many stories between Sḵwx̱wú7mesh families and among other First Nations. We share a summary of S<u>k</u>w<u>x</u>wú7mesh history here, and it does not negate the other histories. We respect the sovereignty and distinctive stories of our neighbours.

Areas of Responsibility

Indigenous Peoples could enter each other's territories through marriage and kinship rights, or with permission. Through intermarriage, many villages were home to more than one language group.

For generations, many of the S<u>k</u>w<u>x</u>wú7mesh whose winter villages were in Howe Sound travelled south in summer into our Burrard Inlet permanent villages and campsites. Oral history and academic research indicate that before Contact we marked our presence southward, living at villages like <u>X</u>wáy̓<u>x</u>way ("mask," at Lumbermen's Arch), Seńá<u>k</u>w ("inside the head of the bay," at False Creek, which also became known as Kitsilano Indian Reserve No. 6), and Xwmélch'stn ("place of rolling waters"; the mouth of the Capilano River). Archaeological sites suggest ten thousand years of occupation in Howe Sound, and four thousand years of occupation in Burrard Inlet. There is some debate on permanent occupation of Burrard Inlet—evidence suggests it began before Contact, but was significantly accelerated with the onset of the wage economy and colonial settlement. Before Contact, seasonal rounds were an integral part of many Indigenous Peoples' economies and livelihood, and it was typical to spend many months in different camps and villages, living according to resource availability.

The importance of reciprocity was central to our trade and culture. Maintaining relationships meant relatives in different villages could rely on each other.

"In years of resource shortage occasional food shortfalls occurred. By accessing a neighbouring territory through kinship relations, S<u>k</u>w<u>x</u>wú7mesh people could make up for these periodic shortfalls," Yum<u>k</u>s (Dr. Rudy Reimer) wrote.

X̱ats'alánexw Siỷám̓ (Chief August Jack Khatsahlano); his wife, Swanamia; and a child canoeing near Sen̓áḵw, 1907.

Yumḵs also described the importance of Sḵwx̱wú7mesh place names. "Sḵwx̱wú7mesh place names are deeply descriptive," he said. "[Sḵwx̱wú7mesh] place names are linked to the wider oral history and traditions of the territory and its past."

This was exemplified in one exchange X̱ats'alánexw Siỷám̓ (Chief August Jack Khatsahlano) had with J.S. Matthews. X̱ats'alánexw Siỷám̓ dismissed Matthews's attempt to adjust a translation to make it more anglicized.

Matthews: August! What does Cheakamus mean?

X̱ats'alánexw: Basket; basket catch fish. Put basket in ripple in river; fish go inside; cannot get out. [August said these baskets were about ten feet long and three feet high.]

Matthews: It could be called "Fish Trap River"?

X̱ats'alánexw: Why call it that when Cheakamus is a better name. It's "Cheakamus," that's "basket catch fish."

6

TELYÉSH IY SÚTICH: SOUTH AND NORTH

ELKSN (POINT GREY) is acknowledged today as the farthest southwest boundary for the S<u>k</u>w<u>x</u>wú7mesh, and the name translates as "point of land." This is where the <u>X</u>aays (Transformer brothers) landed and hurled stones at Nch'<u>k</u>aỷ (Mount Garibaldi), according to S<u>x</u>áaltxw Siỷám̓ (Chief Louis Miranda). Elksn was known for having old-growth cedar, many elk, sturgeon, and smelt. Shellfish dotted the shore. James Point, who was from Xwmétskwiyam (Musqueam), told Wayne Suttles that "northern people" raided the stockaded house of respected leader <u>K</u>iyáplánexw near Point Grey. He said <u>K</u>iyáplánexw Siỷám̓ was leader of the people at Xwmétskwiyam, Iỷál̓mexw (Jericho Beach), and Xwmélch'stn (Capilano River), and had homes at all three places.

The ones who speak S<u>k</u>'emíñem (Halkomelem) are our closest neighbours to the south. Halkomelem is another Coast Salish language and it has many distinct variations but three main groups: Upriver, Downriver, and Vancouver Island. It is believed the Sel̓íl̓witulh (Tsleil-Waututh) spoke a variation of Downriver most closely associated with a dialect spoken by the people from Kw'ikw'tl'ám (Kwikwetlem/Coquitlam), but this variation became extinct because of extreme sickness that killed many people in the 1700s and 1800s. Many surviving descendants wound up speaking S<u>k</u>w<u>x</u>wú7mesh

Sníchim (Squamish Language) after the impacts of sickness and colonization caused closer integration and marriage with the S<u>k</u>wx<u>w</u>ú7mesh.

The Indigenous languages are very rich and unique on this part of the coast. "Musqueam cannot speak to Squamish, but share the Halkomelem tongue with Cowichan and Nanaimo [on Vancouver Island]," Charles Hill-Tout wrote. Some of our place names are similar, and we also share similar stories from our oral history. The ones who speak S<u>k</u>'emíṅem have their own stories about the Transformers and the two-headed serpent, like the S<u>k</u>wx<u>w</u>ú7mesh variations. Our stories place Sínulh<u>k</u>aỷ (the double-headed serpent) in Howe Sound and Burrard Inlet, while Upriver and Downriver Halkomelem stories place the serpent in Indian Arm, near the mouth of the Fraser River and farther upriver.

Trade and Kin Ties

We S<u>k</u>wx<u>w</u>ú7mesh interacted with those who spoke S<u>k</u>'emíṅem around Burrard Inlet and the lower Fraser River, an area rich with fish, animals, and plants. The area now known as Coal Harbour in downtown Vancouver was a perfect place to harvest herring. Oblate records show that both S<u>k</u>wx<u>w</u>ú7mesh and Xwmétskwiyam were staying at Xwmélch'stn in the 1860s. Multiple sources have also said the Xwmétskwiyam depended on the river for chum salmon. Meanwhile, both Peoples plus the Seḷíḷwitulh have oral traditions connecting them with the once-populous village <u>X</u>wáỷ<u>x</u>way at present-day Lumbermen's Arch in Stanley Park.

In terms of archaeology, one of the main signifiers of how we traded across territories are stone objects sourced from stone quarries in our territory. For example, at an archaeological site at Marpole in South Vancouver, Yum<u>k</u>s (Dr. Rudy Reimer) documented many pieces of *smant tl'a Nch'<u>k</u>aỷ* (obsidian, Mount Garibaldi stone) at the site. Yum<u>k</u>s believes this is likely associated with S<u>k</u>wx<u>w</u>ú7mesh people exchanging this stone material for access to the mouth of the Fraser River, where our people regularly participated in the *stséḵi7* (sockeye salmon) fishery. Buffalo Mathias also said some Sḵwx̱wú7mesh helped work on and shared proceeds of a fish trap near Xwmétskwiyam.

There was extensive marriage between the Sḵwx̱wú7mesh and the ones who speak Sḵ'emín̓em. X̱ats'alánexw Siy̓ám̓ (Chief August Jack Khatsahlano) said Ḵiyáplánexw Siy̓ám̓ had three wives: one who was Xwmétskwiyam, one who was Sḵwx̱wú7mesh, and one who was Shishá7lh (Sechelt). Ḵiyáplánexw Siy̓ám̓ was also known as George and is often referred to as "Old Man" Kiapilano, or similar variations, in early 1900s writings. Kiapilano and its variants were further anglicized to "Capilano." Ḵiyáplánexw Siy̓ám̓ is said to have been full Musqueam or half Squamish by different sources.

(As a side note, most people in the region are familiar with Sḵwx̱wú7mesh leader S7ápeleḵ Siy̓ám̓ (Chief Joe Capilano), a prominent chief in the 1800s, and it's important to note here that this is a different person. "Old Man" Kiapilano would have been born in the late 1700s; S7ápeleḵ Siy̓ám̓ was born in 1854.)

Marriage brought together families and expanded kin networks. In her research, Dorothy Kennedy said that the fact that the Sḵwx̱wú7mesh prioritized marrying out of their villages supported the idea that marriage created "allied families" that were an essential part of fostering economics and prestige.

People would also come together through potlatches, travelling from across territories to attend. X̱ats'alánexw Siy̓ám̓ recalled hearing about a large potlatch at Iy̓ál̓mexw:

The big potlatch at Jericho was before my time; all I know about it is what they tell me, but it was the biggest potlatch of all. Indians come from everywhere—Lummi, Victoria, Saanich, Nanaimo, Panall (Cooper Island), Chee-woat-held; no Indians from Sechelt; they not come to potlatches.

Four men give it. Chinalset (Jericho Charlie), Tow-hu-quam-kee, Hey-much-tun, and Charl-tun (Old Tom). They have great big building just other side where air station is now; building about three hundred feet long, ninety feet wide, great big beams. At each end three big posts; high; big as a man's body, then three big beams run the entire length of building on top of posts, each beam eighty to ninety feet long, and butted end to end so as to run whole three hundred feet of building one on each side, one down middle. Split cedar slab sides, laid what you call horizontal, laced together with small posts; roof of great big split cedar slabs fitted together like this so as not to let water in; tell you how big they were. Four kinds (Indians) use one for canoe after they pull it down. Warship come along one day and take a lot of it away; load on scow and take on board; don't know what they did with the slabs; to England, may be, may be burn, don't know. But you see the way they build the roof no water can get in.

He said there was another longhouse at Seṅáḵw ("inside the head of the bay," at False Creek, which also became known as Kitsilano Indian Reserve No. 6) that was between 175 and 200 feet long and 70 feet wide, with platforms all along the edge about 5 feet wide.

Both before and after Contact, the relationships among the Xwmétskwiyam, Sḵwx̱wú7mesh, and Seli̓l̓witulh were defined by peace. Squamish had sought refuge at Musqueam during a northern raid, and people from multiple villages allied together to fight off northern raiders. When the Seli̓l̓witulh were decimated by *kwétsi siy̓ám̓ smex̱wíws* (smallpox), it seems the Squamish assisted and helped build their village, the Burrard Indian Reserve. Randy Bouchard and Dorothy Kennedy noted there was an influx of Sḵwx̱wú7mesh men and women in the village in the 1800s. It is said that when Squamish residents of the Kitsilano Indian Reserve No. 6 (at Seṅáḵw) were pushed off their land in 1913 and moved to the Squamish River, the Xwmétskwiyam helped move their ancestral remains.

The Squamish also used land toward Port Moody at the far east end of Burrard Inlet, where the village Títemtsen stood. This is also the easternmost Sḵwx̱wú7mesh place name. Our spelling of the name "Seli̓l̓witulh" marks the village at the head of Indian Arm and the estuary of Indian River, and it signifies land belonging to Seli̓l̓witulh. This name is possibly derived from *slíl*, which means "a bunch of woven blankets" or "piled up mountain goat blankets." "Seİíİwitulh" also may have been used to refer to the waters of Burrard Inlet, but there were some varying translations. Xwechtáal (Andy Paull) said Seİíİwitulh referred to Burrard Inlet, while others said it referred only to the area around Indian Arm. According to the *Land Use and Occupancy* report, older Sḵwx̱wú7mesh members said the older generations of Seİíİwitulh had special knowledge of Indian medicine.

Across the water from present-day Deep Cove is Belcarra, where the large village Temtemíxwtn once stood; its name means "lots of land place." According to Sx̱áaltxw Siỷám̓, the village was so large that the villagers could all gather together when ducks flew low overhead, and when they yelled loudly the sound would stun ducks and they would fall from the sky. According to the late Sḵwx̱wú7mesh Elder Emma Joe in the *Land Use and Occupancy* report, the Giant Cannibal Woman Ḵáİḵalilh lived around Indian River.

Bouchard and Kennedy recorded some conflicting accounts of exactly what Sḵwx̱wú7mesh resource use would be needed in what proximity to the Seİíİwitulh, and when. In more recent times, as quoted in the *Land Use and Occupancy* report, Sḵwx̱wú7mesh member Ed Nahanee said some Sḵwx̱wú7mesh went to Indian Arm to dig clams and were told to leave. But another community member, Ted Band, said we shared a reciprocal relationship where people from Mission and Capilano also dug clams in front of the Seİíİwitulh Indian Reserve No. 3. As Bouchard and Kennedy described, the protocols in place might have shifted over time with marriage, especially after Contact.

The Stl'áİmexw

To the north, our closest Stl'áİmexw neighbours were the Lúx̱wels (Lil'wat People, also known as Mount Currie People) in the Pemberton Valley. There were about fifty-six kilometres between the northernmost Sḵwx̱wú7mesh village and the southernmost Stl'áİmexw

(St’at’imc, also known as the Lillooets), who are part of the Lower St’at’imc, though we also traded with the Upper St’at’imc farther north.

The Lower Stl’ál̓mexw would gather berries and hunt in the area between the Squamish and Pemberton Valleys, and so would the Sk̲wx̲wú7mesh. Both the Sk̲wx̲wú7mesh and Lúx̲wels have stories that tell of punishment when either party encroached on the other’s territory, illustrating how they respected those boundaries. Charlie Mack from Lúx̲wels told a story about some Sk̲wx̲wú7mesh who had camped near Lúx̲wels territory. The Transformers came upon them and deemed it inappropriate that they camped so close to people who spoke another language, so they changed the Sk̲wx̲wú7mesh into a pile of rocks. Similarly, the Sk̲wx̲wú7mesh have a story about Lúx̲wels being transformed into three distinctive rocks, called Lex̲wlúx̲wels, still visible in Howe Sound today. According to X̲ats’alánexw Siy̓ám̓ (Chief August Jack Khatsahlano), the Lúx̲wels did not know if a canoe was passing, but they were waiting in hope of getting a ride to Squamish. In another version, the X̲aays asked them what they were doing, and when the Lúx̲wels said they were resting, “the Transformers suggested they could have a good rest there and changed them into rock.”

FACING: Transformer mask carving on a X̲aays canoe.

The only instance of hostility between the Sk̲wx̲wú7mesh and Lúx̲wels that Bouchard and Kennedy noted in their research was an incident at Yekw’ápsm that Sx̲áaltxw Siy̓ám̓ (Chief Louis Miranda) shared. Some girls from Yekw’ápsm were picking blueberries around Garibaldi and were killed by Lúx̲wels. Sx̲áaltxw Siy̓ám̓ said that, in revenge, the Sk̲wx̲wú7mesh invited the Lúx̲wels to a feast at Yekw’ápsm and killed them once they were inside the longhouse.

According to oral history shared through the Squamish Lil’wat Cultural Centre, the village Spú7ets’, at the confluence of Rubble Creek and the Cheakamus River, was inhabited by both Sk̲wx̲wú7mesh and Lúx̲wels, and was buried by a Mount Garibaldi volcanic eruption.

As the story goes, for a while the members of both Nations lived peacefully, but eventually the villagers began to disrespect one another and the Thunderbird intervened. He flapped his wings, causing the volcano to erupt and a massive rockslide that buried Spú7ets'. Hundreds were killed instantly. The survivors were sent home with the message that family and neighbours need to work together.

The Yík̲wilhtax̲ (Lekwiltok)

Stories of parties that raided our territory are mostly about the Yík̲wilhtax̲. The Yík̲wilhtax̲ is a name with versions used by different central Coast Salish languages such as Squamish and Halkomelem. It's often thought to refer to one or more tribes from the people today called the Kwakwaka̲'wa̲kw, who were often incorrectly labelled the "Kwakiutl people." One of the Kwakwaka̲'wa̲kw tribes is called the Ligwilda'xw, which some think is where the term "Yík̲wilhtax̲" comes from. While contemporary Ligwilda'xw people are associated with present-day Campbell River and Cape Mudge, historically they migrated south into areas occupied by Comox, Klahoose, Hamalco, and Tla'amin people. Prior to the early nineteenth-century migration, they were more connected to areas around Topaze Harbour near Sayward, BC.

In stories by Squamish, the Yík̲wilhtax̲ are often called Northerners and considered an enemy of the Sk̲wx̲wú7mesh, but many of these stories are quite recent, placed in the early 1800s. It's believed that raids between villages intensified after Europeans arrived, bringing guns with them. In the *Fort Langley Journals* in 1829, Archibald McDonald wrote about the people of the Fraser River: "It is impossible to describe their continual alarm at the very name of this formidable foe [the Yík̲wilhtax̲]."

"It is evident that much which has been written about Indian slaves—as in other matters—has been exaggerated and 'coloured,'" city archivist J.S. Matthews wrote after a conversation with X̱ats'a-lánexw Siy̓ám̓. "It is obvious, for instance, that a Yuclataw [Yíḵwilhtax̱] slave in the possession of the Squamish would be a source of irritation to the Yuclataws; might form an excuse for a reprisal raid on the Squamish, and, regardless of what whitemen have written of the desire of Indians to fight one another, the fact is they feared those raids, and desired peace, no less than we do."

According to Sam Baker, the Yíḵwilhtax̱ travelled up Howe Sound and raided St'á7mes. In Bouchard and Kennedy's research, X̱ats'a-lánexw Siy̓ám̓, Sx̱áaltxw Siy̓ám̓, and Buffalo Mathias all confirmed that Xwmélch'stn (Capilano) was a fortified village in the face of Yíḵwilhtax̱ attacks. They concluded that there was likely a period of intensified hostilities shortly after contact with Europeans. Amateur anthropologist Charles Hill-Tout described the battle won by Ḵiyáplánexw Siy̓ám̓ over the Yíḵwilhtax̱ at Xwmélch'stn, using a surprise volley of musket fire:

It is told that the [Squamish] scouts brought timely warning of the approach of two war canoes of U'keltaws [Yíḵwilhtax̱]. The [Squamish] at that time had a courageous and resourceful leader in their head chief Ḵiyáplánexw Siy̓ám̓. He assembled a number of the bravest men and best shots of the tribe and hid them in a log hut built for the purpose at the mouth of the narrows leading into Burrard Inlet. On the flats immediately in front of the hut he placed some of the women and children, who were to pretend to be gathering driftwood. When the U'keltaws came into the narrows they at once perceived the women and children, and, thinking to secure these for slaves in the apparent absence of the men, they landed. They women and children now fled towards the woods, drawing their pursuers after them close to the hut. The hidden [Squamish] now opened fire upon the U'keltaws and killed every one without harm to themselves.

Buffalo Mathias told a similar version of this story. Hill-Tout also recorded an incident during which residents of Jericho Beach, Capilano River, Musqueam, and Marpole all joined forces with Ḵiyáplánexw Siy̓ám̓ to take revenge on the Yíḵwilhtax̱ at the Battle at Maple Bay.

The Sḵwx̱wú7mesh retaliated. X̱ats'alánexw Siỷám̓ talked about Shishaỷu7áy (Britannia Beach) in Howe Sound. Although there is slight disagreement about the exact spot, he identified it as a tiny island near the shore just north of Britannia Creek. X̱ats'alánexw Siỷám̓ told J.S. Matthews that it was at this site that Squamish warriors "beached their war canoes" and "displayed on poles the heads of their foes decapitated in warfare." Andy Natrall and George Moody also asserted this claim.

According to Sx̱áaltxw Siỷám̓, the area is known for screech owls, and the term *shaỷu7* can mean "screech owl" or "ghost of a dead person." So, in the *Land Use and Occupancy* report, the place was interpreted both as "place of screech owls" and "place of ghosts." "Because of the association between dead people and this bird, Louis Miranda recalled the old people used to talk about the Britannia Beach area as being 'ghosted,'" the report reads.

According to the oral history, at Tsítsusm (Potlatch Creek), the Sḵwx̱wú7mesh and Yíḵwilhtax̱ agreed to end their raiding of each other's villages. Sx̱áaltxw Siỷám̓ told a story of a powerful warrior, his great-great-granduncle Xwepelḵínem, who fought the Yíḵwilhtax̱ until a Yíḵwilhtax̱ woman, Kwelá7wiḵw, was taken captive by the Squamish and married a Squamish warrior, Pítsemeḵ, and she suggested peace so no more of her relatives on either side would be killed.

FACING: A view of the sun setting on Shishaỷu7áy (Britannia Beach).

Háx̱sten (the late Harriet George) told a similar story interpreted by Xwechtáal (Andy Paull) in conversation with J.S. Matthews in 1933. "[Háx̱sten is] my wife's grandmother, who actually saw the bodies of the slain. She is now over 100 years old. It is claimed that she is 112 years old," Xwechtáal said.

Háx̱sten said they had Kwelá7wiḵw and that she was pregnant. Eighteen warriors came and attacked Xwmélch'stn and made off with Kwelá7wiḵw. They ran into three Squamish men in a canoe near Point Atkinson. The Squamish men retreated but successfully turned on

the attackers until just two raiders and Kwelá7wik̲w were left. She told her captors to stop fighting. Only one Squamish man, Sxwelík̲tn, survived. Matthews's recording of Xwechtáal interpreting Háx̲sten's story continues: "Pítsemek̲, half-brother to 'Old Chief' Capilano, said, 'This fighting must stop.' Kwelá7wik̲w's husband said, 'Men tl'i7s lha Kwelá7wik̲w. I am going to Nanaimo, where there is a Nanaimo man married to a woman from the north. I will ask him to go with me, and we will go as ambassadors of peace from the people of the south to the people of the north, and I will ask them to let me have Kwelá7wik̲w.' In due time, the mission proceeded north, their requests were granted, peace was declared, and [here, Xwechtáal laughed as he interpreted] they lived happily ever after.'"

In the *Occupancy* report, Tim Moody said, "The Yík̲wilhtax̲ people [realized] as much as the Squamish that they could not go on indefinitely with those senseless raids where one then the other tribe suffered losses." They went to Tsítsusm to "lay down their arms and forget their tribal enmities."

And it is evident that the names mentioned in this historic event are still with us today. They are carried by people in our community, brought here by marriage and a peaceful reconciliation.

The Last Battle: Chilcotin Raid

The Sk̲wx̲wú7mesh also tell stories about raids by the Stek'ín (Haida) and the Sx̲íx̲nam (Chilcotin), also both coming from the north. Sx̲wálh Siy̓ám̓ (Chief Jimmy Jimmy) was said to be the lone survivor of a Sx̲íx̲nam raid when he was a child.

Sx̲áaltxw Siy̓ám̓ shared the story of the last raid of the Sx̲íx̲nam: "What I will be relating here is something [about] my late stepfather whose ancestral name was Sík̲emkin, known to the white people as Chief Squamish Jim. He said that it was something that he seen when he was in his early teens. I also overheard it when it was related to the other children by the other dear old people. This is how my late stepfather started out to tell me."

The story begins with the stepfather of Sx̱áaltxw Siy̓ám̓ going mountain goat hunting with his father and brother. Síḵemkin's father went to visit some relatives. Here is how Sx̱áaltxw Siy̓ám̓ said Síḵemkin would tell the story about his father: "As we were nearing our destination, our father seemed to be studying things. He was finding it strange that there was no smoke going up from the big house and also, no one seemed to be moving around. We landed on the shore and found it strange that no one came down to see who was arriving...

"Our dad hurried up the bank and I followed closely behind him. When we got up the riverbank we seen the house, there was no smoke coming out and also no one appeared. Our father hurried to the house; we never seen anyone, so we stood in the doorway looking around. It was then that our father seen the two men lying dead on their bed."

The men had been stabbed by a war spear. Back at the water, Síḵemḵin discovered a bunch of arrows in the sand and another relative dead. His father concluded that the women and children had been taken and the men killed. They brought the man in the sand into the canoe, and headed downriver to tell their friends what had happened.

"When we arrived at our home, we found out that the people already were aware of what happened. One of the women, who had been taken away in the raid, had returned to this village after making her escape from the hands of the enemy, which already had her as captive for a few days. It was through the kindness of the man that held her that she was able to escape."

The woman said she saw a stranger come out of the underbrush by the river, then disappear again. She ran back and told her husband, but he didn't believe her. She told some of the other women, but they were afraid to tell their husbands. She saw the man again in the evening, and then by the fire in her own home—both times, her husband still didn't believe her. Finally, she woke to find the tall man was standing there with a spear, and her husband was dying, and he motioned her to get their son. She saw all the other men were dead, except one was missing. The women were taken away, each with a man guarding them. She said her guard was kind, and on the third night he woke her and let her free. Sx̱áaltxw Siỷám̓ continued to recount his stepfather's story: "My stepfather would say, 'That is what that woman told me when she got home with her son after her kindhearted captor helped her and her son to get away.' My father would also say that that was where he got his first arrows and his father made him a bow. I was very young but my father knew that I would be a great hunter. He would say that the woman, who got away from the enemy, became a grandmother of Charlie Douglas and his sister. That boy she had with her grew up to manhood and got a wife, he was the father of Charlie Douglas and his sister...

"This is what I know as I was told and heard others speak of. This is what really happened to those people who were all by themselves many miles up the Squamish River. It is said that this was the last raid of the Chilcotins on the Squamish people."

At the end of this story, it is related that this woman went back to live with her captors. When she was old, some Squamish went to visit her, but she said she was happy where she was.

There are several Squamish historic stories that relate the power of connection through marriage. The following is one example.

Ch'ich'iyúy: The Two Sisters

Here is a story that is shared about how peace was reached with the Stek'ín, as told by Squamish Elders in a book released for the 2010 Olympics:

The Squamish had fierce enemies but none so feared as the Stek'ín. Stek'ín is our name for the Haida. It so happened one day that a party of Stek'ín had travelled successfully down the coast to steal up on the Squamish people in the hopes of raiding a village. The enemy's purpose was to deal a blow to the Squamish; we were their mortal enemy. The Stek'ín had also planned to steal away with young women and children to be taken as slaves or to take the place of some of their own loved ones[;] they may have been lost to other enemies or to accident and illness.

At this time, among the Stek'ín were two young men—twins. They were sons of a highly respected Chief among their people. They were young and this was the first time they had accompanied the warriors on a raid. They had travelled far out in the open ocean. This was how they came to travel from their northern home to the Squamish territory. Once the southern journey was completed, their canoe moved closer-in to shore, travelling by night until the village was reached.

The two young Stek'ín twins were waiting not too patiently near their canoes. Because they were young and inexperienced and to protect them their leaders had left the twins to guard the canoes as the main war party went to watch their target village. The warriors had been gone most of the night and the two young men were grumbling, so they made up their minds to go and look at the village themselves. They moved off silently in the direction the warriors had gone.

With great care, they finally came to a crest where they could look down upon the sleeping Squamish village. Cautiously, they went down to the river that separated the village from their party. Suddenly, they stopped. Two young women had come out of a longhouse. They were the first ones awake in their village. This was unusual. It was usually an Elder who woke first. As the young men watched, the girls went about their morning: bathing, praying and then heading back to their longhouse. The young men looked at one another. In their unspoken way they had decided they would marry these two young women.

They set off to find their raiding party. They found the others just as the raid was about to begin, but they had enough time to let the leader know they had seen two young women, to show him which house they had emerged from and to get his promise that the young women would be captured and not harmed in any way. You see, twins were believed to be very special. If these two young

men-twins, who would be future leaders, saw something of their future in those young women, then the leader knew he must agree to do as they asked.

The raid was successful. The Stek'ín took the village by surprise, killing many and taking many captives, among them the two young women who were immediately turned over to the young men. Upon seeing the young women up close, the men were astonished to recognize that these girls were also twins! They were brought home to the Stek'ín village of their father and treated with great respect. The young women soon came to realize that they were not to be enslaved.

Under the care and protection of the Chief's family, it became clear the young women were to be married to that Chief's twin sons. And so it was. The women carried themselves with such dignity and respect for their adopted family and people that they were well known and liked by all. Indeed, their husbands' families were very proud of them. It was only when someone noticed that sometimes the twins would wander away, off from the other women, where they would cry and become very sad, that their husbands questioned them to try to see how they could help.

The women told them that they were happy in their marriages and said they knew all of their husbands' people treated them well. They were sad because they missed their families and wished that their parents, relatives, and the Squamish people could know their children and could know how well they had been treated.

FACING: A view of Ch'ich'iyúy, known as the Two Sisters or the Lions.

The young men went to their parents and then the Chief went to the other village leaders. Because of the fine example these twin Squamish women had shown, the Stek'ín decided to sue for peace with the Squamish people. So it did happen. When the Stek'ín Chief, his sons and their wives sent word seeking peace, the Squamish people accepted.

When the women had passed away in their old age, the Creator changed them into the mountains we see every day; we call them the Sisters, or now in modern times, the Lions. It is for all Squamish to remember their example and to understand how the women helped to secure peace with the Stek'ín.

7

TELTÍWET IY TELÉTSNECH: WEST AND EAST

IN THE SOUTHWEST, the farthest point of our territory is Ch'k̲w'élhp (Gibsons Landing)—where the story of the brothers Tsek̲ánchtn and Sx̲eláltn and the wooden sea lion took place. Here, our territory is close to that of the Shishá7lh (Sechelt). They are another Coast Salish group, speaking their own language: she shashishalhem.

Dominic Charlie said the White Islets, just northwest of St'elk̲áya (Roberts Creek) was the limit of Sk̲wx̲wú7mesh territory. He told Wayne Suttles, "If Sechelt people saw Squamish go beyond the White Islets, they would kill them." Randy Bouchard and Dorothy Kennedy, however, pointed out they couldn't find any other evidence of this. But X̲ats'alánexw Siy̓ám̓ (Chief August Jack Khatsahlano) also emphasized the importance of this boundary: "Schen̓k̲, that's Gibsons Landing; St'elk̲áya, that's Roberts Creek; that beyond Squamish must not go; beyond St'elk̲áya is Sechelt," he told J.S. Matthews. "Schen̓k̲ is a little creek about three hundred to four hundred yards west of Gibsons Landing; St'elk̲áya is a long way; about three miles to Roberts Creek. There's a creek come down at St'elk̲áya; Indians camp there all the time; but north of that is Sechelt country."

It seems there was extensive marriage between the Sḵwx̱wú7mesh and the Shishá7lh. According to Oblate records from the 1800s analyzed by Bouchard and Kennedy, 10.45 percent of Sḵwx̱wú7mesh marriages were to Shishá7lh. The research also showed 68.5 percent of marriages allied one Sḵwx̱wú7mesh family with another; 7.9 percent were to Halkomelem-speaking people; 2.1 percent were to other Coast Salish groups, and 0.9 percent were to Stl'ál̓mexw (Lillooet). As mentioned earlier, Ḵiyáplánexw Siy̓ám̓ had a Shishá7lh wife.

The area is rich with marine natural resources. Both Sḵwx̱wú7mesh and Shishá7lh would have been active seal and sea lion hunters. X̱ats'alánexw Siy̓ám̓ described what seal hunting would look like: "Squamish go seal hunting in canoe. Seal sleeping on surface; just under surface... sneak up and spear him... Then cook him, little fire, slow, not big fire. Cook on two little logs on ground; about ten inches diameter; lay logs side each other; about twelve inches apart on ground; built little fire of pitch sticks between logs; lay seal across logs so his middle over fire; cook him slowly; just burn the hair off. When the middle's done, catch him by tail or feet, turn him over; two or three times, when he's cooked in middle, cook ends, move him; pull him across logs so he's head over fire; catch him by tail and pull him. Tail's last part cooked."

Marriage and trade meant the Sḵwx̱wú7mesh kept quite close ties with the Shishá7lh. J.S. Matthews noted that Shishá7lh were present when X̱ats'alánexw Siy̓ám̓ received his ancestral name. This relationship continued after Contact. Among both the Sḵwx̱wú7mesh and the Shishá7lh were many converts to the Catholic Church. They were encouraged to renounce spirit dancing and potlatching, and instead take part in church-sponsored gatherings. According to Bouchard and Kennedy's research, the Sḵwx̱wú7mesh and the Shishá7lh "attended such gatherings in large numbers."

The Ones Who Spoke Téytk̲in

Farther east, we would go up the Fraser River for the integral *stsék̲i7* (sockeye salmon) fishery, where Indigenous Peoples came from Vancouver Island, as well, to harvest. This is where we would interact with the ones who spoke Téytk̲in—Stó:lō, the Upriver Halkomelem dialect. The Sk̲wx̲wú7mesh would extensively trade with the Téytk̲in-speaking people. Sockeye was the central resource that brought us to the Fraser River, but we also harvested *wápatu* (Indian potato) and cranberries from the area, resources that belonged to the Katzie.

Smant tl'a Nch'k̲aỷ (obsidian, Mount Garibaldi stone) has been found farther up the Fraser River, in Katzie territory in the Pitt Meadows area. This also suggests similar exchanges of lithic material for access to *wápatu*. X̲ats'alánexw Siỷám̓ (Chief August Jack Khatsahlano) confirmed that Sk̲wx̲wú7mesh would eat freshwater potatoes found at the Fraser River. *Smant tl'a Nch'k̲aỷ* has also been found in the modern town of Port Douglas at the head of Harrison Lake, where a pithouse village was excavated. Some research suggests visiting groups would provide goods in exchange for resources in Chehalis territory, like *sts'úk̲w'i7* (salmon).

We share similarities in our oral histories, though our stories are still distinct. For the ones who spoke Téytk̲in, the Transformers were called Xexá:ls, similar to our name, "X̲aays." They are four bear children—three sons and a daughter born from Red-Headed Woodpecker and Black Bear. Those who spoke Téytk̲in also had their own version of the serpent story, which occurs at a lake near Chilliwack and other parts of the Fraser Valley.

As mentioned earlier on, the Oblate records that Bouchard and Kennedy analyzed showed that 7.9 percent of Sk̲wx̲wú7mesh marriages in the 1800s were to Halkomelem-speaking people, but they didn't break that down further into dialect groups. Háx̲sten (Harriet George) mentioned a Sk̲wx̲wú7mesh woman marrying a man at Kwikwetlem (Coquitlam) in one of her stories. Our word for the Kwikwetlem is "Kw'ikw'tl'ám"; they too were a Téytk̲in-speaking people.

In chapter 3, we established that families often tried to maintain their economic connections if a couple separated or if a spouse passed away. In the *Fort Langley Journals* in 1829, there is a reference to such a situation happening in the area, when a Sḵwx̱wú7mesh wife of a Kwantlen (Fort Langley) man hanged herself, and eight months later her family arrived on the Fraser River with another bride—a means to continue an alliance between families.

The Fishing Village of Ḵiḵáyt

The Sḵwx̱wú7mesh often travelled up the Fraser River to trade, which began before Contact as corroborated in the *Fort Langley Journals* records. Our history is also connected to a village known as Ḵiḵáyt (also qiqá:yt, qəqəyt) on the south bank of the river, in present-day Surrey, BC. Charles Hill-Tout identified Ḵiḵáyt as a fishing village in the Kwantlen area that existed until 1858 or 1859, when New Westminster was established as the capital on the other side of the river. There was a trail connecting present-day Port Moody to New Westminster, which the Sḵwx̱wú7mesh may have used to travel down to Ḵiḵáyt. But, according to Bouchard and Kennedy's *Land Use and Occupancy* report, in 1858 Ḵiḵáyt was identified as a Squamish fishery. By the early 1860s, it was home to Sḵwx̱wú7mesh and Xwmétskwiyam (Musqueam), along with some people from Kw'ikw'tl'ám and Kwantlen.

It seems relations with the ones who spoke Téytḵin were largely peaceful, again with ties maintained through marriage and trade, as with our other neighbours. Only one stand-off was recorded in the *Fort Langley Journals*, which was quickly defused: "A show of force could be enough to make a threatening war party back off. Before dawn on 17 May 1830, two Squamish war canoes went upriver, making the people near the fort uneasy, but the next day the war canoes returned without having done any harm. It was reported that they had been confronted by two Kwantlen canoes, each side fired a few shots 'by way of bravado,' and that was all. Farther upriver, the Sumas had stood their ground, and the Squamish retreated."

There are many other stories and histories that connect us with our neighbours. Our Great Flood story connects us with the Xwsa7k̲ (Nooksack), who are said to be the ones who got loose from Nch'k̲ay̓ (Mount Garibaldi). We are related to those at Pná7lx̲ets' (Kuper Island) by way of the wooden sea lion. We are connected through our oral histories on the origin of the *sx̲wáy̓x̲wey* mask and how it has been shared through marriage between villages. We have witnessed one another's namings and funerals, and both warred and made peace.

These partnerships continued to be integral with the onset of colonization, and continue to be integral today. In 1906, leaders including S7ápelek̲ Siy̓ám̓ (Chief Joe Capilano; Squamish), Chief Charlie Tsulpi'multw (Cowichan), and Chief Basil David (Bonaparte) together went to London to demand King Edward VII's recognition of how Indigenous rights were being violated. In the years to come, neighbours banded together to create the Union of British Columbia Indian Chiefs, the North American Indian Brotherhood, and other organizations. We work with our neighbours, in our present-day governance systems, on land stewardship, archaeological work, and economic opportunities. We participate in canoe races, and share artwork and teachings. The ancient relationships continue.

Just a few centuries would change how these relationships had looked for millennia. First, those boats arrived.

PART THREE

SḴWX̱WÚ7MESH IY XWELÍTN: THE SQUAMISH AND THE EUROPEANS

"As your great explorer [George] Vancouver progressed through the First Narrows, our people threw in greeting before him clouds of snow white feathers which rose, wafted in the air aimlessly about, then fell like flurries of snow to the water's surface . . . It must have been a pretty welcome . . . There was motive behind it. They were expecting a calamity and were anxious to do anything to avoid it."

XWECHTÁAL (ANDY PAULL)

A WAVE OF sickness and oppression swept the world—and it was getting closer to our home. The French first settled in modern-day Quebec in the 1600s. British, Spanish, Russian, and American explorers began to visit modern-day British Columbia in the 1770s, but they wouldn't explore Sḵwx̱wú7mesh Aysáy̓ch (Squamish Territory) until 1791. Sickness preceded *xwelxwalítn* (white people), a sign of what was to come. Melḵws told Charles Hill-Tout about a sickness that tore through the Sḵwx̱wú7mesh before the arrival of settlers, causing a "dreadful skin disease." He said it was borne on *sts'úḵw'i7* (salmon). A Katzie Elder named Old Pierre told another anthropologist that pre-Contact, "news reached them from the east that a great sickness was travelling over the land, a sickness that no medicine could cure, and no person escape." It's likely that news of settlers reached our people before we saw them, since settlers had been in contact with Indigenous Peoples of the east for generations. European goods, and even word of their religion, likely reached our people years before the first men arrived.

Historians believe disease had impacted Indigenous Peoples in British Columbia before settlers arrived, and a significant *kwétsi siy̓ám̓ smex̱wíws* (smallpox) outbreak hit the Coast Salish region around 1780, perhaps because of a pandemic in Mexico that spread northward. The disease hit the Sel̓íl̓witulh (Tsleil-Waututh) particularly hard; they went from a population of ten thousand to just a handful of survivors. This great loss led to closer ties with the Sḵwx̱wú7mesh. Experts have

estimated that this first wave of smallpox could have killed between 50 and 90 percent of Coast Salish populations. According to Melk̲ws, hundreds of Sk̲wx̲wú7mesh died, and the population had only just become "strong and numerous again" when the first white men came.

Geography historian Cole Harris pointed out that early settlers, and North Americans right up to the modern day, had a Eurocentric view that Indigenous cultures were "static" until the arrival of Europeans.

In reality, Indigenous Peoples have lived through many changes pre- and post-Contact, always adapting to a shifting world. Harris argued that Europeans encountered Indigenous Peoples on the West Coast when their populations were unusually small because of the pandemic that had arrived before the settlers had—but that it "was far more convenient to think that the Native population had always been small, and that those who remained would soon die off." The "dying Indian" trope invented at First Contact would remain pervasive until modern day, supporting the colonial concept of *terra nullius*—that this land was empty and up for grabs.

FACING: A model of the HMS *Discovery*—the lead ship during Captain George Vancouver's exploration of the West Coast in the late 1700s.

European settlement would utterly change our day-to-day lives. Settlers altered how we accessed food, measured wealth, brought up our children, and practised spirituality. Resources would be overexploited, completely out of step with our ways of not taking more from the earth than we need. Missionaries took it upon themselves to oversee the Sḵwx̱wú7mesh. They taught our people that our ways were bad or even evil. They moved us from longhouses to single-family homes, breaking up our system of community.

As with many of our First Contact stories here on the coast, it began with a mysterious shape on the sea's horizon.

8

S7A7Ú7 YA TL'IK̲ TA XWELÍTN: THE ARRIVAL OF THE FIRST WHITEMAN

IN THE 1700S, the British and Spanish were both attempting to lay claim to Indigenous territories in present-day British Columbia. In July 1791, a crew of Spanish explorers, led by José María Narváez, were the first Europeans to enter Burrard Inlet. In their records, they made limited commentary on the Indigenous people they saw but they did map some villages, including a village at Ch'ax̲áy̓, which refers to herring breaching the surface during spawning season. Today, the spot is known as Horseshoe Bay. They also mapped Sk̲wx̲wú7mesh homes at Xwmélch'stn (Capilano). J.S. Matthews asked X̲ats'alánexw Siy̓ám̓ (Chief August Jack Khatsahlano) if the Spanish explorers could have seen their homes from afar, and X̲ats'alánexw Siy̓ám̓ said they must have come quite close to the Sk̲wx̲wú7mesh homes, because they were not easy to see:

X̲ats'alánexw Siy̓ám̓: The homes were cedar colour, old cedar colour, no paint. Not quite black, kinda reddish. They not very high, only about twenty feet or bit more. Nobody could see them from Point Grey. If they was

FACING: Sx̲áaltxw Siy̓ám̓ (Chief Louis Miranda) at home on the Mission Reserve, 1983.

white you could see white spots, but theys almost black. The first white men to come must have come pretty close to old cedar houses at Homulchesun [Xwmélch'stn]. You would have to go close. They was hidden by the crab apple trees. Indians don't cut crab apple trees on west side of Capilano Creek. They keep those trees for shelter from the wind. What time of year was the first white man here?

Matthews: July (1791).

X̱ats'alánexw Siy̓ám̓: Oh! He couldn't see those houses at Homulchesun [Xwmélch'stn]. He must have come pretty close. In July the leaves would hide the houses, and the houses was old cedar colour. He must have come close.

A year later, in June 1792, British captain George Vancouver led two ships to Point Grey and then into Burrard Inlet (he named both after his friends). Xwechtáal (Andy Paull) said prophets had predicted a new people would arrive. In the 1930s, he recounted the history that had been relayed to him:

It seems that it was a tradition among the Indians of early days that a calamity of some sort would befall them every seven years; once it was a flood, on another occasion a disease wiped out X̱wáy̓x̱way, now Stanley Park, again it was a snow storm which lasted for three months. The wise men had long prophesied a visitation from a great people, from a very powerful body of men. Captain Vancouver came in 1792, a year which coincided with the seventh year, the year in which some calamity was expected, regarding the form of which there was much trepidation, so that when strange men of strange appearance, white, with their odd boats, etc., arrived on the scene, the wise men said, "This may be the fateful visitation, what may it bring us," and took steps to propitiate the all-powerful visitors.

It was the custom among Indians to decorate or ornament the interior of festival or potlatch houses with white feathers on festive occasions and ceremonials. The softer outside feathers from beneath the coarser outside covering of waterfowl were saved, and these white eiderdown feathers were thrown and scattered about, ostensibly to placate the spirits, in a manner not dissimilar to the decoration of a Christmas tree with white artificial snow at Christmas time.

Captain Vancouver reports that he was received with "decorum," "civility," "cordiality," and "respect," and that presentations were made to him. I will explain to you the true meaning of this, always bearing in mind that I have come to know, it has come to me as knowledge, through my father's devotion to the duty of elders to pass on by word of mouth the great traditions and history of our race.

As your great explorer Vancouver progressed through the First Narrows, our people threw in greeting before him clouds of snow white feathers which rose, wafted in the air aimlessly about, then fell like flurries of snow to the water's surface, and rested there like white rose petals scattered before a bride. It must have been a pretty welcome. Then there were presents of fish, all to invoke the all-powerful arrivals to have pity on them; it was the seventh year. You see, there was motive behind it. They were expecting a calamity and were anxious to do anything to avoid it. Read what Vancouver had to say about the conferences which took place, the meaning of which he did not understand, but which reports as, "they did not seem to be hostile."

I am informed that the ceremony of casting the white eiderdown before him took place as Captain Vancouver's ship passed through the First Narrows and was passing X̱wáýx̱way, the big Indian village in Stanley Park where the Lumbermen's Arch is now. X̱wáýx̱way must have been a very large village, for it spread from Brockton Point to Prospect Point. It must also have been a very ancient village; none know its age, but there must have been hundreds, perhaps thousands living there at one time.

In his published work, Vancouver does not recount this same meeting. He said he was greeted by "fifty Indians" who "conducted themselves with the greatest decorum and civility, presenting us with several fish." It's not completely clear where these people were from, and whether they spoke Sḵwx̱wú7mesh or Sḵ'emíñem (Halkomelem). Some believe it's clear from descriptions that they canoed from Xwmélch'stn. Records show Sḵwx̱wú7mesh and Xwmétskwiyam (Musqueam) were living there much later, in the 1860s. In Vancouver's journals, he said the Coast Salish tribes were "pleasing and courteous."

S7a7ú7 ya Tl'ik̲ ta Xwelítn (The Arrival of the First Whiteman)

Vancouver's crew camped at Port Moody, and then they set sail north into Howe Sound. It was raining, leading Vancouver to conclude that the lush fjords surrounded by snow-capped mountains were "dreary and comfortless." They anchored at a bay known since that time as Xwelxwalítn ("white people").

Just south of Xwelxwalítn, there is a rock bluff called Lex̲wlúx̲wels, where it is said the X̲aays (Transformer brothers) transformed some Lúx̲wels (Lil'wat) to stone. The Lúx̲wels ate a starfish and fell asleep, and their canoe drifted away. Starfish are a taboo food to the Sk̲wx̲wú7mesh. The X̲aays paddled by and woke up the Lúx̲wels, asking why they were so far from their home *temíxw* (lands). They responded that they wanted to sleep and be left alone. They refused to leave, and so the X̲aays turned them into stone.

Near those column-like rocks, thousands of years later, on a June morning in 1792, forty Sk̲wx̲wú7mesh people, eager to trade and with a strong interest in iron, approached the first white people they had ever seen.

X̲ats'alánexw Siy̓ám̓ said that when the Sk̲wx̲wú7mesh first saw white men come up into Howe Sound, they thought the ship was an island "with three dead trees."

"They not know what it was; think it an island, go down in canoe and see. By and bye [*sic*], see men on island. The men in black clothes with high hat over head with sharp point on top. I suppose it was black overcoats with a hood," he said. He said the settlers gave the Sk̲wx̲wú7mesh molasses, which they had no idea what to do with. He said they tried applying it as medicine and as hair oil, unsure of how to use the unfamiliar and sticky substance.

Sx̲áaltxw Siy̓ám̓ (Chief Louis Miranda) recounted a similar history. He said an old man awoke at St'á7mes (Stawamus), looked on the water, and saw what he thought was a floating island with trees on it.

Basket weaver Sewinchelwet (Sophie Frank; front row, left) with her family, c. 1930s.

He alerted the other villagers. They launched their canoes to look at the "drifting island." Then they saw the white men onboard.

They thought they were dead people, for they were very white. Only their faces were showing, so the Indians thought that the white people had their burial blankets wrapped around them... The Indians saw one of the white people walk to the side of the big canoe. They thought that he was eating fire, for there was smoke coming out of his mouth.

Finally, one of the men, who was eating fire, started to talk to the Indians and motioned for them to come aboard...

When all the Indians were aboard, the smoke-blower and fire-eater extended his hand. The Indians said to each other, "Look, they are not dead; he wants to k̲eléxw!" This is an Indian game. The players, using one finger, pull on the competitor's finger. One of the Indians got ready to play. He spat on his finger and offered it to the white man. The smoke-blower shook his head and waved his hand, as if refusing the finger. The Indians said to the man, "You are not a worthy opponent, let someone else try." Another Indian stepped forward and extended his finger. Again the smoke-blower refused. They went down the line until there was only one Indian left. He was the strongest player of this game, and was from Ch'iyák̲mesh. I guess the smoke-blower thought that this was the Indian way of greeting, so he put out his hand. The Indian grabbed his middle finger and pulled it out of the joint. "He couldn't be dead! If he was dead, he wouldn't have been hurt!"

Sx̲áaltxw Siy̓ám̓ said the Sk̲wx̲wú7mesh were also gifted rum, which they believed, because of its effects, must have gone bad; and they used biscuits as toys and silver dollars as buttons.

More Traders Arrive

When Captain Vancouver came back down to Burrard Inlet, he ran into Spanish explorers, this time led by Dionisio Alcalá Galiano and Cayetano Valdés y Flores. They travelled the area together for a time before separating. Captain Vancouver was treated very kindly by those he met and was generously provided food by the Sk̲wx̲wú7mesh and beyond.

Vancouver spoke highly of the many Indigenous people he met. At the same time, his writings show some of the same prejudiced views that other colonizing powers had about societies they didn't understand, calling Indigenous people "uncivilized." It is important to note that the feelings were mutual! In one telling of the first encounter, it is said that the Squamish could "smell that something was strange" in the area. They could smell it but didn't know what it was.

In 1794, when more trade was taking place on the coast, Vancouver criticized what he called the "unjustifiable" conduct of other traders and criticized them for giving Indigenous people guns without fully educating them on their dangerous nature, and even providing faulty guns; he described one young Indigenous man losing his hand because of a faulty gun. But at the same time, he said he was telling Indigenous people that "submitting to the authority and protection of a superior power" would allow them to be "less liable to such abuses." In his own words, he encouraged Indigenous people to submit to those perpetrating abuse as a means to be safe.

Settlement on the coast, in Sḵwx̱wú7meshulh Aysáy̓ch (Squamish Territory) and beyond, was not established for a few more years. The Hudson's Bay Company didn't set up fur trading posts in what is now modern-day British Columbia until the early 1800s (the first post was built at Hudson Bay in 1668). Simon Fraser travelled the Fraser River from 1805 to 1809. S7ápeleḵ Siy̓ám̓ (Chief Joe Capilano) said his father saw the first white man coming down the Fraser in 1808. Háx̱sten, who was also known as Skwétsiy̓a, and by her English name Harriet George, who passed on in 1940 at over one hundred years old, first saw a white man in 1808 when she observed a trader setting up a property on the Fraser.

Fur trade and permanent settlements would continue to increase into the mid-1800s. We began to learn the language, and tried to learn how to live peacefully with this new people. They were still so new to this land, but a time of great change had already begun.

9

NEXW7ÁÝSTWAÝ: TRADE

Word about the West Coast spread through the European world through explorers' writings, and fur traders began to descend on the coast. A pre-Contact gathering place for Indigenous Peoples to trade, Fort Langley was established on the lower Fraser River in 1827. The village became a central trading hub, and through this trading post, the Hudson's Bay Company began exporting *sts'úḵw'i7* (salmon). Daily journals from the traders at Fort Langley, dated 1827 to 1830, record Sḵwx̱wú7mesh people trading fish and salmon oil.

We and our neighbours were already experienced traders pre-Contact—exchanging hides, wool, beads, blankets, foods, tools, and more. First Nations developed Chinook Jargon, a trade language to communicate with each other. First Nations were eager to participate in new commerce and try new technologies, and early Europeans noticed we were shrewd traders. White people traded guns, manufactured wool, and iron, which changed our ancestors' day-to-day lives.

"Land Hunger"

The wealth that the Hudson's Bay Company accumulated, and the booming fur trade, would not have been possible without the skill and labour of Indigenous Peoples from coast to coast gathering goods like beaver and sea otter pelts. Since Europeans were outnumbered at this time, they also largely depended on the peace of First Nations, as well relying on them for food. Trade was mostly peaceful, but it was not without conflict—especially if European trappers were working in First Nations' territories without permission. Hostilities increased as settlers encroached on Indigenous land, and then, with the introduction of firearms, increased between villages; raids continued through the 1800s.

Then trade took its toll on the landscape. The Europeans wanted beaver, mink, otter, fox, and bear pelts. Sea otters were especially sought after, having warm fur of one million hairs per square inch. Scientists estimate that between 150,000 and 300,000 sea otters swam along the coast between Alaska and California in the 1700s. By 1911, about two thousand were left. The last recorded sea otters in British Columbia were shot in 1923 on Vancouver Island. They remained locally extinct until 1969, when sea otters from Alaska were reintroduced on the BC coast.

Our ancestors met the first white men in 1792. In 1808, Há<u>x</u>sten (Harriet George) had just seen a white man for the first time on the Fraser River. But change was happening quickly. By 1827, several trading posts had been established on the coast. Racist attitudes were common. Across Canada, traders voiced their sense of entitlement to the land and their desire to have power over Indigenous Peoples. In 1822, Hudson's Bay Company governor George Simpson wrote that Indigenous Peoples "must be ruled with a rod of iron, to bring and to keep them in a proper state of subordination."

FACING: The Royal Proclamation issued by King George III in 1763 was a first step toward the recognition of existing Indigenous rights.

As one historian put it, Europeans began to feel a "land hunger." Fur trading alone did not satisfy their appetites for wealth anymore—they wanted land. They wanted supremacy over the Indigenous Peoples who blocked their access to resources.

By the KING,

A PROCLAMATION.

GEORGE R.

WHEREAS We have taken into Our Royal Consideration the extensive and valuable Acquisitions in *America*, secured to Our Crown by the late Definitive Treaty of Peace, concluded at *Paris* the Tenth Day of *February* last; and being desirous, that all Our loving Subjects, as well of Our Kingdoms as of Our Colonies in *America*, may avail themselves, with all convenient Speed, of the great Benefits and Advantages which must accrue therefrom to their Commerce, Manufactures, and Navigation; We have thought fit, with the Advice of Our Privy Council, to issue this Our Royal Proclamation, hereby to publish and declare to all Our loving Subjects, that We have, with the Advice of Our said Privy Council, granted Our Letters Patent under Our Great Seal of *Great Britain*, to erect within the Countries and Islands ceded and confirmed to Us by the said Treaty, Four distinct and separate Governments, stiled and called by the Names of *Quebec*, *East Florida*, *West Florida*, and *Grenada*, and limited and bounded as follows; *viz.*

First. The Government of *Quebec*, bounded on the *Labrador* Coast by the River *St. John*, and from ence by a Line drawn from the Head of that River through the Lake *St. John* to the South End of e Lake nigh *Pissin*; from whence the said Line crossing the River *St. Lawrence* and the Lake *Champlain* Forty five Degrees of North Latitude, passes along the High Lands which divide the Rivers that empty emselves into the said River *St. Lawrence*, from those which fall into the Sea; and also along the North oast of the *Baye des Chaleurs*, and the Coast of the Gulph of *St. Lawrence* to Cape *Rosieres*, and from thence ossing the Mouth of the River *St. Lawrence* by the West End of the Island of *Anticosti*, terminates at the oresaid River of *St. John*.

Secondly. The Government of *East Florida*, bounded to the Westward by the Gulph of *Mexico*, and the *Apa-chicola* River; to the Northward, by a Line drawn from that Part of the said River where the *Chatahoucher* and *int* Rivers meet, to the Source of *St. Mary's* River, and by the Course of the said River to the *Atlantick* Ocean; d to the Eastward and Southward, by the *Atlantick* Ocean, and the Gulph of *Florida*, including all Islands thin Six Leagues of the Sea Coast.

Thirdly. The Government of *West Florida*, bounded to the Southward by the Gulph of *Mexico*, including all ands within Six Leagues of the Coast from the River *Apalachicola* to Lake *Pentchartrain*; to the Westward by e said Lake, the Lake *Mauripas*, and the River *Mississippi*; to the Northward, by a Line drawn due East from at Part of the River *Mississippi* which lies in Thirty one Degrees North Latitude, to the River *Apalachicola* or *atahouchee*; and to the Eastward by the said River.

Fourthly. The Government of *Grenada*, comprehending the Island of that Name, together with the *Grenadines*, d the Islands of *Dominico*, *St. Vincents*, and *Tobago*.

And, to the End that the open and free Fishery of Our Subjects may be extended to and carried on upon the oast of *Labrador* and the adjacent Islands, We have thought fit, with the Advice of Our said Privy Council, to t all that Coast, from the River *St. John's* to *Hudson's Streights*, together with the Islands of *Anticosti* and *Madelaine*, d all other smaller Islands lying upon the said Coast, under the Care and Inspection of Our Governor of *ewfoundland*.

We have also, with the Advice of Our Privy Council, thought fit to annex the Islands of *St. John's*, and *Cape* *reton* or *Isle Royale*, with the lesser Islands adjacent thereto, to Our Government of *Nova Scotia*.

We have also, with the Advice of Our Privy Council aforesaid, annexed to Our Province of *Georgia* all the Lands ing between the Rivers *Attamaha* and *St. Mary's*.

And whereas it will greatly contribute to the speedy settling Our said new Governments, that Our loving Sub-ts should be informed of Our Paternal Care for the Security of the Liberties and Properties of those who e and shall become Inhabitants thereof; We have thought fit to publish and declare, by this Our Proclamation, at We have, in the Letters Patent under Our Great Seal of *Great Britain*, by which the said Governments are nstituted, given express Power and Direction to Our Governors of Our said Colonies respectively, that so soon the State and Circumstances of the said Colonies will admit thereof, they shall, with the Advice and Consent the Members of Our Council, summon and call General Assemblies within the said Governments respectively, such Manner and Form as is used and directed in those Colonies and Provinces in *America*, which are under ur immediate Government; and We have also given Power to the said Governors, with the Consent of Our id Councils, and the Representatives of the People, so to be summoned as aforesaid, to make, constitute, and dain Laws, Statutes, and Ordinances for the Publick Peace, Welfare, and Good Government of Our said Colonies, d of the People and Inhabitants thereof, as near as may be agreeable to the Laws of *England*, and under such egulations and Restrictions as are used in other Colonies: And in the mean Time, and until such Assemblies can called as aforesaid, all Persons inhabiting in, or resorting to Our said Colonies, may confide in Our Royal Pro-ction for the Enjoyment of the Benefit of the Laws of Our Realm of *England*; for which Purpose, We have iven Power under Our Great Seal to the Governors of Our said Colonies respectively, to erect and constitute, ith the Advice of Our said Councils respectively, Courts of Judicature and Publick Justice, within Our said Colo-ies, for the hearing and determining all Causes, as well Criminal as Civil, according to Law and Equity, and near as may be agreeable to the Laws of *England*, with Liberty to all Persons who may think themselves ag-rieved by the Sentences of such Courts, in all Civil Cases, to appeal, under the usual Limitations and Restrictions, Us in Our Privy Council.

We have also thought fit, with the Advice of Our Privy Council as aforesaid, to give unto the Governors and ouncils of Our said Three New Colonies upon the Continent, full Power and Authority to settle and agree with e Inhabitants of Our said New Colonies, or with any other Persons who shall resort thereto, for such Lands, enements, and Hereditaments, as are now, or hereafter shall be in Our Power to dispose of, and them to grant any such Person or Persons, upon such Terms, and under such moderate Quit-Rents, Services, and Acknow-edgements as have been appointed and settled in Our other Colonies, and under such other Conditions as shall appear Us to be necessary and expedient for the Advantage of the Grantees, and the Improvement and Settlement of ur said Colonies.

And whereas We are desirous, upon all Occasions, to testify Our Royal Sense and Approbation of the Conduct and Bravery of the Officers and Soldiers of Our Armies, and to reward the same, We do hereby command and impower Our Governors of Our said Three New Colonies, and all other Our Governors of Our several Provinces on the Continent of *North America*, to grant, without Fee or Reward, to such Reduced Officers as have served in *North America* during the late War, and to such Private Soldiers as have been or shall be disbanded in *America*, and are ually residing there, and shall personally apply for the same, the following Quantities of Lands, subject at the Expiration of Ten Years to the same Quit-Rents as other Lands are subject to in the Province within which they are granted, as also subject to the same Conditions of Cultivation and Improvement; *viz.*

To every Person having the Rank of a Field Officer, Five thousand Acres.—To every Captain, Three thousand Acres o every Subaltern or fficer, Two thousand Acres.—To every Non-Commission Officer, Two hundred A —To every Private Man, Fifty Acres.

We do like authorize and require the Governors and Commanders in Chief of all Our said Colonies upon the Continent *North America*, to grant the like Quantities of Land, and upon the same Conditions, to such Reduced Officers of Our Navy, of like Rank, as served on Board Our Ships of War in *North America* at the Times of the Reduction of *Louisbourg* and *Quebec* in the late War, and who shall personally apply to Our repective Governors for such Grants.

And whereas it is just and reasonable, and essential to Our Interest and the Security of Our Colonies, that the several Nations or Tribes of *Indians*, with whom We are connected, and who live under Our Protection, should not be molested or disturbed in the Possession of such Parts of Our Dominions and Territories as, not having been ceded to, or purchased by Us, are reserved to them, or any of them, as their Hunting Grounds; We do therefore, with the Advice of Our Privy Council, declare it to be Our Royal Will and Pleasure, that no Governor or Commander in Chief in any of Our Colonies of *Quebec*, *East Florida*, or *West Florida*, do presume, upon any Pretence whatever, to grant Warrants of Survey, or pass any Patents for Lands beyond the Bounds of their respective Governments, as described in their Commissions; as also, that no Governor or Commander in Chief in any of Our other Colonies or Plantations in *America*, do presume, for the present, and until Our further Pleasure be known, to grant Warrants of Survey, or pass Patents for any Lands beyond the Heads or Sources of any of the Rivers which fall into the *Atlantick* Ocean from the West and North West, or upon any Lands whatever, which, not having been ceded to, or purchased by Us as aforesaid, are reserved to the said *Indians*, or any of them.

And We do further declare it to be Our Royal Will and Pleasure, for the present as aforesaid, to reserve under Our Sovereignty, Protection, and Dominion, for the Use of the said *Indians*, all the Lands and Territories not included within the Limits of Our said Three New Governments, or within the Limits of the Territory granted to the *Hudson's Bay* Company, as also all the Lands and Territories lying to the Westward of the Sources of the Rivers which fall into the Sea from the West and North West, as aforesaid; and We do hereby strictly forbid, on Pain of Our Displeasure, all Our loving Subjects from making any Purchases or Settlements whatever, or taking Possession of any of the Lands above reserved, without Our especial Leave and Licence for that Purpose first obtained.

And We do further strictly enjoin and require all Persons whatever, who have either wilfully or inadvertently seated themselves upon any Lands within the Countries above described, or upon any other Lands, which, not having been ceded to, or purchased by Us, are still reserved to the said *Indians* as aforesaid, forthwith to remove themselves from such Settlements.

And whereas great Frauds and Abuses have been committed in the purchasing Lands of the *Indians*, to the great Prejudice of Our Interests, and to the great Dissatisfaction of the said *Indians*; in order therefore to prevent such Irregularities for the future, and to the End that the *Indians* may be convinced of Our Justice, and determined Resolution to remove all reasonable Cause of Discontent, We do, with the Advice of Our Privy Council, strictly enjoin and require, that no private Person do presume to make any Purchase from the said *Indians* of any Lands reserved to the said *Indians*, within those Parts of Our Colonies where We have thought proper to allow Settlement; but that if, at any Time, any of the said *Indians* should be inclined to dispose of the said Lands, the same shall be purchased only for Us, in Our Name, at some Publick Meeting or Assembly of the said *Indians* to be held for that Purpose by the Governor or Commander in Chief of Our Colonies respectively, within which they shall lie; and in case they shall lie within the Limits of any Proprietary Government, they shall be purchased only for the Use and in the Name of such Proprietaries, conformable to such Directions and Instructions as We or they shall think proper to give for that Purpose: And We do, by the Advice of Our Privy Council, declare and enjoin, that the Trade with the said *Indians* shall be free and open to all Our Subjects whatever; provided that every Person, who may incline to trade with the said *Indians*, do take out a Licence for carrying on such Trade from the Governor or Commander in Chief of any of Our Colonies respectively, where such Person shall reside; and also give Security to observe such Regulations as We shall at any Time think fit, by Ourselves or by Our Commissaries to be appointed for this Purpose, to direct and appoint for the Benefit of the said Trade; and We do hereby authorize, enjoin, and require the Governors and Commanders in Chief of all Our Colonies respectively, as well Those under Our immediate Government as Those under the Government and Direction of Proprietaries, to grant such Licences without Fee or Reward, taking especial Care to insert therein a Condition, that such Licence shall be void, and the Security forfeited, in case the Person, to whom the same is granted, shall refuse or neglect to observe such Regulations as We shall think proper to prescribe as aforesaid.

And We do further expresly enjoin and require all Officers whatever, as well Military as Those employed in the Management and Direction of *Indian* Affairs within the Territories reserved as aforesaid for the Use of the said *Indians*, to seize and apprehend all Persons whatever, who, standing charged with Treasons, Misprisions of Treason, Murders, or other Felonies or Misdemeanors, shall fly from Justice, and take Refuge in the said Territory, and to send them under a proper Guard to the Colony where the Crime was committed of which they stand accused, in order to take their Tryal for the same.

Given at Our Court at *Saint James's*, the Seventh Day of *October*, One thousand seven hundred and sixty three, in the Third Year of Our Reign.

GOD save the KING.

LONDON:
Printed by *Mark Baskett*, Printer to the King's most Excellent Majesty; and by the Assigns of *Robert Baskett*. 1763.

Europeans Lay Claim to Land

According to the Royal Proclamation of 1763, large-scale settlement on Indigenous land was not allowed until the lands were surrendered by treaty. But that's not how things went at that time. By the mid-1800s, Americans and Europeans were drawing borders to chart their claimed colonies, without consideration for the Indigenous Peoples whose territories and resources did not fall within these arbitrary lines on a map. In 1846, the Americans and British drew the border between British North America and the United States at the forty-ninth parallel from the Rocky Mountains to the Pacific Ocean, cutting through Indigenous Peoples' homelands and trade routes.

The Hastings Sawmill was the first commercial endeavour in Vancouver, 1872.

Settlement hadn't fully taken hold in Sḵwx̱wú7mesh territory yet, and the Hudson's Bay Company by and large ran the show for non-Indigenous residents. Then, in the 1850s, the Fraser Canyon Gold Rush took off. Americans flooded the area, passing through Fort Langley. To assert British control over the area, the Crown declared British Columbia a colony in 1858. (Vancouver Island had been declared a Crown colony of British North America in 1849, and this new colony was on the mainland.) The capital of British Columbia, New Westminster, was established a year later.

More industry began operating around Burrard Inlet, and Sḵwx̱wú7mesh people began to work in sawmills and logging, and as migrant farm workers at hop farms. Sḵwx̱wú7mesh women took part in trade and labour, and also married white men to create familial ties with the newcomers. The British set their sights on timber, coal, and fisheries. The natural resource economy that would soon dominate British Columbia had begun.

And then, the 1862 smallpox epidemic hit Indigenous Peoples on the coast horrifically hard. There had been smaller outbreaks before this, but the 1862 outbreak was documented as the fastest and the deadliest.

Experts estimate that when Europeans arrived in the 1770s, between 200,000 and 500,000 Indigenous people were living in present-day British Columbia, and many experts estimate populations were lower than usual because of disease that preceded the arrival of settlers. It's estimated that, by 1900, only twenty-five thousand Indigenous people remained. That means about 95 percent of the population died in just a few generations.

According to one estimate, before Contact the Sḵwx̱wú7mesh numbered between ten thousand and thirty thousand, and by the 1860s, between three hundred and six hundred of us remained.

It's hard to imagine exactly how our ancestors must have felt. It's hard to imagine all the stories and teachings erased amid such devastating loss. One highly respected Elder, Kwítelut (Lena Jacobs), said that she carried five ancestral names because her family did not want the names to be lost or forgotten.

Our world was in upheaval, and settlement was just ramping up. After the gold rush, more white people began to settle permanently. In 1866, Vancouver Island and the Colony of British Columbia united to become a single colony, which eventually became the province of British Columbia.

All this set the stage for the fight over unceded land that continues to this day. Indigenous Peoples were not involved in the conversations about establishing a colony. The British stamped their name on an area that already held names. They were trying to extend power over areas that were already governed. The Royal Proclamation of 1763 forbade settlers from claiming land from Indigenous Peoples unless it had been bought by the Crown—but the settlers violated their own laws for decades to come, as well as the laws of the Indigenous lands they were walking on.

The future City of Vancouver was still largely covered in forest. In 1863, the first sawmill, built by Sewell "Sue" Moody, an American, opened in Moodyville on the north shore of Burrard Inlet in present-day North Vancouver. In 1867, the first sawmill on the south shore of Burrard Inlet opened: Stamp's Mill, which was in the area known to us as K̲'emk̲'emel̓áy̓ ("many maple trees"; at the foot of what is now Dunlevy Avenue in Vancouver). That same year, in the east, the Dominion of Canada was established, initially a much smaller version of the country we know today.

The fur trade was falling to the wayside in favour of other industries, such as coal, gold, fisheries, and timber. The lands and waters around Burrard Inlet already looked different. And the white settlers were encroaching on our lands more and more. They would eventually begin restricting our access to fish and other resources, pushing us to participate in their capitalist economy, and separating us from the resources we relied upon to thrive.

10

STS'ITS'ÁP IY SḴ'AW: WORK AND PAYMENT

"WHITE MAN food change everything," X̱ats'alánexw Siy̓ám̓ (Chief August Jack Khatsahlano) said in transcriptions of his conversations with archivist J.S. Matthews. "Everywhere white man goes he change food; China, other place, he always change food where he goes."

"Indians had plenty food long ago, but I could not do without tea and sugar now," he said. X̱ats'alánexw Siy̓ám̓ described how much things had changed—how Sḵwx̱wú7mesh men who first met white men in Howe Sound had rolled biscuits they were given on the ground as moving targets for arrow practice, and he "laughed heartily" describing how they rubbed molasses on their stiff leg muscles as medicine. By the twentieth century, with the City of Vancouver growing all around us, we were more reliant on commercial food production.

Settlement was disrupting our relationship with the lands, waters, and non-human relatives around us. X̱ats'alánexw Siy̓ám̓ described how Indigenous people wore sea otter garments at the time of Contact—"very valuable furs now, very valuable furs indeed, but quite common

FACING: Hop-drying kiln at the Squamish Valley Hop Company farm, c. 1900.

with the Indians at the time." The introduction of the wage economy placed a dollar value on items instead of their subsistence or intrinsic value. To this day, that capitalist economy does not align with Indigenous values, but it surrounds our territories and our people—the lands once rich with foods now covered in concrete.

A Predatory Economy

As the fur trade began, we still hunted and gathered for enough food independently. But because of settlement and mass depopulation from sickness, all that changed. We became more dependent on the capitalist economy growing around us. And as settlers became more populous, their needs became more predatory and less equal.

"Shall we allow a few vagrants to prevent forever industrious settlers from settling on unoccupied lands? Not at all... Locate reservations for them on which to earn their own living, and if they trespass on white settlers, punish them severely," editor Amor de Cosmos wrote in the *British Colonist* newspaper.

Indigenous people were paid less for their labour than white people—but more than Chinese people, illustrating how racism affected trade and commerce. Chinese people had arrived on the coast in the late 1700s; they helped the British establish trading posts, many in hopes of sending money back to their families. Immigration increased in the 1800s, and Chinese people faced racial discrimination and segregation by white people even as their labour made the colony's dreams of expansion possible.

Indigenous Peoples' labour, resources, and knowledge of the land were integral to developing wealth and the cities and industries we see today. European settlers were offered 160 acres for their families to live on, but by the 1870s, Lieutenant-Governor Joseph Trutch recommended no more than 10 acres per family be allocated for Indigenous families. This meant First Nations in British Columbia had vastly smaller reserves than those allocated in the east—but it also meant we were not pushed into agriculture the way Indigenous Peoples were in the Prairies.

The Sḵwx̱wú7mesh were eager to trade at first, but our ancestors' concerns grew as European influence grew. Our people would get frustrated and concerned when Europeans did not act in good faith, encroaching on our lands or devaluing our resources or labour.

In an 1859 letter from settler Julius Voight, he claimed that he saved New Westminster from an attack by the Sḵwx̱wú7mesh: "with the help of their Chief Kleaplannah [Capilano] last summer I did prevent an attack of those Indians on New Westminster when several of them were taken prisoner for an outrage on white men near Westminster." In her master's thesis, Sḵwx̱wú7mesh member Kirsten Baker-Williams said she was told this attack was planned in response to the rape of a Sḵwx̱wú7mesh woman.

Amateur anthropologist Charles Hill-Tout also told a story that demonstrated that the Sḵwx̱wú7mesh had early distrust of some Europeans. Hill-Tout wanted to "examine" Sḵwx̱wú7mesh people for their "physical characteristics." This was in the heyday of racist pseudoscience, as white people sought to find measurable differences between "races" to support their racist ideologies that people had different abilities and intelligence based on race, and to justify the subjugation and abuse of other races. French anthropologist Georges Vacher de Lapouge popularized the measuring of skulls, and he also spread the belief in the so-called Aryan race that would eventually inform the Nazi regime. The measurement of skulls (called phrenology) has been dismissed as a racist, pseudoscientific practice.

Hill-Tout said he found it "impossible" to examine any Sḵwx̱wú7mesh people because they had been so disturbed by anthropologist Franz Boas's attempts to do the same work. No one would submit to being poked and prodded. A bishop told Hill-Tout that when Boas visited, Sḵwx̱wú7mesh people "ran away and hid themselves in the woods rather than submit to the examinations."

William "Bill" Nahanee (centre) with longshoremen at Moodyville Sawmill dock, 1889.

But Hill-Tout did not listen. He said he asked that same bishop, Pierre-Paul Durieu, to persuade Sk̲wx̲wú7mesh people to submit to examinations, but Durieu died, leaving Hill-Tout "sorely disappointed" that he didn't have someone to help him convince the Sk̲wx̲wú7mesh to be examined.

He said he tried anyway, and particularly on a group of children: "The mothers of them came upon us before I had measured the first boy's head and dragged them all off. After this I gave up the attempt to do anything with them in this way... I regret being unable to secure a good specimen of this type among my photographs."

The disturbing language Hill-Tout uses shows how Sḵwx̱wú7mesh people were treated as industrialization took hold. Our ancestors tried to hold on to our teachings, to our land, to protect our children, and to survive waves of sickness—at the same time, trees were cleared for roads and steamships began docking at the future city of Vancouver.

"Arduous Work"

Around the turn of the century, Sḵwx̱wú7mesh people began to farm hops, and early settlers farmed hops too. Simon Baker of the Sḵwx̱wú7mesh Úxwumixw (Squamish Nation) said it was "arduous work" to carry heavy hop sacks to the kiln for drying. After they were dried, the hops were exported through Vancouver.

Indigenous labour was integral to the fisheries industry, with men working on fishing boats, while women were central to the canneries processing *sts'úḵw'i7* (salmon).

As white people further encroached on our lands, clearing forests and taking over waterways, they also began to confine us to reserves, diminishing our access to land and so creating a situation where we were more dependent on the industrial economy as our access to our traditional fishing, hunting, and plant resource gathering areas was restricted.

In 1880, Hudson's Bay Company began selling farm lots to settlers in western Canada, increasing the population of non-Indigenous settlers. Migrants from around the world were also working in present-day British Columbia, and Chinese migrants were integral to building its infrastructure, especially the transcontinental railway that reached Burrard Inlet in 1885.

In 1886, Vancouver incorporated as a city—only to be destroyed two months later in the Great Vancouver Fire. Sḵwx̱wú7mesh people paddled across the water to help people trapped on the shore. The

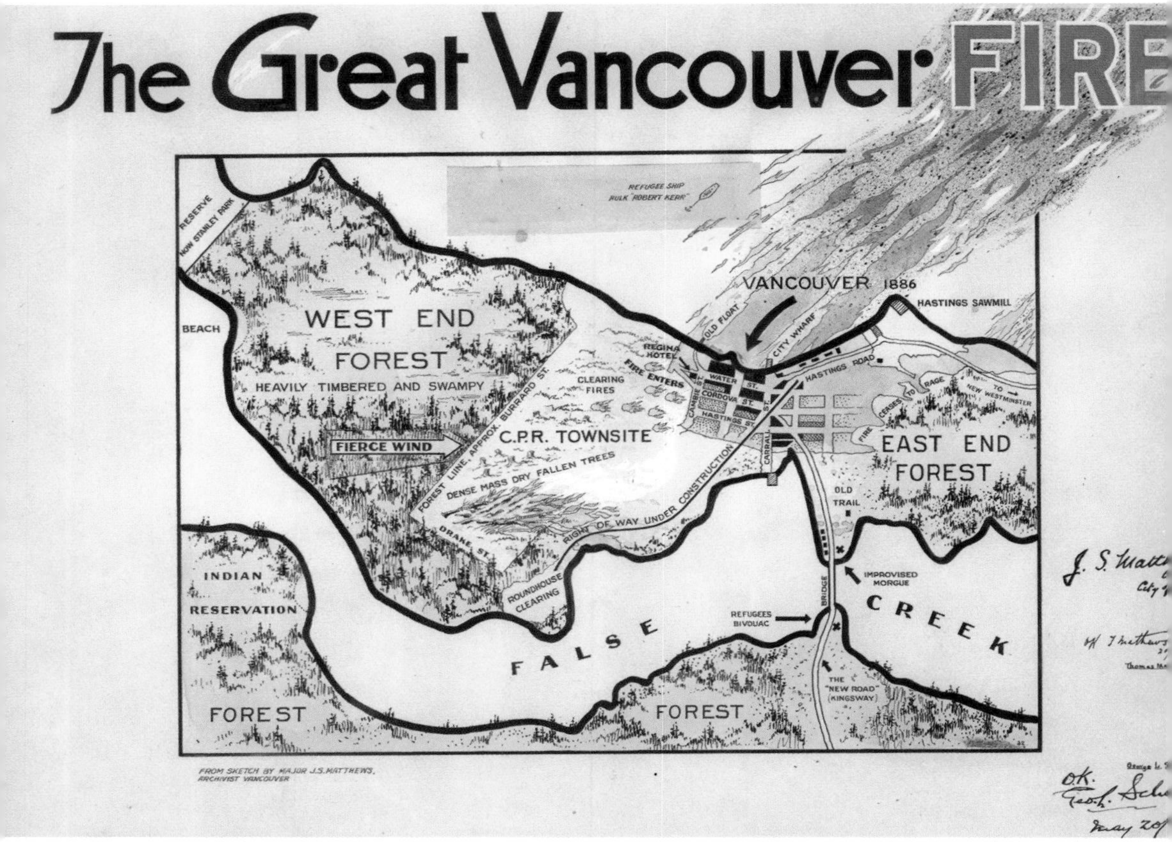

city was rebuilt quickly, and just one year later, the first Hudson's Bay store opened in Gastown. The city was less than a year old, and home to about one thousand people. In 1891, the city established a steamship connection with Asia.

White settlers were taking on large-scale logging in the old-growth forests across the colony of British Columbia, including our territory around English Bay, Burrard Inlet, and in Howe Sound. One Squamish Elder, the late Ed Nahanee, remarked that the initial longshore crews were made up largely of our people because we knew how to move the huge logs!

But the Canadian federal government's Department of Indian Affairs restricted the Sḵwx̱wú7mesh to small-scale hand-logging. This work gave way to the work of longshoremen loading the wood onto ships to be exported—and Sḵwx̱wú7mesh and Səlílwitulh (Tsleil-Waututh) men wound up being the majority of longshoremen on the North Shore.

A Radical Workers Union

The capitalist economy was exploiting the labour of racialized people, and Indigenous men on the waterfront saw the inequality and sought to change it. In 1906, Sḵwx̱wú7mesh and Səlílwitulh men were central to establishing one of the first unions on Vancouver's waterfront. About fifty to sixty handlers formed Local 526 of the Industrial Workers of the World, a larger network that was established in Chicago in 1905 and that centred on racial solidarity and anti-capitalist ideology.

The Sḵwx̱wú7mesh led the way in establishing Local 526, which was informally called "Bows and Arrows." They had their first meeting at the village Eslha7áñ (Mission Reserve) on the north shore of Burrard Inlet, which was allocated as a reserve in 1869.

The Industrial Workers of the World's ideology showed through Local 526: although made up of mostly Indigenous workers, the union brought together nationalities including Chinese, English, Hawaiian, and Chilean workers as well. About a year after it formed, the union broke up following an intense strike, but it retained its legacy as the first example of industrial workers unionizing on Vancouver's waterfront and centring racial equality as integral to worker justice. A number of other "Bows and Arrows" iterations formed and disbanded over the years.

FACING: A hand-drawn map (1932) by Major J.S. Matthews, Vancouver's first archivist, depicting the Great Vancouver Fire of June 13, 1886.

In the early 1900s, First Nations comprised a huge portion of the labour force in British Columbia, even as the white population grew. Indigenous people were increasingly treated as inferior, but Sḵwx̱wú7mesh workers found ways to advocate for themselves and demonstrate the value of their own work.

William "Bill" Nahanee spent fifty-two years as a longshoreman and acted as president of Local 38-57 of the International Longshoremen's Union in the early 1900s. Xwechtáal (Andy Paull) wrote about Nahanee's career in the *Vancouver Daily Province* in 1941: "'I had to find work and earn a living the best way I could,'" Nahanee told Xwechtáal. "'For my Hawaiin [*sic*] father died when I was two years old, and my mother, a Capilano Indian, had a hard time to keep up with the customs introduced by the coming of the white men.'"

Nahanee described how, at fifteen years old, when he was loading ships, he asked the stevedore in charge for $3 a day, which was the standard adult wage. The stevedore refused, offering him only $1 a day, so $30 for the whole month of work. Nahanee refused to accept the offer, and instead told the stevedore "to keep the thirty pieces of silver."

Later, working the less strenuous job of operating lumber rollers, Nahanee accepted $1 a day. But the stevedore asked him to take on unloading wheat. Nahanee refused to do that work for less than $3 a day. He wanted $90 for the month. "By his refusal he staged the first longshore strike, in the Port of Vancouver, for an increase in wages," Xwechtáal wrote.

FACING: A seasonal Indigenous labourer seated in a hop field with her children, c. 1890–1930.

According to Nahanee, a less experienced worker was tasked with moving the wheat, and accidentally dumped some in the inlet. "Wheat in those days was worth its weight in gold, and [Nahanee] was not surprised when the mill foreman returned, told him to go to the office, collect his ninety dollars and get on with the work of discharging the golden cargo," Xwechtáal wrote. "And so the first one-man longshore strike in the history of the port was won."

Xwechtáal himself played a central role in advocating for Indigenous workers' rights, helping to establish the Independent Lumber Handlers' Association in 1926.

Indigenous workers used their labour and earnings to continue to push for sovereignty and justice for their people. They saw the injustice of the world forming around them and sought to use the tools they had available, such as unions. In another example, First Nations veterans from World War I also worked as longshoremen, and they were promised the right to vote as long as they were in the army. These same veterans pushed for the right to vote to be granted to all First Nations people, which would not happen until 1960.

Our ancestors' participation in early labour demonstrated how we still believed in decentralized, collective power and would fight for our rights. It is an early sign of how, in the coming decades, harnessing our collective power would be the only way to stand strong in the face of the colonial state.

The Salish Woolly Dog

Harvesting wool and meticulously creating our own yarn by hand with spindle whorls was an ancient practice of Sḵwx̱wú7mesh culture. A central change during industrialization was in the materials we used for clothing and textiles. Disease and cultural suppression through colonization interrupted our intergenerational teachings, and fewer people were weaving. As well, Europeans brought industrial yarn with them.

These factors led to the extinction of a companion in Coast Salish communities: the woolly dog. The woolly dogs were usually white, with thick, plush fur similar to that of Pomeranians or Shiba Inus today. These dogs were associated with wealth, and families would often name their woolly dogs and give them ceremonial burials. The Sḵwx̱wú7mesh would keep their woolly dogs inside to prevent them

Making a canoe from a tree trunk at Eslha7áń (Mission), c. 1893.

from breeding with hunting dogs. Other tribes would sometimes keep them on nearby islands to prevent breeding with others, and would bring them food. "They were also a beloved pet," said Senaqwila Wyss, who is Sḵwx̱wú7mesh, Tsimshian, Stó:lō, Hawaiian, and Swiss.

Once or twice a year, the dogs were sheared for their "wool," and would be left with just a fuzzy layer. Their hair was mixed with mountain goat wool and plant fibres to create textiles. Researchers estimate woolly dogs existed alongside our people for more than four thousand years.

According to one study, excavation at St'á7mes (Stawamus) revealed an "abundance" of dog remains and burials compared with other, similar archaeological sites in the region. There were 653 canid remains at the village, both woolly and village dogs. The site was rich with other evidence of our ancestors—16,627 artifacts were identified, showing a focus on the manufacture of tools emerging around four thousand years ago. There were mostly stone tools, and some bone and antler tools. There were awls, wedges, chisels, and a large dagger made from a whale rib. Multiple dogs were given burials, most away from the house, but there were also unique examples of dogs being buried under the house floor of a home. The dogs in various communities were fed *sts'úḵw'i7* and elk, the same food people ate.

With the arrival of Europeans, the woolly dog disappeared. Some accounts attribute this to the cheap manufactured wool blankets Europeans brought with them. As we were forced into the capitalist economy around us, we began to rely on colonial currency, and our weavings were often undervalued in that system. As well, our weaving practice was disrupted by colonization. Researchers believe that this combination of factors led to woolly dogs breeding with other dogs and eventually becoming extinct.

Senaqwila Wyss emphasized the colonial impact on our culture, including weaving. As well, in her research into the woolly dog, Wyss heard that many communities "had [the Royal Canadian Mounted Police] or government kill the dogs on the shoreline." Researchers estimate woolly dogs went extinct around 1940.

The art of weaving has been revived, however, largely thanks to the efforts of Chepx̱ímiya Siỷám̓ (Chief Janice George) and her husband, Skwetsímeltxw (Willard "Buddy" Joseph). The materials have changed, but more and more Sḵwx̱wú7mesh people are learning the tradition of weaving.

Ecological Impacts on Burrard Inlet

The rapid industrialization in the late 1800s and right through the 1900s radically changed the land and waters we knew, to the point at which the land is hardly recognizable compared with what it once was.

"There were mussels, sea eggs, cockles and lots of clams where the Lions Gate Bridge is," Syex̱wáltn (Dominic Charlie) said in an interview with the *Vancouver Sun* in 1971. "There were elk at Point Grey. The elk would swim across the bay. Everything was plenty." The beach went right up to the church at Eslha7áṅ (Mission Reserve). Our villages in Vancouver and North Vancouver were surrounded by trees.

Skwé7tsiya (Shellene Paull) described the Burrard Inlet her grandmother Skwé7tsiya (Eva Lewis) knew, in a written submission to the government. "My grand mom [*sic*] swam with a seal, and this seal would wait at the beach just outside of St. Paul's Church, waiting for the children to come out to swim. My mom Lucille Nicholson and her cousin Joyce Joe spent many summer days swimming at the beach where the mud flats were referred to as the Sand Banks."

Today, the beach is gone, dredged in 1963 to create Mosquito Creek Marina. The Port of Vancouver is now the largest port in Canada. Much of the inlet has been dredged. The sand that remains is not as rich as it was. The inlet is dotted with tankers and barges. Whales are now a rare sight in the inlet, when once they were plentiful. Vegetation, like huckleberries and thimbleberries, has also been reduced.

Loggers cleared the mountainsides and valleys of old-growth forests, which caused an ecological cascade. Without those strong roots, soil runs down steep hills, accumulating in creeks and smothering salmon eggs. Creeks are warmer and shallower without the old-growth to keep them cool and retain water in the soil. *Sts'úḵw'i7* have dwindled, which impacts eagles, bears, and whales. In turn, fewer *sts'úḵw'i7* carcasses are dragged into the woods by animals of prey, which means fewer nutrients are fertilizing the forest floor.

A less healthy forest impacts our ability to hunt and fish, and contributes to erosion and flooding. Second-growth forests retain less water and less carbon, and will take centuries to get anywhere close to what an old-growth forest can look like. Whatever forests are left to grow old will still look different in the face of climate change.

Corporations' and settler governments' irresponsible resource management would continue for decades without consultation with First Nations, causing immense and sometimes irreversible damage to the landscape.

11

CHILH SIY̓ÁM̓ SHÍSIK̲LI: RELIGION

IN SYSTEMATICALLY trying to separate us from the land, the settlers sought to divide us from our means of food, independence, culture, and spirituality. They would begin to restrict us to small reserves. And with the arrival of the sailing ships came the missionaries who sought to completely change our spiritual understanding and practice.

The altering of our world as Sk̲wx̲wú7meshulh (Squamish's People) was part of a bigger picture. The global story of Christianization, and the racist narrative of "saving" pagans, had begun centuries before.

Christian missionaries arriving at our territories viewed Christianity as the one true religion, with no tolerance for other beliefs. For wider context, in 1455 Pope Nicholas V wrote the papal bull *Romanus Pontifex*, a public decree that "granted" Portugal's king Afonso V the right to "invade, search out, capture, vanquish and subdue all Saracens and pagans" as his kingdom descended into Africa. Another papal bull, issued by Pope Alexander VI in 1493, "granted" Spain the possession of lands discovered by Christopher Columbus, stating any

FACING: Councillor Sempúlyan (Stewart Gonzales) presents Pope Francis with a blanket at the Vatican.

lands not inhabited by Christians were open to be claimed by Christians, and calling for "barbarous nations [to] be overthrown." These papal bulls demonstrate the very close connection of Christianity and colonialism, and how the desire to spread that religion, and eradicate all other types of spirituality, was connected with colonial powers' desire to exploit land and people for wealth. "The adoption of Christianity within the Roman Empire (which defined itself as 'civilized') reinforced the view that to be civilized was to be Christian," reads the 2015 *Final Report of the Truth and Reconciliation Commission.*

Of course, these papal bulls are based on flawed logic—what jurisdiction did the pope have to "grant" any rights on sovereign lands, and how could white people "discover" lands already inhabited for thousands of years? But this "civilization" narrative was used to justify the occupation of Indigenous lands, and missionaries followed close on the heels of European explorers. In New Westminster, the first mission was established in 1860, just two years after the city was founded, and the Sk̲wx̱wú7mesh encountered oblates there. In 1868, the first St. Paul's Church was built at Eslha7áṅ (Mission Reserve). Many Indigenous people converted—some willingly, some by force.

Xwechtáal (Andy Paull) described the connection between Christianity and colonialism while addressing the Canadian House of Commons in 1946: "Your ancestors came here and you penetrated into the country, and you sent as your ambassadors people with the Bible, with the Book. Now, I am a Christian man and I have no kick against any religion, but that is the way you got in," he said.

The Truth and Reconciliation Commission reached a similar conclusion in its final report: "Christian missionaries played a complex but central role in the European colonial project. Their presence helped justify the extension of empires, since they were visibly spreading the word of God to the heathen."

In an unpublished article, Xwechtáal said Sk̲wx̱wú7mesh people were happy to be acquainted with the church, as their "belief in a supreme being, the Creator, was already paramount," so Christianity resonated with some Sḵwx̱wú7mesh people. Sx̱áaltxw Siy̓ám̓ (Chief Louis Miranda) emphasized that Christian missionaries also espoused values of "love and respect for everyone," which aligned, in theory, with traditional Sḵwx̱wú7mesh beliefs. Those values, however, were not central to the colonization process. The missionaries and government used oppressive and abusive practices to compel Indigenous Peoples to abandon their culture, and would profoundly disrespect Indigenous individuals and Nations.

Our ancestors upheld Sḵwx̱wú7mesh traditions even when they were told to abandon them in the name of Christianity. In the generations of our interactions with the church, Sḵwx̱wú7mesh Christians also influenced our culture. Salish artwork has been incorporated into the church, and hymns were translated into the Sḵwx̱wú7mesh Sníchim (Squamish Language). The historic St. Paul's Church became a gathering place for the community to share stories and food and joy. New Christian traditions were picked up. The Shaker Church was formed, a new religious path that brought together pre-Contact and Christian spirituality. Eslha7áń was a Catholic community, while Xwmélch'stn (Capilano) was seen as pagan.

But Christianity is also part of the legacy of the federal residential school system. The oppressive tactics of residential schools turned some people against the religion because of the damage associated with it. Our people have varied and complex relationships with Christianity today.

After ground-penetrating radar suggested the recovery of 215 children at Kamloops Indian Residential School in 2021, people came together at St. Paul's Church and lined its steps with children's shoes. The structure was built by our ancestors and remains a gathering place for people, a place for many to find comfort and support, and to share memories. The history of St. Paul's Church, and Christianity, is alive and ever-moving with time. That is a teaching of our ancestors: to respect all spiritual beliefs.

The Doctrine of Discovery

The series of papal bulls, mentioned above, contributed to the Doctrine of Discovery—the legal justification that Europeans used to claim the land of Indigenous Peoples. "The Doctrine is built upon this largely racialized philosophy: those who were superior had superior rights to those who were inferior," a group of legal experts wrote in the book *Discovering Indigenous Lands: The Doctrine of Discovery in the English Colonies.*

The authors argued that the Doctrine of Discovery remains core to the Canadian legal system, which constantly assumes Indigenous claims and laws are inferior to Canadian claims. Canada replaced "papal imperialism" with "legal imperialism," casting imperial law as "normal" and Indigenous law as "non-existent or abnormal," and perpetuating the belief that European property laws are the "right" ones. The authors argue that the Canadian judicial system has been unable to "even entertain the notion of Indigenous legal orders as determinants of Indigenous land."

FACING: St. Paul's Indian Residential School (east side), 541 W. Keith Road in North Vancouver, built c. 1898.

Colonizers used the Doctrine of Discovery alongside the idea of *terra nullius*, the legal principle that any land that was not part of a "state" or being "used" in the European sense of the word could be seen as unowned and unoccupied. When Europeans arrived in Indigenous territories, the lands were, of course, occupied—but they decided they were not "owned," since they were not being "used" for European-style agriculture or exploitation.

The idea of the land being "empty," "lawless," and ripe for the taking was closely connected with the idea that Indigenous Peoples needed to be civilized through Christianity.

These concepts would be challenged in the coming decades—but they served as the foundation of Canadian law.

The Origin of St. Paul's

The earliest missionary visited the lower Fraser River in 1841. X̲ats'alánexw Siy̓ám̓ (Chief August Jack Khatsahlano) said the first church in Burrard Inlet was Methodist, built by Indigenous people in Gastown.

In an interview with J.S. Matthews in 1932, Reverend Charles Tate described that first church as a "tiny house of God": "[It] was a little box of a place, perhaps thirty feet long by twenty wide, built on the edge of the low bank, perhaps three or four feet high, of the shore, surrounded by a bit of clearing in the forest, say half an acre, more or less, at a point where the shore line bulged outwards. It was so close to the shore that the Indians used to tie their canoes to the front steps."

St. Paul's Indian Church was built by our people's hard work at Eslha7áń in 1868, under the name Sacred Heart. Sḵwx̱wú7meshulh lived around English Bay and Burrard Inlet when white people arrived, including villages at Xwmélch'stn, X̱wáy̓x̱way ("mask"; Lumbermen's Arch), and Ch'ích'elxwi7ḵw (Seymour Creek). More people began to live at Eslha7áń to work at the sawmills, according to X̱ats'alánexw Siy̓áḿ. He spoke to anthropologist Oliver Wells about religion in 1965:

FACING: St. Paul's Catholic Church, North Vancouver, 1905.

Wells: Well, when the people talked to you about religion, before we had the White man's religion—when I talked to Bob Joe, I talked to him about the word for chief and he says "seeahm"; and then he says there's another word, "cheechel seeahm." This is "the big high chief," like a god.

X̱ats'alánexw: That's a god, chilh siy̓áḿ.

Wells: Did the Indians worship this the same as we worship now? When you become Christian, why, we think we have the God to worship, like.

X̱ats'alánexw: Yeah, much the same. When you believe, you're all right, you'll get what you want. But before the White peoples come, we had our, like, church, just about the middle of the Squamish there, up there they call 'em Yekw'ts. The saltwater peoples go up there, and the peoples from above come down—all meet in that one church. Everybody got his own language and his own grub, and they just trade, like.

Wells: They would have ceremonies, would they, like a program?

X̱ats'alánexw: Yeah, then they have just some kind of a dancing. And they prayed for something, for maybe apples, maybe cherries, or anything like that. Us peoples here, we see the priests coming down in the hop yard, and one fellow says, "They think we're just starting to learn, but we know how the church is before, before the White peoples came to this country."

Wells: Our people, we didn't believe it when we came. My grandfather was Protestant, and my father, and I'm Protestant, and Crosby came in the Chilliwacks, and most of the Indians before this had the priests. Well, my grandfather was a friend of Crosby, so I know the Protestant Indians quite well, you see. But when these men came, why, all the missionaries they tried to tell the Indians about God and the High Spirit, and the Indians already had theirs—the White man thought he had something new, but the Indians already had it.

X̱ats'alánexw: [Laughs] That's right. We know it before, before the Whites come.

In 1890, Father Leon Fouquet said the Sḵwx̱wú7mesh villages had "taken to (Christian) prayer," and noted that the rapid conversion to Christianity struck him as exceptional.

The missionary order that established St. Paul's Church was the Missionary Oblates of Mary Immaculate, who came from France to Canada in 1841, and whose bishop became Father Pierre-Paul Durieu (the same bishop whom Charles Hill-Tout hoped would help him convince Sḵwx̱wú7mesh people to submit to physical examinations). The church and St. Paul's Indian Residential School were named in Durieu's memory. The Missionary Oblates of Mary Immaculate led the way in spreading Catholicism in western Canada, and Durieu spoke with pride about Sḵwx̱wú7mesh converts. "All have embraced with joy the practices of our holy religion," he wrote in an 1865 letter. "The denizens of Heaven are doubtless rejoicing at the transformation of these *sauvages*, only recently children of darkness, into children of light."

"A Troublesome Tribe"

There are different stories of how the mission on Sḵwx̱wú7mesh territory came to be. One often-told version starts with the Sḵwx̱wú7mesh being accused of murders in New Westminster. Here is a letter from the chief commissioner of lands and works, Arthur Bushby, dated July 30, 1869:

SIR,—*I have the honour to report that [Chief Snat and a party of Squamish Indians] came to me yesterday to complain that certain white men were intruding upon land on which they were settled, at Burrard Inlet, and on which they have built: they further tell me that they applied at the Lands and Works Office at the Camp, sometime back, and that they were told that the Inlet would be visited, their case looked into, and if necessary a "zum" or chart made of their land...*

I have not been long enough in charge to have time to make myself aware of the facts; but should there be any truth in the complaint made by the

Indians I would respectfully suggest that the matter be sifted, with as little delay as possible. The Squamish is a troublesome tribe and likely to give the scattered white population of the Inlet a good deal of trouble. The murder of Crosby and the recent murder of Perry will naturally create a very bad feeling between the whites and Indians which any disputes about land will tend to heighten.

According to records, the American trying to seize land at Eslha7áṅ was "Gassy Jack" Deighton, whom the neighbourhood Gastown is named after, a man who married one S<u>k</u>w<u>x</u>wú7mesh woman and then married her twelve-year-old niece.

The land matter was eventually resolved, and the government confirmed the land Deighton wanted as reserved for the S<u>k</u>w<u>x</u>wú7mesh (in fact, Father Durieu would later express frustration that the original reserve granted in the early 1860s had been curtailed and shrunken).

There is no evidence that the S<u>k</u>w<u>x</u>wú7mesh were responsible for the murders of Crosby and Perry. But as the oral history goes, the lieutenant-governor of British Columbia, Richard Moody, threatened to wipe out the S<u>k</u>w<u>x</u>wú7mesh in retaliation for the murders. Then, to protect the S<u>k</u>w<u>x</u>wú7mesh, Chief Snat teamed up with Father Fouquet to petition the government to set up a mission at Eslha7áṅ. Those who "wished to reject their evil ways and become civilized Christians" would be protected.

"Father Fouquet went over and he interceded on behalf of the Indians, and begged and pleaded for the Governor to give him a town to speak to the Indians first. So the people moved over at that time with the understanding that this place would be a Catholic mission, and everyone had to be converted and become a Catholic," S<u>x</u>áaltxw Siỷám said in a 1979 interview. Xwechtáal told a similar history in documents held by the Squamish Nation Archives and Cultural Collections, and in a 1936 article in the *Vancouver Sun*. This is a modern example of oral history, for there are no written records for this part of the story. But the church was built, and a great number of our leaders and community members became dedicated Catholics.

St. Paul's is the oldest surviving mission church in Vancouver, and it was designated a national historic site in 1980. The church was renovated in 1884, had two spires added in 1909, and was again renovated in the 1980s and 2010s.

"Paganish"

The way Xwechtáal and X̱ats'alánexw Siy̓ám̓ described it, many converts to Christianity saw similarities between the new religion's values and their own. But in the views of the missionaries, there wasn't room to hold on to Sḵwx̱wú7mesh culture while taking on new aspects of culture; the traditional culture and spirituality had to be erased.

FACING: ***Supplejack's Grave*, c. 1888. "An ancient Indian clearing, [at] Stanley Park . . . built of cedar slabs split with stone hammers and horn wedges."**

X̱ats'alánexw Siy̓ám̓ told J.S. Matthews about three family masks that he hid away and saved when missionaries attempted to destroy all traces of our culture. The story is summarized in the book *Conversations with Khahtsahlano*:

The Roman Catholic priests instructed Indians to destroy their masks as they were paganish. There is no actual record of any destruction of masks. The three Khahtsahlano masks were hidden in the attic rafters of August Jack Khahtsahlano's house at Capilano Creek for half a century, until in 1942 Major Matthews persuaded August Jack Khahtsahlano to allow them to be photographed by a professional photographer in Vancouver.

Subsequently Major Matthews purchased two of them; one for fifty dollars, a second for twenty dollars, and they are now (1954) in a large glass showcase in the City Archives. Mr. Khahtsahlano would not part with the third, giving as a reason that it "belonged to the peoples."

Kitsilano, a suburb of Vancouver, derives its name from Chief Khahtsahlano . . . A broad interpretation of the name is khahtsah, a lake, and lanough, a man,—hence "Man of the Lakes," a form of nomenclature somewhat similar to the British peerage titles, as in Prince of Wales, and Lord of the Isles . . .

Mr. Khahtsahlano was born at Snauq [Seṅák̲w], False Creek, Burrard Inlet, about 1878, and is the son of Khay-tulk, or "Supplejack", whose wife was Qwywhat (buried at Snauq about 1906), and her father was Quat-saylem. Khay-tulk lived at Chay-thoos [Sch'ílhus], or 'high bank', Prospect Point, First Narrows, Stanley Park, in a very old Indian lodge built with stone hammers and stone chisels of cedar slabs, and at his death the day August, his son, was born, was entombed in a canoe, placed in a mausoleum of wood on four short posts—and windows—his body being wrapped in blankets...

Primary pupils outside St. Paul's Indian Residential School, c. 1905.

At Khay-tulk's death, his widow, Qwywhat, remarried, her second husband being Chinalset, or "Jericho Charlie", a well-known and esteemed Indian of consequence, reliable and God-fearing, and he was a step-father beloved by his step-son August. Before Chinalset's death he charged his step-son to always treasure the three masks. Chinalset died over a half century ago, so the masks have been in Mr. Khahtsahlano's possession that length of time. He says that for many years they were hidden in the rafters of his habitation owing to the Roman Catholic priests having suggested that they should be burned. He also says that his step-father and his own mother told him that the oldest of the masks belonged to "Old Man Chief Khahtsahlanogh," father of Chief Khahtsahlano, who was father of Khay-tulk, who was August's father. August was also named Khahtsahlano, by Indian rite, at the vanished village of Snauq, False Creek, when he was a youth, and at a special potlatch called for the ceremony. Let it be repeated to clarify. The oldest mask belonged to the great-grandfather, the next to the grandfather, the third to the father. As for the son, August, he remarked "I have no mask," and added, "I've already got three"...

It is not known exactly how old the oldest mask is. It is said to be 'very old,' and differs from the other two of cedar wood as it is of British Columbia vine maple and very strong. This mask has never, previous to 5th June, 1942, been on the site of the city of Vancouver. It has been hidden away and never used nor displayed; nor have any of the three masks, previous to 5th June, 1942, been photographed.

The Sḵwx̱wú7mesh were told to give up many traditions, including our traditional burials, which Christians said were "not proper," and we were told to do underground casket burials in the Christian tradition. We were slowly restricted to reserves. Our children were forced to go to residential school, and our fishing and hunting were restricted. We were told to speak English, and children were punished for speaking their language in schools. Potlatches were banned from 1884 to 1951, as part of the effort to assimilate Indigenous Peoples into white Christian culture.

X̱ats'alánexw Siỷám̓ told J.S. Matthews that he paid for a potlatch in 1915 when five children died, but at it, they weren't supposed to give away gifts as was tradition, because of the ban, which could lead to people's arrest. They were expected to follow capitalist culture, and so X̱ats'alánexw Siỷám̓ instead paid the people helping, with money. He described that after the funeral, they had a feast, dance, and potlatch.

When Matthews asked him why feast and dance when people were sad, X̱ats'alánexw Siỷám̓, "(apparently annoyed at the stupidity of the question)" replied, "Well, may be—(pause). You got to pay help. Whitemans give drinks (whisky) after funeral. Indians don't give drinks; he gives eats; something good."

Assimilation Camps

All Sḵwx̱wú7meshulh are impacted by residential schools, and we all know it is a painful and often triggering thing to speak about. The rest of this chapter looks at the Sḵwx̱wú7mesh experience of residential schools.

The 1879 Davin Report, commissioned by Prime Minister Sir John A. Macdonald and written by Nicholas Flood Davin, looked at Indian Industrial Schools in the United States and recommended that a similar system be brought to Canada. Davin said children were still too influenced by their homes and families; they needed to be separated from their parents to be indoctrinated into settler society. These schools served the government end of assimilating Indigenous Peoples—but the "schooling" would be carried out mostly by the Roman Catholic, Anglican, Methodist, Presbyterian, and United Churches.

The first residential school opened in 1834 in Brantford, Ontario (Haudenosaunee and Anishinaabe territory). In 1867, the first residential school in British Columbia opened: the St. Mary's Residential School in Mission, BC (Stó:lō territory). St. Paul's Indian Residential School was established at Eslha7áṅ in 1899. There were 139 federally funded schools across Canada, and the last one closed in 1996.

The schools systematically tried to separate children from everything they knew about their culture and who they were. Children were subjected to terrible abuses as well as deplorable conditions, all of which are well documented. They were starved, molested, beaten, restrained, and experimented upon. Sickness tore through the schools. Children were not given quality education, and were largely put to labour. They were mostly fed religious doctrine and nationalist propaganda. Today, many people refuse to call these institutions schools and instead call them assimilation camps. The Truth and Reconciliation Commission concluded that these schools amounted to cultural genocide: the systematic destruction of all the traditions, language, and values of a distinct people.

"I left there not knowing how to be a sister. I left there not knowing how to be a mother. I left there not knowing how to be a grandmother. I left there not knowing how to be a friend," Jo-Ann Nahanee said about attending Kamloops Indian Residential School as a child.

In establishing residential schools, the colonial government showed it knew the power of our language, culture, and teachings—and that's why it wanted to destroy them. The goal was to have unfettered control of Indigenous lands by wiping out their diverse cultures. As Indian Affairs official Andsell Macrae said in 1886, "It is unlikely that any Tribe or Tribes would give trouble of a serious nature to the Government whose members had children completely under Government control."

"There [at residential school], we did not learn our traditions. We didn't learn our language. We were made to forget it," said the late Sḵwx̱wú7mesh chief Alana Andrews, who was sent to residential school at seven years old.

"It Wasn't a School"

"It wasn't a school. It was a place to kill the Indian in us," Sḵwx̱wú7mesh Elder Sam George said about St. Paul's Indian Residential School. He was brought there at seven years old.

Children at St. Paul's were often not allowed to see their family members at the school. They were punished for speaking their language or practising their traditions. About seventy-five children were living at the school at any given time, and there was evidence of overcrowding. In 1931, a local Indian agent—these agents were the Canadian government's representatives on Native reserves—reported that he suspected children weren't being fed properly. In 1933, the Indian Commissioner for British Columbia described the school as a "death-trap" and a "firetrap." The students at the school suffered an epidemic of smallpox in 1935.

More than two thousand children from Sḵwx̱wú7mesh, Xwmétskwiyam (Musqueam), Sel̓íl̓witulh (Tsleil-Waututh), and Lúx̱wels (Lil'wat) Nations and other communities were institutionalized at St. Paul's from grades one to eight. Survivors remember children who disappeared without explanation. After leaving St. Paul's, many older children were forced to attend Kamloops Indian Residential School.

"I am deaf in my right ear from being slapped in the ear and the head, and my left ear rings constantly," Sḵwx̱wú7mesh Elder Sam George told CTV News in 2021. He said they were "always hungry." He endured physical and sexual abuse. He attempted to run away twice.

"The RCMP came and I was introduced to these small handcuffs," he said. "They put the handcuffs on me and put me in the back of the car. They drove me up to the residential school and took the handcuffs off in front of everybody and I was brought in front of all the boys and I got struck."

FACING: Dozens of children's shoes line the stairs of St. Paul's Catholic Church in honour of the children at Kamloops Indian Residential School, 2021.

The pain that survivors went through led to trauma cycles of abuse, addiction, and loss. Survivors continued to be oppressed by the colonial state, making recovery and healing extremely difficult while they tried to survive. Shame was instilled in survivors for practising their own culture and speaking their own language.

"When I came out, I did not want to be an Indian," Sam George said. But returning to his culture saved him. Only later in life did he begin to share his experiences. He said this helped with his healing. "I was finally realizing why I was the way I was," he said. "Why I had anger and why I rebelled against authorities, or, you know, why authority made me angry."

Sḵwx̱wú7mesh survivors all have stories of enduring residential school and day school. Their children and relatives carry forward their stories, and the legacy of those who didn't survive.

"You got to wonder how these people could be so mean, you know? And they were supposed to be closer to God than anybody," Elder

Shirley Toman said. "They were telling me how bad I was going to be when I grew up... pretty soon it starts to sink in, you know, that maybe I'm not going to be a very good person."

Sḵwx̱wú7mesh Elder Gwen Harry went to St. Michael's Indian Residential School in Alert Bay and recalled being separated from her sisters. "We were strangers in a way," she said. "I was a stranger with my own family. I was a stranger to the cousins that I didn't know were my cousins." She described how this impacted the next generation: "We were not parents. We didn't know how to raise babies."

Many people didn't feel they could talk about what they went through. This resulted in mental health crises, all while facing oppression by the colonial government. People were limited in where they could work, and white people segregated places where Indigenous people were allowed to go.

St. Paul's Indian Residential School was condemned in 1957. Two years later, it was closed and torn down. The current St. Thomas Aquinas Regional Secondary School, a Catholic private school, was erected on the site.

Language as Identity

Immense efforts have gone into reclaiming the language that the government sought to destroy, and healing the impacts of trauma on generations. In many ways, Indigenous children were stripped of choice for generations. That impacted the choices of their children and their children's children. Several residential school survivors and language speakers spoke to Kirsten Baker-Williams for her master's thesis about the revival of the S<u>k</u>wx̱wú7mesh Sníchim (Squamish Language).

"It's your identity, every nationality has a language," said Kwinák̲atemat (Lucille Nicholson). "I worked in a daycare and I could hear them talking to the babies in their language. And I think that gives a person a sense of security and a sense of who you are, who you really are."

Residential and day school survivors preserved the language despite the state's attempt to take it away, and there are more and more speakers every year.

"I feel the language is so important... It just overwhelms me, the thought of having our language come back. And it may be different, a little bit different sounding, but it's still our language that's going to be saved for our own children's children," said Chiyálhiya (Lila Johnston), Kwinák̲atemat's sister.

"I think it is important to speak the Squamish [Language]. To me it's a *rebirth* of our Squamish ancestors. Keep it alive," Tiyáltelut (Audrey Rivers) said.

"I was glad I was able to come to speak again... I enjoyed it. It was a little scary, I didn't know how to come out with it [speaking the language]. I'm still learning," said Nekwsáliya (Margaret Locke).

These Elders, and others, were among those who joined the Squamish Language Elders Group: Ta na wa Nexwniw̓n ta a Ímats (Teachings for Your Grandchildren). They contributed to the Squamish–English dictionary published in 2011 and helped pass the language to the next generations.

Truth

The last residential school in Canada was in Saskatchewan, and it closed in 1996. Twenty years later, in 2006, the Indian Residential Schools Settlement Agreement was reached, and the class action established a fund to help survivors.

While Indigenous Peoples knew the truth of what happened at residential schools, the Canadian public still largely did not understand the full extent of the abuse that took place, and perpetrators had not been held accountable. The agreement, which was the largest class action settlement in Canadian history to date, sought to address that. The Truth and Reconciliation Commission of Canada was established out of the settlement to uncover the full truth of what happened and to facilitate reconciliation.

The commission spent six years travelling across Canada and hearing from over 6,500 witnesses. The government of Canada provided more than five million records to the commission, which are now stored at the National Centre for Truth and Reconciliation at the University of Manitoba in Winnipeg.

In June 2015, the commission presented its findings, concluding that the residential schools amounted to cultural genocide. The report included ninety-four calls to action to further reconciliation between Canada and Indigenous Peoples. The report contributed to Canadians' awareness of the atrocities that took place at these schools, or camps, and the intergenerational effects the trauma has on families. But as of December 2022, only eleven of the ninety-four calls to action had been fulfilled.

The commission provided ample evidence that children died at residential schools, but public attention faded after the report was released—until 2021, when ground-penetrating radar detected 215 potential unmarked graves at Kamloops Indian Residential School. National and international attention was wide-reaching. Neighbours, including a delegation of S<u>k</u>wx̱wú7mesh members, visited the former school site.

This spurred many Canadians to recognize the depth of the horror that had occurred at residential schools, which many had not been taught about in their own education. But racism persists, and there are still deniers who refuse to acknowledge the violence perpetrated at these schools. A red cedar memorial outside of the former St. Paul's Indian Residential School, carved by survivor Jason Nahanee, was vandalized in both 2020 and 2022, first with graffiti, then with an arm being broken off. The concrete base shows ancestors travelling in a canoe through waves, representing the challenging journey of survivors. Some surviving children's names are engraved in the waves. The monument was created in collaboration with the Sḵwx̱wú7mesh Úxwumixw (Squamish Nation), the Roman Catholic Archdiocese of Vancouver, the Sisters of the Child Jesus, the Assembly of First Nations, and the City of North Vancouver, and was unveiled in 2014.

More communities took on surveys of former residential school sites. The Sḵwx̱wú7mesh Úxwumixw launched an archival and land-based investigation into St. Paul's in 2021, alongside the Selílwitulh and Xwmétskwiyam Nations. The project is called Yúusnewas, which means "taking care of spirit, taking care of one another, taking care of everything around us."

According to public records, twelve unidentified students died while attending St. Paul's between 1904 and 1913. The investigation aims to find these children and lay them to rest.

Truth and Reconciliation Commissioners unveiling the final report, 2015.

In July 2022, the Nation oversaw its first LiDAR (light detection and ranging) scans. Yúusnew̓as completed phase one of the project, which was planning how to care for Elders and survivors and establishing a research process, and entered phase two, which is truth discovery: listening to and recording the oral histories of survivors.

As of the end of 2022, the National Centre for Truth and Reconciliation had documented 4,118 children who died at residential schools. According to the head of archives for the centre, Raymond Frogner, they hadn't gone through even one-fifth of their records at that time. He told the CBC that he anticipated the number of children on the death register will increase "by five-fold," at least.

One of the Truth and Reconciliation Commission's calls to action in 2015 was for the pope to apologize for "the Roman Catholic Church's role in the spiritual, cultural, emotional, physical, and sexual abuse of First Nations, Inuit, and Métis children in Catholic-run residential schools." People advocated for that apology for years. Finally, in April 2022, council Chairperson Khelsilem (Dustin Rivers) and Councillor Sempúlyan (Stewart Gonzales), a residential school survivor, went to Rome to meet Pope Francis, alongside a large group of Indigenous delegates, to address the harms caused by residential schools in Canada. From the Vatican, Pope Francis apologized for the Catholic Church's role in the schools—an apology many survivors and family members had been awaiting for a very long time.

Pope Francis then visited Canada, and Sḵwx̱wú7mesh deacon Rennie Nahanee attended the pope's address in the community of Maskwacis, south of Edmonton, near Ermineskin Indian Residential School. The pope once again apologized on behalf of the Catholic Church.

"I was thinking of my parents who went to residential school, and my siblings, and my two sisters who have passed away," Rennie Nahanee told *North Shore News*. "And my eyes started watering as I was listening to his apology and I kind of wished they were there to hear that." But, he added, the apology was only a first step. "And it's different for each and every person who was affected by the residential schools," Nahanee said. "It's not a blanket thing, that they heard the words and now everything's going be okay. There have to be some actions there."

Jo-Ann Nahanee, survivor of the Kamloops Indian Residential School, also said the apology is meaningless without action. "His apology means nothing to me," she said. "He hasn't said anything about what he will do in the future... For me it's a little bit too late."

Recovery

Our ancestors had to bear more pain than anyone should, just to survive. But our culture was not destroyed.

"It was the duty of the more responsible Indians to see that the history and traditions of our race were properly handed down to posterity," Xwechtáal said about our traditions before colonization. "It was the responsible duty of responsible elders."

In the face of so much pain and oppression, our ancestors took on that duty. Knowledge, stories, and loved ones have been unjustly lost in the face of colonization—but Indigenous Peoples have not disappeared.

"We still carried on our potlatches, our Indian culture... We still kept on using our own language," Sx̱áaltxw Siy̓ám̓ said about residential schools. People held on to their language in their minds, even if they could not speak it. They hid masks in attics. They did whatever they could. Our people are still facing the impacts of social upheaval, but healing is taking place.

In 2014, in the *Tsilhqot'in Nation v. British Columbia* case, the Supreme Court of Canada made the important decision to wipe out the concept of *terra nullius* in Canada—the idea that had been foundational to the spread of Christianity and colonization. But while the court concluded that the Indigenous lands known as Canada were not unoccupied when white people arrived, the Doctrine of Discovery was not overturned.

In 2021, under Justin Trudeau's Liberal government, Canada finally rejected the Doctrine of Discovery when it introduced legislation to adopt the United Nations Declaration on the Rights of Indigenous Peoples. On March 30, 2023, the Vatican also formally repudiated the doctrine. That kind of public denunciation would not have happened even one decade prior. But while Canada publicly renounced it, the doctrine still underlies the very foundation of the country.

PART FOUR

SḴWX̱WÚ7MESH IY ḴÁNATA: THE SQUAMISH AND CANADA

"I have things that I just know because of who I am and where I came from. It's because of my ancestors . . . Some of that has been lost through residential schools and due to other forces of colonization. Some of the parents haven't passed on what they could because they were not allowed to. Others have, though. All that is needed to take care of the land and work on the land exists inherently within us."

ORENE BROWN

AT THE SAME TIME industrialization and Christianization were taking place in our communities, settlers were building the infrastructure of modern-day Canada around us. The improvised settlement of trading posts would give way to the province of British Columbia, which would eventually join the nation of Canada.

It's hard to emphasize enough how quickly things changed. After first contact in 1792, there's no written record of our activities until 1827, with the *Fort Langley Journals* describing our visits to the Fraser River. There was little European settlement in Burrard Inlet until the 1860s. One account suggests the Sḵwx̱wú7mesh in the Squamish Valley didn't see another white person until 1857. About a decade later, in 1871, British Columbia joined Confederation. The province began fixing Indian reserve boundaries in 1875, and the Indian Act came into effect in 1876.

Settlers cut up and divided Indigenous land without respect for Indigenous occupation and without treaty in most of the province. They displaced Indigenous Peoples from their villages and destroyed their homes and the traditional resource gathering sites they relied on. The settler government banned and suppressed Indigenous cultures and practices and limited Indigenous people's livelihoods, all while sickness continued to weaken our communities. The government restricted Indigenous people to smaller and smaller land parcels, and residential schools took children from their homes. In Vancouver, into the 1900s, Indigenous people weren't allowed in certain parts of town.

For decades, Indigenous people weren't allowed to vote or retain a lawyer. As culture, language, and families were being suppressed and ripped apart, and the world of Indigenous Peoples eroded—their Indigenous and human rights violated—social issues among us, like addiction, began to rise.

Amateur anthropologist Charles Hill-Tout noted that it seemed much of Sḵwx̱wú7mesh history and traditions had already been "forgotten" by the time he tried to record information from elder Sḵwx̱wú7mesh people around 1900—though some of our people also resisted sharing information to protect our knowledge. All the while, traditional knowledge transmission was interrupted by the need to work wage jobs, the devastation of disease, and the social upheaval of colonialism.

S7ápelek̲ Siy̓ám̓ (Chief Joe Capilano; fifth from left) and delegates, 1908.

In British Columbia, settlement looked different from other parts of Canada. While other Indigenous Peoples had large reserves, First Nations on the coast were allocated small and scattered reserves that would continue to be dismissed as such and further cut up over decades. Today, Indian reserves represent only 0.4 percent of the province. As with Indigenous populations all over North America, Sk̲wx̲wú7mesh faced increasingly oppressive laws. But the more structured the oppression became, the more structured our resistance became. The twentieth century also saw the evolution of Indigenous organizations and the Sk̲wx̲wú7mesh movement toward presenting an amalgamated presence, whereas the colonial outlook was to deal with each community as a separate populace instead of a united Sk̲wx̲wú7mesh Úxwumixw (Squamish Nation) government.

12

Í7X̲WIX̲WAT STÉLMEXW: ALL OF US "INDIANS"

CORRESPONDENCE SUGGESTS that, in the years leading up to Confederation, British Columbia's first governor, James Douglas, tried to generously allot Indigenous lands. The influx of Americans during the Fraser Canyon Gold Rush had rapidly increased the non-Indigenous population, which was leading to rising tensions. Douglas was instructed to negotiate treaties with the "Indians," which resulted in fourteen treaties on Vancouver Island in 1850. The next treaty in British Columbia wouldn't be signed until 1899: Treaty 8, which spans parts of northeastern BC, Alberta, Saskatchewan, and the Northwest Territories. These were the only treaties that would be signed in British Columbia until the modern day. While Douglas was more generous than some of his contemporaries, he still "created reserves throughout the colony without either negotiation nor [*sic*] extinguishing Aboriginal Title," the Union of British Columbia Indian Chiefs wrote. The reserves created under Douglas would later be reduced by politicians who did not care about Indigenous rights.

The 1850s and 1860s were still early days in trade. There are records of gold seekers interacting with the Sk̲wx̲wú7mesh as they

FACING: First ever photograph of X̲ats'alánexw Siy̓ám̓ (Chief August Jack Khatsahlano).

headed into BC's Interior. Apparently, some were escorted up the Squamish River by a son of "Old Chief" K̲iyáplánexw. Another account notes that settlers exchanged tobacco, clothing, and a basket for a canoe and dried salmon; yet another said the Sk̲wx̲wú7mesh were "apprehensive" and kept their muskets at the ready.

In 1859, the first survey of Burrard Inlet took place. Written reports show that in that same year, Captain George Henry Richards was sent by Governor Douglas to see if Sk̲wx̲wú7mesh followers of "Old Chief" K̲iyáplánexw were holding Englishmen hostage. It turns out those men, Robert Burnaby and Walter Moberly, were simply camped at Coal Harbour, searching for coal. Settlers' search for natural resources to exploit continued with the more intensive mapping of the land they now called British Columbia.

Four Stakes to Claim the Land

To establish their control over the land, the British wanted to increase the rate of settlement. In 1860, Governor Douglas issued a land reform act to attract settlers. Any British subject, or foreigner who had sworn allegiance to the queen, could go almost wherever they wanted in the colony, plant four stakes, and claim that land. The only places they couldn't acquire land this way was within townsites, mineral sites, or Indigenous settlements. Once the land was surveyed, they would be given the first opportunity to purchase it for ten shillings an acre. They had to prove they made "permanent improvements" to the land. Use like agriculture and extraction was considered "improvement." Indigenous use of the land was not considered valuable—settlers did not see how Indigenous stewardship and care had maintained the land's richness.

In the eyes of the British, settlers could essentially acquire any lands they wanted. But these were unceded Indigenous territories; they had not been surrendered by or purchased from Indigenous

Peoples. As such, the act was in conflict with the 1763 Royal Proclamation of King George III, which forbade settlers from claiming land from Indigenous Peoples unless it had first been bought by the Crown and then sold to settlers. As Randy Bouchard and Dorothy Kennedy concluded, this wide-open land policy would "provoke abuses." Settlers began to pre-empt land in Burrard Inlet, often without living on it, which was against the land act. Settlers were laying claim to "the same lands from which the Indian people had gained their subsistence for thousands of years," Bouchard and Kennedy wrote. As early as 1865, a settler attempting to pre-empt land east of the Capilano River burned Indigenous people's potato patches at the site. As we discussed in chapter 11, "Gassy Jack" Deighton also tried to pre-empt land at the Mission Reserve, which led to tensions with the Sḵwx̱wú7mesh. While these two attempts weren't successful, others did successfully encroach on Indigenous settlements.

As more settlers imposed upon their land, the cultural and physical health of Indigenous communities was significantly weakened. Still, Bouchard and Kennedy point out that the Sḵwx̱wú7mesh did not give up in the face of these challenges, which also included smallpox and the opening of residential schools. They rallied behind their leaders. While colonialism often took a "divide and conquer" approach, neighbours found ways to unite. Whether from the reserves, politicians' offices, or Indigenous organizations, they fought for the recognition of their rights, which were being ignored and violated.

Trying to Secure Our Land

Our Sḵwx̱wú7mesh chief and council consented for Bouchard and Kennedy to access the Oblate Archives, where they found evidence of missionaries assisting our people in "claiming" some of our own land. Missionary Louis-Joseph D'Herbomez checked if Indigenous people could claim land under Douglas's new land act, and he and others helped S̲k̲wx̲wú7mesh people make so-called improvements to the land, such as agriculture, so that their pre-emptions would be approved. At the same time, correspondence shows that settlers favoured leaders they approved of. The *Fort Langley Journals* describes how Hudson's Bay Company "created" a new S̲k̲wx̲wú7mesh chief. The HBC provided their chosen person with valuable trade items and treated them as "chief," as opposed to the way we recognized someone as a *siy̓ám̓* before colonization. Missionaries also selected chiefs and refused to recognize those who carried on the traditional ways as *siy̓ám̓*. Some accounts say Skwatatwámk̲in was seen as a leader in Eslha7án̓, but because his wife was a spiritual dancer, missionaries appointed his nephew, Chief Snat, as leader instead. Squamish people at Mission Reserve who didn't convert to Catholicism were sent to Capilano. All this change profoundly affected leadership in villages and access to land.

Governor Douglas believed First Nations should be allowed to choose their reserves. In one letter, he wrote that surveying officers should meet Indigenous Peoples' wishes "in every particular," and reserves should include village sites, fishing stations, burial grounds, cultivated lands, and "all the favourite resorts of the tribes." He said each tribe's "natural or acquired" rights should be secured, and settlers should not do anything to cause complaint or unjustly deprive Indigenous people of land.

Douglas's stand put him at odds with others, such as Colonel Richard Clement Moody, commissioner of lands and works and a land speculator. Moody directed missionaries to stop assisting First Nations in pre-empting land. Meanwhile, allotment was disorganized. Reserve allocations began in the 1850s, but were often unrecorded, leading to conflicts with settlers trying to pre-empt land that Indigenous people had been promised as reserves.

Policy drastically changed after Governor Douglas retired. In 1864, chiefs in the Lower Mainland approached the new governor, Frederick Seymour, for help protecting their land. But the new commissioner of lands and works, Joseph Trutch, was emphatically against Indigenous rights and reduced reserved lands. Bouchard and Kennedy described Trutch as the "archetypal colonialist." He saw British Columbia as "a frontier to be developed," as most white people did at the time.

"The Indians have really no right to the lands they claim, nor are they of any actual value or utility to them and I cannot see why they should either retain them to the prejudice of the general interests of the colony, or be allowed to make a market of them either to the Government or to individuals," Trutch wrote in 1867. When land conflicts arose between Indigenous people and settlers, he sided with the settlers in almost every instance. Trutch maintained that previous agreements never acknowledged Indigenous title. "These presents were, as I understand, made for the purpose of securing friendly relations between those Indians and the settlement of Victoria, then in its infancy, and certainly not in acknowledgement of any general title of the Indians to the lands," he said. The province refused to discuss Indigenous title or treaties and supported Trutch's policies that increasingly carved away at the lands and rights of Indigenous people.

British Columbia Joins Confederation (1871)

The Dominion of Canada formed in 1867 and British Columbia joined in 1871, after Canada promised the province a railway. The railway significantly shifted the population balance between non-Indigenous and Indigenous people in the region.

Indigenous people outnumbered settlers when British Columbia joined Confederation, but no Indigenous people were present at the negotiations. The Government of Canada assumed responsibility for the Indigenous population and reserves. Unceded Indigenous lands were viewed as provincial Crown lands "burdened" with Indian interest. Indigenous people were excluded from any role in government and voting.

Dominion Day canoe races near the foot of Carrall Street, c. 1890.

British Columbia and Canada agreed the province would retain control over land allocation. They also agreed that Indian land would be allocated in a policy as "liberal" as BC had already been pursuing—only ten acres per family. Meanwhile, Europeans could pre-empt 160 acres and then buy more. Indigenous people began to organize and advocate for their interests.

In 1873, at a celebration of the queen's birthday in New Westminster, Indigenous leaders approached an Indian Affairs official, Israel Wood Powell, with a petition. This was organized by Catholic priests, and only the church's approved leaders were allowed to be present. So-called pagan leaders were not invited, so the petition had no signatures from individuals representing Xwmélch'stn (Capilano) or Ch'ích'elxwi7kw (Seymour Creek), which were seen as "uncivilized" because of their lower number of converts to Catholicism.

About three to four thousand Indigenous people attended the event. A spokesperson addressed Powell: "The white man have taken our land and no compensation has been given [to] us, though we have been told many times that the great Queen was so good, she would help her distant children the Indians. White men have surrounded our villages so much so in many instances, especially on Fraser River, but few acres of land have been left [for] us. We hope that you will see yourself our wants, and our desires, and you will remove that veil of sorrow which is spreading over our hearts." This address was signed by many chiefs, including "Peter Chief of Skwamish" and "Kwatat kwamkren Chief of Stames." Powell visited several communities and heard complaints that people had insufficient reserve land or no land at all. The Sḵwx̱wú7mesh had only three small reserves at the time, all in Burrard Inlet. The federal government was expected to hold reserve land in the interest of Indigenous people, rather than the communities having control. The land had never been surrendered, but to the colonial governments, the underlying title lay with the province. This meant the province claimed ownership over any land removed from Indian reserves.

Author Bob Joseph, hereditary chief of the Gwawaenuk Tribe, noted that Confederation led to a conflict of interest: "On the one hand, [Canada] was responsible for 'Indians and lands reserved for Indians,' while, on the other hand, it was the responsible party for negotiating treaties and purchasing their land for the Crown," he wrote. As well, claiming responsibility over Indigenous Peoples did not respect their sovereignty.

13

TA XWELÍTN K̲WELK̲WÁLWN: THE XWELÍTN WAY OF THINKING

Indigenous peoples were banned from pre-empting land or recording claims to unsurveyed land without direct federal permission. Then, a piece of legislation was passed that would shape Canada's relationship with First Nations for decades to come: the Indian Act of 1876. The intention behind the act was to wipe out Indigenous cultures and assimilate First Nations into Canadian society.

This act came after the Gradual Civilization Act of 1857, which outlined "voluntary enfranchisement," meaning a First Nations person could get land and voting rights—if they chose to give up their status as an "Indian." Obviously, Indigenous people did not want to give up their identity—some say only one person in all of Canada voluntarily enfranchised. And so, the Gradual Enfranchisement Act of 1869 removed the voluntary nature of enfranchisement. If an Indigenous person received a university degree or became a doctor, Christian minister, or lawyer, they were unilaterally enfranchised. Any woman who married a non-Indigenous man was stripped of her status. This act also

FACING: X̲ats'alánexw Siy̓ám̓ (Chief August Jack Khatsahlano; right) and others at the Stanley Park rededication, 1943.

Dwellings at Eslha7áń (Mission), 1888.

introduced elected "band" councils, which were to be composed of men over twenty-one years old only. No Indigenous person could live on reserve unless permitted by the superintendent of Indian Affairs.

With the Gradual Enfranchisement Act, Indigenous people could either retain membership in their communities or give up membership to exercise full legal and political rights in Canadian society. They couldn't do both.

When the Gradual Civilization Act and Gradual Enfranchisement Act were folded into the Indian Act of 1876, the paternalistic view Canada had of Indigenous people was on full display. "Indians" should be "treated as wards or children of the State," the new act stated. The many diverse forms of traditional Indigenous governance across First Nations were actively unrecognized; in 1880, it became illegal for First Nations to practise ceremonies and cultural gatherings. In 1884, the potlatch was banned, and people could be imprisoned for engaging in them. In 1895, "any festival, dance or other ceremony" was banned.

In 1900, the pass system, which restricted the movement of First Nations people off reserve, was introduced. The Indian Act required children to attend residential schools.

A large Chinese population had grown on the mainland, mostly working in prospecting and on the railway. Other people from around the world, like Hawaiians and South Americans, gathered in Burrard Inlet. The Canadian Pacific Railway was completed in 1885, built mostly by Chinese Canadians. The railway ended in Vancouver, ushering in a rapid increase in population. In 1884, about nine hundred settlers lived in Burrard Inlet; by 1891, the number had grown to fourteen thousand. At the same time, the Indigenous population declined by one third. In 1891, Vancouver established a steamship connection with Asia. The City of Vancouver was being built around the Indigenous Peoples of Burrard Inlet—a hub of trade and industry, where sawmills were central to the town's economy. Eventually, it would become one of the most populous cities in Canada.

Joint Indian Reserve Commission (1876)

In 1874, the federal government appointed a board to oversee Indian Affairs in British Columbia, to sort out reserves. Canada had promised eighty acres per family; British Columbia countered with proposing a mere ten acres per family. Indigenous leaders wrote a petition in support of eighty acres. The two levels of colonial government agreed on twenty acres, to the frustration of Indigenous people; a group of leaders told Indian Agent Israel Wood Powell they felt "the aim of the White men is to exterminate us as soon as they can." This number would be further reduced to ten acres per family. This is a stark contrast from the Prairies, where 160 acres per family were allocated.

In 1875, to allot reserves, the provincial and federal governments established a three-man commission, called the Joint Indian Reserve Commission (JIRC), which began its work a year later. At this time, many Indigenous people were still travelling and using resources from the land. With this shift to reserves, Indigenous people would be more and more constricted to permanent residence on a single reserve.

The JIRC immediately turned down the Sk̲wx̲wú7mesh claim to the entire Squamish Valley because of the white population's interest in building a cattle road between the coast and Stl'átl'imx (Lillooet), though no white people resided in the valley yet. Because the Sk̲wx̲wú7mesh had been given very little land around Burrard Inlet, the JIRC allocated larger reserves around the mouth of the Squamish and Cheakamus Rivers to compensate.

FACING: Plan showing parcels of the Kitsilano Indian Reserve No. 6 of the Squamish Nation, surveyed by George Frederick Fountain.

Sk̲wx̲wú7mesh chiefs met with the Commission at St'á7mes (Stawamus) and asked about the right of Sk̲wx̲wú7mesh people to move about freely. Committee member A.C. Anderson assured them that any land that was not fenced by white men "was as free to them as ever and the more white men mixed amongst them, the better they would be."

Overall, however, the JIRC left Indigenous communities unsatisfied. As discussed in Parts One and Two, marriage, kinship, and use of resources established where people lived. Some areas were exclusive, while others were shared. Different language groups were the majority in a village at different times because of the sharing of resources as a result of intermarriage. Other villages would clearly belong to one people.

"It is no wonder, then, that the Indian reserve commissioners in the 1870s, with their European notions of land tenure and ownership, struggled futilely to determine the sole 'owners' of Burrard Inlet," Randy Bouchard and Dorothy Kennedy wrote. This lack of understanding impacted Indigenous people for decades to come. Settlers called the Squamish "squatters" for residing in Burrard Inlet. As one geography professor put it, these surveys flattened and reduced "topographically and culturally distinct" spaces into a homogenized grid.

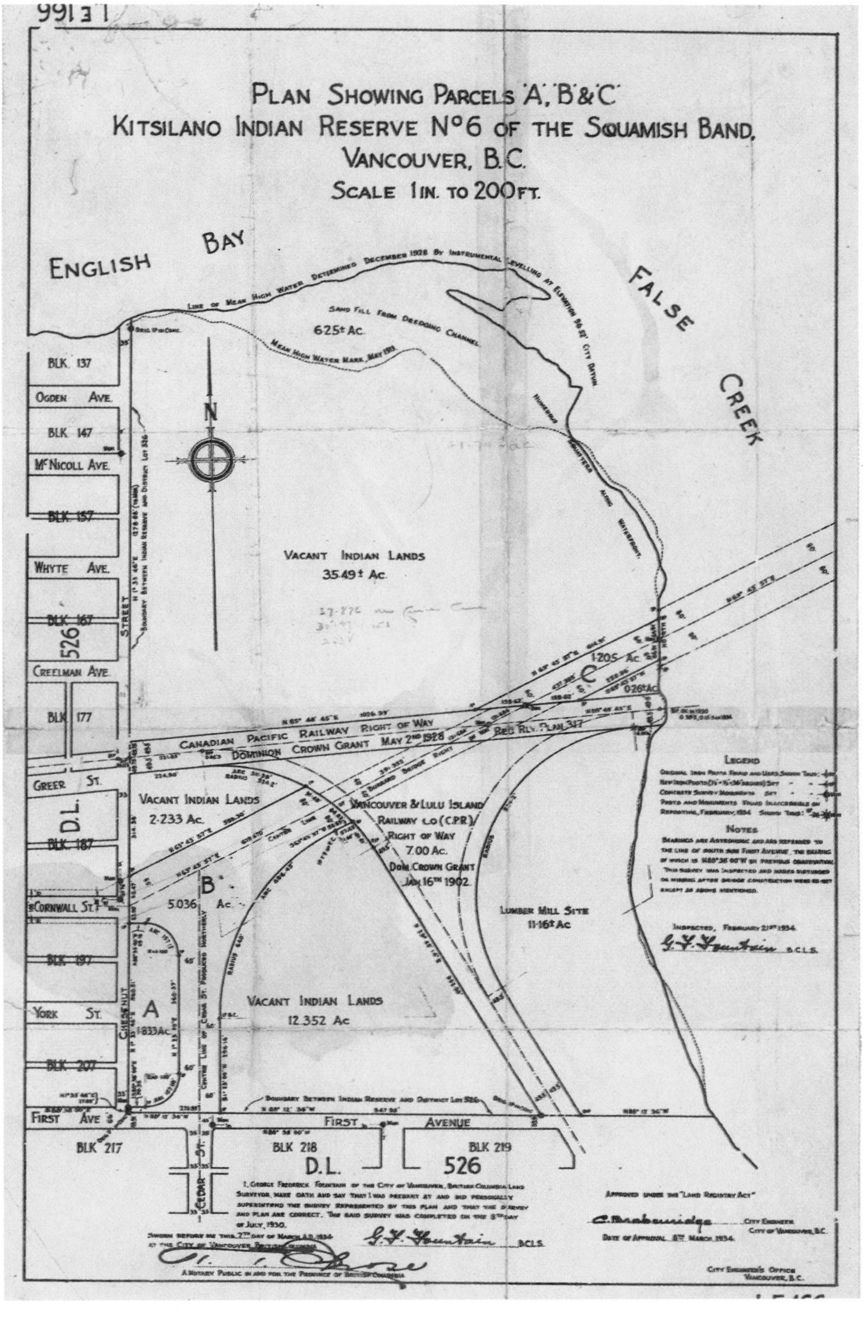
PLAN SHOWING PARCELS 'A', 'B' & 'C'
KITSILANO INDIAN RESERVE Nº6 OF THE SQUAMISH BAND,
VANCOUVER, B.C.
SCALE 1 IN. TO 200 FT.
ENGLISH BAY
FALSE CREEK
6.25± Ac.
VACANT INDIAN LANDS
35.49± Ac.
1.205 Ac.
C
CANADIAN PACIFIC RAILWAY RIGHT OF WAY
DOMINION CROWN GRANT MAY 2ND 1928
VACANT INDIAN LANDS
2.233 Ac.
VANCOUVER & LULU ISLAND RAILWAY CO (C.P.R.) RIGHT OF WAY
7.00 Ac.
DOM. CROWN GRANT JAN 16TH 1902
B
5.036 Ac.
LUMBER MILL SITE
11.16± Ac
VACANT INDIAN LANDS
12.352 Ac
A
1.833 Ac.
BLK 137
OGDEN AVE.
BLK 147
McNICOLL AVE.
BLK 157
WHYTE AVE.
BLK 167
526
CREELMAN AVE.
BLK 177
GREER ST.
D.L.
BLK 187
CORNWALL ST.
BLK 197
YORK ST.
BLK 207
FIRST AVE
BLK 217
CHESTNUT
STREET
CEDAR ST.
FIRST AVENUE
BLK 218
BLK 219
D.L. 526
LEGEND
NOTES
INSPECTED, FEBRUARY 21ST 1934.
B.C.L.S.
APPROVED UNDER THE "LAND REGISTRY ACT"
CITY ENGINEER
CITY OF VANCOUVER, B.C.
DATE OF APPROVAL 8TH MARCH 1934.
CITY ENGINEER'S OFFICE
VANCOUVER, B.C.
A NOTARY PUBLIC IN AND FOR THE PROVINCE OF BRITISH COLUMBIA

The Loss of Seṅáḵw

The Sḵwx̱wú7mesh lived in a village called Seṅáḵw ("inside the head of the bay," at False Creek) in the present-day Kitsilano neighbourhood in Vancouver. The village allowed families access to the water. Chepx̱íṁ Siỷáṁ (Chief William George) lived at Seṅáḵw. Chepx̱íṁ Siỷáṁ was born around 1830, and also lived in the Ch'éḵch'eḵts community on the Squamish River. He was respected as a *siỷáṁ* in those communities, as well as in the nearby Squamish River communities of Yelhíxw and P'uỷáṁ. In the summer, people from the three Squamish Valley communities lived together at Seṅáḵw.

Chepx̱íṁ Siỷáṁ stated that the land at False Creek "belonged to his grandfather" and that his "dead relatives" were buried there.

Seṅáḵw became known as Kitsilano Indian Reserve No. 6. It first appeared on a surveyor's map in 1869 at 37.45 acres. The village was home to at least eighteen families, and it was expanded to eighty acres in 1877 by the Joint Indian Reserve Commission. At this point in time, each reserve the government recognized was treated as a separate "band," so people living at Seṅáḵw were known as the False Creek Indian Band. Each band had a chief that the federal government recognized as a leader in the community, even though a "chief" was not a Squamish concept. Chepx̱íṁ Siỷáṁ passed away in 1907; his sister's son Kwenáx̱tn (Andrew) became regarded as a *siỷáṁ*, and he became chief of the False Creek Indian Band. The imposition of reserves had eroded traditional seasonal rounds, and by the 1920s, most people were living in one place, permanently. Many people can identify family members who lived at Seṅáḵw, such as Squamish Charley, X̱ats'alánexw Siỷáṁ (Chief August Jack Khatsahlano) and his mother Xwaywat, Old Jim Samelton, Willie Jack, Jacob Louis, Monica Williams, Pierre Jim, and Háx̱sten (Harriet George).

FACING: Canoes at the foot of Richards Street, c. 1898.

Little time would pass before settlers began to eye the land and slice it into pieces. In 1886, 3.62 acres were expropriated for rail, and another 7 acres in 1901. The provincial government and City of Vancouver wanted to buy the land and use it for development, but the federal government pushed back, though its efforts were inconsistent and communication was spotty. In early 1904, when discussions of a surrender first arose, Chepx̱íṁ Siỷáṁ was opposed. His relatives were buried there, and he did not want to sell.

The province, and some people in the city, were determined to eradicate the village. According to one businessman, the village was an "eyesore." Indian Agent Frank Devlin said, "False Creek is anything but a suitable place for the Indians as they are too close to town."

Chunks of land continued to be leased by the federal government from 1901 to 1913, since they controlled the land for the "benefit" of the residents. Then, in 1911, Canada passed the Oliver Act, an amendment to the Indian Act. The government claimed authority to remove Indigenous people without their consent if they were living next to a town with a population of eight thousand or more. Indigenous groups and critics called the act an abuse of power.

FACING: Seṅáḵw residents with their belongings on a barge, after being forced to leave their homes and relocate to other reserves, 1913.

In 1913, British Columbia and the False Creek Indian Band agreed to a "sale" of what was left of the reserve—a transaction that, decades later, all parties agreed was illegal. In reality, the families were threatened, misled, and coerced into selling. They were promised $11,500 per family, but not everyone got that payment. The province loaded the families on a barge to be sent across the inlet to join the population of the reserves in North Vancouver or go up to the town of Squamish.

"The remains of those buried in the graveyard on the reserve [Seṅáḵw] close to First Avenue about the foot of Fir or Cedar Street were exhumed and taken for reburial at Squamish," X̱ats'alánexw Siỷáṁ (Chief August Jack Khatsahlano) told J.S. Matthews.

"The orchard went to ruin, the fences fell down, and the houses were destroyed. A few hops survived and continued to grow until the

building of the Burrard Bridge covered them up. I received a formal invitation to be present at the opening of the great bridge as a guest of the city."

The homes of the Sḵwx̱wú7mesh were burned to the ground. Much of the reserve would remain empty for years after the families were forced out. But slowly, over time, it would continue to be divided among settlers, who created a park, apartment buildings, and the large Molson brewery on the land; it was also leased to the military during World War II.

Inspector for the province William Ditchburn, later commissioner of Indian Affairs in British Columbia, saw the eradication of "Indians" from Burrard Inlet as inevitable. "These chiefs fully realize that they will eventually have to move off the reserves close to the cities and move up to the Squamish River, where they have plenty of reserves, and I am of the opinion that no difficulty would be met within the matter of getting them to surrender their present reserves, providing they get a good value for the land," he wrote.

Eventually, in 1946, the Sḵwx̱wú7mesh Úxwumixw (Squamish Nation) surrendered the False Creek reserve for lease or sale. The federal government accepted surrender for sale only, and sold the land off in six parcels. The government was supposed to manage these sales to the benefit of the Sḵwx̱wú7mesh Úxwumixw, but did not. By 1965, the entire reserve had been sold for a net revenue of $1 million.

The dissolution of Seńáḵw is only one story among many of displaced Indigenous people and their destroyed villages. The story of Seńáḵw remains a painful memory for the Sḵwx̱wú7mesh. But the non-Indigenous population in the generations to come would have little awareness of the history behind the beautiful beach, and the land beneath Burrard Street Bridge.

The Sḵwx̱wú7mesh were also removed from X̱wáy̓x̱way ("mask," also known as Lumbermen's Arch), where the village was demolished to build a road around the perimeter of Stanley Park. The Sḵwx̱wú7mesh had not been allocated a reserve there.

"We was inside this house... when the surveyors come along, and they chop the corner of our house... when we was eating inside," X̱ats'alánexw Siy̓ám̓ told J.S. Matthews. "We all get up and go outside see what was the matter. My sister Louise, she was only one talk a little English; she goes out ask whiteman what's he doing that for. The man say, 'We're surveying the road.' My sister ask him, 'Whose road?'"

Human remains, shell middens, and archaeological evidence of Indigenous life at Stanley Park were buried underneath the road. Not only was it grossly disrespectful of the remains of our ancestors, let alone the people who lived there at the time, but it also disrupted archaeological study, to which the shell middens and other remains are integrally important.

Chief George Tom from Brackendale also described the loss of his land in a letter, written on his behalf, to the Indian agent in the early 1900s. This letter exemplifies how the stated principles of not encroaching on Indigenous settlements did not happen in practice. The letter describes how the Squamish Valley Hop Company claimed twenty feet of Chief Tom's land and ordered him to move his fence back. He moved it, but then they ordered him to move it back another fifteen feet. "George Tom objects to move it any more," the letter reads. "George wants you [the Indian agent] to come up at once & bring maps and compass with you & decide as to the line, for the Company are after him to move it again."

Chief Billy also wrote a letter, in 1910, to the Indian agent about Howe Sound & Northern Railway's development in Brackendale: "I am afraid that we will have a quarrel, or rather a fight and if such things happen may be [*sic*] one of us would be killed, and you have the trouble of fixing up the trouble in this place. Of all my friends there is none who have said not a word of me. They said why I have let the railway company work on this reserve. When there is no money laid at our side that's the reason, that there is lots of talk of anger. You know very well that I never get angry at anybody."

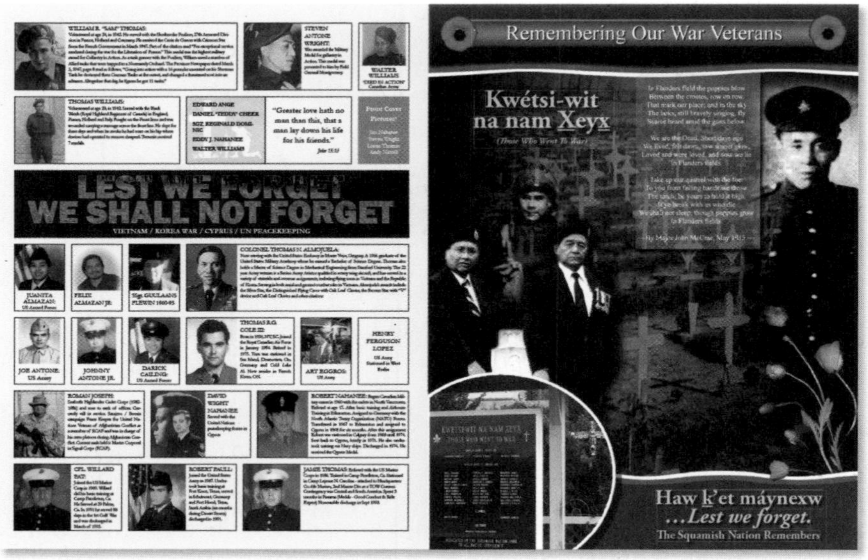

The Sk̲wx̲wú7mesh Úxwumixw (Squamish Nation) remembers its veterans.

A year later when the railway was completed, Chief Billy expressed frustration that the railway company had not fixed his gate, and said, "I don't wish to be locked up as if I were in prison after the Railway Co. has destroyed my place."

Taking Concerns to the King

Indigenous leaders never stopped pushing for recognition of their rights. In 1906, S7ápelek̲ Siy̓ám̓ (Chief Joe Capilano; Squamish), Chief Charlie Tsulpi'multw (Cowichan), and Chief Basil David (Bonaparte) travelled to London to air their grievances with King Edward VII. They brought a petition protesting the lack of treaties and the inadequate allocation of reserves in British Columbia.

"In the past few years white men have so increased that they are like a storm of locusts, leaving the earth bare where they pass by," S7ápelek̲ Siy̓ám̓ told the *Vancouver Daily World* at the time.

In their petition, the three chiefs said they desired to "live in harmony with the white people who are filling up our country," but that titles were issued upon Indigenous lands by the provincial government. "The Indians, being without votes, they can get no redress so they trust His Majesty's ears will be open to their cry," the petition read.

After waiting several days, they had a fifteen-minute meeting with the king. The king advised the chiefs to approach Prime Minister Wilfrid Laurier. The trip was a success in terms of getting media attention and inspiring pride in the Indigenous community. When the chiefs returned, they were greeted with a parade.

In 1910, the same year Chief Billy wrote his letter to the Indian agent requesting support, Laurier finally visited British Columbia to settle the conflict between the federal and provincial governments. Canada had been pushing for larger reserve sizes, while the province refused. BC Premier Richard McBride made it clear he didn't want to address any question of Aboriginal title, arguing it would impact British Columbia's finances.

By 1914, with the onset of World War I, there were 450,000 people living in the province, with more than 111,000 people in Vancouver. Veteran Robert Nahanee spoke with the *Toronto Star* about the impact of the war, about how Indigenous veterans pushed for their Indigenous rights as well as their veteran rights, having served in the war at the same time potlatches and ceremonies were banned. "They weren't being treated as equal to other veterans," Nahanee said. "[Indigenous veterans] said this imbalance of rights has to be changed."

It was abundantly clear that the province was systemically disregarding Indigenous title and status. And it wasn't anywhere near over. The next step in reserve allocation would take away more productive land from First Nations.

14

SḴWX̱WÚ7MESH ÚXWUMIXW: THE SQUAMISH NATION

British Columbia halted reserve allotments in 1908, believing Indigenous people had quite enough land. In 1901, reserve land around the mouth of the Squamish River had already been sold to the Howe Sound, Pemberton Valley and Northern Railway, reducing the landholdings of the Sḵwx̱wú7mesh (Squamish), St'á7mes (Stawamus), and Kaw̓tín (Kowtain) reserves.

The fact that settlers were taking Indigenous land contributed to the thirteen-year process of meetings, correspondence, and discussions among the leaders of the sixteen Sḵwx̱wú7mesh bands. The federal government treated each Sḵwx̱wú7mesh community as an individual entity, but with the Amalgamation document signed on July 23, 1923, Sḵwx̱wú7mesh Úxwumixw (Squamish Nation) leadership exerted our people's political strength in pursuit of better relations with the provincial and federal governments.

Indigenous leaders had been frustrated with their rights being trampled on, and their complaints being ignored. The early 1900s were a time of organizing and resistance. Indigenous people fought in unions on the waterfront in the 1920s, and began to create Indigenous organizations like the North American Indian Brotherhood in the decades to follow.

McKenna-McBride Commission (1913–1916)

To settle the allocation of reserves issue, the federal and provincial governments agreed to form a royal commission. The McKenna-McBride Commission was named for Richard McBride, the premier of British Columbia, and Joseph McKenna from the Dominion's government, co-signers of the agreement that stated that when governments reduced a reserve, they would share the profit from selling the land. Each level of government got 50 percent; the Dominion would keep half of its portion, and allocate the other half "in trust for the benefit of British Columbia Indians." So, while Indigenous land was being taken and sold, our people were getting only one quarter of the profit, and we did not have control over the funds.

The McKenna-McBride Commission surveyed from 1913 to 1916, and its recommendations were adopted in 1924. Notably, the Commission refused to meet any organized body of Indigenous representatives, such as the Indian Rights Association. The chiefs pushed for title to their lands but were told that title was not in the scope of the Commission. The Commission assured the S<u>k</u>wx<u>w</u>ú7mesh leaders that their land was protected, even as the North Vancouver City Council and rail companies eyed it. The mayor wanted to acquire the Seymour Reserve and offered $600 per acre, when off-reserve land went for $2,500 per acre. Chief Jimmy Harry asked for this off-reserve price, and the mayor called his request "absurd."

One can easily imagine how frustrating these discussions must have been for the S<u>k</u>wx<u>w</u>ú7mesh leaders. In one 1913 meeting, the Commission said the Pacific Great Eastern Railway Company wanted to build through the Mission and Capilano reserves, as well as in Howe Sound. The company offered $150,000 for the land. On one hand, the chairman told the S<u>k</u>wx<u>w</u>ú7mesh representatives that the land couldn't be sold without consent. On the other hand, they implied that the railway would likely be approved either way: "As this country progresses and is settled more and more, and as commerce and trade increases, there will always be demands for facilities to carry it, and the law provides that property of this character may be taken possession of without consent of the owner for the construction of these public works. I don't make the law, but there it is, and I want to tell you that this not only applies to the lands of Indians but it also applies to the lands of whitemen," the chairman of the Commission said. The Sḵwx̱wú7mesh leadership was basically told to either come to an agreement with the railway company, with the consent of the majority of the band, or not give consent and risk receiving less money and the railway going through anyway. The Sḵwx̱wú7mesh leaders were assertive in their response. Xwechtáal (Andy Paull), one of the leaders, acted as interpreter:

Chief Joseph: I don't think this is quite right, as we told you at your last visit that we would not consider any offers until the question of Title had been settled, and we are still waiting for your decision on that.

Chairman: We cannot give you that decision until we get through with our work—we have not yet even visited your reserve.

Paull: Well I think your Lordship stated that no portion of the Reserves of the Squamish Tribe would be sold until the question of Title had been settled, and all the majority of the male members of the Squamish Tribe voted on that resolution.

Chairman: That is quite true, but we cannot stop a railway for two or three years until we get this question settled as to the British Columbia Government surrendering their right of reversion.

Paull: What we would have to do your Lordship is to hold a proper meeting, as the Indians you see here are not a majority and we cannot state anything today that would be official from the majority of the Squamish Tribe.

Chairman: I would just state that if the Band considers the price a good one, are you not as well off as if you get a clear title—would you not be as well off?

Paull: If the price was satisfactory the Indians would be as well off, but the Indians will not surrender their reserves until the price is satisfactory.

Xwechtáal said they would need to call a meeting with as many representatives from each Sḵwx̱wú7mesh band as possible. The

Commission pressured them to set a date to resolve the issue quickly. Xwechtáal pushed back, saying they couldn't make any decisions without a majority of male members from the band present.

Paull: In the event of the Indians refusing the offer of the Railway Company altogether for good reasons, what protection have the Indians got insofar as the land marked "red" [i.e., Railway] on the plan is concerned?

Chairman: So far as the ground marked "green" is concerned as I said before, we have nothing to do with, you own that and it is for you to say whether you want to dispose of it, but insofar as the land marked "red" is concerned, the Commission will recommend that the Railway Company have permission to enter upon the land and take it for railway purposes.

Paull: The regulations would have to be altered before the Indians would be satisfied to a surrender of their lands. It has been well understood that 50 percent of the purchase money would go to the Government to be held in trust for the Indians. That has been the custom for years, and money has been in Ottawa in trust for the Indians for years, but that is one of our greatest grievances. It was very difficult for the Indians to make use of that money that is in Ottawa. There is a lot of things for public purposes that we could use this money for. We have asked the Government to appropriate the money for certain public things and we have been refused time after time. That system has not given us very much encouragement—why should the Government get 50 percent? That is one of the cases the Indians cannot make out.

Chairman: That is the law Andrew. We can only make recommendations to the Government, that is all we can do if we think it is proper to do so.

Today, the railway runs through the Mission and Capilano reserves, and led to the sale of several reserves in Howe Sound. The St'á7mes Reserve was reduced from 141.5 acres to 50 acres; the Yekw'ápsm Reserve went from 154 acres to 4 acres.

The McKenna-McBride Commission shaved 150 acres off the Capilano Reserve. Over thirty acres were cut from Mission Reserve. Indigenous people sought a meeting with the Privy Council of England, but the federal government intervened, saying that "Indian" claims could go to Canadian courts, but with conditions. The Indigenous

Eslha7áń (Mission Reserve), opposite Vancouver, c. 1886.

people had to be represented by legal counsel appointed and paid for by the government. If the courts decided Indigenous people in British Columbia had title, they had to agree to surrender it. They also had to accept compensation "in accordance with past procedure." And they had to give up future claims. If the court decided they had no title, "the Indians would continue to be governed by the federal government."

Of course, Indigenous leaders refused these conditions. The issue of title was kicked down the road.

The reserves that the Sḵwx̱wú7mesh *were* allocated presented challenges. The Sḵwx̱wú7mesh were encouraged to use the land for agriculture, to make the land "productive," but some lacked the tools. Several reserves, such as Skowishin and Kaw̓tín (Kowtain), faced significant erosion. The Poquiosin and Skamain Reserve also had "severe" erosion. Two years after the McKenna-McBride Commission, surveyors found that only 55 of the original 110 acres of that reserve remained intact. Back in 1876, the government had already recognized that Siy̓ích'em (Seaichem) Reserve was experiencing serious erosion, but nothing was done. By the 1940s, roughly half the original reserve was lost to erosion.

According to one historian, in total, the McKenna-McBride Commission removed forty-seven thousand acres of mostly good land from reserves in return for eighty-seven thousand acres of generally poor land. The original land allocations had been three times as valuable. By the Commission's end (its recommendations were adopted in 1924), First Nations had 843,000 acres of land allocated as reserves—less than 0.4 percent of the province. The Sḵwx̱wú7mesh have ownership over 0.423 percent of our entire traditional territory today. Only 45 percent of land applications put forward by Indigenous Peoples during the Commission were granted, and some were only granted in part. Commission minutes show Sḵwx̱wú7mesh chiefs made four applications, and all were rejected.

The Amalgamation (1923)

All these frustrations regarding land and title motivated Xwechtáal to look for a solution. He had been engaged in Sḵwx̱wú7mesh rights since he was twenty-three, and was a strong leader. He fought to invalidate the sale of Seṅáḵw. He got involved in Indigenous rights organizations, and studied law—but he refused to go to the bar to become a lawyer because that would mean giving up his status as an Indian. After the loss of Seṅáḵw, Xwechtáal felt more than ever that Indigenous leaders needed a way to shift the power dynamic that had been subjugating them for decades. He wanted to "strengthen the hand" of the Sḵwx̱wú7mesh "by giving them the opportunity for greater participation in their own affairs," author E. Palmer Patterson wrote.

Proposal for Unity

Before the Amalgamation, any profit made from land transactions on a reserve could be claimed only by the members of the "Indian

Band" who lived on that reserve. But since the Sḵwx̱wú7mesh saw themselves as one people, some felt this was unfair. Reserves were allotted for the benefit of the families who traditionally lived in that area, but increased industrialization near some reserves meant those "Indian Bands" had more opportunity to profit. Meanwhile, people on reserves that were less "desirable" areas for development profited less.

In 1913, Xwechtáal wrote a proposal for amalgamation in which thirty-five Sḵwx̱wú7mesh band members petitioned Indian Affairs for an elected council. A more developed proposal was written two years later, when fifty-eight Sḵwx̱wú7mesh people requested amalgamation of reserve interests and finances. It stipulated that the profits from the sale of any Sḵwx̱wú7mesh reserve "shall be divided equally between each man, woman and child, irrespective of age or occupation or position, on condition that the participants in the proceeds of such sale shall have established their qualifications to participate in any sale."

Chief Harry, who was known as Kwíselshn, was born 1831 and became a government-appointed chief for Eslha7áṅ (Mission Reserve). He wanted consensus among the Sḵwx̱wú7mesh before submitting the proposal. Meeting minutes recording the proposal's development show other Sḵwx̱wú7mesh leaders supporting the amalgamation. Chief Harry passed in 1918, and that proposal was never sent.

That same year, Xwechtáal joined with Haida leader Peter Kelly to establish an organization called the Allied Tribes of British Columbia. Indigenous Peoples across British Columbia donated to the organization to fight for the recognition of Indigenous title. With an elected council of chiefs, Xwechtáal was determined to bring about unification of Sḵwx̱wú7meshulh (Squamish's People) as well.

He would raise the issue of amalgamation again in 1921 in a letter to Deputy Superintendent General Duncan Campbell Scott. Xwechtáal wrote, "It is now the prayers of the Squamish Tribe that the old (custom) of every Squamish Reserve to be joint and common property of the Tribe... Under the present system in the event of any sale would lead to a lot of discontent among the Indians and it is questionable what the results would be, because if each Indian looks back far enough, each Indian by (heritage) has an interest in each Squamish reserve," he said.

Xwechtáal wrote more letters to Indian Affairs. In 1922, he told Inspector William Ditchburn, "It is the unanimous desire of the Skwawmish Tribe to have ownership of our reserves to the credit of the Squamish Indians, and I am instructed by the Skwawmesh tribe to represent them in establishing [this] for the tribe." He pushed for Indian Affairs to consider amalgamation before any more land was surrendered, and before any existing or new profits from sales were distributed.

In 1922 and 1923, four transactions sparked controversy among the S<u>k</u>w<u>x</u>wú7mesh. Three were already completed: the sale of timber from Ch'iyá<u>k</u>mesh (Cheakamus) Indian Reserve, the sale of reserves in the Squamish Valley to the Pacific Great Eastern Development Company, and the sale of Seṅá<u>k</u>w. One was proposed: the sale of reserve lands at Ch'ích'elxwi7<u>k</u>w (Seymour) to the Burrard Inlet Tunnel and Bridge Company. People were concerned about the sales and how the profits had, or had not, been shared, and how much money had been made in total. In particular, some people with interests in Seṅá<u>k</u>w had not been paid at all. Indian Agent Charles Perry said he heard complaints that chiefs of the Cheakamus Reserve No. 11 had drawn up a pay list "in their own personal pleasure," meaning some people from Cheakamus did not receive a payout. Xwechtáal reportedly warned the Indian agent there would be "a revolution and hard feelings" unless distribution was made equitable.

The Votes

The S<u>k</u>w<u>x</u>wú7mesh held several mass meetings between 1922 and 1923 to discuss amalgamation. Chiefs and leaders designated Xwechtáal the official spokesperson for the meetings with the federal government. Kwenáxtn Siỷáṁ (Chief Andrew) of Seṅá<u>k</u>w said he did not want to block amalgamation and was willing to relinquish all rights

Members of Squamish musical band at the Indian Affairs building, 1921.

and claim to the False Creek reserve, “providing that by doing so we would become amalgamated.”

Leaders discussed amalgamation at a meeting at Cheakamus Reserve (attended by forty-one Sḵwx̱wú7mesh men over twenty-one years old) and a meeting at Mission Reserve (attended by twenty-seven Sḵwx̱wú7mesh men over twenty-one years old and four chiefs from Cheakamus). A meeting at Mission Reserve in January 1923 hosted forty-eight Sḵwx̱wú7mesh men. According to a handwritten note, twenty-nine voted in favour of amalgamation, and eighteen voted against.

Later, another meeting was held at Cheakamus Reserve, which twenty-three men attended. According to the minutes, all men in attendance voted in favour of amalgamation and for profits from the Cheakamus timber sale to be distributed to all Sḵwx̱wú7mesh people. Xwechtáal and Indian Agent Perry collected four additional votes in favour from people who weren't present at the meeting. Another twelve men wrote letters to Indian Agent Perry voting in favour of amalgamation.

That same day, another meeting was held at the Mission Reserve. According to the minutes, nine chiefs and five headmen made speeches about amalgamation. By this meeting, 119 eligible votes were cast, with 78 in favour and 15 opposed. Of those opposed, 13 were Sel̓íl̓witulh (Tsleil-Waututh).

The Sel̓íl̓witulh

After disease and colonialism had devastated communities, the Sel̓íl̓witulh were closely connected with the Sḵwx̱wú7mesh at the time of the Amalgamation. They were administratively connected as well—Sel̓íl̓witulh men received payments for the sale of portions of reserve land at Eslha7áń, and Slix̱wel̓tx̱w Siỷáḿ (Chief George) was on a pay list in 1910. Slíx̱weltx̱w Siỷáḿ, Dan George, Joseph Thomas, and Aleck Gus were on pay lists in 1919, which meant the men were on a band list for the Mission Reserve in addition to the Sel̓íl̓witulh reserves. However, the Sel̓íl̓witulh voted to retain their independence and not join the Amalgamation—fourteen eligible men who attended the latest meeting sent a letter to the superintendent general in opposition. The letter expressed concern that with amalgamation, "our Chief, as a leader, would be void of power. The majority would always rule."

The Document

After the meeting at Cheakamus Reserve, the Sḵwx̱wú7mesh brought their petition—the "Prayer for Amalgamation"—to Indian Affairs. It bore the signatures of seventy-six Sḵwx̱wú7mesh people, including thirteen chiefs. It asked for the consolidation of reserves, trust funds, and distributions for the benefit of the "whole" people.

It was at this meeting, on July 23, 1923, attended by all recognized Sḵwx̱wú7mesh chiefs, that Deputy Superintendent General of Indian Affairs Scott approved all the meeting resolutions, including the "Prayer for Amalgamation" petition.

The document reads:

Dr. Duncan C. Scott
Deputy Superintendent General of Indian Affairs

Sir:

We the undersigned on behalf of the Squamish Indians beg leave to respectfully convey the prayer of the Squamish Indians for your consideration and approval.

In the preamble we take the liberty to acquaint you with the fact that the Squamish Nation of Indians have had numerous conversations for the past eight years [on] the question of the amalgamation of the several bands of the tribe and after a series of meetings recently, during which we considered and digested the question of amalgamation and with a view of illuminating for all that to overcome any inequality or disagreement among the Squamish tribe, it was unanimously agreed by the members and Chiefs of the under mentioned reserves, that the amalgamation of the several is the only solution for the good government of the tribe, which would have as an ultimate result the abolishment of ill feeling that has arisen in past transactions, and which we know will henceforth bring about a brotherly feeling among each and every member of the Squamish people.

With a view of properly conducting the affairs of the Squamish Indians we have unanimously agreed to have a council to transact the affairs of our people in cooperation with the Indian Department, said council to be composed of all the chiefs of the Squamish Nation of Indians, and we say that said council has met with the approval of every chief of the Squamish Indians and the people.

Commemorating Sk̲wx̲wú7mesh Úxwumixw (Squamish Nation) Amalgamation, 1923.

The above is [the] true and sincere desire of the Squamish people for their future welfare, and we are thankful in having the honour of meeting you in person, to most sincerely pray that you approve of the amalgamation of the Squamish Indians, . . . [and thus] the consolidation of funds.

We further and respectfully pray that you approve . . . and give due recognition of chiefs of the Squamish Indians to act as a council for the Squamish people, and we hope that any representations that the council may make in the future receive a sympathetic and attentive hearing from the government, and especially the Department of Indian Affairs to whom we look for protection, guidance, and assistance in the good government of our affairs.

That power be granted [to] the council of chiefs to enact bylaws for the good government of the members.

It is the desire of the people that the superintendent general or his deputy would by his most generous consideration to such representation and recommendation as council of the tribe may from time to time make, having in view the improvement of development of any its reserves and expenditure of tribal funds for this purpose. The council will give due regard to practice the economy and will endeavour to make restriction of foolish or extravagant nature.

We beg to say that the above are principal requirements of the Squamish people, and that we again say that we will ever pray for the amalgamation of the Squamish Indians and that consolidation of the funds, that in our opinion the only and proper manner of administering the affairs of our people is through a council of the chiefs in cooperation with the Department, and again pray that you give our council recognition, to this we ever pray, and then hereby affix our signatures and mark to certify that the above, on behalf of the Squamish Nation of Indians, are humbly but respectfully,

Gus Band
Jacob Lewis [his x mark]
Harry Disscon [his x mark]
Julian August [his x mark]
Old William [his x mark]
George Johnny [his x mark]
Jim August [his x mark]
Isaac Dick [his x mark]
Joe Thomas [his x mark]
Old Timothy [his x mark]
Basil Charley [his x mark]
Alfonse William [his x mark]
Louie Lewis
Harry George [his x mark]
Stanley Joseph
George Tom
Antone John
Isaac Jacob
Captain Jack
Denny Mack
Dan Jacob
Jim Dick
John Julian
Isidor Pierre
Napoleon Moody [his x mark]
Harry Moody [his x mark]
Wm Baker Jr [his x mark]
A. Mack
A.R. Baker
Gabriel Moody [his x mark]
Aleck Julien [his x mark]
Thos. Johnston
Denny Jack
Louie Charley
Wm Nahanee Jr
Robert Baker [his x mark]
Henry Baker
J. Johnston
Dan Paull [his x mark]
B. Miranda
F Johnston
John Gonzales
Charlie Antone
Charlie Stewart [his x mark]
Moses Billy [his x mark]
Isaac Joseph

Andrew Natrall
Patrick Sells [his x mark]
Christie Lewis [his x mark]
Old Tommy [his x mark]
Cronie [his x mark]
Billy Williams [his x mark]
Peter Gray [his x mark]
Charlie Douglas [his x mark]
Dominic Charley
Andrew Louie [his x mark]
August Jack [his x mark]
Tommy Moses [his x mark]
August George
Squamish Charley [his x mark]
Tommy Johnny [his x mark]

Squamish Mission No. 1 and Stawamus No. 24 reserve—Chief Moses Joseph
Seymore Creek No. 2—Chief Jimmy Harry
Burrard No. 3 and Inlailwatash No. 4—[no signature]
Capilano No. 5—Chief Mathias Joe Capilano
Kitsilano or False Creek No. 6 and Cheakamus No. 11—Chief Andrew [his x mark]
Skowishin No. 7 and Graveyard No. 10—Chief Jimmy Jimmy [his x mark]
Chuchuck No. 8 [and] Puyam No. 8—Chief Jimmy Jimmy [his x mark]
Cheakamus No. 11—Chief Tom [his x mark]
Cheakamus No. 11—Chief Charley [his x mark]
Cheakamus and Yookwitz No. 12—Chief Frank Baker
Poquisen and Skamain No. 13—Chief Edward Joseph [his x mark]
Waiwaikum No. 14 and Aikwucks No. 15—(act) Henry Jack [his x mark]
Seachem No. 16—Chief George Williams [his x mark]
Kowtain No. 17—Chief Billy [his x mark]
Yekwaupaum No. 18 and Burial Ground No. 19—Chief Ed Williams
Kaikalahun No. 25—Chief Wm Baker [his x mark]
Chekwelp No. 26 and Burial Ground—Chief Louis Miranda
Defence Island No. 28—Chief Squamish Jacob [his x mark]

The sixteen Sḵwx̱wú7mesh bands, with a population of 412 members, were united that day as a newly formed Sḵwx̱wú7mesh Úxwumixw. They had a consolidated trust of about $167,740.

This "new" Nation built a council of chiefs from the previously separated bands. For this first council, the chiefs were not elected and held these positions for life. After a council member died, the council and the deceased member's family decided who would succeed them. Elections of new members began in 1932, and these chiefs also held office for life. They were then considered councillors instead of chiefs.

Since the Amalgamation, the Sḵwx̱wú7mesh population has grown almost 900 percent, from just over 400 members to over 4,100. The Nation began with a trust account worth almost $3 million in 2023 dollars. In 2020, the Nation reported $102 million in revenue.

Of course, even after the triumph of the Amalgamation, the world around us continued to present challenges, particularly regarding land claims. The McKenna-McBride Commission's recommendations were adopted in 1924. First Nations challenged the Commission's authority to reduce reserves, which had been reduced without their consent, even though the McKenna-McBride agreement stipulated that consent was necessary. The lack of consent was also in violation of the Royal Proclamation of 1763. In the coming years, First Nations would fight for the return of the reserve land that had been taken without their consent.

The Allied Tribes of British Columbia, the organization Xwechtáal and Peter Kelly had founded, served as "a training ground" for individuals in the Indigenous rights movement, author E. Palmer Patterson wrote. They brought land claims to a parliamentary special joint committee in 1927 and were rejected. That same committee recommended that Canada make it illegal to raise funds for Indigenous people to pursue land claims. That same year, Canada followed the recommendation and amended the Indian Act to criminalize soliciting funds in pursuit of a land claim. The amendment was "aimed directly at the British Columbia Indians and was intended to suppress political activity," one historian wrote.

The Allied Tribes of British Columbia dissolved then, but the resistance couldn't be stopped. The Sḵwx̱wú7mesh and other First Nations would continue organizing and challenging the oppressive system they faced.

Columbia, Inc.
ishing Co., Ltd.
MArine 7434.
, Vancouver, B.C.
LORNE NAHANEE
ED. NAHANEE
PER HILL (Toronto)
, REGINALD COOK,
WILLIAM PASCAL
ARMYTAGE-MOORE
MATT FEE

ishing Ltd.

Ottawa.

› two categories, ish Columbia are cured to them by lizing or losing if ite inhabitants to y should not be

e a long step for- They have given s an end in itself natives need no ıey now go with thers demanding eed they be satis- an's table.

ay not be far dis- ead of the table. and maintain the s.

provisions of the of Canada from eedom from want,

ld be a reproach ny of the original and by their lack n inferior people,

ad put into their dgment they can ation and in other fatives showing a

THE FIRST X

CHIEF ISAAC JACOBS

Chief Isaac Jacobs of the Squamish tribe proudly reaps the harvest of his faith in the efforts of the NATIVE BROTHERHOOD of B.C. as he marks his first cross in the Provincial Election.

Chief Jacobs resides at Capilano and at an early hour of June 15th, arrived at the Polling Booth in North Vancouver and was the FIRST Indian to vote for the candidate of his selection.

In full costume for this occasion and resting assured that this event will long remain a pleasant memory. This was a day long awaited by these aboriginal people who for many years had been denied the right to vote. A truly historic event and the first step to freedom.

AN OPEN LETTER

15

SWAT MELH TA NEW: NOW WHO ARE YOU?

WHEN BRITISH COLUMBIA joined Confederation, it was required to transfer title over most Indigenous reserves to Canada, but by and throughout most of the 1930s, the province was still delaying the transfer. In 1938, BC finally transferred reserve lands to the king in trust for First Nations, including the Sḵwx̱wú7mesh.

At this time, Indigenous people still couldn't become doctors or lawyers, and Indigenous women couldn't marry a non-Indigenous person, without losing their status. By the mid-twentieth century, however, this would begin to change.

Author Bob Joseph connected the shift in public views in Canada with the impacts of World War II. With the world's attention on the treatment of Jews in concentration camps in Europe, people in Canada began "to judge how the government treated Indians." Indigenous soldiers had also served in both World Wars, and information about residential school deaths was increasing.

A special committee between the Senate and House of Commons reviewed policies and management of Indian Affairs from 1946 to 1948. The committee recommended the complete revision or repeal

FACING: Tnaxwtn Siy̓ám̓ (Chief Isaac Jacobs), BC's first Indigenous voter, 1949.

of the entire Indian Act. It made several recommendations, including shifting away from "wardship" to citizenship, giving women a political voice in band affairs, and more financial assistance for bands.

Sḵwx̱wú7mesh veteran Robert Nahanee, who served in the Canadian Forces from 1963 to 1977, agreed that World War II was a turning point for Indigenous Peoples in Canada. His uncle had served in World War II and helped found the Indigenous Veterans Day ceremony in Vancouver.

"By the time 1951 came, they changed the law," Nahanee said. "That's when our people started recovering, reclaiming and reusing traditional and cultural ceremonies that were taken away," he said. "They wanted freedom of choice and recognition of who we are as a people. That's what our veterans gave us."

FACING: BC Senior B Champions. First Nations baseball team, 1929.

In 1945, Xwechtáal (Andy Paull) founded the North American Indian Brotherhood, which advocated for special rights for Indigenous Peoples. He had "imagination and vision" that made him a central figure in Indigenous rights through the first half of the twentieth century, E. Palmer Patterson wrote. Xwechtáal emphasized international solidarity with the North American Indian Brotherhood. Indigenous Peoples still faced tremendous discrimination, but their movement was gaining momentum.

At the same time as the Sḵwx̱wú7mesh were strengthening their political hand, they were making a name for themselves in sports. Xwechtáal helped establish the Buckskin Gloves, a boxing program at St. Paul's Indian Residential School. He also assembled a First Nations lacrosse team in 1935, the famous North Shore Indians, to compete for the national Mann Cup. "The Indians were so talented, so entertaining, so much fun to watch, that they were able to pack 8,000-plus fans into Vancouver's Denman arena at 25 cents a head, even during the Great Depression," a *North Shore News* article reported. The All Native Basketball Tournament was established in 1959 and remains a cultural touchpoint of pride and celebration of Indigenous talent.

For his contributions, Xwechtáal was inducted into the Canadian Lacrosse Hall of Fame in 1966 and the North Shore Sports Hall of Fame in 2019. Henry Baker of Sḵwx̱wú7mesh was a member of the Olympic lacrosse team representing Canada in the 1932 Los Angeles games. Several other Sḵwx̱wú7mesh individuals have been honoured in the Canadian Lacrosse Hall of Fame, the BC Sports Hall of Fame, and the North Shore Sports Hall of Fame.

Reforms to the Indian Act (1951)

Although the federal government had proposed a slew of reforms to the Indian Act, First Nations had rejected the changes because the government did not involve them in the process. Finally, Canada consulted with First Nations to bring about changes to the Indian Act. After consultation, the revised Indian Act was enacted on June 20, 1951.

The reforms lifted the ban on potlatches and other ceremonies, such as the sun dance. Women were allowed to vote in elections, and communities were permitted to bring about land claims. But people with Indian status were still prohibited from possessing intoxicants or being intoxicated unless a province specifically sought to overturn that law within its jurisdiction. The concept of Indian blood and status didn't change. Women still lost status for marrying a person without status.

Over the following decades, the Indian Act continued to change. Significantly, in 1960, First Nations people with Indian status were able to vote without losing status. A year later, the compulsory enfranchisement clause that could strip people of their status if they did things such as gain a university education or leave the reserve for too long was removed.

FACING: **Lacrosse team outside St. Paul's Church, North Vancouver. In 1936, the famous North Shore Indians competed nationally for the Mann Cup.**

Cultural Survival

Children were still going to residential schools, though the schools were being phased out. But in the 1960s, the Sixties Scoop would begin, when children—often babies—were taken away from their homes and put into the child welfare system. This was informed by the 1951 amendments to the Indian Act that allowed a province to provide services to Indigenous Peoples where none existed federally, including child welfare. Between 1951 and 1964, Indigenous children went from making up 1 percent of children in care in British Columbia to representing 34 percent of children in care. In 1951, just 29 Indigenous children were in care; in 1964, that increased to 1,466 children. And the number would only get higher. These systems caused immense damage to the well-being of our people and the way we would normally pass on our cultural teachings. Yet people did pass on what they could.

Sx̱áaltxw Siy̓ám̓ (Chief Louis Miranda) talked about how there were far fewer traditional dancers by the late 1960s. Practices like weaving had also decreased, as well as speaking our language, largely because of residential schools. At this time, Sx̱áaltxw Siy̓ám̓ began to extensively record the Sḵwx̱wú7mesh Sníchim (Squamish Language), oral stories, and other traditional knowledge. Hundreds of pages of his transcripts and handwritten translations are held in the Squamish Nation Archives. In every family, adults passed on stories and teachings to children as much as they could in the circumstances they were in.

Indigenous Women's Rights

Despite a special committee review of the Indian Act in the 1940s, the law dictating that Indigenous women would lose their status if they married a non-Indigenous person remained in place until 1985. The 1951 amendments introduced the "Double Mother" clause, which revoked status from a person whose mother and grandmother had acquired status through marriage.

In the years before the law was finally repealed, Indigenous women fought hard against this discrimination. The fight was not easy—in 1973, the Supreme Court of Canada maintained that connecting an Indigenous woman's status to her husband's "did not discriminate against women." A few years later, in 1981, the United Nations Human Rights Commission disagreed, reporting that Canada had violated international civil and political rights with the law.

The Amendment Bills

Indigenous women, including Sḵwx̱wú7mesh Elder Theresa Anne Nahanee, continued to push for reform. Finally, in 1985, the government submitted to public pressure and passed Bill C-31 to address inequality in the Indian Act. This bill amended the Indian Act to align with the Canadian Charter of Rights and Freedoms that had been introduced a few years earlier, in 1982. The Charter guarantees every individual is equal under the law "without discrimination based on race, national or ethnic origin, colour, religion, sex, age or mental

Swanamia, X̲ats'alánexw Siy̓ám̓'s (Chief August Jack Khatsahlano's) wife, c. 1930.

or physical disability." People who had been enfranchised under the Indian Act for any other reasons were allowed to apply to regain their status as well. The bill allowed women to apply to regain their and their children's Indian status. As well, marriage could no longer affect a woman's status. Non-Indigenous women no longer gained status for marrying an Indigenous person, but those who had already gained it were allowed to keep it.

"For well over one hundred years, the Act legalized discrimination against aboriginal women," the Aboriginal Women's Council of BC

S<u>k</u>w<u>x</u>wú7meshulh Aysáy̓ch (Squamish Territory) before the white men came.

wrote in 1992. "A process that has been entrenched for several generations is not easily reversed. Therefore, although Bill C-31 provided official recognition of the discriminatory behaviour against aboriginal women and legally abolished such behaviour, this is merely a first step on a long road to recovery." The council described how women had lost property, had suffered a loss of "purpose, pride and dignity," and experienced a high level of family violence. "Although the Indian Act has not achieved its ultimate purpose of assimilation, it has nevertheless left behind a trail of destruction."

In her 1995 study of criminal justice issues, Teressa Nahanee, who worked with the British Columbia Native Women's Society and the Native Women's Association of Canada, wrote: "It is under Indian Act governments that Aboriginal women have been suppressed. That oppression of Indian women's rights, in particular, comes not from the Indian communities themselves, but from the imposition of the federal machinery of government. It is mainly the white state that has imposed its laws upon the Indian community and forced Indian women to leave their communities. It is the Indian Act that has resulted in mainly men being elected to Indian Act Chiefs and Councils. It is mainly the Indian Act that has ensured that property on reserves is held by men and not by women. Clearly the Indian Act, as a law of the federal government is subject to the Charter, is discriminatory against Indian women and requires changes through legislation or litigation."

Bill C-31 introduced new problems, such as the second-generation "cutoff." For example, if a status parent and a non-status parent had children together, their children had status too—but if their status child eventually had children with a non-status person, that third generation could not register for status.

Another issue was that although Bill C-31 made more than 174,500 people eligible to register for Native status, the federal government didn't provide band governments the funding necessary to provide services and housing to all their new members. T'echux̱ánm Siỷám̓ (Chief Joe Mathias) said that by 1991, about four hundred members were added to his band population of two thousand. Over half of band members were under twenty years old. Across British Columbia, more than ten thousand Indigenous people regained their status, and nationwide, more than seventy-three thousand people. Bill C-31 did allow bands to create and control their membership. In 1987, the Sḵwx̱wú7mesh Úxwumixw (Squamish Nation) created its own membership code.

Bill C-3, the Gender Equity in Indian Registration Act, passed in 2011 to make section 6 of the Indian Act more inclusive. Bill C-3 did not completely rid the act of discrimination, but it allowed thirty-seven thousand people to register.

In 2017, Bill S-3 was introduced, which addressed more issues of unequal treatment. In 2019, further amendments to Bill S-3 came into effect. They were intended to address some of the remaining inequities in registration under the Indian Act and extend the ability to pass on status to descendants. The journey to eliminate gender discrimination continues, with further amendments that were tabled in January 2023 with Bill C-38.

There are many resources that dive deeper into all the issues around status, and into the critique that status is, at its core, an attempt to legislate First Nations out of existence.

Looking Forward

The mid-1900s increased the political tools and public awareness available to the Sḵwx̱wú7mesh to push forward their inherent rights. While still healing from the trauma of residential schools and cultural genocide, the people gathered to pursue a prosperous future.

About nine years after the Amalgamation, vacancies on council were filled more generally by men who were members of the Nation, rather than through the original proposal of a council of hereditary chiefs. This continued informally until 1976, when Sḵwx̱wú7mesh members gathered at a community meeting and voted to create a fully elected council on four-year terms, to be chosen through election regulations approved by members. In 1981, the Nation elected its first fully democratic council.

Up until 1962, an Indian agent still oversaw the band council, but then the Nation took over leadership. Community leaders emerged, such as Sxwpílem Siy̓ám̓ (Chief Philip Joe), Simon Baker, and T'echux̱ánm Siy̓ám̓, who was passionate in calling out the legislative oppression Indigenous Peoples faced. "How do you destroy a people? You attack their political rights. You attack their cultural rights. You attack their legal rights. You attack their languages and religions. You take away their ability to self-determine their own destiny," he said.

As the City of Vancouver and its municipalities grew, settlers still discriminated against Indigenous people in many ways. First Nations faced poverty and unemployment because of all the ways economics, education, and laws were stacked against them. Council was focused on how to bring wealth into the communities.

In 1969, municipal government representatives from Squamish, West Vancouver, and North Vancouver met with the Sḵwx̱wú7mesh in a conference to reach a "better understanding" of each other. The Sḵwx̱wú7mesh asked that Indigenous history be taught in schools, and that intergovernmental agreements be honoured. They also asked to work together on an economic development plan. The Nation emphasized the need to benefit from reserve lands, rejecting an idea that the land should be used for parks. "They did not object to parks—their main concern was the financial benefit of the members. [Lawyer Paul] Reecke said the Indian lands had to be used to the best possible advantage so that the band could obtain money to finance its economic development program," the conference minutes read.

One of the greatest opportunities the mid-twentieth century brought was the chance to pursue legal recourse for past and ongoing activities taking place on our lands without consent. Several significant court cases were led by BC First Nations to assert Indigenous rights. The Sḵwx̱wú7mesh had battled colonization from the shipyards, from our homes, from the classroom. Now we would begin our battles from the courtroom.

PART FIVE

SḴWX̱WÚ7MESH STITÚYNTSAM̓: SQUAMISH INHERITANCE

"Ottawa needs to hear loud and clear that they can't just run roughshod over Aboriginal rights and title. That era has come and gone."

X̱ÁLEḴ'/SEḴ'YÚ SIY̓ÁM̓ (CHIEF IAN CAMPBELL)

FROM 1927 UNTIL 1951, under section 127 of the Indian Act, the federal government banned Indigenous people from hiring lawyers. During that period, an Indigenous person, group, or government needed the permission of Indian Affairs to pursue a legal claim. This racist policy prevented Indigenous people from participating equally in the legal system that had been imposed upon them, while their own pre-existing legal systems were ignored.

The federal ban had been lifted for over a decade by the year 1965, when the Sḵwx̱wú7mesh Úxwumixw (Squamish Nation) approached lawyer Paul Reecke of law firm Ratcliff, Kitchen and Reecke (now Ratcliff). But it was still one of the first times a First Nation retained legal counsel to protect its lands. The Indigenous leaders had an incredible story to tell about being wrongfully displaced from their land, and they wanted legal help to win it back. They told Mr. Reecke about being forced off Sen̓áḵw ("inside the head of the bay," at False Creek, which also became known as Kitsilano Indian Reserve No. 6) in 1913; now the land was going to be leased, and the Sḵwx̱wú7mesh wanted to claim their interest in it.

This initiated a decades-long legal battle to reclaim Sen̓áḵw, which lasted from the 1970s until 2001. It also began a long relationship between Ratcliff and the Sḵwx̱wú7mesh Úxwumixw. The Nation returned to court many times over the following decades to fight for recognition of title and the duty to consult, and to assert our place as a leader on our lands.

The courts are an imperfect tool, but they've proved to be an important space to advance Indigenous rights. The federal government has an ongoing legacy of breaking its promises and duties to Indigenous Peoples, and often, using the judicial system to hold Canada accountable to its own laws has been the only way for Indigenous Peoples to move the country forward in acknowledging Indigenous rights. And yet, the judicial system remains another arm of a colonial state. In courtrooms, Canadian law is supreme, not Indigenous laws. Going to court drains years of resources and often millions of dollars. And even if Indigenous rights are upheld in court after all that money and effort and fighting, sometimes the government still does not act on the court's decision. The status quo remains, the government drags its feet, and the Indigenous party is left wondering if it's worth it to go to court all over again.

FACING: Khelsilem (Dustin Rivers) at "Many People, One Canoe" to protect the Salish Sea, 2012.

Nonetheless, courts are a tool that have led to major advancements for the S<u>k</u>wx<u>w</u>ú7mesh and other Indigenous Peoples. The S<u>k</u>wx<u>w</u>ú7mesh have been part of several significant court cases, and it is beyond the scope of this book to cover them all in detail (the *Mathias et al. v. Canada* hearing alone lasted two hundred days and the decision is almost five hundred pages), but it's possible to summarize some of the cases and their significance, which is the focus of Part Five.

Looking closely at our legal paths is important because Squamish leadership and individuals have used the courtroom to demonstrate our inherent rights. Through the courts, the Nation has reclaimed control over aspects of our education, child and family services, health care, and lands. Leadership continues to go to court to push for recognition of our jurisdiction as a sovereign Nation. We have used the courts to prove our capacity to advocate for ourselves in our own words.

16

HAW K̲'AT MÁYNEXW SEṅÁK̲W: WE NEVER FORGOT SEṅÁK̲W

As discussed in chapter 13, Sk̲wx̲wú7mesh families were displaced from the village of Seṅák̲w ("inside the head of the bay," at False Creek, which also became known as Kitsilano Indian Reserve No. 6) in the twentieth century. But we didn't forget. In the 1960s, the Sk̲wx̲wú7mesh Úxwumixw (Squamish Nation) prepared to launch a case to reclaim Seṅák̲w. As a guest on the CBC podcast *Land Back*, Chepx̲ímiya Siỷáṁ (Chief Janice George) told host Angela Sterritt about how, when she was a child in the 1960s, her father would drive her and her sisters in his truck to see Seṅák̲w:

Chepx̲ímiya Siỷáṁ: He said, "This is Squamish. This is Squamish land. This is where your ancestors lived. We're working on getting this place back; we're going to court for this." I was like, Wow, that's Squamish. I always thought it was so amazing.

Angela Sterritt: It was a moment of pride.

Chepx̲ímiya Siỷáṁ: Yeah, it was a moment of pride. And I could see what it meant to him. It meant so much to him. And to do that work, it's serious emotional labour to talk about what our ancestors went through.

FACING: Khelsilem (Dustin Rivers) and Sxwíxwtn (Wilson Williams) at the Seṅák̲w site.

More than sixty years after Squamish people were put on a barge and their homes were burned, on June 30, 1977, chiefs and the council—led by T'echuxánm Siỷáṁ (Chief Joe Mathias)—launched a series of legal claims, known as the Omnibus Trust Action. This Action pursued compensation for being displaced and to prove our claim to Seńáḵw, along with other sites in the town of Squamish and North Vancouver. The sites had become covered in private homes and businesses. The former village of Seńáḵw had quickly become a desirable piece of real estate in the middle of rapidly growing Vancouver.

The Sḵwx̱wú7mesh Úxwumixw argued that the federal government had neglected its fiduciary duty to act in the best interest of the Nation while managing Kitsilano Indian Reserve No. 6 and by allowing the seizure of their lands. Leaders like T'echux̱ánm Siỷáṁ and Xwechtáal (Andy Paull) dedicated their lives to seeking justice for the loss of Seńáḵw.

FACING: Yamschloot (Mary), Chinalset (Jericho Charlie), William Green, Peelass George, Jimmy Jimmy, and Towhumquamkee (Jack) at Seńáḵw, 1891.

On July 23, 2000, their dreams came to fruition. Nation members voted in favour of a $92.5 million settlement that addressed compensation for historical wrongdoing and for abandoning claim to the whole of Seńáḵw and the other sites in Squamish and North Vancouver. Remember, we were addressing the abuse of trust that both local and federal governments had enacted when their representatives, the Indian agents, controlled how our lands, under their legal term of "reserves," were used, leased, or partitioned.

A total of 1,488 of 1,940 eligible Sḵwx̱wú7mesh voters approved the settlement, and it was signed on July 27, 2000. T'echux̱ánm Siỷáṁ had died suddenly on March 10, 2000, just months before Nation members voted in support of the settlement—but his legacy in fighting for Seńáḵw lived on. This settlement secured an investment in the Nation's future, with the funds held in the Squamish Nation Trust. So far, some of it has been used to support housing, education, language and culture, and other community services. The interest on 20 percent

of this income was set aside for direct distribution to members. In exchange, the Nation promised to no longer claim the lands in question or sue the government in relation to those lands.

"Unconscionable" Management

The Xwmétskwiyam (Musqueam) and Sel̓íl̓witulh (Tsleil-Waututh) also claimed interests in the Sen̓ák̲w reserve, and their chiefs and councillors, along with some individuals, were added as defendants in *Mathias et al. v. Canada* in 1993. They took on different arguments but mostly had a similar focus to that of the Sk̲wx̱wú7mesh: the federal government had breached its fiduciary duty to them by improperly allocating and mismanaging the reserve.

The various actions in the case were referred to collectively as the "Mathias Litigation." The Squamish Action, although dismissed after the settlement was reached in 2000, claimed that the Crown had breached its duty by not preventing the 1913 sale of the reserve, as well as by failing to collect rents owed to the Sk̲wx̲wú7mesh, and by entering into "unconscionable leasing arrangements" that did not provide "reasonable leasing revenues." As a Nation, we also claimed that the Crown had breached its duty in promoting and accepting the (coerced) Surrender of the Reserve for sale. The Surrender agreement required $350,000 of the proceeds from the sale to go to the province instead of to the Sk̲wx̲wú7mesh, to address the province's supposed interest in the reserve. The Sk̲wx̲wú7mesh claimed the Crown had further breached its duty by selling off the reserve in "uneconomic parcels" rather than long-term leases, which would have provided long-term revenue for the Nation.

The Xwmétskwiyam argued that the reserve had been Musqueam and they had a right to it since it was within their traditional territory. They said their use of the territory had continued after the Seṅák̲w reserve was established, and that not including the Xwmétskwiyam in the allotment of the reserve was a "mistake" on the part of the Joint Indian Reserve Commission.

The Seli̓́l̓witulh claim was different. At the time the Seṅák̲w reserve was created, the Seli̓́l̓witulh were known as the Burrard Indian Band, and they were administratively considered Sk̲wx̲wú7mesh by the colonial government. In 1923, the Burrard Band chose to not join the Sk̲wx̲wú7mesh amalgamation that brought our sixteen bands together as one Nation in dealings with municipal, provincial, and the federal governments. The Seli̓́l̓witulh argued that the Crown had "breached its fiduciary duty to them by assenting to the Amalgamation and by failing to protect the interests of the Burrard People in the reserve."

The battle for Seṅák̲w required the Sk̲wx̲wú7mesh Úxwumixw to demonstrate continuous use of the land. Notably, this was also one of

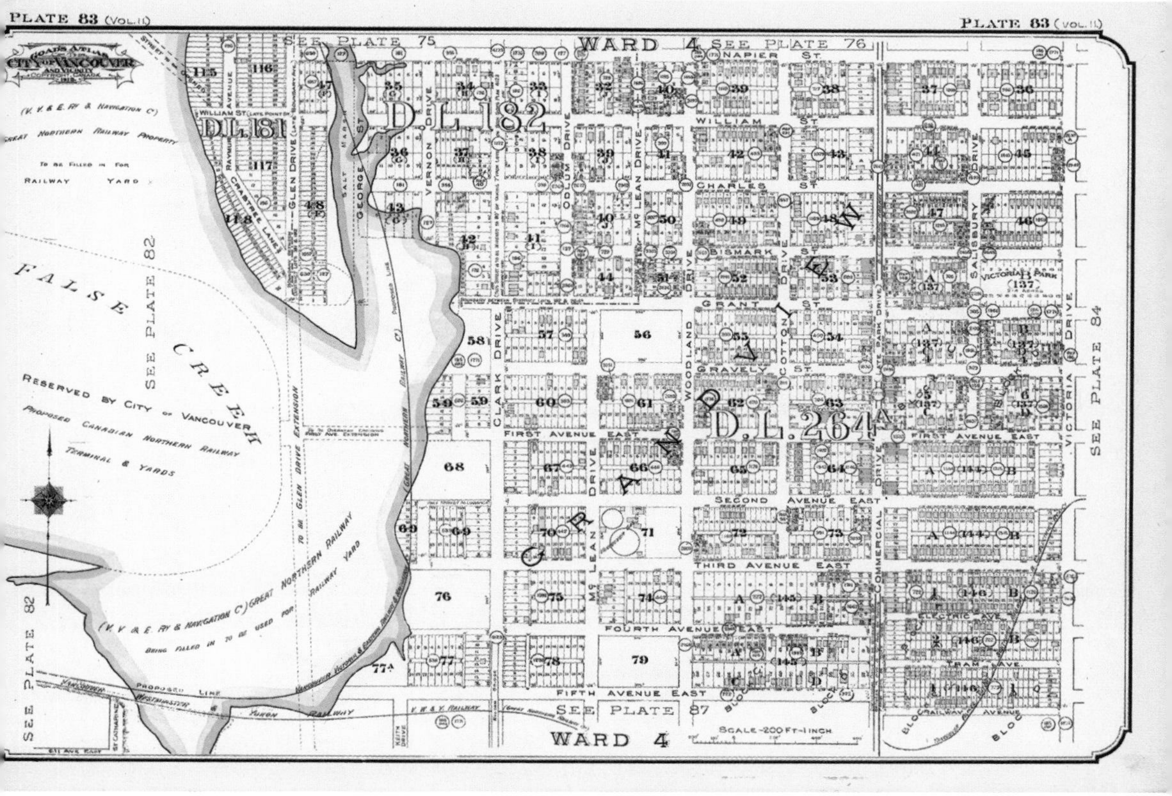

The proposed railway development through Seňáḵw, 1912.

the first court cases to rely heavily on oral evidence, since *Delgamuukw v. British Columbia* (1997) had set precedent in accepting oral history as evidence in the colonial court system. The court acknowledged the importance of oral history as evidence, since it is an "unbroken chain across the generations." But the judge also said this case required historical specificity. The reserve was allocated in 1869 to the "False Creek Indian Band." In 1877, in new documentation, it was clearly allocated to the Sḵwx̱wú7mesh. So, the court argued, the clear, specific question of the case was: Who was a resident of the reserve from 1869 to 1877?

Seṅáḵw, Granville, CPR Kitsilano bridges, and other buildings.

To achieve this specificity, the case relied on census records, the records of the Oblate Order of Catholic missionaries, and other archival materials. The evidence presented showed just how complex our relationship with the past can be. Family histories differed; dates and locations varied within stories. The origin of the place name, Seṅáḵw, was not agreed upon. And it was a colonial construct to be a member of only one band—people intermarried and their identities were not exclusive to one people. Some people at Seṅáḵw had both Xwmétskwiyam and Sḵwx̱wú7mesh heritage, and both Nations would claim them. The judge had to assess, based on the evidence, if they lived their life as a Sḵwx̱wú7mesh person.

There were more uncertainties. The exact year the Sḵwx̱wú7mesh set up a permanent village and the time the Xwmétskwiyam had or had not stopped using the site were not agreed upon either. This viewpoint disregards that Indigenous Peoples have always moved within their territories, and that the onset of colonialism impacted where people travelled, where they lived, and how they harvested food. Indigenous Peoples don't live in a vacuum or in the past—we are always adapting and changing with the world around us. Our resourcefulness and responsiveness are how we survived as the very ground beneath our feet and air around us shifted. The colonial paradigms of a reserve, a courtroom, and the Indian Act don't allow for the full expansiveness of our lived experiences.

But the judge made it clear that Aboriginal title, Aboriginal rights, treaty rights, and constitutional rights were not on the table in this court case. Similarly, she said the purpose of the case was not to address the flaws of the reserve system, or the traditional rights to the area. The purpose was to answer the direct question of who, according to the government's paper trail, the Seṅáḵw reserve's historical residents were—which, the judge concluded, were the forty-two people living there at the time in question. The other question was whether the Crown had indeed breached its fiduciary duty.

Relying on census data and genealogical research done by the Squamish Nation's expert witness Dorothy Kennedy, the judge found substantial evidence that the vast majority of people living at the reserve were Sḵwx̱wú7mesh or spouses of Sḵwx̱wú7mesh people. Looking at several letters and legal documents, she also concluded that evidence existed to show that the government had intended to allocate the Seṅáḵw reserve to the Sḵwx̱wú7mesh. For example, one report by the Joint Indian Reserve Commission describes how many acres of the reserve the Xwmétskwiyam and Sḵwx̱wú7mesh had, and the numbers added up only if the reserve was considered Sḵwx̱wú7mesh.

Everyone in court agreed that the Burrard Band (Seli̓l̓witulh) was widely considered by outside parties as Sḵwx̱wú7mesh at the time, but evidence showed they had still considered themselves a distinct band and operated independently. The judge concluded that separate Sḵwx̱wú7mesh bands—like the False Creek Band or the Burrard Band—did not automatically share funds from selling or leasing reserve land. The Seli̓í̓lwitulh also alleged that the Crown had failed to ensure the Burrard Band had understood the Amalgamation or to implement it in a way that protected the interests of their people. But the judge disagreed, concluding that, based on evidence, the Burrard Band had been well informed about the Amalgamation and they knew they would have to give up any potential interest in the other reserves. She also concluded that the government had taken the steps necessary to ensure the Burrard Band, and all the other Sḵwx̱wú7mesh bands, reached an informed decision about Amalgamation.

The impacts of colonialism created the conditions for these disagreements. But there was another key point everyone agreed on in court—that prior to colonization, friendly First Nations like the Xwmétskwiyam, Sḵwx̱wú7mesh, and Seli̓í̓lwitulh would share resources and did not control territories with linear boundaries. These relationships have existed for generations, and this peaceful coexistence is foundational as the three host Nations claim space in Vancouver after being sidelined for so long.

Canadian Pacific Railway

At the same time *Mathias et al. v. Canada* (2001) moved through the courts, there was another loose end: the Canadian Pacific Railway.

The company had acquired 10.5 acres of Seṅáḵw reserve land for railway use in 1886 and 1902, but it did not gain absolute title to the land. Once railway use was no longer necessary, the land was meant to be returned to the Crown, which had the duty to manage it for the benefit of the Squamish Nation. About a century later, Canadian Pacific sought to sell the land.

In *Canada v. Canadian Pacific Ltd.* (2002), Canada challenged the sale, claiming title lay with the federal government. In the 1980s, the Sḵwx̱wú7mesh, Xwmétskwiyam, and Seli̓í̓lwitulh had each launched

Welcoming canoes back to the shore in celebration of the return of Seṅáḵw.

actions against Canada and Canadian Pacific, claiming the land had reverted to reserve land and that they had interests in the Seṅáḵw reserve. In 2000, the Supreme Court of British Columbia concluded that the interest of the land lay with whichever of the three bands was entitled to it. As we know, in 2001, through *Mathias et al. v. Canada*, that was established as the Sḵwx̱wú7mesh.

Both Canadian Pacific and Canada appealed the decision that 10.5 acres be reverted to reserve land, but the Court of Appeal for British Columbia upheld the decision in 2002.

The last of the obstacles was overcome. The last portion of the reserve was officially returned to our Nation.

The Joy of Returning Home

Now, after years of planning and community consultation, the Sk̲wx̱wú7mesh Úxwumixw has begun building homes at Seňák̲w. The Nation caused a stir in Vancouver, and internationally, when it announced it was building what the *New York Times* called the biggest Indigenous development in North America. Since the development is taking place on reserve land, it doesn't have to follow the city's zoning rules. In a city that is in the middle of a desperate housing crisis, with people unable to find affordable homes to rent or buy, the Seṅák̲w development will provide about six thousand homes in downtown Vancouver. The development will allow the Sk̲wx̲wú7mesh Úxwumixw to benefit from its land, from which the City of Vancouver has extracted and built wealth for decades, often to the detriment of First Nations. The development centres on Sk̲wx̲wú7mesh values, with a focus on public space, cultural programming, and integrating nature. The eventual completed project will present a clear, strong representation of Indigenous presence on the land that was returned to our safekeeping.

On September 6, 2022, the Nation broke ground at the site, alongside the federal government. Canada announced a $1.4 billion loan to launch construction—the largest loan ever offered by the Canada Mortgage and Housing Corporation. The project is expected to bring a $10 billion return to the Nation.

"While we were displaced, we fought hard to reclaim Seṅák̲w, and now it will once again provide for our people and for the future of the Sk̲wx̲wú7mesh peoples," Councillor Sxwíxwtn (Wilson Williams) said at the groundbreaking ceremony. That same day, council Chairperson Khelsilem (Dustin Rivers) said, "The fact that we're coming home is a type of joy that is hard to describe."

FACING: A happy crowd gathered at the Seṅák̲w development site.

Our reserves have been used as tools to contain. They were supposed to provide the bare minimum—not abundance. They were a closed door, where "Indians" were expected to stay and eventually disappear. But none of this worked. Reserves have remained a place to share community and culture. Indigenous Peoples in British Columbia retain claim to their unceded land beyond reserve borders. And Seṅák̲w is an example of a reserve, and Indigenous Peoples, expanding beyond what the federal government intended. The vision of Seṅák̲w is one of thriving and abundance—an open door to a brighter future.

17

I7X̱W STS'ÚḴW'I7: ALL SALMON

AT THE CENTRE of many of our people's court cases is the duty to consult, as was the case in *Squamish Nation v. Canada (Fisheries and Oceans)* (2019). On July 5, 2011, to accommodate our growing population, the Sḵwx̱wú7mesh Úxwumixw (Squamish Nation) requested an increase in its allocation of Fraser River *stséḵi7* (sockeye salmon), which Fisheries and Oceans Canada (referred to as DFO) rejected. Instead, it increased the Nation's allotment of other salmon stocks, which confused us: the government was saying we could catch more of different salmon stocks we had not even requested. Thus began a years-long battle over our right to fish according to our Nation's needs.

Harvesting Sts'úḵw'i7 (Salmon)

According to Sx̱áaltxw Siy̓ám̓ (Chief Louis Miranda), the X̱aays (Transformer brothers) went to visit the Salmon People for a feast. The Spring Salmon Chief, Kwu7s, said to be careful with fish bones and

FACING: ***snékwem*****, a mural by Xwalacktun (James Harry) and Lauren Brevner, 2020.**

not throw them away. The X̱aays passed on the instructions to the Sḵwx̱wú7mesh, and the people agreed. Bones must always be thrown back into the river, and if we don't follow that condition, the salmon won't return. Since then, our relationship with *sts'úḵw'i7* (salmon) has been central to our culture and livelihoods.

The Sḵwx̱wú7mesh participated in the Fraser River salmon fishery for sustenance long before settlers arrived. Before colonization, Indigenous Peoples in present-day British Columbia practised a wide range of sustainable fishing techniques that allowed them to simultaneously monitor the fish, notice how well different populations were doing, and fish accordingly. With the establishment of British Columbia and Canada, fishing transformed dramatically. Marine fisheries began catching as many fish as they could, while integral habitat was degraded. Old-growth forests, which provide shade and cool water for migrating *sts'úḵw'i7*, were clear-cut, leaving dried-up rivers with shallow, warm water. Rather than nutrient-rich fallen logs creating cool pools for *sts'úḵw'i7* to rest in, many rivers were blocked with boulders and debris from unstable valleys that were once held in balance by the roots of old-growth trees.

Similarly, estuaries were cleared in the name of development. Estuaries are integral for young salmon entering the ocean as places to rest, eat, and grow while adjusting from freshwater to saltwater. The Fraser River estuary alone has lost 70 percent of its *sts'úḵw'i7* habitat because of development.

Overfishing, habitat degradation, climate change, and other factors caused Fraser *stséḵi7* to decline. An average of 9.6 million *stséḵi7* were expected to return to the Fraser River between 1980 and 2014, ranging from 2 million to 28 million per year. In 2020, only 291,000 returned, the lowest run ever recorded. First Nations that have long had relationships with these salmon aren't able to harvest enough to feed their entire communities through winter.

The salmon also support other life, like eagles, bears, and orcas. Syetáx̱tn (Chris Lewis) spoke about the importance of *sts'úḵw'i7* to the orcas near Xwmélch'stn (Capilano), which doesn't carry *stsé<u>k</u>i7* but does support other salmon species:

My grandfather, along with my uncles and myself have observed... resident killer whales... training their young in the narrows [near Lions Gate Bridge] where they line up side by side in the narrows as the tide comes out of Burrard Inlet... They're like a firing line almost... How we know if they're residents is they start flipping the fish around. You start seeing the fish flipping around. And they're teaching their young how to hunt and how to catch fish... That connection to that way of life is alive and well and has been passed down. I'm not that old. I don't have white hair. And I've been fortunate to hear those stories and... I hope my kids see the [yéw̓yews (*orcas*)] *hunting and teaching their little ones how to hunt the seals or hunt the fish in the narrows at Xwmélch'stn.*

Sts'ú<u>k</u>wi7, *which is our word for salmon, is a keystone species to the S<u>k</u>w<u>x</u>wú7mesh people. Everything we do from the time they arrive to the time they spawn is in relation to harvesting salmon. We have many stories from many Elders where we would leave a village and travel to the Fraser River to harvest sockeye, to harvest chinook, to harvest eulachon, to harvest smelts. We would go to a village we know as <u>K</u>i<u>k</u>áyt, which is now known as the Pattullo Bridge. We had a village on the north side. We were forcibly removed from the north side because New Westminster became the capital of British Columbia. Under the Oliver Act, there couldn't be any Indians close to a non-Indian settlement. So they moved us across the river and created a reserve.*

In the meantime, they tore down any of our structures, killed any of our cattle, anything we had... And that village of <u>K</u>i<u>k</u>áyt was an interaction place. We were there with our relatives, the Musqueam, the Tsleil-Waututh, the Kwikwetlem, our Stó:lō relatives up the River. We got to think of a time 200 years ago where what we now know as Richmond was probably all river mud. We have to think differently in terms of what the land looked like, and hence, why we would go upriver where the river narrowed to harvest sts'ú<u>k</u>w̓i7, *salmon.*

Indigenous Peoples in Canada have a constitutionally protected right to fish, which was reinforced in an important Supreme Court case, centred on a Xwmétskwiyam (Musqueam) fisherman, called *R. v. Sparrow* (1990). The case upheld our Indigenous right to fish for nutritional, social, and ceremonial purposes. The court held that the Indigenous right to fish was second in importance only to conservation and came before any other use of the resource. Although this has had a lasting effect, some Indigenous leaders have also questioned how it's being practised. While First Nations in British Columbia are having to pare back how many fish they harvest in order to conserve *sts'úḵw'i7*, commercial and recreational fisheries sometimes continue to fish—which some argue is in contradiction to *R. v. Sparrow.*

The Duty to Consult

Because the DFO has restricted how many *sts'úḵw'i7* can be harvested by First Nations for nutritional, social, and ceremonial purposes, in recent years, many First Nations have had to go without enough of it, because of low returns. In the case of the Sḵwx̱wú7mesh Úxwumixw, the catch limit hadn't been increased in a long time, while our population had grown substantially. In the 1990s, the Sḵwx̱wú7mesh were allocated a twenty-thousand-piece annual catch limit on *stséḵi7*. At the time, the Nation had about 1,900 members. By 2011, we had about 3,500 members. To allow for our growing membership, on July 5, 2011, the Sḵwx̱wú7mesh requested an increase from twenty thousand to seventy thousand Fraser River *stséḵi7*. The DFO didn't meet the Nation's request—instead, it allowed for only 10,000 additional Fraser *stséḵi7*, along with 4,500 chum and 9,000 pink salmon, despite the fact that the Nation had not requested an increase for pink or chum salmon.

FACING: Whonoak (Wilfred Baker Sr.) demonstrates a traditional method of grilling *sts'úḵw'i7* (salmon).

In 2012, the Sḵwx̱wú7mesh described the issue further, explaining that members were receiving only about five fish per person, "which

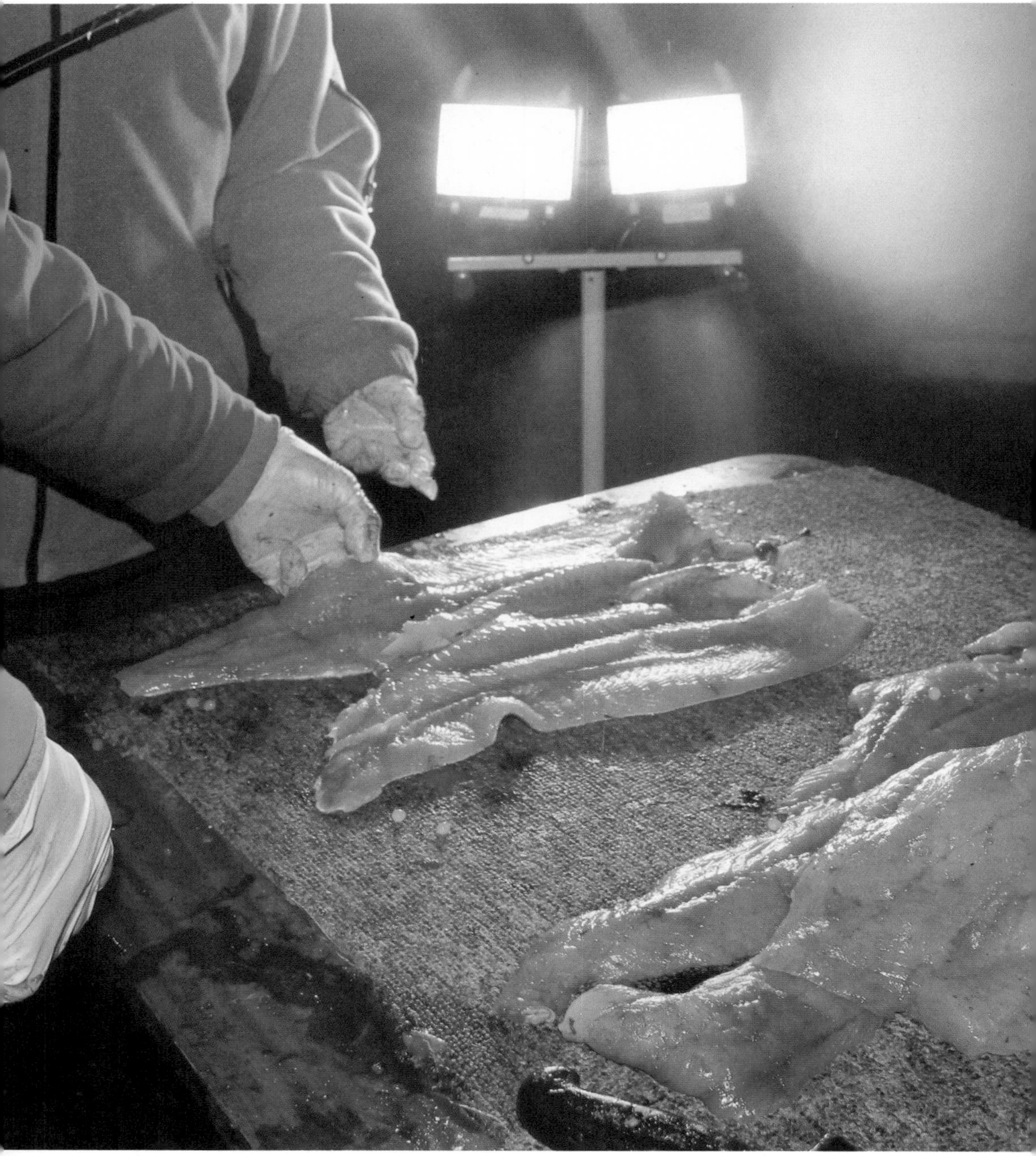

is not meeting our community's needs" and meant that not enough *stsé<u>k</u>i7* could be stored for social and ceremonial purposes. According to Xwechtáal (Andy Paull), historically, a family needed about 250 dried salmon and 75 to 100 salted salmon for sustenance through the winter. At that time, *sts'ú<u>k</u>w'i7* were plentiful—which is evidenced in the S<u>k</u>w<u>x</u>wú7mesh word for the Capilano River, Xwmélch'stn, which means "rolling at the mouth with fish."

The Nation sought a judicial review, which the Federal Court of Canada dismissed in 2017. The court said the Nation had failed to prove that the DFO's decision adversely impacted its right to fish Fraser *stsé<u>k</u>i7*. The court also concluded that the DFO's decision was reasonable, and that the S<u>k</u>w<u>x</u>wú7mesh did not demonstrate how the existing allocation of *stsé<u>k</u>i7* was insufficient. Given the "lack of evidence of an adverse impact" on the Nation, the federal court decided the duty to consult was not triggered. The court added that even if the duty to consult had been triggered, it was "at the low end of the spectrum" and Canada had met that duty. The idea of a "spectrum" of consultation was introduced in *Haida Nation v. British Columbia (Minister of Forests)* (2004), describing how the scope of the duty to consult could be high or low, in proportion to the weight of the adverse impacts and strength of the claimed title.

FACING: Filleted *sts'ú<u>k</u>w'i7* (salmon), a S<u>k</u>w<u>x</u>wú7mesh mainstay, being prepared for traditional grilling.

The S<u>k</u>w<u>x</u>wú7mesh appealed the decision and were successful: on April 8, 2019, the Federal Court of Appeal unanimously ruled that the DFO had been unreasonable in denying the Nation's request, and had breached its duty to consult. The court decided that the S<u>k</u>w<u>x</u>wú7mesh Úxwumixw had provided enough information to demonstrate a possible adverse impact, which triggered the duty to consult. This duty extended beyond the S<u>k</u>w<u>x</u>wú7mesh, and the court concluded the DFO should also consult with other First Nations that rely on Fraser *stsé<u>k</u>i7* whose rights could be adversely affected if the S<u>k</u>w<u>x</u>wú7mesh Úxwumixw was allocated more fish.

The court also concluded that the DFO had not communicated its decision-making process clearly. For example, why had the department increased the Nation's allocation of chum and pink salmon, though that had not been requested, when it had data showing the Sḵwx̱wú7mesh were not catching even 25 percent of its existing chum allocation? The court could find no rationale for the decision in the documents available. The court also concluded that the DFO had failed to demonstrate that the Nation's concerns had even been considered or why it had decided upon thirty thousand pieces of *stséḵi7*.

In addition, the Court of Appeal maintained that the DFO had "passively" requested and received information from the Nation, instead of taking part in a "meaningful two-way dialogue." Even if the need to consult was considered to be "lower on the spectrum" in scope, the government was "required to make a meaningful effort to act in a manner consistent with the honour of the Crown." In this case, the DFO did not dispute that the Sḵwx̱wú7mesh had a constitutionally protected right to fish, and the Sḵwx̱wú7mesh had voiced concerns that its right was being adversely impacted—hence, the DFO had a duty to consult. The court explained that this duty is also grounded in the protection of Aboriginal and Treaty Rights, as described in subsection 35(1) of the Constitution Act, 1982, and that the duties of consultation are part of "the process of reconciliation and fair dealing."

The question of consultation is still thorny and, many Indigenous Peoples would argue, flawed—the court described how the process has to be "reasonable" but not "perfect," and that the process "does not give Indigenous groups a veto" or require parties to "agree." In addition, many experts have argued that consultation without free, prior, and informed consent means Indigenous groups can still simply be told what is going to happen on their territory by the colonial government without being treated as equal decision-making powers, and consultation is just another box to tick. But even as a flawed process, it is not always followed or upheld, such as the court found in this case.

The Federal Court of Appeal went on to describe how good faith is required on both sides during consultation, and both sides must be "reasonable." As we'll see in chapter 18, issues around the duty to consult were also central to the Nation's court battle against the Trans Mountain pipeline.

The Legacy

Ultimately, the Court of Appeal found that any decision the DFO made about the Nation's request for an increase in *stsé<u>k</u>i7* would impact, potentially adversely, its ability to exercise the Nation's constitutionally protected rights; therefore, consultation was necessary. The case confirmed that consultation must be done in good faith at all times, whether it's considered low or high on a "spectrum." The court called for a fresh round of consultation, and said additional information was needed from both sides to facilitate good faith discussions.

The consultation mandated by the court hasn't taken place yet. Unfortunately, the results of this case are closely tied with the impacts of climate change and habitat degradation. With further consultation, the path is still open to increase our Fraser *stsé<u>k</u>i7* allocation on paper—but the salmon are still struggling and have been in decline for years. It's unclear when a harvest of seventy thousand sockeye salmon will be possible. First Nations are reclaiming their role as stewards in their territories to do habitat restoration and salmon monitoring, but the threats of climate change and the biodiversity crisis loom large and require collaboration across all peoples to mitigate the impacts.

18

S7ULH CHIY̓ÁXW: OUR PROTOCOL

THE BOLD FIGHT against the Trans Mountain Expansion Project—through *Tsleil-Waututh v. Canada (Attorney General)* (2018) (2020); *Squamish Nation v. British Columbia (Environment)* (2018); and *Coldwater First Nation v. Canada (Attorney General)* (2020)—may be the most famous litigation the Sḵwx̱wú7mesh Úxwumixw (Squamish Nation) has been involved in. The project, now under construction, will increase the Trans Mountain pipeline's capacity from 300,000 to 890,000 barrels per day. The pipeline runs from Edmonton, Alberta, to the Westridge Marine Terminal in Burnaby, British Columbia, where oil tankers can bring the crude oil to markets like Asia and California. The expansion will increase the terminal's exports from five tankers per month to up to thirty-four tankers per month.

Experts have warned that the increased tanker traffic will impact *yéw̓yews* (orcas), who rely on sonar to communicate and forage for food. They have also expressed concern about the damage a spill would cause to the living habitats of Burrard Inlet, such as those of *sts'úḵw'i7* (salmon) and other fish and birds. A cohort of First Nations

FACING: X̱álek̲'/Sek̲'yú Siy̓ám̓ (Chief Ian Campbell) at "Many People, One Canoe," 2012.

and other parties challenged the project in federal court, arguing that the approval process was flawed and that Canada had failed in its duty to consult with impacted First Nations.

The Seli̓íl̓witulh were the representative Nation in *Tsleil-Waututh v. Canada (Attorney General)* (2018) (2020); and the Squamish Nation was an equal participant that made its own arguments. The rest of the plaintiffs included: The City of Vancouver; City of Burnaby; X̱áleḵ'/Seḵ'yú Siy̓ám̓ (Chief Ian Campbell), on his own behalf and on behalf of all members of the Squamish Nation; Coldwater Indian Band; Chief Lee Spahan in his capacity as Chief of the Coldwater Band, on behalf of all members of the Coldwater Band; Aitchelitz; Skowkale; Shxwhá:y Village; Soowahlie; Squiala First Nation; Tzeachten; Yakweakwioose; Skwah; Chief David Jimmie on his own behalf and on behalf of all members of the Ts'elxwéyeqw Tribe; Upper Nicola Band; Chief Ron Ignace and Chief Fred Seymour on their own behalf and on behalf of all other members of the Stk'emlupsemc Te Secwepemc of the Secwepemc Nation; Raincoast Conservation Foundation; and Living Oceans Society.

While the battle in federal court was underway, the Sḵwx̱wú7mesh also challenged British Columbia in provincial court for issuing an environmental assessment certificate. First Nations raised concerns that the expansion would increase the amount of diluted bitumen entering Burrard Inlet; at the same time, the science is clear that Canada and the rest of the world must reduce its greenhouse gas consumption to halt climate change. A number of biologists, climate scientists, insurers, health workers and physicians, engineers, and private landowners have questioned or criticized the approval process and economic viability of the pipeline expansion. Of course, a breadth of First Nations, individuals, oil and gas proponents, and the Alberta government voiced their support and pushed for its approval. The Squamish Nation fought the pipeline expansion all the way to the Supreme Court of Canada, because of the risk it carries for the land, water, animals, and resources we have long relied upon. In the end, Canadian law was not on our side.

The case put the duty to consult under the microscope, along with the National Energy Board's process of approving the pipeline expansion. It also brought attention to cumulative impacts of industry on endangered species like *stséḵi7* (sockeye salmon), *yéw̓yews*, and Thompson and Chilcotin steelhead.

When the original proponent, Kinder Morgan, eventually backed out of the project, Prime Minister Justin Trudeau's federal government purchased the pipeline in 2018 for $4.5 billion to ensure it would be built. All the while, the cost of the pipeline has steadily increased, soaring to $21.4 billion. This is a stark contrast from the $6.8 billion that Kinder Morgan had originally estimated the expansion would cost in 2013. As of 2022, Canada's parliamentary budget officer concluded the pipeline had a net value of negative $600 million.

The Risk of a Spill

The pipeline expansion was originally proposed by Kinder Morgan in 2013. It will carry diluted bitumen to Trans Mountain's Westridge Marine Terminal in Burrard Inlet for export. It will twin the existing 1,147-kilometre Trans Mountain pipeline and expand its terminal. The Sḵwx̱wú7mesh were immediately concerned about the health of Burrard Inlet—the health of the water, the salmon, the resident orcas—and the ability to harvest resources that have already been significantly impacted by the cumulative effects of industrialization across our territory.

In 2012, the Sḵwx̱wú7mesh Úxwumixw chiefs and council passed a motion opposing the project. The Nation participated as an intervenor in the National Energy Board hearing for the project, including reviewing Trans Mountain's application and submitting information about the Nation's use and occupation of the project area. The Nation described our relationship with *sts'úḵw'i7* and with places around Burrard Inlet, including Burnaby Mountain, called Lheḵw'lhúḵw'ay̓tn, which refers to the peeling bark of arbutus trees. The Sḵwx̱wú7mesh would travel by canoe between Xwmélch'stn (Capilano) and Indian Arm to hunt for bear, deer, elk, and ducks—following the same waterway that is now dotted by tankers, ferries, and cargo ships. The Sḵwx̱wú7mesh described how travel through the territory had already been profoundly disrupted, and would also undermine restoration efforts in the area.

Elder Paítsmuḵ (David Jacobs) described how our access to food had changed after the inlet was dredged and industrialized in the 1950s:

FACING: Members of the Sḵwx̱wú7mesh and Səlílwitulh Nations gather in canoes at the Kinder Morgan–Burnaby Terminal to protest the expansion of the Trans Mountain pipeline, September 1, 2012.

My father brought us down to the beach, digging clams, getting oysters, crab, codfish, seaweed. So basically when the tide went out, our table was set. It was abundance of seafood for us... We would preserve them for winter use. During residential school, at times when we would get allowed to get home, we would still go down and dig clams and oysters.

Then in the mid-fifties, the industrial age began in the harbour. The dredges came in and destroyed those beds, clam beds. They destroyed them forever. We cannot go down the beach anymore, get clams, or anything in front of our village. It's gone. I go over to Snuneymuxw [Nanaimo] to my cousins', my family over there, and I get some from them. They give me buckets of clam, and oysters, and it's the only way I can enjoy that food anymore.

In May 2016, after hearing from the Sḵwx̱wú7mesh, Səlílwitulh, and other First Nations and intervenors, the National Energy Board recommended to the federal governor-in-council that the project be approved, subject to 157 conditions. The board concluded the project was in the "public interest," which became another thorny question. Whose interest was protected? Who was considered the public? Who profited, and who carried the risk? Squamish and the other First Nations that intervened saw that their interests, values, homes, and futures were carrying the risk of an oil spill in Burrard Inlet; they

received none of the benefits of the project. A consultation process followed, and the Nation found that the Crown did not engage meaningfully or address their outstanding concerns.

"Squamish have long occupied, governed and been the stewards and protectors of our traditional territory... and want to ensure our territory is able to support generations to come," X̱álek̲'/Sek̲'yú Siỷám̓ (Chief Ian Campbell) wrote in the Squamish Nation's final submission to the governor-in-council in January 2016, a few months before it greenlit the project. "Trans Mountain proposed to locate the Project within the heart of Squamish territory—our home—without consulting the Squamish," he continued. "[The project will] pose significant risks to Squamish people, culture and ways of life."

X̱álek̲'/Sek̲'yú Siy̓am̓ (Chief Ian Campbell) opposes the Trans Mountain pipeline, 2017.

He went on to say the Squamish's concerns had not been addressed, and criticized the National Energy Board process, noting it "proved to be an inappropriate and inadequate forum for discharging the constitutional obligation owed to the Squamish, and for providing a robust, science-based assessment of the Project." X̱álek̲'/Sek̲'yú Siy̓ám̓ wrote, "The Board's process was driven by Trans Mountain and constrained by the need to review the Project within statutory timelines, and did not provide the opportunity to thoroughly assess the risks and impacts." He asked the governor-in-council to direct the National Energy Board to assess the impacts of the expansion on our rights and title, and to explore alternate terminal locations and further investigate the dangers of a diluted bitumen spill. Instead, the governor-in-council approval came through in November 2016.

That very same day, the Sḵwx̱wú7mesh Úxwumixw began to consider whether it would challenge the decision in the Federal Court of Appeal. Council only had fifteen days to file an application for leave to appeal. That same year, the Federal Court of Appeal had concluded that Canada had breached its duty to consult with the Gitxaala Nation about the proposed Enbridge Northern Gateway Pipelines, so the Nation's legal counsel was hopeful its case could go the same way. But they warned our council that Canada's duty to consult is "not a high bar to get over," and there was a risk the court would conclude that Canada had fulfilled its obligations. The legal counsel knew that the project may still be approved but that the Nation could be successful in demanding more meaningful consultation that may result in additional measures to accommodate its concerns. Council weighed the risks of going to court or allowing the project to continue unchallenged and decided the risk to the land and water was greater.

Bitumen itself is a heavy crude oil that is too thick to flow in a pipeline on its own, so it needs to be diluted with a lighter, conventional oil. Trans Mountain continues to argue that diluted bitumen will float, but this type of oil eventually did disintegrate and sink during the disastrous 2010 Kalamazoo River oil spill, when an Enbridge pipeline burst in Michigan. Other reports have shown that in natural settings impacted by environmental factors, diluted bitumen will sink.

The combination of risk to endangered species, along with the cumulative impacts of industrialization on our territory that impacts our access to resources and ability to practise our culture, meant the Squamish Nation committed to challenge the project.

A Stand for the Water

In October 2017, with the Selíl̓witulh as the representing Nation, Sḵwx̱wú7mesh and other First Nations launched their challenge to the pipeline project. A month later, the Sḵwx̱wú7mesh Úxwumixw challenged the province in the BC Supreme Court over a flawed consultation process in issuing an environmental certificate as well.

In May 2018, the BC Supreme Court rejected the challenge. Meanwhile, debate over the Trans Mountain Expansion Project filled the news and online discourse. British Columbia, Vancouver, Burnaby, and other nearby municipalities opposed the project alongside First Nations in the province. Alberta pushed fervently for the pipeline to go through.

In early 2018, facing such widespread opposition and having spent $1.1 billion on the project, Kinder Morgan threatened to abandon the pipeline. It demanded that Trudeau's Liberal government find a way to guarantee a path forward. So, Trudeau's government did: Canada would repay Kinder Morgan the money it had spent on the expansion, plus another $3.4 billion for the existing pipeline.

FACING: Jamie Antone of the Squamish Nation protests outside National Energy Board hearings on the Trans Mountain pipeline expansion, 2016.

On August 30, 2018, the Federal Court of Appeal struck down Canada's approval of the project. The court found that the National Energy Board had not included tanker traffic in its review, so the governor-in-council could not rely on that report. The court also concluded that Canada "fell short" in the last stage of consultation: "Canada failed in Phase III to engage, dialogue meaningfully and grapple with the real concerns of the Indigenous applicants so as to explore possible accommodations of those concerns. The duty to consult was not adequately discharged," the decision reads. The court ordered the National Energy Board to do another review as well as conduct the Phase III consultation again.

Just thirty minutes after the decision, Kinder Morgan shareholders voted to approve the sale of the pipeline and expansion to Canada for $4.5 billion. Construction was halted until further notice.

It was a moment of joy and celebration for the Seli̓ĺ̓witulh, Sḵwx̱wú7mesh, Coldwater, and their allies, and people had hope that their concerns would be meaningfully addressed. But the joy was short-lived.

Jack Woodward, a lawyer with years of experience in Indigenous law, raised concerns from the get-go about the government's potential conflict of interest as the new owner of the pipeline. "How can Canada go back to the First Nations and listen and accommodate properly? The government has made its case so much more difficult now because the question of good faith consultation is now front and centre because the government has said we don't care what this decision says, it is going ahead," Woodward said to *The Narwhal* after the decision.

A second round of consultation began, and the Sk̲wx̲wú7mesh found that, again, the process was inadequate. In 2019, it happened all over again. That February, the National Energy Board recommended approval. In June, the federal government greenlit the project. In September, six First Nations challenged the consultation process.

But this time, in February 2020, the Federal Court of Appeal concluded that Canada had fulfilled its duty to consult. "The applicants' submissions are essentially that the Project cannot be approved until all of their concerns are resolved to their satisfaction," the decision reads. "If we accepted those submissions, as a practical matter there would be no end to consultation, the Project would never be approved, and the applicants would have a *de facto* veto right over it."

The court's decision was largely based on the federal cabinet's evaluation of its own consultation.

"To let the federal government be its own judge and jury of its consultation process was flawed in so many ways," Syetáx̲tn (Chris Lewis) told CBC News at the time.

The case highlighted the sovereignty at the heart of these court battles. The Sk̲wx̲wú7mesh argued that after sharing their concerns, Canada unilaterally proposed accommodation measures without any effort to collaborate with the Nation in developing them. The court dismissed this, agreeing with Canada that it had significantly improved its initial suggestions. But at the heart of the Nation's grievance was the idea of being treated as a sovereign nation and decision-maker within its territory.

In July 2020, the Supreme Court of Canada refused to hear an appeal to this decision. The legal road had been exhausted. Construction of the pipeline resumed.

Win in Provincial Court

Meanwhile, the incumbent NDP government in the province was in a sticky situation. The previous Liberal government had issued the environmental certificate for Trans Mountain. The NDP had opposed the project since before the party was elected. The provincial government was fighting the pipeline in court, but at the same time, the Sḵwx̱wú7mesh Úxwumixw was challenging the provincial certificate that the Liberals had issued. The NDP government was in a legal bind to defend the certificate issued under the previous government. The province wound up in the bizarre situation of defending and fighting the pipeline's approval at the same time.

The Sḵwx̱wú7mesh Úxwumixw lost its provincial court challenge in the early days of the court saga. But after the National Energy Board process was found to be flawed in 2018, the Nation was able to argue that the BC environmental assessment had also been flawed, since it was based on a faulty report from the board. The court decided the provincial ministers should have the chance to consider the changes in the National Energy Board's updated report.

In the end, the Sḵwx̱wú7mesh Úxwumixw had some impact by appealing this court decision. Now that the government was directed by the court to revisit its decision, the provincial Environmental Assessment Office invited the Nation and the City of Vancouver to participate in the review. After this review, additional conditions were added to the certificate, requiring additional research into bitumen behaviour, spill response, and restoration and recovery. The conditions require consulting with Indigenous Nations and local governments in plans to address human health impacts from spills.

It wasn't what the Nation had hoped for. But in one significant way, it enabled some new environmental conditions to be added to the project.

19

STETA7ÁTELTWAY CHET: WE'RE ON EVEN GROUND

ALONGSIDE WANTING to protect and exercise title to land, another key focus of the Sḵwx̱wú7mesh Úxwumixw (Squamish Nation) is regaining its ability to economically benefit from the land, which was taken away or restricted by colonization. The City of Vancouver, the three municipalities of the North Shore of Vancouver, the District of Squamish, and the Resort Municipality of Whistler continue to reap financial benefit from the use of unceded Sḵwx̱wú7mesh lands and waters. *Squamish Nation v. British Columbia (Community, Sport and Cultural Development)* (2014) demanded recognition that First Nations also have the right to economically benefit from their lands.

The Resort Municipality of Whistler was unique in that it required provincial approval of its official community plan (OCP). Whistler had a more direct relationship with the province than other municipalities because it was not just a town but a town operating like a corporation. The province approved Whistler's proposed official community plan in 2011, but the Sḵwx̱wú7mesh and Lúx̱wels (Lil'wat) Nations challenged the approval. While Whistler had undertaken consultation, the Nations argued that the province had not met its duty to consult, since a provincial minister made the ultimate decision.

The case was significant because it confirmed that the Squamish and Lil'wat had a strong claim to Aboriginal title in Whistler, because of the presence of village and cultural sites. The case also verified that economic interests are a part of Aboriginal title. A municipality's or corporation's actions can adversely impact a First Nation's rights, such as whether a First Nation wants to develop land or conserve it.

The court ultimately agreed with the Squamish and Lil'wat that the province had not fulfilled its duty to consult with the Nations and had underestimated the scope of consultation needed to address the potential adverse impacts on their Indigenous rights. In court, the province had argued that the official community plan would not adversely impact the rights of the two First Nations because it was restricting development and the imprint of Whistler on the land, but the court disagreed.

The two First Nations argued that the community plan would infringe on their economic interests by restricting their ability to develop lands. The court agreed that the plan had the potential to adversely impact their economic interests and, therefore, substantial consultation by the province was needed.

The court emphasized that Indigenous title is not restricted only to the preservation of lands, citing the landmark decision in *Delgamuukw v. British Columbia* (1997) that Aboriginal title has "an inescapable economic component."

The Squamish Nation's territory has been profoundly developed. Like many BC First Nations, we received much less reserve land than Treaty Nations to the east. For the S<u>k</u>wx<u>w</u>ú7mesh Úxwumixw, the way to benefit from our land looks different. Sustainable development in Whistler, the sustainable building of homes in Kitsilano—these are integral paths forward for us to prosper on our land. Our territory looks different today, woven with concrete, machinery, and glass. While our core values remain the same, our means of abundance and vitality have changed as the world around us has changed.

Jurisdiction

Official community plans are not binding legislation, but they do inform the decision-making of local governments. Because it is a resort town, Whistler measures development by "bed units," and it was looking to enact a bed limit in its community plan. In 2011, both the Squamish and Lil'wat Nations expressed concern that this limit would restrict their ability to develop their lands and take advantage of economic opportunities. They explained that, in the near future, they were likely to obtain First Nations' private lands on Crown land within Whistler, and they wanted equal opportunity to develop and prosper from tourism taking place on their lands.

"We have a substantial legal and cultural interest in relation to the future of Provincial Crown lands within [Whistler's] boundaries," the Squamish and Lil'wat wrote in a letter addressing Whistler and the province on August 23, 2011. "Those lands also represent potential economic interests important to our Nations' futures," the letter continued. "We respect [Whistler's] desire to control development... but we ask that those policies also respect the legitimate aspirations of our Nations as well as our Aboriginal rights and title." The Nations also made the point that the Sḵwx̱wú7mesh and Lúx̱wels have title that "precedes the jurisdiction" of the Resort Municipality of Whistler.

More consultation between Whistler and the Nations took place to discuss the Nations' proposed amendments to the official community plan. The Nations reiterated that they had economic, environmental, and cultural aspirations within Whistler's boundaries, and that most development in Whistler by that date had occurred without the participation of the Sḵwx̱wú7mesh or the Lúx̱wels.

The Nations asked that Whistler and BC work with them to explore economic opportunities, plan sustainable developments on future First Nations private lands within Whistler, and work together on land use planning. Whistler made substantial revisions to the official community plan, but the changes still did not address the Sḵwx̱wú7mesh and Lúx̱wels concerns about economic development or the bed unit limit.

Whistler argued that the future of First Nations reclaiming Crown lands was beyond its jurisdiction as a municipality—it argued this was an issue to be worked out between the Nations and the province.

In a 2012 letter to Whistler, the Sḵwx̱wú7mesh and Lúx̱wels explained to Whistler why the municipality couldn't claim that it didn't have a part in the equation:

We understand the difficulty that RMOW [Resort Municipality of Whistler] faces in its desire to have its planning process encompass large amounts of Crown land, while wanting to defer to the Province the responsibility to address unresolved aboriginal rights and title on those Crown lands.

We believe this is a shared problem. We are willing to work with you to resolve it, and to include the Province in those discussions. We have, however, expressed our firm resolve that RMOW cannot proceed unilaterally and either ignore the problem, or delegate it back to the Province to resolve.

If you believe that it is the Province's sole duty to resolve our concerns, then it would not be appropriate for you to claim to the Province that you are fulfilling consultation with us. If you direct us to the Province for consultation on the OCP, then we believe that will greatly increase the time for the OCP to be approved, and it will require the Province to have the power to make amendments to your OCP.

We prefer to work together.

New Partnerships

On July 24, 2012, Whistler sent its official community plan draft to the provincial minister of Community, Sport and Cultural Development. On August 1, the Sḵwx̱wú7mesh Úxwumixw wrote to the minister, reminding that consultation was required at the earliest stage of decision-making. A representative for the minister responded that the Crown encouraged local governments to "dialogue directly with First

The Squamish Lil'wat Cultural Centre in Whistler, BC.

Nations" for local government matters. The province would only review Whistler's own account of consultation and the Nations' concerns.

In January 2013, the assistant deputy minister told the Squamish and Lil'wat Nations that the official community plan had "fairly low potential impacts" on their rights. The province concluded that consultation fell at the "lower end of the spectrum," and requested that the Nations send along any "new" information, not anything that had already been shared. The province assured the Nations that

the community plan would have no impact on BC's future decision-making regarding Crown lands.

The BC Supreme Court found that the consultation process that followed was "short and unproductive." The Nations reminded the province that it had a duty to consult, particularly based on previous land use and development agreements. The province didn't budge. By April 2013, the minister approved the plan, which Whistler adopted in May.

The court struck down Whistler's arguments that since the community plan was not legally binding, the duty to consult was unnecessary. In fact, the duty to consult does not arise only for new laws but also whenever the Crown "contemplates conduct or a decision." The court also struck down Whistler's argument that the 2011 official community plan had no more adverse impacts than the 1993 plan. In this regard, the court pointed out that the Nations were not consulted for that plan, and a past wrong does not mean there is no duty to consult later. The court said it was no surprise that the 1993 community plan did not address any concerns of the Squamish and Lil'wat since it had been created a decade before the *Haida Nation v. British Columbia Minister of Forests* (2004) decision that established the duty to consult.

FACING: A view of the Sḵwx̱wú7mesh (Squamish) River.

The official community plan that the province had approved was quashed. In 2017, the province, Whistler, and Sḵwx̱wú7mesh and Lúx̱wels Nations signed a Memorandum of Understanding; a year later, they signed a protocol agreement. A revised official community plan was finally passed in 2020, which included the goal that "the Lil'wat Nation and Squamish Nation participate in a meaningful way in the economic development of fee simple lands in which they have an ownership interest."

Referencing this court challenge, Whistler's chief administrative officer at the time, Mike Furey, told *Pique Newsmagazine*: "I think we all sort of stepped back and realized that, going forward, working with the Nations required more investment in terms of building the relationship with them."

"I really believe there is going to be more opportunities for the Nation, but there is also going to be a willingness from all parties to work together for things of mutual interest," said Squamish Nation Councillor Syetáx̱tn (Chris Lewis).

Shortly after the community plan was approved, the three levels of government also released an in-depth framework agreement that recognized the "social, cultural, spiritual, [and] economic" interests of the two First Nations and established an economic development committee, as well as a slew of other agreements.

In the end, however, British Columbia amended legislation so that Whistler no longer needed provincial approval to pass community plans. As such, the scenario that led to this court case won't arise again—Whistler has the power to pass its own community plans. But the court case confirmed the economic interest the Squamish and Lil'wat Nations have in their lands, as well as the fact that both Nations have strong claims to title within the boundaries of the Resort Municipality of Whistler, which is almost the size of Greater Vancouver. It led to a true recognition of Sḵwx̱wú7mesh and Lúx̱wels rights to the area, and the foundation of a more positive relationship between Whistler and the two First Nations.

Victories and Losses

This is just a small sample of the many court cases the Sḵwx̱wú7mesh Úxwumixw has been involved in. In a decision that set the foundation for all the above cases, the province had approved the Garibaldi at Squamish resort without consulting with the Nation. The development is at Nch'ḵay̓ (Mount Garibaldi), the mountain that provided the Squamish safety during Sḵw'ats' (the Great Flood). The Sḵwx̱wú7mesh Úxwumixw called for a judicial review, forcing the province and the company to consult with and accommodate the Nation. This case came hot on the heels of *Haida Nation v. British Columbia* (2004), the case that had established the duty to consult, and built on that precedent that changed the landscape for First Nations in British Columbia. "Judge (Marvyn) Koenigsberg's decision is a significant victory for the Squamish Nation and for all First Nations in British Columbia," Ratcliff counsel wrote to Kákeltn Siy̓ám̓ (Chief Gibby Jacob) after the decision came down.

In another case, which went all the way to the Supreme Court of Canada, three Sḵwx̱wú7mesh members sought to establish that the Sḵwx̱wú7mesh Úxwumixw fishing bylaw applied on the Squamish River, arguing that the river fell within the Cheakamus Reserve. The reserve is on the bank of the river, and the Nation argued that Canada had intended to allow them access to fish on the reserve by drawing the boundaries that way. They lost in the Supreme Court, but the case set out parameters that wound up establishing the Capilano River as part of the Capilano Reserve at the village Xwmélch'stn; therefore, Sḵwx̱wú7mesh bylaw applies on the river.

The Sḵwx̱wú7mesh have had both major wins and disappointing losses in court. Courts governed by Canadian law cannot allow for Indigenous law to have equal footing. But the Sḵwx̱wú7mesh, and other First Nations, have used the courts to hold Canada accountable to its own laws and duties and for acting in good faith in the "honour of the Crown." Even in losses, the Sḵwx̱wú7mesh Úxwumixw has tried to find ways to push the needle in recognizing Indigenous rights and title.

These court cases have been integral to establishing parameters around the duty to consult. These cases have demonstrated the possibilities and limitations of that duty. These cases have established claims to lands and waters, and shown that Indigenous title goes beyond lines on a map. Our right to thrive and our right to be included as an equal decision-making power are at the heart of every legal fight.

PART SIX

SḴWX̱WÚ7MESH TEMÍXWCHT: OUR SQUAMISH LANDS

"We look at the maps. We show the territories of the Squamish. I don't like to use the word 'territory.' I say, 'That is our home. That is our home.' That land will never go away. Our Squamish people will never go away, so we've got to be careful what we do today."

PAÍTSMUK̲ (DAVID JACOBS)

AFTER 2000, the Sḵwx̱wú7mesh Úxwumixw (Squamish Nation) began to evolve from having to fight in courts to having a seat at the negotiating table, and even to a position in which the Nation set the table. The Nation began to negotiate accommodation agreements and take back ownership and stewardship of our homelands.

The Squamish Nation had closely watched the Nisga'a Tribal Council's fight for recognition of title, which went to court in 1968. In 1973, the Supreme Court of Canada recognized the possible existence of Indigenous rights to lands and resources. The federal government decided it needed to develop a new policy to address land claims. In 1976, the Nisga'a Tribal Council and Canada began treaty negotiations.

British Columbia joined the Nisga'a negotiations in 1990 and then established a provincial Treaty Commission in 1992. The Squamish pursued a modern treaty until 2005, when the Nation changed course.

20

CH'XWITAS CHET KWI ÚXWUMIXWCHT: WE'RE ADDING ON TO OUR COMMUNITIES

T'ECHUX̱ÁNM SIỶÁṀ (Chief Joe Mathias) emerged as a leader for the Sḵwx̱wú7mesh in the 1960s and acted as a spokesperson for the Nation until his death in 2000. In a 1992 profile in the *Vancouver Sun*, T'echux̱ánm Siỷám̓ talked about his roots.

As a boy, Mathias sat in the family kitchen while native leaders from around the province talked about their frustration in dealing with the government.

"I didn't know what was happening, but I was there. Those things were sinking in, about our water rights, our land rights, our treaties, Indian agents, this whole thing they were trying to grapple with and understand with no educational backgrounds.

"As time went on, it became clearer to me and clearer to my family that this is the role I would be undertaking as soon as I was old enough, as soon as my grandfather moved on."

FACING: T'echux̱ánm Siỷám̓ (Chief Joe Mathias), photographed by David Neel, 1990.

Mathias' great-grandfather, Chief Joe Capilano, was one of the three delegates who travelled to London in 1906 to petition King Edward for treaties between Indians and European settlers.

Over the course of his life, T'echuxánm Siýám̓ helped review Ottawa's land claims policy, and significantly contributed to the creation of the BC Treaty Commission. He worked with the First Nations Summit, representing the group on issues like treaties, fisheries, and education. In 1981, when Canada proposed a constitution that did not include Indigenous or treaty rights, the Assembly of First Nations' constitutional working group, of which T'echuxánm Siýám̓ was a part, fought furiously alongside other Indigenous groups for their recognition. Leaders ensured that the Constitution Act legally guaranteed Indigenous rights in section 35 of the constitution. They fought for further clauses in the following years.

"It's a logical follow-through, once Indian Rights are entrenched, to exercise those rights over traditional territory, not just Reserve land," T'echuxánm Siýám̓ said in 1985. Section 35 has been pivotal in court challenges and public understanding of Indigenous Peoples' pre-existing rights.

"Chief Joe Mathias" became synonymous with the fight for Indigenous rights, one journalist wrote. The Sḵwx̱wú7mesh Úxwumixw (Squamish Nation) was constantly pushing the government on its failure to rectify land issues, including the McKenna-McBride Commission's cut-off lands from reserves.

For example, in 1972, the Squamish and Sechelt Nations co-wrote a letter to the Department of Indian Affairs claiming that they could not "achieve self-sufficiency" because of the Department of Indian Affairs' failures and inconsistencies. Letters were being unanswered and issues were left unresolved.

"Our band councils and our people are totally frustrated in their efforts to advance the welfare of their band members and to assume a greater degree of responsibility for, and control over, our own affairs in the face of administrative and policy delay and indecision. We have tried the path of reasonable discussion and we have been rejected," the letter reads. It was signed by T'echux̱ánm Siy̓am̓ and Simon Baker of the Squamish Nation, and Chief Henry Paul and Clarence Joe of Sechelt.

T'echux̱ánm Siy̓am̓ fought tirelessly for Squamish land claims on the North Shore, in Vancouver, and in Squamish, demanding land back or adequate compensation. "We're not in a position to kick everyone back to Europe," he said in a 1985 *Vancouver Sun* article. "But we want a negotiated settlement." This laid the groundwork for the $92.5 million settlement that was completed in 2001.

Through the late 1900s, the Nation was fighting for the return of cut-off reserve lands on the Capilano Reserve. Eventually, it successfully regained control over ten acres of land, as well as $900,000 in compensation from Ottawa and $545,520 from the province. But the Ambleside land was valued at around $75 million at the time. "An element of English common law is that if you take someone else's land, you pay for it," lawyer Gary Yabsley said at the time.

In 1950, the Sḵwx̱wú7mesh Úxwumixw opened the Park Royal mall as a revenue stream on the Capilano Reserve. The Nation also planned additional residential developments on the reserve. Still, there was some resistance and misunderstanding from the public. In 1971, the *Vancouver Sun* published editorials dismissing the projects as poor urban planning and suggesting the Squamish Nation was being taken advantage of. Again, T'echux̱ánm Siy̓am̓ was quick to call out the hypocrisy he saw.

"Chief Joe Mathias of the Squamish Indian Band thinks it's odd that people seem to want Indians to get ahead but throw up roadblocks when they try," the article reported. "Indians are certainly aware they have been exploited in the past," T'echux̱ánm Siy̓am̓ said in the article. "We have vast experience in it. So we're making decisions for ourselves. We're examining the direction we're going into and there's no way we are going to be exploited again."

Leaving the Treaty Process

After the constitution recognized Aboriginal rights and title, the Sḵwx̱wú7mesh Úxwumixw created a land claims department in 1986. The department established the detailed geographic boundaries in the Nation's assertion of Aboriginal title in 1993. From 1993 to 1996, our people worked on treaty negotiations and began to draft a framework agreement with the provincial and federal governments.

For a long time, T'echux̱ánm Siy̓ám̓ was at the forefront of advocating for treaties in British Columbia. But in the late 1990s, he decided to pursue accommodation agreements instead. Because the Sḵwx̱wú7mesh Úxwumixw was launching the Kitsilano court case, the federal government halted negotiations in 1996. The government would not negotiate treaty with a First Nation that was in court for Aboriginal title.

In 1997, the federal government agreed to resume negotiations, but T'echux̱ánm Siy̓ám̓ began to doubt if treaty would help the Nation meet its objectives. "Chief Mathias came to the conclusion that the Squamish Nation might achieve many of its objectives prior to the conclusion of a treaty without having to incur the financial burden and political risks that go with making a treaty, while treaty offers remain unacceptable," reads a 2010 Sḵwx̱wú7mesh Úxwumixw document. A series of court cases affirmed Indigenous rights, further suggesting jurisdiction could be established without treaty. And it appeared that treaties might not bring all the rights leaders had hoped.

"We learned in the first two years of negotiating with the federal government what limitations the federal government was actually giving the tribes, in terms of benefits [in treaties]," Telálsemḵin Siy̓ám̓ (Chief Bill Williams) said. "And, we determined at that time, that it was more beneficial to leave our title to our whole traditional territory, rather than claiming one quarter of our territory through the treaty process. That's when we decided to break away from the treaty and never go back."

At the same time, T'echuxánm Siy̓ám̓ tried to share our story more widely. In 1990, the Sḵwx̱wú7mesh opened up their *tl'áḵtax̱anaw̓txw* (longhouse) to the public. "What we are trying to do is give people a better understanding of our culture," Sxwpílem Siy̓ám̓ (Chief Philip Joe) said. T'echux̱ánm Siy̓ám̓ explained the history of Indigenous land claims to the non-Indigenous attendees. In a *Vancouver Sun* article, a politician at the time admitted there was "so much misinformation and lack of understanding" around Indigenous title among non-Indigenous people. A non-Indigenous attendee said, "I think there has been too much speculation about what land claims are about and it's time that we sat and listened to what native people have to say." Many still had very limited understanding of what our people had endured, what we had lost, and how policy had maligned us and continued to do so. Despite that we had only 0.4 percent of our traditional lands, some people still held the belief that we already had too much.

For a long time, the government ensured Indigenous Peoples were cut off from the rest of society. While the Sḵwx̱wú7mesh lived in the city, veterans weren't allowed in legions because they served alcohol and the law prohibited serving alcohol to Indigenous people. We were restricted in our movements and where we could work. As Saskatchewan Premier Tommy Douglas put it in 1960, "We are reaping the harvest of 50 years or more of making the Indian a second-class citizen." He said the country had to decide whether it wanted to maintain "a sort of Canadian apartheid."

Opening the *tl'áḵtax̱anaw̓txw* to the public was one example of the wider Sḵwx̱wú7mesh effort to form partnerships and relationships to break down the walls that had been built and reinforced by the by government for so long. The Sḵwx̱wú7mesh wanted people to understand our history and what we wanted for our future.

Going ahead without treaty, the Sḵwx̱wú7mesh Úxwumixw negotiated several accommodation agreements, such as the Sea-to-Sky Highway Agreement. The highway that connects Greater Vancouver with Squamish-Lillooet was improved for the 2010 Olympics, and the

Squamish Nation received compensation for a right-of-way through St'á7mes Reserve No. 24, as well as employment training funds, six hundred acres of fee simple lands at no cost, and the option to purchase six hundred more acres. The new highway incorporated Sḵwx̱wú7mesh place names into the road signs.

The Sḵwx̱wú7mesh also made an agreement with the ski resort Garibaldi at Squamish to protect the integrity of culturally significant areas and receive fee simple land, as well as the option to purchase additional lands.

Additions to Reserve

The Sḵwx̱wú7mesh Úxwumixw built rapid momentum to develop reserve lands to increase the Nation's revenue, partly through Additions to Reserve. These additions may expand an existing reserve or create a new reserve. Sometimes there was a legal obligation for the government to consider Additions to Reserve, such as remedying cut-off lands, or an expansion was necessary to accommodate community growth. Getting the land itself didn't always have to be difficult, but the process to change those parcels to reserve land proved to be slow-going through the late twentieth century, sometimes taking decades. An improved process was updated in 2016.

By 2000, the Sḵwx̱wú7mesh Úxwumixw had reached an agreement with BC Rail, BCR Properties, and British Columbia—called the Umbrella Agreement—to introduce protections and co-management to Skwelwíl̓em (the Squamish Estuary) and provide the Nation opportunities to acquire land. The province also agreed to support Sḵwx̱wú7mesh Additions to Reserve, including 1,200 acres of land in the lower Squamish Valley. Chiefs, Elders, and council selected the land with the goal of being able to also provide housing for Sḵwx̱wú7mesh members. This included adding the Mortenson property to the St'á7mes (Stawamus) reserve in the Squamish Valley.

Kákeltn Siỷám̓ (Chief Gibby Jacob) canoes the Olympic flame to Victoria, 2009.

In 2011, the Nation began planning the Cheekye Fan development of more than five thousand homes over twenty-five to forty years. The Cheekye development is meant to address the need for affordable family housing and "attract new residents and promote economic and employment growth." The plan includes building a barrier to block debris flow from the Cheekye River that threatens the Sea-to-Sky Highway.

The Sḵwx̱wú7mesh have pursued several developments, some still in the proposal phase, at the existing Xwmélch'stn (Capilano), Ch'ích'elxwi7ḵw (Seymour), and Ch'ḵw'élhp (Gibsons Landing) reserves. All developments must be approved by membership.

Past councils held the vision of building revenue from developments at reserves mainly to facilitate member housing. Back in 1968, Simon Baker wrote, "The development of the existing reserves should

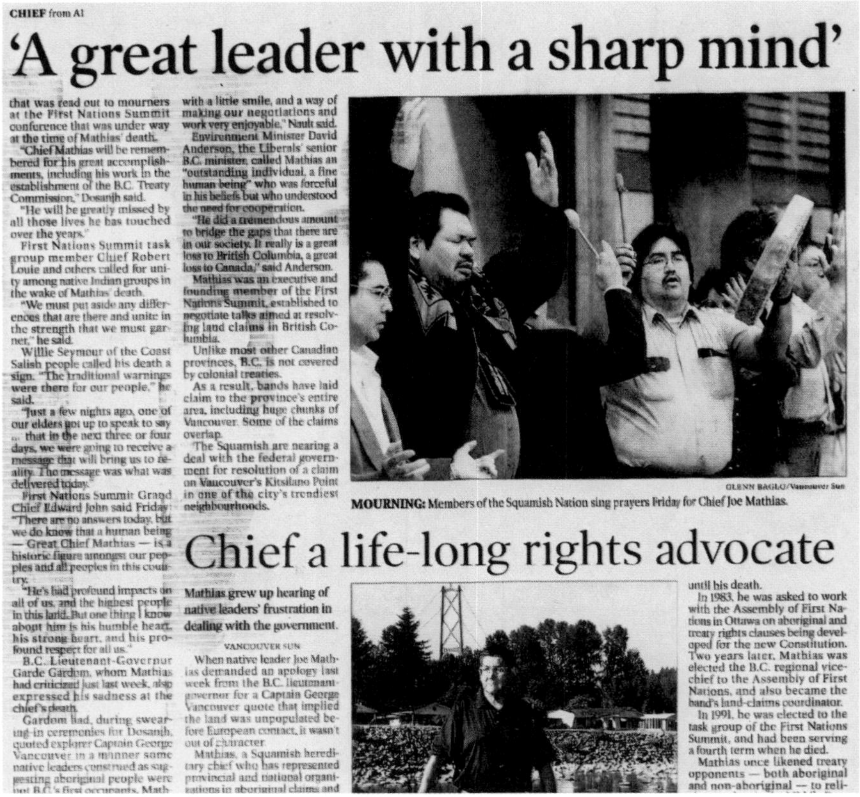

CHIEF from A1

'A great leader with a sharp mind'

that was read out to mourners at the First Nations Summit conference that was under way at the time of Mathias' death.

"Chief Mathias will be remembered for his great accomplishments, including his work in the establishment of the B.C. Treaty Commission," Dosanjh said.

"He will be greatly missed by all those lives he has touched over the years."

First Nations Summit task group member Chief Robert Louie and others called for unity among native Indian groups in the wake of Mathias' death.

"We must put aside any differences that are there and unite in the strength that we must garner," he said.

Willie Seymour of the Coast Salish people called his death a sign. "The traditional warnings were there for our people," he said.

"Just a few nights ago, one of our elders got up to speak to say ... that in the next three or four days, we were going to receive a message that will bring us to reality. The message was what was delivered today."

First Nations Summit Grand Chief Edward John said Friday: "There are no answers today, but we do know that a human being — Great Chief Mathias — is a historic figure amongst our peoples and all peoples in this country.

"He's had profound impacts on all of us, and the highest people in this land. But one thing I know about him is his humble heart, his strong heart, and his profound respect for all us."

B.C. Lieutenant-Governor Garde Gardom, whom Mathias had criticized just last week, also expressed his sadness at the chief's death.

Gardom had, during swearing-in ceremonies for Dosanjh, quoted explorer Captain George Vancouver in a manner some native leaders construed as suggesting aboriginal people were not B.C.'s first occupants. Math-

with a little smile, and a way of making our negotiations and work very enjoyable," Nault said.

Environment Minister David Anderson, the Liberals' senior B.C. minister, called Mathias an "outstanding individual, a fine human being" who was forceful in his beliefs but who understood the need for cooperation.

"He did a tremendous amount to bridge the gaps that there are in our society. It really is a great loss to British Columbia, a great loss to Canada," said Anderson.

Mathias was an executive and founding member of the First Nations Summit, established to negotiate talks aimed at resolving land claims in British Columbia.

Unlike most other Canadian provinces, B.C. is not covered by colonial treaties.

As a result, bands have laid claim to the province's entire area, including huge chunks of Vancouver. Some of the claims overlap.

The Squamish are nearing a deal with the federal government for resolution of a claim on Vancouver's Kitsilano Point in one of the city's trendiest neighbourhoods.

GLENN BAGLO/Vancouver Sun

MOURNING: Members of the Squamish Nation sing prayers Friday for Chief Joe Mathias.

Chief a life-long rights advocate

Mathias grew up hearing of native leaders' frustration in dealing with the government.

VANCOUVER SUN

When native leader Joe Mathias demanded an apology last week from the B.C. lieutenant-governor for a Captain George Vancouver quote that implied the land was unpopulated before European contact, it wasn't out of character.

Mathias, a Squamish hereditary chief who has represented provincial and national organizations in aboriginal claims and

until his death.

In 1983, he was asked to work with the Assembly of First Nations in Ottawa on aboriginal and treaty rights clauses being developed for the new Constitution. Two years later, Mathias was elected the B.C. regional vice-chief to the Assembly of First Nations, and also became the band's land-claims coordinator.

In 1991, he was elected to the task group of the First Nations Summit, and had been serving a fourth term when he died.

Mathias once likened treaty opponents — both aboriginal and non-aboriginal — to reli-

Newspaper article commemorating the life of T'echuxánm Siỳám̓ (Chief Joe Mathias).

generate considerable revenue which the Band has intended to be used in part for the acquiring and construction of land and new homes." However, retaining culture has also been central to land development plans, with the intent to use revenue "to fund cultural programs and services for membership," reads a 2010 community development plan. "Ensuring there are opportunities for Squamish people to live together will provide opportunities for the Squamish language to be spoken and cultural traditions [to] continue." The 2010 plan also recognized that, with a growing population, revenue was necessary to maintain the same level of programs and services for future generations.

The land acquisitions continued. In 2011, the Sḵwx̱wú7mesh Úxwumixw announced the purchase of 467 acres of land, using a loan, with the intention of creating reserve land. "This is an historic day for the Squamish Nation," Kákeltn Siy̓ám̓ (Chief Gibby Jacob) said at the time. "The amount of land we are acquiring is roughly equal to the amount of land that was taken from us by the Pacific Great Eastern Railway in 1913."

In 2001, the Sḵwx̱wú7mesh and Lúx̱wels (Lil'wat) signed a protocol agreement that set the stage for eventually signing an agreement to support the 2010 Vancouver Olympics bid. Together, they built the Squamish Lil'wat Cultural Centre, which opened in 2008.

In return for their support of the Olympic Games (through the Shared Legacies Agreement), the two Nations acquired three hundred acres of fee simple land, making them the largest private landholder in Whistler. The land allowed the Sḵwx̱wú7mesh and Lúx̱wels to reach a development deal at Baxter Creek. In combination with a contribution from the province, this cleared the debt from building the Squamish Lil'wat Cultural Centre. The Shared Legacies Agreement also included housing units for the Olympic Villages that then became property of the Sḵwx̱wú7mesh and Lúx̱wels Nations after the Games. In addition to the legacy lands, the agreement supported skills and training for Nation members, as well as ensuring the recognition of First Nations heritage and an endowment fund to create the Indigenous Youth Sport Legacy Fund.

In some cases, the process of Additions to Reserve is rectifying the wrongs of land taken through the McKenna-McBride Commission and the Oliver Act. The ancient village of St'á7mes, home to some of the first Sḵwx̱wú7mesh ancestors, was restricted to a reserve. That reserve was further cut up in the twentieth century. In the 1990s, the BC Rail agreement set the stage for the land to be transferred back, but the government dragged its feet on creating a process to return the land. Decades later, in 2021, the Nation added twenty acres to the St'á7mes Reserve, bringing more Sḵwx̱wú7mesh back to the ancient village.

21

SWIỶÁT: WOODFIBRE

WITH ALL the significant court cases like *Delgamuukw*, *Tsilhqot'in*, and *Haida* that affirmed Indigenous title and consent, companies took more notice of the importance of obtaining consent for projects. Further attention to Indigenous consent came in 2007, when the United Nations adopted the Declaration on the Rights of Indigenous Peoples. The declaration recognized Indigenous Peoples' distinct rights to self-determination, with an emphasis on collective rights versus individual rights. The declaration also recognized the Indigenous right to free, prior, and informed consent before lands are taken or used, catalyzing a conversation about what "informed consent" means. Many communities criticized the process of getting consent in Canada as merely checking boxes and then telling the Nations the project was happening whether they said yes or no.

Communities also pointed out the flaws within provincial and federal environmental assessments of industrial projects. In a document written for the Sk̲wx̲wú7mesh Úxwumixw (Squamish Nation), Sk̲wx̲wú7mesh lawyer Kelts'tkínem (Aaron Bruce) and lawyer Emma Hume of Ratcliff wrote that assessments often did not consider First Nations' land management objectives or values.

These assessments also do not consider the cumulative effects of industry. One individual project can say it has a specific "footprint," and that it won't impact the environment too much. Cumulative effects consider how industry can impact the land far more significantly than one project estimates when all the different industrial activities in the same area are considered together. Kelts'tkínem and Hume also pointed out that the federal and provincial environmental assessments do not adequately weigh cultural values, that Indigenous rights are often oversimplified, and that data is often presented in a way that is "impossible to accurately understand." Significantly, the decision to approve a project lies solely with the provincial and/or federal government in these processes.

FACING: Development of the Woodfibre LNG facility, being built on Swiy̓át, which is also the site of the former Woodfibre pulp mill.

The Woodfibre LNG project and associated Eagle Mountain pipeline wound up being an experiment in addressing the many flaws of these industrial assessments. The Sḵwx̱wú7mesh Úxwumixw established its own environmental assessment process to review the project.

Woodfibre LNG first sought a BC environmental assessment (EA) in 2013 for its proposal to construct a liquefied natural gas (LNG) production, storage, and marine carrier transfer facility on the former village of Swiy̓át. The site was also home to a sawmill, most recently the Woodfibre pulp and paper mill. Industrial activity took place at Swiy̓át throughout the twentieth century without consent from the Squamish Nation. Syetáx̱tn (Chris Lewis), a councillor at the time, spoke about the decision to create the Sḵwx̱wú7mesh process:

We were involved in many other EA processes at the time and we were very unhappy with how Squamish concerns, our voices, in the environmental assessment process, had been written down. We felt that it was very much a "check box" kind of process where the federal government or the provincial government would come to Squamish Nation and say, "What are your issues?" and they would write down notes, and our concerns would get lost in the macro EA process. But there would be a checked box saying, "We spoke to Squamish Nation and these are their concerns," and maybe there would be mitigation—maybe there wouldn't be.

The EA *process was completely absent of Squamish Nation follow-up in terms of what the environmental management plans would be. No recognition or implementation of our culture and our spirituality—there is no space in that* EA *process for it. So, at that time we were quite frustrated with the* EA *processes.*

The Conditions

The process began with a framework agreement with the proponents, Woodfibre LNG and FortisBC. The Nation built strict confidentiality into the process so the companies couldn't share information, the act of which might be viewed as having met the Crown's duty to consult under the Crown's assessment process. "[The Nation] did not want the Squamish Process to be viewed by the Crown as a vehicle through which the proponents would fulfill the Crown's consultation requirements," law professor Jennifer Sankey wrote in her PhD dissertation. The two proponents agreed. So the Sḵwx̱wú7mesh Úxwumixw took its first step in pursuing its own independent assessment in a confidential process, paid for by the proponents. It would not participate in the Crown process beyond sending a consultant to obtain technical information. The Crown was nervous about the First Nation not participating in its process, and about Woodfibre engaging in confidential negotiations.

The Nation then had to create its own assessment method, grounded in Sḵwx̱wú7mesh values, such as interconnectedness within the environment. Community consultation was central, including focus groups and larger community meetings. The assessment included a traditional use and occupancy study that involved interviewing knowledge-holders. Many Nation members were concerned about the project.

Syetáx̱tn spoke to this in Sankey's PhD dissertation: "There was concern that if there was a catastrophe, our village would be destroyed... even though the science said if there was a big explosion the village is far enough away that it wouldn't be impacted. Our people didn't believe it. They said, 'I don't believe them. I don't believe that guy.'... People would say, 'I know you are trying to do a different process[,] Chris, and we thank you for it, we think it's great. But, not on this project. It just needs to go.'... So for some, it was more of a principle thing, but other people had actual issues with the technology, with what the companies were doing, and we extracted all that through our consultation process."

The technical review focused on concerns from the community like the impacts on marine life, or potential impacts on Skwelwíl̓em (the Squamish Estuary), or possible accidents. The team prepared an assessment report confidential to the Sḵwx̱wú7mesh community, which recommended mitigation measures for all the community's concerns.

Our community discussed the challenges of saying no to the Woodfibre LNG project—which would mean launching into a court battle—and the possibilities and limitations of the Squamish Nation Environmental Assessment Process as a future path to dealing with industrial projects. Council voted in favour of proceeding with the project in 2015 and drew up an Environmental Agreement, in which the Nation issued its own environmental certificates and outlined twenty-five conditions for Woodfibre LNG, FortisBC, and the province of BC. The Sḵwx̱wú7mesh could revoke its environmental certificates if any of the conditions were breached. Woodfibre was first in accepting all of its conditions, which included further studies on ecological impacts and providing insurance coverage in case of loss or injury resulting from an accident, directly addressing concerns from our community members.

Woodfibre set a precedent for the Sḵwx̱wú7mesh Úxwumixw acting as an environmental regulator independent of the federal and provincial governments. The province promised several parcels of Crown land will be returned to the Nation in exchange for its support of Woodfibre LNG.

The Issue of Consent

Kelts'tkínem (Aaron Bruce) and Emma Hume from Ratcliff described in depth what reaching consent means for the Sḵwx̱wú7mesh Úxwumixw. They wrote: "In order to get to consent, two key objectives must be met: an informed decision by the Squamish Nation and a shared decision-making process with the Crown." The Crown proved resistant to shared decision-making, leading the Nation to create its own process. In a Squamish process, "It is not the responsibility of the Squamish Nation to prove that the project will or will not have significant adverse effects on the environment. Rather, the burden of proof is on proponents to prove that a project will not have adverse effects on the environment and Squamish interests."

The Sḵwx̱wú7mesh Úxwumixw process for the Woodfibre project emphasized the traditional land use and occupancy study, and how "Squamish Nation members exist as part of the land base." Another key component is what is determined as a "significant" impact. In a traditional Crown assessment, the death of a single fish from a stable population may not be considered a "significant loss," Kelts'tkínem and Hume wrote. But according to Sḵwx̱wú7mesh values, that one death may be "very significant."

Kelts'tkínem and Hume wrote that in a Sḵwx̱wú7mesh process, to truly obtain consent, the Crown cannot make a decision until the process is complete, and the Nation and Crown must discuss the Nation's decision prior to the Crown issuing its decision: "The Environmental Agreement allows the Squamish Nation to enforce compliance, and should the proponent fail to comply, the Nation would have the opportunity to seek damages, an injunction or specific performance of obligations...

FACING: An aerial view showing Sḵwx̱wú7mesh River industry.

"The Squamish Nation Process allows the opportunity for the Squamish Nation to provide its 'free, prior and informed consent' to projects proposed in its territory...

"The key to making the Process successful is a cooperative project proponent that understands the importance of obtaining the Squamish Nation's consent... Obtaining the Nation's consent is also an important aspect of social licence and the goal of reconciliation, which courts have recognized as the purpose of the Crown's duty to consult and accommodate."

They emphasized that the Sḵwx̱wú7mesh assessment process is not complete—it is still evolving, and "lessons will be learned as the Nation continues to assess major projects."

22

SEṈÁḴW: INSIDE THE HEAD OF THE BAY

IN 2018, the Sḵwx̱wú7mesh Úxwumixw (Squamish Nation) established Nch'ḵaỷ Development Corporation, the economic development arm of the Nation. The corporation allows for the separation of business and politics within the Nation. Nch'ḵaỷ manages the Nation's existing businesses: multiple gas stations, two marinas, an RV park, forestry operations, and property leasing and development. The board is led by four independent directors, two council directors, and one Nation member director. Nch'ḵaỷ's goal is to maximize the Nation's economic development potential.

Nch'ḵaỷ's most well-known and precedent-setting project so far is the development of the Seṅáḵw village.

After a decades-long legal battle (see chapter 16), the Sḵwx̱wú7mesh Úxwumixw won back the land at Seṅáḵw in *Mathias et al. v. Canada* (2001). However, the Nation only won back a portion of its land. The original reserve at Seṅáḵw was eighty acres. The court decision in 2003 that returned the Nation's land only returned a small, misshapen parcel—10.5 acres of the original 80.

The Nation knew the land had immense development potential, right in the middle of the City of Vancouver. The Nation proposed to build market housing at the Kitsilano reserve. In 2019, 87 percent of voting members voted in support of the development, and 81 percent voted in support of the business terms with the developer, Westbank Projects Corp.

The 10.5-acre site is set to host eleven towers up to fifty-seven storeys, with the intention of being the largest net-zero operational carbon residential project in Canada. The new Seṅáḵw village will provide commercial space and an estimated 6,077 rentals, with 20 percent affordable rental units, and 250 homes set aside for Nation members at affordable rates. The project is expected to bring a long-term return of more than $10 billion for the Nation, while providing rentals in a city facing a housing shortage. Phase one includes three towers and 1,408 units, with 219 affordable units, and the first residents are expected in 2025. The project is set to provide jobs and training to members.

FACING: Chepx̱ímiya Siỷám̓ (Chief Janice George) stands where Seṅáḵw will be built, January 31, 2022.

The Kitsilano reserve as it exists today is less than half the size it was when people were displaced, but it will be the largest First Nations–led development in Canada.

The Squamish people, having won back their lands after being forcibly removed, are returning, and rebuilding their village into a modern neighbourhood in the heart of a global city.

Government Support

Seṅáḵw is located on Squamish land, and therefore it is not subject to the land use regulations of any other government. The development doesn't have to abide by the City of Vancouver's zoning bylaws. But other levels of government have still stepped up to support the project and praised the Nation for its vision and how the project will benefit the region.

Attendees of the Seṅáḵw site ceremony with Justin Trudeau (centre), 2022.

On May 25, 2022, the Sḵwx̱wú7mesh Úxwumixw and City of Vancouver signed a Services Agreement that created a framework to guide government-to-government relations between the Nation and the City to ensure access to municipal services in the Seṅáḵw neighbourhood, such as water and storm sewer services and investment in transit. "Seṅáḵw has been a Sḵwx̱wú7mesh village site for thousands of years. With the overwhelming support of our Squamish people, the Seṅáḵw development will generate enormous wealth for our community and see the return of Squamish people to our village that past Canadian governments forcibly evicted us from," one of the council spokespersons, Sxwíxwtn (Wilson Williams), said at the time.

The incumbent mayor, Kennedy Stewart, called it "an honour" to support the Nation's sovereignty. "Seṅáḵw will deliver more than six thousand homes to address our critical need for rental and below market housing. I couldn't be more proud to support such an historic and visionary project—the largest First Nations economic development in Canadian history," he said.

Construction began in September 2022, after a groundbreaking ceremony on September 6. Liberal prime minister Justin Trudeau attended and announced a $1.4 billion construction loan to support Seṅák̲w, which is the largest-ever loan from the Canada Mortgage and Housing Corporation for residential development, and the largest economic partnership between a First Nation and the federal government in Canadian history.

"Today's announcement not only builds more much-needed homes for Vancouverites, it supports the Squamish Nation's vision for their traditional lands and their path to continued economic independence and self-determination. When we all work together as partners—federal and Indigenous governments, private sector, local communities—we innovate, and we find solutions to the challenges we face," Trudeau said.

Seṅák̲w will leave its mark on Vancouver's skyline. It is set to feature architecture and design inspired by Squamish visual culture, and over half of the ten-acre site will be publicly accessible with green spaces and plazas. "The vision of Seṅák̲w will demonstrate how humanity and nature can co-exist, and the development aims to be the largest net-zero residential project in the country," the Nation said in a statement.

In the coming years, we will see how Seṅák̲w impacts the local economy and the community, and what precedent it may set as a zero-carbon project. We will see Squamish leadership in action.

"The wealth generated from these lands can then be recirculated into our local economies and communities to address our people's urgent needs for affordable housing, education, and social services," council Chairperson Khelsilem (Dustin Rivers) said.

23

CHET WA NSÉYX̱NITAS WA LHTIM̓ÁCHT: WE ARE PROTECTING OUR WAYS OF LIFE

INDUSTRIALIZATION AND development continued with even more speed through the late 1900s and early 2000s, and drastically changed the lands and waters throughout the twentieth century. Sḵwx̱wú7mesh Elder Paítsmuḵ (David Jacobs) spoke of his experience with the harvest of seafood near Xwmélch'stn (Capilano Reserve): "In my wildest dreams I would never have thought they would destroy that, take our food away from our mouths. But that happened. I can't teach my grandchildren, my great-grandchildren, how to dig clams, get crab, cook the crab, dry the seaweed. I can't do that. It's gone. I don't know how to explain that to my grandchildren."

It's true that some clam beds, elk, and old-growth forests have been wiped out. But the Sḵwx̱wú7mesh began reclaiming their roles as stewards. From land use planning to permanent protections, the early 2000s brought a wave of Sḵwx̱wú7mesh-led stewardship on the land.

Logging in the Elaho Valley

Beginning in 1997, Skwxwú7mesh Úxwumixw (Squamish Nation) members joined others in protesting Interfor's logging at Tree Farm Licence 38 (TFL 38), which encompasses 240,000 hectares in the Elaho and Squamish River Valleys. Interfor had begun logging monumental old-growth trees. Protesters gathered at the confluence of Sims Creek and Elaho River in 1999. Logging was destroying wildlife habitat, eradicating irreplaceable old-growth forest, and disrupting water retention in forests. Clear-cuts increase the risk of floods and landslides by destabilizing the soil.

In 1997, a group of environmentalists with the Wilderness Committee began to take the public camping at Nexw7áy̓antsut (Sims Creek) to inspire people to care about the forest. After Telálsemkin Siy̓ám̓ (Chief Bill Williams) pointed out they were operating on Skwxwú7mesh homelands without permission, the Wilderness Committee and Skwxwú7mesh members initiated a collaborative effort called Utsám̓ (the Witness Project), aimed at protecting the Elaho Valley. This alliance lasted ten years.

On weekends, groups would travel from Vancouver to Nexw7áy̓antsut and hold witness ceremonies. They shared other activities like drum-making and learning about traditional medicines. For some Skwxwú7mesh members, it was the first time they had visited that part of their homelands. The project led Telálsemkin Siy̓ám̓ to invite artist Tawx'sin Yexwulla/Púlxtn (Aaron Nelson-Moody) to carve on the land. One of his *Cedar Women* house posts was placed at the end of the logging road at Nexw7áy̓antsut. The project became an opportunity to educate non-Indigenous people on Skwxwú7mesh rights and values. "There was nothing else to do but engage in ceremony. This was how the land was going to be taken back," T'uy't'tanat (Cease Wyss) said.

FACING: Ethnobotanist Styawat (Leigh Joseph) believes forest biodiversity is connected to the traditional knowledge of Indigenous Peoples.

Harvested 1963
Planted 1973
Rotary

But logging continued. Yumks (Dr. Rudy Reimer) discovered culturally modified trees in the area, demonstrating cultural use generations ago. In April 2001, about four hundred people gathered for a ceremony by a cutblock that Interfor planned to log. Interfor vice-president Ric Slaco attended.

A few years later, in 2005, the Nation purchased TFL 38 from Interfor. The licence grants exclusive rights to harvest timber over 218,000 hectares. This made the Nation the largest forest licencee in the Squamish Forest District. That same year, Sims Creek was protected through an agreement with the province.

X̱ay Temíxw Land Use Plan

In 2001, the Sḵwx̱wú7mesh Úxwumixw created the X̱ay Temíxw [Sacred Land] Land Use Plan, identifying fifty thousand hectares of Ḵw'áyḵw'ay̓ex̱ Kw'elh7aynexw ta Sḵwx̱wú7mesh Temíxw (Wild Spirit Places of the Squamish Nation's Land) to protect. For our people, the creation of this plan was another exercise in self-governance as stewards of Sḵwx̱wú7mesh territory. The Nation spoke to the community about the issues facing the land, and the values and goals members had to protect it.

Chepx̱ímiya Siy̓ám̓ (Chief Janice George) talked about the cultural impact of a degraded environment. "It is harder for our carvers to get wood. For our basket weavers it is also hard to get materials," she said. "Our weavers should be able to go and access the parts of the trees that we use but that the forest companies don't use."

In the plan, Nation members emphasized protecting access to resources and the teachings of respect around using those resources. "It's important to show other people how to respect the animals and hunt in a good way," Tsewḵwílem (Byron Joseph) said in the report. "All hunters should have to abide by that protocol and practice ways of respect for the life they are taking."

The land is still alive with deer, elk, black bears, mountain goats, birds, plants, berries, and fish and sea mammals. People still fish, harvest, and remain connected with the changed landscape. The plan emphasized how the Sḵwx̱wú7mesh are inherently related to the land. "Without this land, there is no Squamish culture," it reads.

This X̱ay Temíxw Land Use Plan establishes a forest stewardship zone within all forests in the territory, as well as important cultural sites, including 180 archaeological sites in the territory. The plan also identifies the need to establish corridors for animals to pass between habitats without being interrupted by development.

According to this plan, Sims Creek, where the Witness Project took place, is a Wild Spirit Place. In 2007, the Nation entered an agreement with British Columbia to protect the area. The Land Use Agreement with the province designated three non-industrial development areas: the Ns7éyx̱nitem tl'a Sútich Wild Spirit Place (Upper Elaho Valley), Nexw7áy̓antsut (Sims Creek Watershed), and the Estétiw̓ilh Wild Spirit Place (Sigurd/West Side of Squamish River). It also ensured co-management of conservancies within the Ns7éyx̱nitem tl'a Sútich and Estétiw̓ilh Wild Spirit Places. The agreement further protects twenty-two smaller Siiy̓ám̓in ta Sḵwx̱wú7mesh (Squamish Cultural Sites) and village sites from Crown tenures being issued. The agreement added over 11,000 hectares of new protected areas—nearly thirty times larger than Stanley Park.

Skwelwíl̓em (Squamish Estuary)

The Nation also took on restoring Skwelwíl̓em (the Squamish Estuary), starting in the 1990s. As it grew during the twentieth century, the town of Squamish had chipped away at the estuary. Without consulting with the Sḵwx̱wú7mesh, BC Rail had dredged the estuary in the 1970s for a proposed coal port project. It built a five-kilometre spit that blocked water coming from the Squamish River and thus dried

View of the Sḵwx̱wú7mesh River from the Siy̓ám̓ Smánit (Stawamus Chief).

up part of the estuary. And after all that, the federal government rejected the coal port proposal. BC Rail left massive piles of dredged soil abandoned. Skwelwíl̓em remained that way for thirty years. Juvenile salmon need to access the estuary as a space to rest, grow, and feed, and get used to saltwater before going to the ocean, but the spit blocked *sts'úḵw'i7* (salmon) from accessing the shallow water. According to Fisheries and Oceans Canada, more than seventeen thousand chinook salmon on average returned to the Squamish River between 1962 and 1972. By the 1980s, they counted fewer than five hundred chinook. (It's worth noting that decline hasn't been attributed to the spit alone—many *sts'úḵw'i7* have faced challenges with habitat degradation and wide-scale industrial development.)

In the 1990s, the Sḵwx̱wú7mesh Úxwumixw, Squamish River Watershed Society, and Fisheries and Oceans Canada partnered up to restore the estuary. They removed the fifteen-hectare dredge pile and replanted vegetation. In 2007, the estuary was designated as the Skwelwíl̓em Squamish Estuary Wildlife Management Area under provincial law.

In 2022, the coalition removed part of the spit to revitalize the ecosystem. The goal was to open the way for *sts'úḵw'i7* to access the estuary again. Removing the spit "opens the lungs of the river," Councillor Sxwíxwtn (Wilson Williams) said. "It brings back the natural being of it."

The Sḵwx̱wú7mesh Úxwumixw also funded a study that discovered the estuary provides $12.6 million every year in ecosystem goods and services, like water filtration. And that's not including the cultural value of the estuary. "As our lands heal and are revitalized, so is our culture and connection to it," Joyce Williams, also a councillor, wrote in 2021.

Selective Logging at Cheakamus Community Forest

The Sḵwx̱wú7mesh Úxwumixw also partnered with the Lúx̱wels (Lil'wat) Nation and the Resort Municipality of Whistler to manage the Cheakamus Community Forest Licence. The partners prioritized small-scale logging, not clear-cuts. They planned for conservation and cultural use. In 2009, the community forest partners began selling carbon offsets that the forest generates from greenhouse gas reductions. Offsets are purchased by greenhouse gas emitters to compensate for their emissions.

As of 2022, the two First Nations and Whistler keep the equivalent of fifteen thousand tonnes of carbon dioxide out of the atmosphere per year by harvesting more selectively than the province legally requires. They log to imitate blowdowns from wind, rather than clear-cutting, the latter being the most cost-effective but destructive way to log. The community forest partners leave a buffer around riparian areas that is double what is required by provincial regulations.

The revenue from carbon offsets has been integral to financing the partners in managing the forest according to their values, since they make less income from timber. As of 2023, the project was the only community forest developing carbon offsets in British Columbia.

The Nation also asserted its sovereignty by declaring a two-year old-growth deferral across the entire territory in 2021, stating that the province had taken "no meaningful action" to adapt unsustainable old-growth logging. That year, Cheakamus Community Forest focused instead on a sustainability strategy. In 2021, the Nation also protected the Dakota Bowl in Sechelt, which is home to old-growth trees, removing the area completely from timber sales. The preserved forest is important for harvesting cedar and plants.

Sínulhk̲aỷ, the Double-Headed Sea Serpent of Átl'k̲a7tsem (Howe Sound)

In 2021, Átl'k̲a7tsem (Howe Sound) was declared a UNESCO Biosphere Region, which means it is an area recognized for its global ecological significance. A biosphere is intended to pursue conservation, sustainable development, and reconciliation with Indigenous Peoples. Átl'k̲a7tsem is central to our history. One of our important stories is about Sínulhk̲aỷ, the double-headed serpent that lay across Átl'k̲a7tsem.

According to X̲ats'alánexw Siỷáṁ (Chief August Jack Khatsahlano), Sínulhk̲aỷ was three miles long. X̲ats'alánexw said people wouldn't travel by canoe to get to Xwmélch'stn (Capilano); instead they would go through the bush to avoid the serpent. Here is the story as told by Sx̲áaltxw Siỷáṁ (Chief Louis Miranda):

Long ago, in the Squamish village of St'á7mes, there lived a young man, his name was Xwechtáal and he had just married a young bride. Because it was custom, he took his new wife to live with him in his father's house.

At this time a huge two-headed serpent called Sínulhk̲aỷ lived near St'á7mes. Its loud and terrible cries could be heard as it slithered around the mountains and rivers. One morning the people heard it coming down the mountain across from them. As it travelled, it shrieked and groaned, coming closer and closer.

It reached the flat land then slithered into the Squamish River and swam across. The people were terrified. But after a while, they could see it climbing up a mountain, its cries becoming fainter and at last dying away.

Xwechtáal's father knew that it must be his son, and his son only, who could get the power to kill the horrible beast. Even though Xwechtáal had just married, his father would have to wake him and send him on the quest to find and slay the serpent.

Xwechtáal and his new wife were sleeping peacefully on their bullrush mat. His father called him, but Xwechtáal didn't stir. After the long wedding feast and ceremonies, he was exhausted. His father called him again and again, but still there was no reply. Finally the father picked up a container of cold water and spilt it all over his son.

Xwechtáal sat up suddenly. His father spoke. "Xwechtáal, you must go and follow the serpent and slay it. No matter how long it takes, you must do it. I know you would rather stay here with your wife but you must go now."

Xwechtáal felt ashamed in front of his bride, but he didn't dare say anything back to his father. He lifted the mat to let the water drain through, then leaned over and kissed his bride goodbye. He promised to come back as soon as he killed Sínulhk̲aỷ, and told his wife not to get tired waiting for him.

He started out to follow the serpent, but as soon as he picked up its trail he began to feel strange and faint, as if he was going to have a convulsion. Finding a creek, he began to cleanse himself, then dried himself with hemlock boughs. Day after day while he tracked the serpent, he bathed himself, but every time he came near it, he felt strange. Xwechtáal continued to bathe constantly, in order to get the power to come close to Sínulhk̲aỷ, so that he could kill it.

One day he watched Sínulhk̲aỷ crossing a lake. Its whole body was never submerged entirely. When one head was in the water, the other head was looking around, so that Xwechtáal had no chance of sneaking up on it. The serpent travelled on and on. Xwechtáal kept following, mile after mile. After crossing many lakes, the serpent finally found one that he was able to cover his whole body with entirely. Day after day, Xwechtáal cleansed himself and pursued the serpent.

After a year had passed this way Xwechtáal had a dream. In his dream the serpent appeared before him and said, "Go and look for some pitch and then prepare four good spears. Put the pitch on the end of the spears."

The next day Xwechtáal did as his vision told him and gathered the pitch. Every day he bathed. Again the serpent appeared to him in a dream. This time he said, "Make a raft for yourself. I will come to the surface of the water, and when I do, spear one of my heads with two of your pitched spears. Then quickly paddle to the other side of the lake. I will surface my other head there. You spear it with your other spears."

Xwechtáal walked until he came to a big lake, then as he had been told, he made a raft and waited. Suddenly the serpent raised one of its ugly heads. Xwechtáal was ready, and thrust the spear as hard as he could at it. Paddling over to the other side of the lake, he saw the other head and speared it with all his strength. Then he fainted and fell into the water.

When he came to, the lake had risen very high and he found himself up on the mountainside. Slowly the water went down until the lake itself dried up. There on the bottom lay the body of Sínulhk̲aỷ. Xwechtáal waited. He kept on bathing and cleansing himself all the time. Finally all that was left of the serpent was its bones. Following the advice of another dream, Xwechtáal climbed down and searched for one special bone. In his dream he had been told he could use it to help search for food for his people.

After he found the bone, he cut across the mountains and went over to the head of the Squamish River. The people on the other side were enemies. Xwechtáal waved his magic bone at them, and they all fell down as though they were dead. Then he went ashore and touched them one by one, to revive them.

The people then knew that Xwechtáal was very powerful because of this gift. After he had stayed with them a few days, the chief gave him one of his daughters for a wife. All the way down to St'á7mes the same thing happened. At every village he was given a wife after he had waved that magic bone at the people, and then awakened them again.

The Cheakamus Community Forest generates massive carbon storage.

Finally, Xwechtáal arrived back at St'á7mes. When the people saw Xwechtáal and his wives coming, they ran out to see who was beaching his canoe. Again Xwechtáal waved that bone, and all the people fell down. Then he touched everyone and they all came back to life. All were touched except his first wife, who had grown tired of waiting and had remarried.

From the head of the Squamish River, to the mouth at St'á7mes, all the Squamish people are now related, because of Xwechtáal.

Sesémiya (Tracy Williams) explained the importance of these stories in our connection to the land. "I think all the old stories about the legendary creatures are important: Smáyl̓ilh [the Wild People], K̲ál̓k̲alilh [the Giant Cannibal Woman], Sk̲weyk̲wtáy̓mesh [the Little People], Sínulhk̲ay̓ [the double-headed serpent] all fit into a natural landscape. We need a natural landscape to be able to understand those stories and to keep them alive. These stories exist all over and tell of a time that we might have forgotten," she said.

"These stories show our connection to the land. [They] show how long we have been here and where we came from."

"I stand before you to speak on behalf of the Squamish people and all the unborn generations to come. This is a teaching that we value—to always look to that unknown place that we call the future where our children and grandchildren and great-grandchildren must live. What we do and say today must be done and said with their well-being in mind."

T'ECHUX̱ÁNM SIY̓ÁM̓ (CHIEF JOE MATHIAS)

WĄNÁXWSW̓IT CHAT EḴ' TKWI AW̓T STÉLMEXWCHT: WE HONOUR OUR FUTURE GENERATIONS

DESPITE THE incredible challenges the S<u>k</u>w<u>x</u>wú7mesh have faced, we have never completely given up our land. In the face of a totally changed world, we have retained our culture and values. The state government has often acted as if we need to be static. But we have always been fluid and adapting. We have always been moving, and using the newest technologies. The S<u>k</u>w<u>x</u>wú7mesh are anything but static.

The S<u>k</u>w<u>x</u>wú7mesh have been working hard to revitalize the S<u>k</u>w<u>x</u>wú7mesh Sníchim (Squamish Language) and cultural practices that were weakened because of residential schools and other oppressive measures.

The link to our past that is our language has been kept alive through the hearts and minds of countless Elders. The recent work of bringing our language to new generations began in the mid- to late 1960s. Our late Elder, Sye<u>x</u>wáltn (Dominic Charlie) was the first one to teach classes for our language at Totem Hall in the late 1960s. When his health prohibited further work for him, the late S<u>x</u>áaltxw

Siy̓ám̓ (Chief Louis Miranda) was asked to hold evening classes in North Vancouver. And work to teach, learn, and share our language was carried on in the Squamish Valley by the late P'ek̲áltn (Ernie Harry) in the 1970s.

Because of his work with the BC Native Language Project, which included four other southern Indigenous languages, Sx̲áaltxw Siy̓ám̓ and the other Elder language speakers developed writing systems to compile old written records of their languages into one writing system. From these years of work, thousands of pages of our language were handwritten by Sx̲áaltxw Siy̓ám̓. With this work he was able to transcribe many different written records of Squamish Language beginning in the 1890s up to the 1990s.

In 1972, chief and council approved language classes being offered at St. Thomas Aquinas Regional Secondary School, and in the years to follow the program expanded to include three high schools, two alternate programs, and five elementary schools, in addition to daycare programs. In recent years, post-secondary classes have been held as community-based programs, where our own people teach, and the students come from our population. These classes began in 2007 through Capilano University with our linguistics instructor and Squamish Nation member T'nax̲wtn (Dr. Peter Jacobs).

FACING: Published in 2011, this dictionary is the first compilation of Sk̲wx̲wú7mesh Sníchim by the Squamish Nation.

While there were only a handful of speakers just a decade or two ago, there were 349 learning language speakers as of 2022. The Sníchim Foundation (previously Kwi Aw̓t Stélmexw) runs the Squamish Language Proficiency Certificate Program at Simon Fraser University alongside the Sel̓íl̓witulh (Tsleil-Waututh) Nation to provide an intensive language program. Sk̲wx̲wú7mesh Sníchim classes are now available for children in elementary and high school grades. Members can also learn words through remote classes done by the Nation and online resources like YouTube.

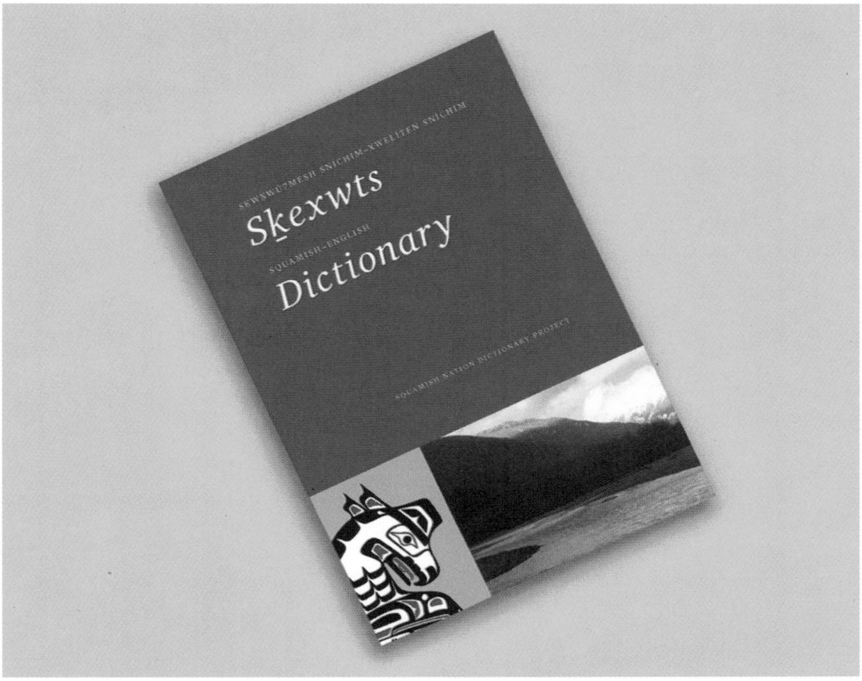

In Sḵwx̱wú7mesh member Kirsten Baker-Williams's study on language revitalization in 2006, speakers talked about the significance of the language coming back, within them and within others: "It's my language. And it's just that some words, it evades me, I've forgotten, but it comes back," said Kwítelut (Lena Jacobs) at the age of ninety-five. "It's better if we speak our language, like if you see somebody that speaks your language, talk to them in our language, what you know. *'Chexw men wa ha7lh,' 'Wa chexw yuu.'* You know those few words, 'How are you?' and 'take care.'"

Canoe journeys have taken off since 1993, and Chepx̱ímiya Siy̓ám̓ (Chief Janice George) and Skwetsímeltxw (Willard "Buddy" Joseph) sparked a revival in weaving. They co-founded the Lhen̓t Aw̓txw (Weaving House) to share teachings, and they have shared knowledge with thousands of students.

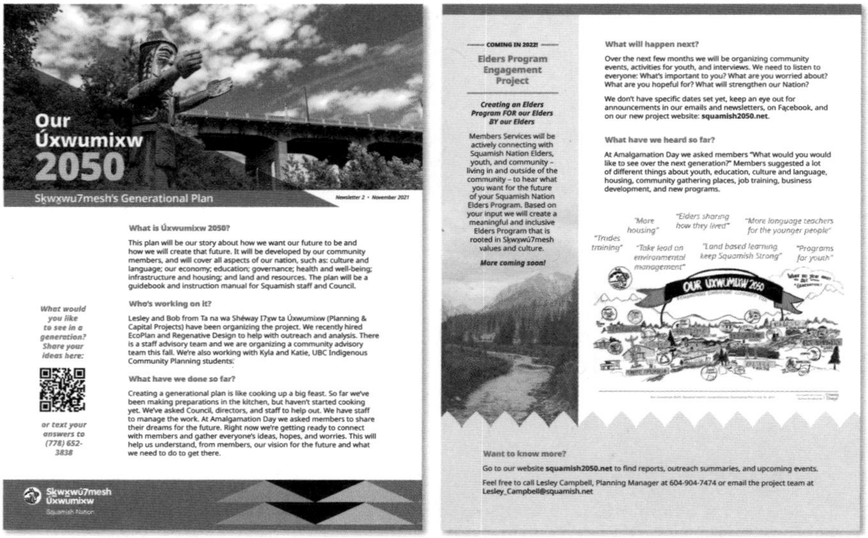

Úxwumixw 2050, the S̲kwx̲wú7mesh Generational Plan.

Planning for Generations

The S̲kwx̲wú7mesh Úxwumixw is planning for the future—partly through Úxwumixw 2050: S̲kwx̲wú7mesh Generational Plan, which is a comprehensive community plan. The Nation has said it will be a "holistic" plan to pursue "sustainability, self-sufficiency and improved government capacity," and will be based heavily on the community engagement process. The wide-spanning plan is set to include things like housing, wellness, fisheries, and land use, building on all the Nation's past planning efforts.

The Nation's most recent strategic plan (2022–2026) identifies the importance of a healing centre; addressing gaps in health care; support for Elders; jobs and training; a S̲kwx̲wú7mesh Sníchim strategy; expanding facilities; developing a constitution; and—as leaders have been doing for generations—engaging with the Crown to affirm and implement S̲kwx̲wú7mesh rights and title.

In creating a plan for future community, homes, and services, the Squamish Nation hosted its first-ever independent census in 2021. The census was meant to ensure equitable distribution of resources, but it was also an act of data sovereignty and self-government, to have ownership over its own information—a stark contrast to the surveys and censuses of the 1800s, done without consent and often used to strip communities of lands and resources.

A consultant hired by the Nation called it "the first First Nations–run census of this scale and kind." A major goal was to inform the Hiy̓ám̓ Housing Society project to provide housing to every Sḵwx̱wú7mesh member.

Housing

In 2019, Nexwsxwníw̓ntm ta Úxwumixw (Squamish Nation Council) approved the creation of a non-profit housing society called Hiy̓ám̓ ta Sḵwx̱wú7mesh, which means "The Squamish Are Coming Home." Through community engagement in 2018 and 2019, the Nation heard that the number one priority for members was housing all members in a generation, which is exactly what Hiy̓ám̓ Housing has set out to do. The society is pursuing the goal of bringing home every Squamish member who wants to live on the territory within twenty-five years.

As of 2023, the housing program intended to build fifteen homes per year. The demand for housing is much higher, with about one thousand members on the waitlist. Like everyone else in the Vancouver and Squamish area, members have been impacted by drastically rising housing costs and costs of living, making it hard for people living off-reserve to stay on their homelands. Hiy̓ám̓ Housing wrote a strategic plan centring gathering spaces and developments that "support community connections."

In a landslide 2021 referendum, Sḵwx̱wú7mesh members approved more than four hundred affordable housing units to be built on

Styawat (Leigh Joseph) and her son Jake in the Cheakamus Community Forest.

reserve land in North Vancouver and within our villages in the municipality of Squamish: North Vancouver at Xwmélch'stn (Capilano Reserve, along Mathias Road), Ch'ích'elxwi7k̲w (at Seymour Reserve, on Orwell Street), and on Siy̓ích'em (Seaichem Reserve). The Nation is pursuing more multi-unit housing, and all the projects bear Sk̲wx̲wú7mesh names, such as:

Estítkw Place (Safe Place): Fifty-five affordable homes at Xwmélch'stn with supports and priority for people with disabilities, LGBTQAI2S+ people, and those experiencing homelessness or mental health issues and addictions

Eskékxwi7ch tl'a Sp'ákw'us Place (Gathering Place of Eagles): Twenty-seven affordable homes at Siy̓ích'em, prioritizing women and their children

Chenk̲w em̓út (I Am Home): Ninety-five units at Xwmélch'stn prioritizing independent Elders, youth, and families

Maṅalhánenawtxw (Feeling Respected House): a thirteen-plex at Wíw̓kem (Waiwakum)

In addition to Hiy̓ám̓ Housing, the Sk̲wx̲wú7mesh are continuing their ancient relationships with the Xwmétskwiyam (Musqueam) and Selíl̓witulh in many other ways, notably through the MST Development Corporation, which, as of 2023, owned six properties throughout Metro Vancouver. In 2022, the MST Corporation topped *Vancouver Magazine*'s Power 50 List, which acknowledges Vancouver's most influential figures.

Chet Men Wanáxwsténemut
(We Treat Ourselves with Respect)

This book contains the details of many events of Sk̲wx̲wú7mesh history, and many words from Sk̲wx̲wú7mesh people. At the same time, it truly only scrapes the surface of our history and who we are. There are many stories behind the names that people and places carry.

This book brings together many of our records. There are even more records available for Sk̲wx̲wú7mesh people—many pages of academic, historical, and cultural works. The archives of the Sk̲wx̲wú7mesh Úxwumixw contain in-depth studies of our utilization of our lands, detailing exactly how we used every part of each type of fish, and how our ritualists conducted their work in the old days. One can see the richness in Sk̲wx̲wú7mesh names—like *sx̲wex̲wek̲wíchen* (spider), derived from *x̲wk̲wíchen*, which means "to make a fish net or a spider's web." According to Sx̱áaltxw Siy̓ám̓, spiderwebs could be used as gauze for wrapping cuts and burns. Nation members can access these recordings, and hear the voices of Sx̱áaltxw Siy̓ám̓ or Syex̱wáltn. We can read the books, academic papers, and stories, and marvel at the deep knowledge of our people.

So much of who we are is off the page, in oral stories and culture. This book is not an end or a summary. It's just the first sliver of light in a sunrise. The first beat in a song. The first branch of a tall tree. Just one step in a lifelong journey of learning about who we are, and asserting who we are. Every Sḵwx̱wú7mesh person is at a different place in their journey. The classrooms are on the land, in the *tl'áḵtax̱anaw̓txw* (longhouse), at the kitchen table with our aunts, uncles, cousins—and today, even online. Teachings come from our time together. Learning and hearing our legends, stories, and history in our ancestors' own words gives us the opportunity to see the world as they did. From everyday activities, to sacred rituals, to how we learn from all the other creatures with whom we share our world.

FACING: Sḵwx̱wú7mesh Nation basketball team players Payton Mack (left) and Eden Joseph (right).

Sḵwx̱wú7mesh history is within every Sḵwx̱wú7mesh person. Sḵwx̱wú7mesh history is where your relatives took you as a kid. Sḵwx̱wú7mesh history is feeling the cold water in the rushing rivers and knowing your ancestors bathed there before you. Sḵwx̱wú7mesh history is our first teaching about respecting our Elders and family. It's the story of how we got where we are today.

These are all beginnings of journeys—not ends.

"We have the same connection to the land our ancestors had, for the land has always provided for us, whether it be physically or spiritually," Chepx̱ímiya Siy̓ám̓ said.

Our ancestors went to tremendous lengths to maintain this knowledge. Ceremonies in secret, whispered words, hours of interviews, pages of handwritten notes. All to save what we had, after so much had been taken. After being forced to whisper, our people took the

NORTH SHORE
INDIANS
VB
15

Na tsixw kwétsi nch’u7 syel̓ánem, nekw nta7áw̓n álhi Sealiya kwis nam̓s k̲w̓ú7ntsut ta síiyay̓s, ta es7ásxw.
After a year it occurred to Sealiya to go and join her friends the seals.

A page from the illustrated tale *Sealiya*, by Kwítelut (Lena Jacobs).

power to speak loudly—*we are here*. We will never give up what our ancestors have passed on to us.

As T’echux̲ánm Siy̓ám̓ (Chief Joe Mathias) said, each one of us can pass on these beautiful gifts we have been given, as our people have fought to do generation after generation: “In our world, where we come from, there is the great circle that we call a medicine wheel. We walk into the future backwards because we are looking to our ancestors. If you are listening to your elders you are learning our traditions and culture. What was given to you is now in your arms. So that sometime in the future you can turn around and give it to your grandchildren.

“What took place you can give to your children. That is the value of our circle.”

Sealiya

We leave with one last story, a *syets* (true story) that happened to and was told by Kwítelut (Lena Jacobs) and written for a children's book. It's a story about beginnings:

I am telling the story of a seal. One time when my late Uncle Isaac was hunting, he shot a seal on the beach.

The seal died. When my uncle went to take a closer look he saw that it was carrying a baby. So right away he went to deliver the baby seal.

We all went closer to see . . . he got out his knife . . . he made a cut . . . and out came the baby seal! All of us kids got to see! Out she came from her mom! Just like that! The seal pup was born! A little girl seal!

But oh! She was so strong! And big! That little girl seal! She was swimming right away! And she would follow the children! All the kids! She would swim with us! If you went swimming . . . there she'd be following us around!

Oh! We all loved that baby seal so much! We went fishing for it to get little fish to feed it!

And so it went . . . if you went swimming there she was following us around! She'd get on our backs and she'd hold on!

One Sunday my Uncle came and told all of us children, "Go and pray! All of you go and pray!" And so we all went off to church.

And there she was! . . . Sealiya was following us! She climbed the steps, following along after us to the Church! And all the time she was hollering, bellowing as she followed us! She really wanted to come along into the church.

But Uncle yelled out, "Don't bring her in!!! Don't bring her in!!!" But she wouldn't obey! So Uncle had to put her outside! She hollered and hollered! Oh . . . we loved that baby seal so much!

And the baby seal grew! Soon she wasn't a baby seal anymore! She was a seal!

After a year it occurred to Sealiya to go and join her friends the seals.

And so all of us watched as she went off . . . but oh we were so sad hearted as we saw our playmate leave. So this is the end of my story.

AFTERWORD

HOW DID WE GET to where we are today? It was really nation-building.

When we first met our lawyer, Paul Reecke, he said, "You have wonderful lands, beautiful lands. You're land-rich, cash-poor. So, how do we turn this around?" He said, "The first thing you need is to service your land. You need sanitary water, traffic, access to provincial and city roads."

We had to do that in order to take the next step, and the next step, and the next step. Where we are today, this is the movement of our people.

It has been said that a good chief listens to the people. That's what sticks in our minds. Listen to the people. I feel so satisfied with not only the achievements of our leaders, but also the recognition of those leaders in the past, like Simon Baker—the recognition that we have for them. There are always stories of leadership.

We have a responsibility to share these stories. Speakers or storytellers like me—where did I learn these stories? From my grandfather, and his grandfather, and his grandfather. That's where the stories come from. My responsibility is to move them, because those stories could die if our people don't continue to tell them. There are histories and stories you won't learn from a book. This is why we have potlatches. We gather the people, feed the people, and we tell them stories. This is why we tell stories in our longhouses. That's why we call witnesses in the longhouses. It's a responsibility, being called a witness. You take that home to your family, to your community, and you tell them, "I witnessed. I was there."

And when you learn Squamish ways and Squamish history, you go back to your community, and you start teaching. You start talking to the kids. *Here's who you are. You're Squamish.* That's an important thing we've got to do.

When you go into the longhouse, if you're new and you don't know too much about it, you go there as a guest; you sit and watch. It's going to take you a long time to learn, because there's a meaning to everything. Then you go home and you ask questions of someone you know in the longhouse. I've been in the longhouse for eighty years and I still don't know it all.

Everything happened in the longhouse before the white men came. The longhouse, from birth to death.

When I grew up, I learned from my grandfather and my mother and father. We were taught *chiỷáxw*: the way of being; the protocol, the practice, the training, the education of our people. Teach them young so they'll be able to understand Squamish, like I do with my children. It's like any other ethnic group that comes to Vancouver and settles here—their traditions and values are with them. That's what we have to maintain.

For example, if you wanted to do a celebration of your father, you would hire a person who will tell you and teach you what to do. Gather the people in the longhouse, have a feast, a celebration in the longhouse with the families. Then you and your speaker would say, "This is the family, this is where our connection is. Our connection is relatives over here, over there." So, they're always bonded. We had a feast for my grandfather—we have to keep that alive. We have to gather the people, give them a feast, give them gifts if you want. Just a celebration to say: *This is the way of the Squamish people. This is what we've always done. That is what we have to continue.* I know a lot of people are not involved in longhouses, but that doesn't mean they can't have a feast. They can still take part and learn.

All those traditions are not written in a book. Things are going to change. But it's up to the people to say, "We'll change, but how much are we going to change?" So, we've got to practise; we've got to continue to tell the stories of our people. We have to keep it strong.

And you use the names. If you say my name, the old-timers will know that name, Paítsmuk̲. They called him the peacekeeper. He was noted for when there was war between the Yík̲wilhtax̲ (Lekwiltok) and the Squamish.

It's so important to learn the name, where it came from, and how you use the name. You never drag that name through the mud. My children follow the family names. All my grandchildren: they all use their Squamish names when they talk to each other. It's so important.

And some of our English names have funny stories. For example, my great-great-grandfather: the settlers did surveys and a census; they went to his place and they couldn't say his name, so the surveyor just said, "We'll put Jacob." And my great-great-grandfather's brother: "We can't write that either," the surveyor said, so he called him Antone. When my grandfather was born, they called him Isaac. His father was Jacob, so he became Isaac Jacob. That two-name system started with the government: "Indian Act Indians." They had to have something in their reports. That's how they started the names. Some of the names would change. I never even knew August was my great-granduncle Khatsahlano's name.

My great-great-grandfather Khaytulk—he lived in Stanley Park at Sch'ílhus (Chaythoos). He had a huge canoe he used for clam digging and all that stuff. He used to haul supplies from the Vancouver area to the lumber mill at Jericho. So, they said, well, we hired this guy, we can't say his name, so they called him Jack. He hauls supplies—so they call him Supply Jack. Our people hadn't ever heard the names "Supply" or "Jack," so the old Indians called him Supplejack!

Another fellow they called Willow Snow. When they first started a saloon, he worked in the kitchen. He never saw spoons before, so he used to put them in his pocket. The Indian agents were doing the census again, and they went to his place, and he had a whole pocket full of spoons. They couldn't say his ancestral name—so, they called him Billy Spoon. That's so funny to me.

So many stories. There are lots of good stories about our people—lots of good stories and traditions. They tell us who we are.

These stories belong to all the people—and they're all part of the story.

PAÍTSMUK̲ (David Jacobs) · *Elder*

GLOSSARY OF SQUAMISH WORDS, TERMS, AND NAMES

Átl'ḵa7tsem: Howe Sound
Áx̱achu7: Beaver Lake
Ch'ax̱áy̓: "herring breaching the surface during spawning season"; an area at Horseshoe Bay
Ch'éḵch'eḵts: "dirty mouth"; the area on Squamish River near Turbid Creek
Ch'ích'elxwi7ḵw: Seymour Creek, also Seymour Reserve
Ch'ich'iyúy: "twins"; the two mountains up the top of Capilano Valley, now also known as the Lions/the Two Sisters
Ch'iyáḵmesh: "basket catch fish"; name of the former village along the Cheakamus River and the entire area of the Cheakamus River
Ch'ḵw'élhp: Gibsons Landing, also known as Schen̓ḵ
Chat: "we"
Chenḵw em̓út: "I Am Home"; a Sḵwx̱wú7mesh housing development at Xwmélch'stn
Chepx̱ím̓ Siy̓ám̓: Chief William George
Chepx̱ímiya Siy̓ám̓: Chief Janice George
Chet men wanáxwsténemut: "we treat ourselves with respect"
Chief Snat: a late chief
Chinalset: Jericho Charlie
Chiyálhiya: Lila Johnston
Chíyatmixw: first-born child of X̱i7lánexw
Chiy̓áxw: protocol
Elksn: "point of land"; a settlement in the area of what is now Point Grey, Vancouver
Esḵéḵxwi7ch tl'a Sp'áḵw'us Place: "Gathering Place of Eagles"; a Sḵwx̱wú7mesh housing development at Siy̓ích'em
Esḵí7ḵel: unskilled, ignorant, not knowing how to do something
Eslha7án̓: Mission Reserve
Estétiw̓ilh: protected; safe. Also, a "Wild Spirit Place"—a place that should not be developed; i.e., Sigurd/West Side of Squamish River
Estítkw Place: "Safe Place"; an affordable housing development at Xwmélch'stn, with supports and priority for people with disabilities, LGBTQAI2S+ people, and those experiencing homelessness or mental health issues and addictions
Esyéw: prophet
Etl'ím̓ lhḵaych': short month, December
Háx̱sten: the late Harriet George, also known as Skwétsiy̓a
Hiy̓ám̓ ta Sḵwx̱wú7mesh: "The Squamish Are Coming Home"; a non-profit housing society
Huy chexw a: thank you
In̓inyáx̱a7n: Thunderbird; a large supernatural bird depicted as having horns, causing thunder when it flaps its wings and lightning when it opens and closes its eyes
Iyálḵp: Alaska blueberries
Iy̓ál̓mexw: Jericho Beach
Iy̓álshn: a former bay near the foot of Davie and Denman Streets
Ḵ'áwatshn: a stick that fish are hung from during cooking
Ḵ'emel̓áy̓: broadleaf maple tree
Ḵ'emḵ'emel̓áy̓: "many maple trees"; an area where the first sawmill on the south shore of Burrard Inlet opened, at the foot of what is now Dunlevy Avenue in Vancouver

Kákeltn Siy̓ám̓: Chief Gibby Jacob
K̲ál̓k̲alilh: Giant Cannibal Woman
K̲álx̲ay̓: ironwood
Kaw̓tín: also known as Kowtain Reserve
K̲él̓etstn: Lions Bay
K̲eléxw: finger game where players, using one finger, pull on the competitor's finger
Kelts'tkínem: Aaron Bruce
Khelsilem: Dustin Rivers, also known as X̲elsílem and Sxwchálten
Kik̲áyt: a Sk̲wx̲wú7mesh fishing village on the south bank of the Fraser River in present-day Surrey, BC, also known as qiqá:yt or qəqəyt
K̲iyáplánexw Siy̓ám̓: a renowned leader; he was also known as George but is often referred to as "Old Man" or "Old Chief" Kiapilano, or similar variations, in early 1900s writings; "Kiapilano" and its variants were further anglicized to "Capilano"
K̲tin: back eddy on the river
K̲w'áyk̲w'ay̓ex̲ Kw'elh7aynexw ta Sk̲wx̲wú7mesh Temíxw: "Wild Spirit Places of the Squamish Nation's Land" that are designated as protected areas
K̲w'émk̲w'em: "lots of kelp"; Defence Islands
Kw'enlh wa x̲aam: "those who weep together"; co-parents-in-law when one of the married couple dies
Kw'ikw'tl'ám: Kwikwetlem, also known as Coquitlam
k̲w'k̲iw'tl'us: a training arrow
Kwálk̲in: a man from St'á7mes, who X̲ats'alánexw Siy̓ám̓ said hosted a ceremonial potlatch at Iy̓álshn
K̲wek̲wu7úpay̓: "place with many wild crab apple trees"; present-day Locarno Beach
Kwelá7wik̲w: a Yík̲wilhtax̲ woman taken captive by the Sk̲wx̲wú7mesh and who married Pítsemek̲
Kweṅám̓in: shells used by masked dancers
Kwenáx̲tn Siy̓ám̓: Chief Andrew
Kwétsi siy̓ám̓ smex̲wíws: smallpox
Kwinák̲atemat: Lucille Nicholson
Kwíselshn: Chief Harry, born in 1831 in Cheakamus and died in 1918; government chief of Mission Reserve
Kwítelut: Lena Jacobs
Kwtsi7ts: a medicine man or ritualist
Kwu7s: spring salmon, also Spring Salmon Chief
Lex̲wlúx̲wels: a rock bluff where it is said the X̲aays transformed some Lúx̲wels to stone
Lhék̲'lhak̲'elk̲: Doctor Jim
Lhek̲w'lhúk̲w'ay̓tn: "peeling bark of arbutus trees"; Burnaby Mountain
Lhemlhémelch': Clemclemluts, a Cowichan Tribe village
Lheṅt Aw̓txw: Weaving House, an organization founded by Chepx̲ímiya Siy̓ám̓ and Skwetsímeltxw to share teachings; they have shared knowledge with thousands of students
Lúx̲wels: Lil'wat People, also known as Mount Currie People
Maṅalhánenawtxw: "Feeling Respected House"; a housing development at at Wíw̓kem (Waiwakum)
Melk̲ws: an old man who was a storyteller; the first Squamish man to be recorded, in 1879
Mím̓na lhk̲aych': child month, January
Nch'áy̓uw̓am: descendants of one head/headman
Nch'k̲ay̓: Mount Garibaldi, the largest peak in Sk̲wx̲wú7meshulh Aysáy̓ch, where Sk̲wx̲wú7mesh canoes tied up after Sk̲w'ats' (the Great Flood)
Nekwsáliya: Margaret Locke
Nepítl': Buck Mountain; an archaeological site, a rock shelter, where hunters would seek cover from the elements under an overhanging boulder
Nexw7áy̓antsut: verb meaning "to transform oneself"; area identified in X̲ay Temíxw as Sims Creek, also known as Sims Creek Watershed
Nexwsxwníw̓ntm ta Úxwumixw: Squamish Nation Council

Nkwu'7say: "place of the spring salmon"; close to Shovelnose Creek

Ns7éyx̱nitem tl'a Sútich: phrase meaning "Be watched over by the north wind"; a Wild Spirit Place in the Upper Elaho Valley, designated to be protected

P'eḵáltn: Ernie Harry

P'ekwchá: Spanish Banks

P'uy̓áṁ: "blackened from smoke"; area near the Squamish River–Elaho River confluence

Paítsmuḵ: David Jacobs

Pítsemeḵ: a Sḵwx̱wú7mesh warrior, married to a Yíḵwilhtax̱ woman, Kwelá7wiḵw

Pná7lx̱ets': Kuper Island

S7ápeleḵ Siy̓áṁ: Chief Joe Capilano

S7ens: the wife of Slhx̱í7lsh

Sch'á7miḵw: great-grandchild, great-grandparents, siblings of the great-grandparents

Sch'ílhus: Chaythoos, near Prospect Point

Scheṅḵ: Second name for Gibsons Landing

Sekéṁkem: bumble bee

Seli̓ílwitulh: Tsleil-Waututh (also previously known as the Burrard Indian Band)

Selsála7ech: campsite on Anvil Island

Séli̓seltn: spindle whorl

Sempúlyan: Stewart Gonzales

Seṅáḵw: "inside the head of the bay"; an area in the mouth of False Creek, which became known as Kitsilano Indian Reserve No. 6

Senlháliya: Lizzie Joseph (née Baker)

Sequailyah: Mrs. Chief George

Sesémiya: Tracy Williams

Sewinchelwet: Sophie Frank

Sh'ḵweṅ: ocean

Shay̓u7: "screech owl" or "ghost of a dead person"

Shishá7lh: Sechelt

Shishay̓u7áy: Britannia Beach

Siiy̓áṁin ta Sḵwx̱wú7mesh: Squamish Cultural Sites

Síḵemkin: Chief Squamish Jim

Sínulhḵay̓: the two-headed serpent, an enormous supernatural double-headed snake that caused convulsions in humans when in close proximity

Siy̓áṁ: highly respected person

Siy̓áṁ Smánit: "Chief Mountain"; a rock formation where the two-headed serpent passed and left a mark across the stone, near St'á7mes

Siy̓ích'em: also known as Seaichem Reserve

Sḵ'ay: smoked fish

Sḵ'emíṅem: Halkomelem language; the ones who speak Sḵ'emíṅem are our closest neighbours to the south

Sḵew̓ḵ: the trickster character depicted as a Raven

Sḵw'ats': the Great Flood

Sḵw'élem: barbecued salmon

Sḵw'élemxw: blackberries

Skw'ikw'íwas: co-parents-in-law

Skw'iyúts: slave taken in a raid of an enemy tribe who is raised as a member of the community

Skwé7tsiya: Eva Lewis

Skwé7tsiya: Shellene Paull

Skwelwíi̓em: Squamish Estuary

Skwetsímeltxw: Willard "Buddy" Joseph

Sḵweyḵwtáy̓mesh: the Little People

Sḵwx̱wú7mesh: Squamish

Sḵwx̱wú7mesh chat: "We are Squamish"

Sḵwx̱wú7mesh Sníchim: Squamish Language

Sḵwx̱wú7mesh Úxwumixw: Squamish Nation; Squamish People

Sḵwx̱wú7meshulh: Squamish's People

Sḵwx̱wú7meshulh Aysáy̓ch: Squamish Territory

Slhx̱í7lsh: standing up man, standing rock, Siwash Rock

Slíl: "a bunch of woven blankets" or "piled up mountain goat blankets"

Slix̱weli̓tx̱w Siy̓áṁ: Chief George

Sluxw: arrowhead

Smaṅálh: a high-class person or noble people; a person who is considered the opposite of a person who is *smáts'en* (proud) or *eskí̱7ḵel* (unskilled, ignorant)

Smant: rock

Smant tl'a Nch'ḵaẏ: obsidian, Mount Garibaldi stone
Smáts'en: proud, stuck up
Smáyl̇ilh: Wild People
Smekw'a7ál: burial sites
Sná7em: inner power
Sníchim Foundation: a non-profit society dedicated to revitalizing the Squamish Language, formerly known as Kwi Aẇt Stélmexw
Sosahlatch: a well-known sheltered place on Gambier Island; also any place with multiple woven mats used for shelter for travellers
Spú7ets': a village at the confluence of Rubble Creek and the Cheakamus River
St'á7mes: an ancient village site and a current reserve at the mouth of the Squamish River, also known as Stawamus
St'ashem: a child of a slave, someone considered a low-class person, illegitimate child
St'elḵáya: Roberts Creek, Gibsons, BC
Staḵw: freshwater
Stáyalh: child of a sibling (niece or nephew)
Stek'ín: Haida
Stḵáya: wolf (term used in longhouse)
Stl'ál̇mexw: St'at'imc, also known as the Lillooets
Sts'úḵw'i7: salmon
Stséḵi7: sockeye salmon
Styawat: Leigh Joseph
Swanamia: X̱ats'alánexw Siẏáṁ's wife
Swanimáylh: "next parents"
Swelwá7lt: streams
Swiẏáṯ: place name in Howe Sound at Woodfibre
Sx̱áaltxw Siẏáṁ: Chief Louis Miranda
Sx̱eláltn: second man to land at Gibsons
Sx̱el̇tsḵwú7: "painted face"; Ice Cap Peak on the Ashlu/Elaho divide
Sx̱íx̱nam: Chilcotin
Sxw7úmten: Indian doctor
Sx̱wálh Siẏáṁ: Chief Jimmy Jimmy, also known as Ḵwatayálh
Sx̱wáymelh: Fraser River
Sx̱wáẏx̱wey: ceremonial mask
Sxwelíḵtn: a Squamish man
Sx̱wex̱weḵwíchen: spider
Sx̱wex̱wiẏáṁ: a legend, a mythical story
Sxwíxwtn: Wilson Williams
Sxwpílem Siẏáṁ: Chief Philip Joe
Syetáx̱tn: Chris Lewis
Syets: a true story
Syex̱wáltn: Dominic Charlie
T'aḵ't'aḵ'muẏíṅ tl'a iṅinyáx̱a7n: "landing place of the Thunderbird" or "Thunderbird's perch"; Black Tusk in Whistler
T'áḵa7: salal berry
T'echux̱ánm Siẏáṁ: Chief Joe Mathias
T'eḵt'ḵáẏ: vine maple trees
T'eḵw't'aḵw'emaẏ: "place of thimbleberry bushes" near Evans Creek and the Squamish River–Cheakamus River confluence
T'nax̱wtn: Dr. Peter Jacobs
T'uy't'tanat: Cease Wyss
Ta na wa Nexwniẇn ta a Ímats: "Teachings for Your Grandchildren"; the Squamish Language Elders Group
Tawx'sin Yexwulla/Púlxtn: Aaron Nelson-Moody
Tax̱ch: cattail mats
Techtechnís: hummingbird
Telálsemḵin Siẏáṁ: Chief Bill Williams
Tem eḵwáyanexw: time when animal hide changes, November
Tem eshcháwm: time for salmon to spawn, approximately mid-August to mid-November
Tem kwu7s: time of spring salmon, approximately July
Tem t'áḵa7: salal berry time, August
Tem tsá7tsḵay: plant-shoot time, April
Tem wélhx̱s: frog time, February
Tem yetwán: salmonberry time, May
Temcháyilhn: fish time, September
Temíxw: land; dirt; earth
Temḵw'éleṁxw: blackberry time, July
Temkw'eskw'ás: hot time, June
Temlháwt': herring time, March

Temp'í7twáy: time of animals rutting, October

Temtemíxwtn: lots of land place; Belcarra

Tétemat: Josephine, Mrs. Chief Tom

Téytk̲in: Stó:lō, the Upriver Halkomelem dialect; the ones who speak Téytk̲in are our neighbours to the east

Títem̓tsen: village toward Port Moody at the far east end of Burrard Inlet

Tiyáltelut: Audrey Rivers

Tiyáx̲eltx̲w: Howe Sound Jim

Tl'ák̲tax̲anaw̓txw: longhouse

Tl'e7énk̲: big-time potlatch

Tnaxwtn Siy̓ám̓: Chief Isaac Jacobs

Ts'ets'ik̲áy̓: spring ceremony

Ts'x̲wém̓k̲sen: Gabriola Pass

Tsek̲ánchtn: First man to land at Gibsons

Tsewk̲wílem: Byron Joseph

Tsitsáyx̲emaat: Rebecca Duncan

Tsítsusm: Potlatch Creek

Tyee: Floyd Joseph

Utsám̓: a verb meaning "call witnesses"; the Witness Project, an effort of Sk̲wx̲wú7mesh members and the Wilderness Committee to protect Elaho Valley

Úxwumixw: people, generally or collectively; also refers to a community with groups of houses and inhabitants

Wápatu: Indian potato

Whonoak: Wilfred Baker Sr.

X̲aays: Transformer brothers who travelled throughout the world causing transformations

X̲álek̲'/Sek̲'yú Siy̓ám̓: Chief Ian Campbell

X̲áp'ay̓ay: red cedar

X̲ats'alánexw Siy̓ám̓: Chief August Jack Khatsahlano

X̲ay Temíxw: "sacred land"; the name for a land use plan aimed to protect fifty thousand acres of K̲w'áyk̲w'ay̓ex̲ Kw'elh7aynexw ta Sk̲wx̲wú7mesh Temíxw (Wild Spirit Places of the Squamish Nation's Land)

X̲echx̲áchu7: lakes

X̲epiyúwelh: shallow dish for dry meat or fish

X̲i7lánexw: one of the first men; also known as X̲í7nexwtn or Xí7nexwtn̓

Xwalacktun: James Harry

Xwalacktun: Rick Harry

X̲ínexwtn: another one of our First People

X̲wáy̓x̲way: "mask"; an ancient village at what is known today as Stanley Park near the Lumbermen's Arch

Xwechtáal: a serpent-slayer, the first ancestor at the village St'á7mes

Xwechtáal: Andrew "Andy" Paull, also known as X̲wepelk̲ínem

Xwelxwalítn: "white people"; also the name for bay where the Squamish met Captain George Vancouver

Xwepelk̲ínem: a powerful warrior

Xwet: Swainson's thrush

X̲wk̲wíchen: "to make a fish net or spider's web"

Xwmélch'stn: "place of rolling waters"; the village at the mouth of the Capilano River, also a village and a reserve

Xwmétskwiyam: Musqueam

Xwsa7k̲: Mount Baker; also refers to the Nooksack Indian Tribe

X̲wúk̲wem: deep dishes for soup

Xwyekw'áyak̲'in: "farthest up the river"; just north of T'ek̲w't'ak̲w'emay̓

Yáw̓ilh swáy̓wi7k̲a: bachelor

Yekw'ápsm: "upper part of the river"; a village on the Squamish River

Yelhíxw: Ashlu Creek, also an old village in the Ashlu Valley

Yéw̓yews: orcas

Yík̲wilhtax̲: Lekwiltok; refers to one or more tribes from the people today called the Kwakwaka̲'wa̲kw, who were often incorrectly labelled the "Kwakiutl people"

Yumk̲s: Dr. Rudy Reimer

Yúusnew̓as: "taking care of spirit, taking care of one another, taking care of everything around us"; an archival and land-based investigation into St. Paul's Indian Residential School

NOTES

Part One. Sḵwx̱wú7mesh Chat: We Are Squamish

p. 9 When the world was created: Sx̱áaltxw Siy̓ám̓ (Chief Louis Miranda), "Seagull, Raven, and the Daylight Box," ARC.CULM.01.0057, Squamish Nation Archives and Cultural Collections, North Vancouver, BC.

p. 10 *Our oral literature and archaeological sites:* Yumḵs (Rudy Reimer), "The Mountains and Rocks Are Forever: Lithics and Landscapes of Sḵwx̱wú7mesh Úxwumixw" (PhD dissertation, McMaster University, 2012), 198, hdl.handle.net/11375/11794.

p. 10 *We are over 4,100 people: The Squamish Nation Strategic Plan 2022–2026*, Sḵwx̱wú7mesh Úxwumixw, 2022, reports.squamish.net/wp-content/uploads/2022/08/Strategic-Plan-2022-2026_web-1.pdf.

p. 11 *You will hear variations of stories:* Reimer, "The Mountains and Rocks Are Forever."

1. Wa p'i7ḵsím̓cht Itti: We Begin Here

p. 15 *Some of us likely spent about six months:* Wilson Duff, *The Upper Stalo Indians of the Fraser River of BC* (Victoria, BC: British Columbia Provincial Museum, 1973), 26, cited in Randy Bouchard and Dorothy Kennedy, *Squamish Indian Land Use and Occupancy*, report submitted to the Squamish Nation Chiefs and Council (Victoria, BC: BC Indian Language Project, 1986), chap. 1, 15.

p. 15 *Distinct stone materials from our territory:* "Trans Mountain Expansion Project: Final Argument of Squamish Nation," January 12, 2016, Canada Energy Regulator, 16, docs2.cer-rec.gc.ca/ll-eng/llisapi.dll/fetch/2000/90464/90552/548311/956726/2392873/2449925/2451054/2905662/C319-40-2_-_Final_Argument_of_the_Squamish_Nation_%2801164829%29_-_A4X5E7.pdf?nodeid=2905007&vernum=-2.

p. 16 *"Members of the Squamish tribes:* Cited in evidence provided by Randy Bouchard and Dorothy Kennedy in Mathias et al. v. Canada, 2000 CanLII 16282 (FC).

p. 19 *Families were also likely to move between villages:* Bouchard and Kennedy, *Squamish Indian Land Use and Occupancy*, 13.

p. 19 *Anthropologists Randy Bouchard and Dorothy Kennedy wrote:* Bouchard and Kennedy, 13, 53.

p. 20 *Everything but the frames:* Squamish Lil'wat Cultural Centre, *Where Rivers, Mountains and People Meet* (Whistler, BC: Spo7ez Cultural Centre & Community Society, 2010), 136.

p. 20 *We used mat shelters regularly:* Bouchard and Kennedy, chap. 1, 15.

p. 20 *Archaeological sites within our territory:* "Trans Mountain Expansion Project," 7; Yumḵs (Rudy Reimer), "The Mountains and Rocks Are Forever: Lithics and Landscapes of Sḵwx̱wú7mesh Úxwumixw" (PhD dissertation, McMaster University, 2012), 50, 203, hdl.handle.net/11375/11794.

p. 20 *X̱ats'alánexw Siy̓ám̓ said the Sḵwx̱wú7mesh:* Wayne Suttles, Squamish fieldnotes, 1951, cited in Bouchard and Kennedy, chap. 2, 15.

p. 20 *In Howe Sound, the Sḵwx̱wú7mesh could hunt:* Bouchard and Kennedy, chap. 2.

p. 20 *Squamish harvested the plentiful elk:* Homer Barnett, Coast Salish fieldnotes, 1935–1936, University of British Columbia Special Collections, Vancouver, cited in Bouchard and Kennedy, 14; J.S. Matthews, *Conversations with Khahtsahlano: 1932–1954* (Vancouver: self-published, 1955), 37.

p. 20 *According to anthropologist Homer Barnett's work:* Bouchard and Kennedy, 396.

p. 20 *Bouchard and Kennedy analyzed mid-1800s data:* Bouchard and Kennedy, chap. 2, 13.

p. 21 *X̱ats'alánexw Siy̓ám̓ said people would reside:* Matthews, *Conversations with Khahtsahlano*, 41; Suttles, Squamish fieldnotes, and Buffalo Mathias, cited in Bouchard and Kennedy, chap. 2, 15.

p. 22 *We call Black Tusk in Whistler T'aḵt'aḵ'muy̓ín̓ tl'a in̓inyáx̱a7n:* This spelling of "Thunderbird" is from Peter Jacobs and Damara Jacobs, eds., *Sḵwx̱wú7mesh Sníchim–Xwelíten Sníchim Sḵexwts (Squamish–English Dictionary)* (Seattle: University of Washington Press and Squamish Nation Education Department, 2011); Reimer spells it differently in "The Mountains and Rocks Are Forever."

p. 22 *Our growth to attaining extensive woodworking abilities:* Richard Hebda and Rolf Mathewes, "Holocene History of Cedar and Native Indian Cultures of the North American Pacific Coast," *Science* 225, no. 4663 (1984): 711–13, doi.org/10.1126/science.225.4663.711.

p. 25 *About six thousand years ago:* Hebda and Mathewes.

p. 25 *We called Burnaby Mountain Lheḵw'lhúḵw'ay̓tn:* "Trans Mountain Expansion Project," 16.

p. 26 *Clams were steamed open:* Randy Bouchard and Dorothy Kennedy, "Utilization of Fish, Beach Foods, and Marine Mammals by the Squamish Indian People of British Columbia," 1976, ARC.CULM.06.01, Squamish Nation Archives and Cultural Collections, North Vancouver, BC.

p. 26 *Ironwood flowers and hemlock helped:* Sx̱áaltxw Siy̓ám̓ (Chief Louis Miranda), Andy Natrall, and Syex̱wáltn (Dominic Charlie), "Squamish Plant Names," 1972, ARC.CULM.0101f, Squamish Nation Archives and Cultural Collections, North Vancouver, BC.

p. 27 *Our relationship with the earth:* "Squamish Classified Word List—Revised Version," 1978, ARC.CULM.04.0133, Squamish Nation Archives and Cultural Collections, North Vancouver, BC; Jacobs and Jacobs, *Squamish–English Dictionary*.

p. 27 *We have other phrases like:* Jacobs and Jacobs, 342.

2. Na7 tkwi Kwekwín̓: In the Long Ago

p. 29 *Oral history is integral to our culture:* Yumḵs (Rudy Reimer), "The Mountains and Rocks Are Forever: Lithics and Landscapes of Sḵwx̱wú7mesh Úxwumixw" (PhD dissertation, McMaster University, 2012), 45, hdl.handle.net/11375/11794.

p. 29 *For example, in one* sx̱wex̱wiy̓ám̓: Definition from Peter Jacobs and Damara Jacobs, eds., *Sḵwx̱wú7mesh Sníchim–Xwelíten Sníchim Sḵexwts (Squamish–English Dictionary)* (Seattle: University of Washington Press and Squamish Nation Education Department, 2011).

p. 29 *Yumḵs (Dr. Rudy Reimer) suggested:* Reimer, "The Mountains and Rocks Are Forever," 196.

p. 30 *This was Hill-Tout's first impression of Melḵws:* Charles Hill-Tout, *Notes on the Cosmogony and History of the Squamish Indians of British Columbia* (Ottawa: Royal Society of Canada, 1897). All quotes in this section can be found on pages 85–88.

p. 33 By means of this fish and bird: Franz Boas records a very similar version: "Legends of the Squamish—Chief Joseph," in *Indian Legends of the North Pacific Coast of America Collected by Franz Boas*, ARC.CULM.01.0003, Squamish Nation Archives and Cultural Collections, North Vancouver, BC.

p. 34 *Syex̱wáltn told Wells about Melḵws:* Oliver Wells, *The Chilliwacks and Their Neighbors* (Vancouver: Talonbooks, 1987), 179.

p. 36 *X̱ats'alánexw Siy̓ám̓ said he did know about the big snow:* Wells, 175.

p. 36 *"This Thunderbird he come down:* Wells, 176; X̱ats'alánexw Siy̓ám̓ told the same story to amateur anthropologist Charles Hill-Tout in X̱ats'alánexw Siy̓ám̓ (Chief August Jack Khatsahlano) and SyeX̱wáltn (Dominic Charlie), "The First of the *cheek-AWK-ah-mish People," *Squamish Legends*, ed. Oliver Wells (Vancouver: C. Chamberlain and F.T. Coan, 1967).

p. 37 *According to Sx̱wálh Siy̓ám̓ (Chief Jimmy Jimmy):* Randy Bouchard and Dorothy Kennedy, *Squamish Indian Land Use and Occupancy*, report submitted to the Squamish Nation Chiefs and Council (Victoria, BC: BC Indian Language Project, 1986), chap. 1, 3; "Jimmy, Jimmy," JJ01, Squamish History Archives, Squamish Public Library, squamishlibrary.digitalcollections.ca/chief-jimmy-jimmy.

p. 37 *They noted the variety of stories:* Bouchard and Kennedy, chap. 1, 3–4.

p. 38 *Syex̱wáltn talked about a man:* Bouchard and Kennedy, chap. 1, 4.

p. 39 *The story of Sḵw'ats' (the Great Flood):* "Some Squamish Nation Historical Facts," Squamish Language (YouTube), May 17, 2021, youtube.com/watch?v=N4jugefCe7g.

p. 39 *Here is how Sx̱áaltxw Siy̓ám̓ told the story:* Sx̱áaltxw Siy̓ám̓ (Chief Louis Miranda), *Squamish Legends: As Told by Louis Miranda Typed by Linda Rivers for Squamish Nation Education 1985* (Sḵwx̱wú7mesh Sníchim, 1994), 99–103.

p. 42 *It would take about seven thousand years:* Reimer, "The Mountains and Rocks Are Forever," 47.

p. 42 *Anthropologist Wayne Suttles theorized that there was little worship:* Wayne Suttles, "Plateau Prophet Dance," *Coast Salish Essays* (Vancouver: Talonbooks, 1987), loc. 3374–75 of 7573, ebook.

p. 44 *It's a good example of how a storyteller:* Different versions of the story told by the same two men are also in *Squamish Legends* (by X̱ats'alánexw Siy̓ám̓ and Syex̱wáltn, ed. Oliver Wells) and *The Chilliwacks and Their Neighbors* (Oliver Wells).

p. 47 *Sx̱áaltxw Siy̓ám̓ said the people drifted:* Miranda, 39; X̱ats'alánexw Siy̓ám̓ (Chief August Jack Khatsahlano) also said there are "many" mask stories. See Wells, *The Chilliwacks and Their Neighbors*, 177.

p. 47 *He said there were three couples:* Miranda, 33.

p. 47 *In some tellings there are three brothers called X̱aays:* Khatsahlano and Charlie, *Squamish Legends*.

p. 47 The Transformers paddled along: Sx̱áaltxw Siy̓ám̓ (Chief Louis Miranda), "X̱áays (Creator)," 1974, ARC.CULM.01.0048, Squamish Nation Archives and Cultural Collections, North Vancouver, BC; Miranda, "The Legend of Siwash Rock," ARC.CULM.01.0051, Squamish Nation Archives and Cultural Collections, North Vancouver, BC.

p. 48 *The Sḵwx̱wú7mesh are taught not to point:* "Siy̓am̓ Smánit: The Stawamus Chief," Squamish Lil'wat Cultural Centre, slcc.ca/siyam-smanit-stawamus-chief.

p. 48 *"They're hard to spot:* Drew Copeland, "Siy̓ám̓ Smánit: Stories of the Chief," *Squamish Chief*, September 24, 2015, squamishchief.com/local-arts/siyam-smanit-stories-of-the-chief-3344213.

3. Úxwumixw: Squamish Society and Social Structure

p. 51 *According to anthropologist Wayne Suttles:* Randy Bouchard and Dorothy Kennedy, *Squamish Indian Land Use and Occupancy*, report submitted to the Squamish Nation Chiefs and Council (Victoria, BC: BC Indian Language Project, 1986), chap. 1, 5; Wayne Suttles, "Private Knowledge, Morality, and Social Classes among the Coast Salish," *Coast Salish Essays* (Vancouver: Talonbooks, 1987); Charles Hill-Tout, "Notes on the Sk-qo'mic of British Columbia, a Branch of the Great Salish Stock of British Columbia," *70th Report of the British Association for the Advancement of Science for 1900*, Appendix II (London: 1900), 475.

p. 51 *These classes were not "absolutely rigid":* Bouchard and Kennedy, *Squamish Indian Land Use and Occupancy*, chap. 1, 5; Hill-Tout, 475.

p. 52 *People adhered to a strict moral code:* Bouchard and Kennedy, chap. 1, 5, 12.

p. 52 *The Sḵwx̱wú7mesh were exogamous:* Hill-Tout, "Notes on the Sk-qo'mic of British Columbia," 477; Bouchard and Kennedy, 20.

p. 52 *Jimmy Frank said a marriage:* Bouchard and Kennedy, 20.

p. 52 Nch'áy̓uw̓am *(descendants of one head/headman):* Bouchard and Kennedy, 10.

p. 52 *Longhouses were large:* For example, at Seymour and Stanley Park the longhouses were two hundred feet long. J.S. Matthews, *Conversations with Khahtsahlano: 1932–1954* (Vancouver: self-published, 1955), 279.

p. 52 *Long planks were held in place:* Wayne Suttles, "Productivity and Its Constraints: A Coast Salish Case," *Coast Salish Essays* (Vancouver: Talonbooks, 1987), loc. 2688 of 7573, ebook.

p. 52 *If a man had more than one wife:* Bouchard and Kennedy, chap. 1, 10.

p. 53 *One of Charles Hill-Tout's more comical observations:* Hill-Tout, 477.

p. 53 *"Ties of marriage linked one village:* Bouchard and Kennedy, chap. 1, 11.

p. 53 *"The Squamish terms for blood kin:* Bouchard and Kennedy, chap. 1, 11.

p. 56 *A siy̓ám̓ was highly respected:* Bouchard and Kennedy, 7.

p. 56 *He said, "Each man boss in his own family:* Matthews, *Conversations with Khahtsahlano*, 51.

p. 56 *But if one retained their traditional ways:* Bouchard and Kennedy, 8.

p. 56 *Those who were considered chiefs:* Bouchard and Kennedy, 9.

p. 56 *But after that:* Hill-Tout, 476.

p. 57 *This is demonstrated in the story:* Sx̱áaltxw Siy̓ám̓ (Chief Louis Miranda), "The Deer Who Was a Wolf Slave," 1978, ARC.CULM.01.0012, Squamish Nation Archives and Cultural Collections, North Vancouver, BC.

p. 57 *Hill-Tout described there being a "supreme siam":* Hill-Tout, 476.

p. 57 *He said Hill-Tout was wrong:* Matthews, 34.

p. 57 *"Respect your elders:* Sx̱áaltxw Siy̓ám̓ (Chief Louis Miranda), "Referring Mostly to a Boy's Upbringing but It Also Includes a Girl's," ARC.CULM.01.0001, Squamish Nation Archives and Cultural Collections, North Vancouver, BC, 2.

p. 58 *"It was the duty of the more responsible:* J.S. Matthews, *Early Vancouver*, vol. 2, rev. ed. (1933; repr., Vancouver: City of Vancouver, 2011), 56, archives.vancouver.ca/projects/EarlyVan/SearchEarlyVan/Vol2pdf/MatthewsEarlyVancouverVol2_ArrivalOfCaptainVancouver.pdf.

p. 60 *They could choose to focus on saltwater hunting:* Miranda, 9.

p. 60 *Children were taught how:* Miranda, 11–12.

p. 60 *The outer rough part of the bark:* Miranda, 11.

p. 62 *Upper-class men:* Hill-Tout, 477.

p. 62 *According to Sx̱áaltxw Siy̓ám̓, if a couple:* Sx̱áaltxw Siy̓ám̓ (Chief Louis Miranda), "The Life Cycle of the Squamish People: Say̓xw Sx̱áaltxw t Siy̓ám̓—The Words of the Late Chief Louis Miranda," unpublished, n.d., Squamish Nation Archives and Cultural Collections, North Vancouver, BC.

p. 62 *For the duration of the marriage:* Bouchard and Kennedy, chap. 1, 13.

p. 62 *Suttles argued that exogamous marriage:* Bouchard and Kennedy, chap. 1, 13.

p. 63 *Some animals were never eaten:* "Squamish Indian People: Guide," prepared for North Vancouver School Board, 1975, 7, 34, BC Native Language Project.

p. 63 *To cook the fish:* Randy Bouchard and Dorothy Kennedy, "Utilization of Fish, Beach Foods, and Marine Mammals by the Squamish Indian People of British Columbia," 1976, ARC.CULM.06.01, Squamish Nation Archives and Cultural Collections, North Vancouver, BC, 43, 46, 94.

p. 63 *Once dried, the* sts'úḵw'i7: Bouchard and Kennedy, "Utilization of Fish, Beach Foods, and Marine Mammals," 53.
p. 63 *Smoked and dried salmon:* Miranda, "The Life Cycle of the Squamish People," 19.
p. 63 *A fish would be woven:* Squamish Lil'wat Cultural Centre, *Where Rivers, Mountains and People Meet* (Whistler, BC: Spo7ez Cultural Centre & Community Society, 2010), 61.
p. 63 *The fish was stored in boxes:* Miranda, "The Life Cycle of the Squamish People," 20.
p. 63 *A whole morning could be spent:* Miranda, 20.
p. 65 *When the eggs were ready to be eaten:* Bouchard and Kennedy, "Utilization of Fish, Beach Foods, and Marine Mammals," 55.
p. 65 *People smoked and prepared food:* Bouchard and Kennedy, *Squamish Indian Land Use and Occupancy*, chap. 2, 18.
p. 65 *Some people had some simple tattooing:* Charles Hill-Tout, *The Squamish and the Lillooet*, vol. 2 of *The Salish People: The Local Contribution of Charles Hill-Tout*, ed. Ralph Maud (Vancouver: Talonbooks, 1978), 45.
p. 65 *Crushed mica gave that paint:* Hill-Tout, 45; Leslie H. Tepper, Chepx̱ímiya Siỷám̓ (Chief Janice George), and Skwetsímeltxw (Willard "Buddy" Joseph), *Salish Blankets: Robes of Protection and Transformation, Symbols of Wealth* (Lincoln, NE: University of Nebraska, 2017), 85.
p. 66 *The box is laid down:* Miranda, "The Life Cycle of the Squamish People," 38; Hill-Tout, *The Squamish and the Lillooet*, 31; Suttles, "Productivity and Its Constraints," loc. 2833; as well, "Documented accounts of Coast Salish burial practices during the ethnographic and ethnohistorical period report the use of baskets, boxes, and canoes to inter the remains of single or multiple persons. Mortuary containers were suspended from trees at heights of up to four meters," Dave Hall and Chris Springer, "Archaeological Overview Assessment (AOA) of Proposed Water Storage Facility Replacements in the Village of Lions Bay," Arrowstone Archaeological Research and Consulting Ltd., 2017, lionsbay.ca/sites/2/files/docs/related/aoa_lions_bay_2017-11-23.pdf.
p. 66 *"[He] tells of how his father:* Matthews, *Conversations with Khahtsahlano*, 123.
p. 67 *The food was then burned:* Miranda, "The Life Cycle of the Squamish People"; Hill-Tout, *The Squamish and the Lillooet*, 32.
p. 67 *The family would be reminded:* Hill-Tout, 33.

4. Wa lhtim̓ácht: Lifeways

p. 70 *"Our longhouse is very important:* Squamish Lil'wat Cultural Centre, *Where Rivers, Mountains and People Meet* (Whistler, BC: Spo7ez Cultural Centre & Community Society, 2010), 136.
p. 70 *Sx̱áaltxw Siỷám̓ (Chief Louis Miranda) recalled:* Sx̱áaltxw Siỷám̓ (Chief Louis Miranda), "Referring Mostly to a Boy's Upbringing but It Also Includes a Girl's," ARC.CULM.01.0001, Squamish Nation Archives and Cultural Collections, North Vancouver, BC, 3.
p. 70 *In the spring ceremony* ts'ets'iḵáỷ: Miranda, 3; also in Wayne Suttles, "The Plateau Prophet Dance among the Coast Salish," *Coast Salish Essays* (Vancouver: Talonbooks, 1987), loc. 3767 of 7573, ebook.
p. 70 *In the morning, the chief saw:* Sḵáaltxw Siỷám̓ (Chief Louis Miranda), "Raven Goes to Look for a Wife," 1974, ARC.CULM.01.0016, Squamish Nation Archives and Cultural Collections, North Vancouver, BC.
p. 73 *The circle often represents unity:* Gerald Bruce Subiyay Miller and D. Michael CHiXapkaid Pavel, "Traditional Teachings about Coast Salish Art," in *S'abadeb/The Gifts: Pacific Coast Salish Art*, ed. Barbara Brotherton (Vancouver: Douglas & McIntyre, 2008), 24.
p. 73 *He argued that early settlers:* Suttles, "The Recognition of Coast Salish Art," 50, 52.
p. 73 *Much of Coast Salish art was carved:* Michael Kew and Susan Point, "A Dialogue about Coast Salish Aesthetics," in Brotherton, *S'abadeb/The Gifts*, 143.

p. 73 *Bark shredder tools, bowls, house posts:* Kew and Point, 154–57.
p. 73 *Mat creasers, used to crimp:* Kew and Point, 163–65.
p. 74 *"They are protective garments:* Leslie H. Tepper, Chepx̱ímiya Siỷám̓ (Chief Janice George), and Skwetsímeltxw (Willard "Buddy" Joseph), *Salish Blankets: Robes of Protection and Transformation, Symbols of Wealth* (Lincoln, NE: University of Nebraska, 2017), xiii.
p. 74 *These textiles symbolically separate:* Tepper et al., 57.
p. 74 *Mountain goat hair was used:* Tepper et al., 6–7.
p. 74 *Nettle and hemp provided materials:* Paula Gustafson, *Salish Weaving* (Vancouver: Douglas & McIntyre, 1980), 72.
p. 74 *Cattail was woven into sleeping mats:* Oliver Wells, *Salish Weaving: Primitive and Modern* (Sardis, BC: self-published, 1969).
p. 74 *Fern could act as a natural black dye:* Tepper et al., *Salish Blankets*, 14.
p. 74 *Beating diatomaceous earth into the fibres:* Tepper et al., 85; Wells, *Salish Weaving*, 10.
p. 74 *Patterns are most often made up of squares:* Tepper et al., 16, 83, 152.
p. 75 *Woven strips of fabric:* Tepper et al., 23; J.S. Matthews, *Conversations with Khahtsahlano: 1932–1954* (Vancouver: self-published, 1955), 44.
p. 75 *Today, weavers continue to carry responsibility:* Tepper et al., 55, 57.
p. 76 *For cedar weaving:* Tepper et al., 8.
p. 76 *For apparel, cedar bark:* Gustafson, *Salish Weaving*.
p. 76 *Charles Hill-Tout said he was told:* Charles Hill-Tout, "Notes on the Sk-qo'mic of British Columbia, a Branch of the Great Salish Stock of British Columbia," *70th Report of the British Association for the Advancement of Science for 1900*, Appendix II (London: 1900), 476.
p. 76 *We relied on cedar dugout canoes:* Squamish Lil'wat Cultural Centre, *Where Rivers, Mountains and People Meet*, 40.
p. 76 *The other half remained in the ground:* Squamish Lil'wat Cultural Centre, 46.
p. 77 *"We would travel by canoe:* Squamish Lil'wat Cultural Centre.

5. Swa7ám̓: Ancestors

p. 79 *The one exception was the "Little Ice Age":* Javier Barbuzano, "The Little Ice Age Wasn't Global, but Current Climate Change Is," *Eos*, July 24, 2019, eos.org/articles/the-little-ice-age-wasnt-global-but-current-climate-change-is.
p. 81 *Analysis of these lithics in Burrard Inlet:* Yumḵs (Rudy Reimer), "The Mountains and Rocks Are Forever: Lithics and Landscapes of Sḵwx̱wú7mesh Úxwumixw" (PhD dissertation, McMaster University, 2012), 172, hdl.handle.net/11375/11794.
p. 81 *The site's high elevation:* Andrew Latimer, communication with author, February 2023, citing Reimer, "The Mountains and Rocks Are Forever," 259.
p. 82 *The Locarno Archaeological Management Plan:* Tsleil-Waututh Nation, "Tsleil-Waututh Nation Annual Report 2019–2020," 2020, twnation.ca/wp-content/uploads/2020/12/Final-TWN-Annual-Report-2019-2020-1.pdf.
p. 84 *Almost five thousand years later:* Latimer, citing ARCAS Consulting Archaeologists Ltd., "Archaeological Investigations Carried Out in Sḵwx̱wú7mesh (Traditional Territory). Under Park Use Permit #2535," report submitted to Squamish Nation Chiefs and Council, 1999, and DkRs-6 Archaeology Site Inventory Form.
p. 85 *An archaeological site nearby:* Reimer, 263.
p. 85 *This site, above the Squamish River:* Latimer, communication with author, citing Reimer, 70–71, and EaRu-2 Archaeology Site Inventory Form.
p. 85 *People from P'uỷám̓ were considered:* Latimer.

p. 85 *X̱wáy̓x̱way means "mask":* Reimer, 183, 231.

p. 85 *There was a large village here:* J.S. Matthews, *Conversations with Khahtsahlano: 1932–1954* (Vancouver: self-published, 1955), 31.

p. 85 *The highly spiritual and significant masks:* Reimer, 239.

p. 86 *In the past few years:* Latimer, communication with author.

p. 86 *The X̱aays took his spear:* Reimer, 71, 259.

p. 87 *In one* syets *(true story):* Latimer, communication with author, citing ARCAS, "Archaeological Investigations Carried Out in Sḵwx̱wú7mesh (Traditional Territory)," Reimer, 246, and DjRt-5 Archaeology Site Inventory Form.

p. 87 *Our stories include giants:* Sx̱áaltxw Siy̓ám̓ (Chief Louis Miranda), *Squamish Legends: As Told by Louis Miranda Typed by Linda Rivers for Squamish Nation Education 1985* (Sḵwx̱wú7mesh Sníchim, 1994).

p. 87 *Our ancestors called on animals:* Story from Miranda, *Squamish Legends*; spelling from Peter Jacobs and Damara Jacobs, eds., *Sḵwx̱wú7mesh Sníchim–Xwelíten Sníchim Sḵexwts (Squamish–English Dictionary)* (Seattle: University of Washington Press and Squamish Nation Education Department, 2011).

Part Two. Síiy̓am̓, Síiyay̓, Síiyuxwa7, Mén̓men: Chiefs, Friends, Elders, Children

p. 91 *Distinct stone materials from our territory:* "Trans Mountain Expansion Project: Final Argument of Squamish Nation," January 12, 2016, Canada Energy Regulator, 16. docs2.cer-rec.gc.ca/ll-eng/llisapi.dll/fetch/2000/90464/90552/548311/956726/2392873/2449925/2451054/2905662/C319-40-2_-_Final_Argument_of_the_Squamish_Nation_%2801164829%29_-_A4X5E7.pdf?nodeid=2905007&vernum=-2.

p. 91 *Stone artifacts from as far as Oregon:* Yumḵs (Rudy Reimer), communication with author, February 2023.

p. 91 *On the one hand, boundaries were:* Randy Bouchard and Dorothy Kennedy, *Squamish Indian Land Use and Occupancy*, report submitted to the Squamish Nation Chiefs and Council (Victoria, BC: BC Indian Language Project, 1986), chap. 2, 49.

p. 92 *For generations, many of the Sḵwx̱wú7mesh:* Squamish Lil'wat Cultural Centre, *Where Rivers, Mountains and People Meet* (Whistler, BC: Spo7ez Cultural Centre & Community Society, 2010), 136.

p. 92 *Oral history and academic research indicate:* Mathias et al. v. Canada et al. (2001) 207 FTR 1 (TD), 37; J.S. Matthews, *Conversations with Khahtsahlano: 1932–1954* (Vancouver: self-published, 1955), 40, 76–77; "Trans Mountain Expansion Project," 7.

p. 92 *Archaeological sites suggest ten thousand years:* "Trans Mountain Expansion Project," 7; Yumḵs (Rudy Reimer), "The Mountains and Rocks Are Forever: Lithics and Landscapes of Sḵwx̱wú7mesh Úxwumixw" (PhD dissertation, McMaster University, 2012), 50, hdl.handle.net/11375/11794.

p. 92 *"In years of resource shortage:* Also, "Coast Salish families protected themselves from sporadic and unpredictable shortages in their food supply, and from other groups who may have coveted these same resources, by forming networks … and through the act of marriage, patterned exchange linked such groups residing in different communities where other resources might be available," Wayne Suttles, cited in Dorothy Kennedy, "Quantifying 'Two Sides of a Coin': A Statistical Examination of the Central Coast Salish Social Network," *BC Studies* 153 (2007): 3–34, doi.org/10.14288/bcs.v0i153.657.

p. 93 *This was exemplified in one exchange:* Matthews, *Conversations with Khahtsahlano*, 167.

6. Telyésh iy Sútich: South and North

p. 95 *This is where the X̲aays (Transformer brothers) landed:* Squamish Atlas, squamishatlas.com; Randy Bouchard and Dorothy Kennedy, *Squamish Indian Land Use and Occupancy*, report submitted to the Squamish Nation Chiefs and Council (Victoria, BC: BC Indian Language Project, 1986), "Place Names," 1–3.

p. 95 *He said K̲iyáplánexw Siỷám̓ was leader:* Suttles, "Stories from James Point," 1963, cited in Bouchard and Kennedy, chap. 2, 21; Jesse Morin, "Tsleil-Waututh Nation's History, Culture, and Aboriginal Interests in Eastern Burrard Inlet [Redacted Version]," report prepared for Gowling Lafleur Henderson LLP, 2015, 98, twnsacredtrust.ca/wp-content/uploads/2015/05/Morin-Expert-Report-PUBLIC-VERSION-sm.pdf.

p. 95 *It is believed the Sel̓íl̓witulh:* Morin, "Tsleil-Waututh Nation's History," 67–68.

p. 96 *"Musqueam cannot speak to Squamish:* Charles Hill-Tout, *The Mainland Halkomelem*, vol. 3 of *The Salish People: The Local Contribution of Charles Hill-Tout*, ed. Ralph Maud (Vancouver: Talonbooks, 1978), 11.

p. 96 *The ones who speak Sk̲'emíñem:* Bouchard and Kennedy, *Squamish Indian Land Use and Occupancy*, 116; Sx̲áaltxw Siỷám̓ (Chief Louis Miranda), "Say-noth-kay: The Two-Headed Serpent," ARC.CULM.0055, Squamish Nation Archives and Cultural Collections, North Vancouver, BC; Sx̲áaltxw Siỷám̓ (Chief Louis Miranda) and Dorothy Kennedy, "The Transformers," ed. Randy Bouchard, 1972, ARC.CULM.0004b, Squamish Nation Archives and Cultural Collections, North Vancouver, BC.

p. 96 *Our stories place Sínulhk̲aỷ:* Howe Sound: X̲áts'alánexw Siỷám̓ (Chief August Jack Khatsahlano) in Oliver Wells, *The Chilliwacks and Their Neighbors* (Vancouver: Talonbooks, 1987), 144, and Miranda, "Say-noth-kay"; Burrard Inlet: Syex̲wáltn (Dominic Charlie) in Wells, 183–84; Fraser River: Bouchard and Kennedy, chap. 2, 37; further upriver: Stó:lō Heritage Trust, *A Stó:lō Coast Salish Historical Atlas* (Vancouver: Douglas & McIntyre, 2001), 6.

p. 96 *The area now known as Coal Harbour:* Bouchard and Kennedy, chap. 2, 18, 25, 216.

p. 96 *Multiple sources have also said:* Bouchard and Kennedy, 28–29, 230.

p. 96 *Yumk̲s believes this is likely associated:* Yumk̲s (Rudy Reimer), "The Mountains and Rocks Are Forever: Lithics and Landscapes of Sk̲wx̲wú7mesh Úxwumixw" (PhD dissertation, McMaster University, 2012), 168, hdl.handle.net/11375/11794.

p. 97 *Buffalo Mathias also said:* Bouchard and Kennedy, chap. 2, 16.

p. 97 *X̲áts'alánexw Siỷám̓ (Chief August Jack Khatsahlano) said:* J.S. Matthews, *Conversations with Khahtsahlano: 1932–1954* (Vancouver: self-published, 1955), n140.

p. 97 *K̲iyáplánexw Siỷám̓ is said to have been:* Matthews, 108, 208; J.S. Matthews, *Early Vancouver*, vol. 2, rev. ed. (1933; repr., Vancouver: City of Vancouver, 2011), 55, archives.vancouver.ca/projects/EarlyVan/SearchEarlyVan/Vol2pdf/MatthewsEarlyVancouverVol2_TheNameCapilano.pdf.

p. 97 *In her research, Dorothy Kennedy said:* Dorothy Kennedy, "Quantifying 'Two Sides of a Coin': A Statistical Examination of the Central Coast Salish Social Network," BC *Studies* 153 (2007): 3–34, doi.org/10.14288/bcs.v0i153.657: "allied families," 23; "prestige," 7.

p. 97 The big potlatch at Jericho was before my time: Matthews, *Conversations with Khahtsahlano*, 42.

p. 98 *Randy Bouchard and Dorothy Kennedy noted:* Bouchard and Kennedy, chap. 2, 41.

p. 98 *It is said that when Squamish residents:* Dorothy Kennedy, "Threads to the Past: The Construction and Transformation of Kinship in the Coast Salish Social Network" (PhD thesis, University of Oxford, 2000), 60, ora.ox.ac.uk/objects/uuid:56bba9a5-d44f-4146-ae65-1451755dee51/files/m7db80fb8d57395c4d7d80e12519fa80e.

p. 98 *This name is possibly derived:* Squamish Atlas, squamishatlas.com.

p. 99 *Xwechtáal (Andy Paull) said Selílwitulh referred:* Bouchard and Kennedy, *Squamish Indian Land Use and Occupancy*, "Place Names," 124.

p. 99 *According to the* Land Use and Occupancy *report:* Bouchard and Kennedy, 42.

p. 99 *Across the water from present-day Deep Cove:* Bouchard and Kennedy, "Place Names," 113–14, 130.

p. 99 *In more recent times:* Bouchard and Kennedy, "Place Names," 149.

p. 99 *As Bouchard and Kennedy described:* Bouchard and Kennedy, chap. 2, 45.

p. 99 *There were about fifty-six kilometres:* Trefor Smith, *Our Stories Are Written on the Land: A Brief History of the Upper St'át'imc 1800–1940* (Lillooet, BC: Upper St'át'imc Language, Culture and Education Society, 1998), 13.

p. 100 *Charlie Mack from Lúx̱wels:* Randy Bouchard and Dorothy Kennedy, eds., *Lillooet Stories* (Victoria, BC: Provincial Archives of British Columbia, 1977), 17, cited in Bouchard and Kennedy, *Squamish Indian Land Use and Occupancy*, chap. 2, 48.

p. 100 *Similarly, the Sḵwx̱wú7mesh have a story:* Bouchard and Kennedy, *Squamish Indian Land Use and Occupancy*, 262–63, 307–19; Charles Hill-Tout, *The Squamish and the Lillooet*, vol. 2 of *The Salish People: The Local Contribution of Charles Hill-Tout*, ed. Ralph Maud (Vancouver: Talonbooks, 1978), 85–90.

p. 100 *According to X̱áts'alánexw Siỷám̓:* Matthews, *Conversations with Khahtsahlano*, 428.

p. 100 *In another version, the X̱aays asked:* Bouchard and Kennedy, *Squamish Indian Land Use and Occupancy*, 262–63.

p. 100 *Sx̱áaltxw Siỷám̓ said that, in revenge:* Bouchard and Kennedy, 335.

p. 100 *According to oral history:* Squamish Lil'wat Cultural Centre, *Where Rivers, Mountains and People Meet* (Whistler, BC: Spo7ez Cultural Centre & Community Society, 2010), 6.

p. 102 *The survivors were sent home:* "History," Squamish Lil'wat Cultural Centre, slcc.ca/history.

p. 102 *In stories by Squamish, the Yíḵwilhtax̱:* Wayne Suttles, "Central Coast Salish," in *Northwest Coast*, vol. 7 of *Handbook of North American Indians*, ed. Wayne Suttles (Washington, DC: Smithsonian Institute, 1990), 457; Kennedy, "Threads to the Past," 212. Raiders sometimes targeted individual houses within villages. See Wayne Suttles, Squamish fieldnotes, 1951, 323, cited in Bouchard and Kennedy; Homer Barnett, *The Coast Salish of British Columbia* (Eugene, OR: University of Oregon Monographs, Studies in Anthropology 4, 1955), 267–71, cited in Bouchard and Kennedy.

p. 102 *"It is impossible to describe their continual alarm:* Morag Maclachlan, ed., *The Fort Langley Journals, 1827–30* (Vancouver: UBC Press, 1999), 101.

p. 102 *"It is evident that much:* Matthews, *Conversations with Khahtsahlano*, 68.

p. 103 *In Bouchard and Kennedy's research:* Bouchard and Kennedy, 14, 215.

p. 103 It is told that the [Squamish] scouts*:* Hill-Tout, *The Squamish and the Lillooet*, 50.

p. 103 *Buffalo Mathias told a similar version:* Bouchard and Kennedy, 230.

p. 103 *Hill-Tout also recorded an incident:* Hill-Tout, 49; Suttles, "Stories from James Point," 1963, cited in Bouchard and Kennedy, chap. 2, 21; Bouchard and Kennedy, 24, 37; Kennedy, "Quantifying 'Two Sides of a Coin.'"

p. 104 *X̱áts'alánexw Siỷám̓ told J.S. Matthews:* Matthews, *Conversations with Khahtsahlano*, 429.

p. 104 *Andy Natrall and George Moody:* Bouchard and Kennedy, "Place Names."

p. 104 *According to the oral history:* Bouchard and Kennedy, 294–96.

p. 104 *Sx̱áaltxw Siỷám̓ told a story:* Bouchard and Kennedy, 21; Sx̱áaltxw Siỷám̓ (Chief Louis Miranda), "Xwepelḵinem," ARC.CULM.0004a, Squamish Nation Archives and Cultural Collections, North Vancouver, BC.

p. 104 *"[Háx̱sten is] my wife's grandmother:* Matthews, *Conversations with Khahtsahlano*, 186.

p. 106 *"Pítsemek, half-brother to 'Old Chief' Capilano:* Matthews, *Early Vancouver*, 59, archives .vancouver.ca/projects/EarlyVan/SearchEarlyVan/Vol2pdf/MatthewsEarlyVancouverVol2_ConversationWithAndrewPaull.pdf.

p. 106 *They went to Tsítsusm:* Bouchard and Kennedy, "Place Names," 296.

p. 106 *The Skwxwú7mesh also tell stories:* Peter Jacobs and Damara Jacobs, eds., *Skwxwú7mesh Sníchim–Xwelíten Sníchim Skexwts (Squamish–English Dictionary)* (Seattle: University of Washington Press and Squamish Nation Education Department, 2011); Bouchard and Kennedy, "Place Names," 208, 398.

p. 106 *Sxwálh Siýám̓ (Chief Jimmy Jimmy) was said:* "Editorial: Look Back to See Ahead, Squamish," *Squamish Chief*, September 24, 2020, squamishchief.com/opinion/editorial-look-back-to-see-ahead-squamish-3351858; Al Price, "Pioneers Should Be Honored Before Environmentalists," *The Chief*, July 8, 1997, squamishlibrary.digitalcollections.ca/uploads/r/squamish-public-library/2/1/21792/19970708_The_Chief_Squamish_B_C.pdf; Squamish Centennial Committee, *A Centennial Commentary upon the Early Days of Squamish, British Columbia*, 1958, squamishlibrary.digitalcollections.ca/uploads/r/squamish-public-library/3/7/37649/centennial_history_complete.pdf.

p. 108 The Squamish had fierce enemies: Tawx'sin Yexwulla/Púlxtn (Aaron Nelson-Moody) and Glenn George, *People of the Land: Legends of the Four Host First Nations: Lil'wat, Musqueam, Squamish, Tsleil-Waututh* (Penticton, BC: Theytus Books, 2009), 81–90. Excerpt reproduced with permission.

7. Teltíwet iy Telétsnech: West and East

p. 113 *They are another Coast Salish group:* "Language," Shíshálh Nation, shishalh.com/culture-language/sechelt-language.

p. 113 *He told Wayne Suttles:* Randy Bouchard and Dorothy Kennedy, *Squamish Indian Land Use and Occupancy*, report submitted to the Squamish Nation Chiefs and Council (Victoria, BC: BC Indian Language Project, 1986), 274n14.

p. 113 *"Schen̓k, that's Gibsons Landing:* J.S. Matthews, *Conversations with Khahtsahlano: 1932–1954* (Vancouver: self-published, 1955), 90.

p. 114 *The research also showed:* Bouchard and Kennedy, *Squamish Indian Land Use and Occupancy*, 20.

p. 114 *"Squamish go seal hunting in canoe:* Matthews, *Conversations with Khahtsahlano*, 63.

p. 114 *According to Bouchard and Kennedy's research:* Bouchard and Kennedy, 20–21.

p. 115 *This is where we would interact:* Spelling of "Téytkin" from Peter Jacobs and Damara Jacobs, eds., *Skwxwú7mesh Sníchim–Xwelíten Sníchim Skexwts (Squamish–English Dictionary)* (Seattle: University of Washington Press and Squamish Nation Education Department, 2011).

p. 115 *Sockeye was the central resource:* Wayne Suttles, "Affinal Ties, Subsistence, and Prestige among the Coast Salish," *Coast Salish Essays* (Vancouver: Talonbooks, 1987), loc. 589 of 7573, ebook; Bouchard and Kennedy, chap. 1, 11; Wayne Suttles, "The Early Diffusion of the Potato among the Coast Salish," *Southwestern Journal of Anthropology* 7 (1951): 272–88, cited in Bouchard and Kennedy.

p. 115 *Xats'alánexw Siýám̓ (Chief August Jack Khatsahlano) confirmed:* Matthews, *Conversations with Khahtsahlano*, 102.

p. 115 *Some research suggests visiting groups:* Yumks (Rudy Reimer), "The Mountains and Rocks Are Forever: Lithics and Landscapes of Skwxwú7mesh Úxwumixw" (PhD dissertation, McMaster University, 2012), 168–69, hdl.handle.net/11375/11794.

p. 115 *They are four bear children:* Stó:lō Heritage Trust, *A Stó:lō Coast Salish Historical Atlas* (Vancouver: Douglas & McIntyre, 2001), 6.

p. 115 *Those who spoke Téytkin:* Stó:lō Heritage Trust, 6.

p. 116 *In the* Fort Langley Journals *in 1829:* Morag Maclachlan, ed., *The Fort Langley Journals, 1827–30* (Vancouver: UBC Press, 1999), 187.

p. 116 *There was a trail:* Bouchard and Kennedy, 111.

p. 116 *By the early 1860s:* George Gibbs, *Map of Lower Fraser*, International Boundary Commission, RG 76, Series 68, folder 1, map 1 (Washington, DC: National Archives of the United States, 1858), cited in Bouchard and Kennedy, chap. 2, 41.

p. 116 *"A show of force:* Maclachlan, *The Fort Langley Journals*, 202.

p. 117 *Our Great Flood story:* X̱áts'alánexw Siỷám̓ (Chief August Jack Khatsahlano) interviewed in Oliver Wells, *The Chilliwacks and Their Neighbors* (Vancouver: Talonbooks, 1987), 141; Dorothy Kennedy, "Threads to the Past: The Construction and Transformation of Kinship in the Coast Salish Social Network" (PhD thesis, University of Oxford, 2000), 2, ora.ox.ac.uk/objects/uuid:56bba9a5-d44f-4146-ae65-1451755dee51/files/m7db80fb8d57395c4d7d80e12519fa80e; Bouchard and Kennedy, 371.

p. 117 *We are connected through our oral histories:* Wayne Suttles, "Productivity and Its Constraints: A Coast Salish Case," *Coast Salish Essays* (Vancouver: Talonbooks, 1987); Claude Lévi-Strauss, *The Way of the Masks* (Seattle: University of Washington Press, 1988), 49; Bouchard and Kennedy, 28.

p. 117 *The ancient relationships continue:* Ian Campbell, "Traditional Knowledge in a Modern Context: Squamish, Musqueam, and Tsleil-Waututh Collaboration in Land Development" (master's thesis, Simon Fraser University, 2015), citeseerx.ist.psu.edu/document?repid=rep1&type=pdf&doi=1c58297eb902b17533bbfc305e4e8a2630fc7069.

Part Three. Sḵwx̱wú7mesh iỷ Xwelítn: The Squamish and the Europeans

p. 121 *Melḵws told Charles Hill-Tout about a sickness:* Charles Hill-Tout, *Notes on the Cosmogony and History of the Squamish Indians of British Columbia* (Ottawa: Royal Society of Canada, 1897), 88.

p. 121 *A Katzie Elder named Old Pierre:* Cole Harris, *The Resettlement of British Columbia: Essays on Colonialism and Geographical Change* (Vancouver: UBC Press, 1997), 8.

p. 121 *European goods, and even word:* Sean Wilkinson, "Missionization and Sḵwx̱wú7mesh Political Economy, 1864–1923" (master's thesis, Simon Fraser University, 2013), 48, summit.sfu.ca/_flysystem/fedora/sfu_migrate/12683/etd7664_swilkinson.pdf.

p. 121 *Historians believe disease had impacted:* Cole Harris, "Voices of Disaster: Smallpox around the Strait of Georgia in 1782," *Ethnohistory* 41, no. 4 (1994): 606.

p. 121 *The disease hit the Seli̓lwitulh:* "Our Story," Tsleil-Waututh Nation, twnation.ca/our-story.

p. 121 *This great loss led to closer ties:* Jesse Morin, "Tsleil-Waututh Nation's History, Culture and Aboriginal Interests in Eastern Burrard Inlet [Redacted Version]," pt. 2, vol. 2 of *Tsleil-Waututh Nation's Record of Written Evidence*, Gowling Lafleur Henderson LLP, 2015, para. 506; Mathias et al. v. Canada (2001) FCT 480 (CanLII), para. 10.

p. 122 *Experts have estimated:* Morin, "Tsleil-Waututh Nation's History."

p. 122 *According to Melḵws:* Hill-Tout, *Notes on the Cosmogony and History of the Squamish Indians of British Columbia*, 88.

p. 122 *Geography historian Cole Harris:* Harris, "Voices of Disaster."

8. S7a7ú7 ya Tl'iḵ ta Xwelítn: The Arrival of the First Whiteman

p. 125 *They also mapped Sḵwx̱wú7mesh homes:* Randy Bouchard and Dorothy Kennedy, *Squamish Indian Land Use and Occupancy*, report submitted to the Squamish Nation Chiefs and Council (Victoria, BC: BC Indian Language Project, 1986), chap. 1, 5–7.

p. 125 *J.S. Matthews asked X̱áts'alánexw Siỷám̓:* J.S. Matthews, *Conversations with Khahtsahlano: 1932–1954* (Vancouver: self-published, 1955), 140.

p. 126 It seems that it was a tradition: J.S. Matthews, *Early Vancouver*, vol. 2, rev. ed. (1933; repr., Vancouver: City of Vancouver, 2011), 56–57, archives.vancouver.ca/projects/EarlyVan/SearchEarlyVan/Vol2pdf/MatthewsEarlyVancouverVol2_ArrivalOfCaptainVancouver.pdf.

p. 127 *He said he was greeted:* Edmond S. Meany, *Vancouver's Discovery of Puget Sound: Portraits and Biographies of the Men Honored in the Naming of Geographic Features of Northwestern America* (New York: Macmillan Company, 1907), 186.

p. 127 *Some believe it's clear:* Bouchard and Kennedy, *Squamish Indian Land Use and Occupancy*, chap. 3, 7.

p. 127 *Records show S<u>k</u>wx̱wú7mesh and Xwmétskwiyam:* Bouchard and Kennedy, chap. 2, 25, 216.

p. 127 *In Vancouver's journals, he said:* Wade Baker and Mary Tasi, *The Hidden Journals: Captain Vancouver and His Mapmaker* (North Vancouver, BC: Sky Spirit Studio Books, 2015), 59, 75.

p. 128 *It was raining:* Baker and Tasi, *The Hidden Journals*; Bouchard and Kennedy, chap. 1, 11; Meany, *Vancouver's Discovery of Puget Sound*, 91; Gary Little, "George Vancouver 1757–2007: 250th Birthday Anniversary Survey of the Southwest Coast of BC: June 1792," Gary Little (website), garylittle.ca/van250.html ("Near Woodfibre"); George Vancouver, *A Voyage of Discovery to the North Pacific Ocean and Round the World*, vol. 1 (London: G.G. and J. Robinson, 1798), 305.

p. 128 *They refused to leave:* Yumks (Rudy Reimer), "The Mountains and Rocks Are Forever: Lithics and Landscapes of Skwxwú7mesh Úxwumixw" (PhD dissertation, McMaster University, 2012), 200, hdl.handle.net/11375/11794.

p. 128 *X̱ats'alánexw Siỷám̓ said that when:* Matthews, *Conversations with Khahtsahlano*, 13.

p. 129 They thought they were dead people: Sx̱áaltxw Siỷám̓ (Chief Louis Miranda), "The First White Men at Squamish," ARC.CULM.0022a, Squamish Nation Archives, North Vancouver, BC.

p. 130 *Sx̱áaltxw Siỷám̓ said the Skwx̱wú7mesh:* Aert H. Kuipers, *The Squamish Language: Grammar, Texts, Dictionary* (Boston: De Gruyter Mouton, 1967), 240.

p. 130 *Captain Vancouver was treated very kindly:* Kuipers, *The Squamish Language*, 103, 108–9.

p. 130 *At the same time, his writings show:* George Vancouver, *A Voyage of Discovery to the North Pacific Ocean and Round the World*, vol. 3 (London: G.G. and J. Robinson, 1798), 30.

p. 131 *The Hudson's Bay Company didn't set up:* The first permanent settlement in what would become British Columbia was Fort St. John, up in the northeast, which was established in 1794.

p. 131 *S7ápelek Siỷám̓ (Chief Joe Capilano) said:* Matthews, 120, 226–27.

p. 131 *Háx̱sten, who was also known as Skwétsiỷa:* "Centenarian Indian Woman Dies in City," *The Province* (Vancouver, BC), February 9, 1940.

9. Nexw7áỷstwaỷ: Trade

p. 133 *The village became a central trading hub:* Parks Canada, "History," Fort Langley National Historic Site, November 19, 2022, parks.canada.ca/lhn-nhs/bc/langley/culture/histoire-history.

p. 133 *Daily journals from the traders:* Morag Maclachlan, ed., *The Fort Langley Journals, 1827–30* (Vancouver: UBC Press, 1999), 33, 181.

p. 133 *We and our neighbours:* Rennie Warburton and Stephen Scott, "The Fur Trade and Early Capitalist Development in British Columbia," *Canadian Journal of Native Studies* 5, no. 1 (1985): 34, cjns.brandonu.ca/wp-content/uploads/5-1-Warburton.pdf.

p. 133 *First Nations were eager:* Warburton and Scott, "The Fur Trade and Early Capitalist Development"; George Vancouver, *A Voyage of Discovery to the North Pacific Ocean and Round the World*, vol. 3 (London: G.G. and J. Robinson, 1798), 305.

p. 133 *White people traded guns:* Warburton and Scott.

p. 134 *Since Europeans were outnumbered:* Warburton and Scott, 38.
p. 134 *Hostilities increased as settlers:* Randy Bouchard and Dorothy Kennedy, *Squamish Indian Land Use and Occupancy*, report submitted to the Squamish Nation Chiefs and Council (Victoria, BC: BC Indian Language Project, 1986), chap. 2, 21, 23.
p. 134 *Sea otters were especially sought after:* Sydney Gass, "10 Amazing Facts about Sea Otters," Oceana, September 19, 2022, oceana.ca/en/blog/10-amazing-facts-about-sea-otters.
p. 134 *The last recorded sea otters:* Donald A. Blood, "Sea Otter," Ministry of Environment, Lands and Parks (Victoria, BC: Province of British Columbia, 1993), www2.gov.bc.ca/assets/gov/environment/plants-animals-and-ecosystems/species-ecosystems-at-risk/brochures/sea_otter.pdf.
p. 134 *Háx̱sten (Harriet George) had just seen a white man:* "Centenarian Indian Woman Dies in City," *The Province* (Vancouver, BC), February 9, 1940.
p. 134 *In 1822, Hudson's Bay Company governor:* Melissa Gismondi, "The Untold Story of the Hudson's Bay Company," *Canadian Geographic*, May 2, 2020, updated May 17, 2022, canadiangeographic.ca/articles/the-untold-story-of-the-hudsons-bay-company.
p. 134 *As one historian put it:* Arthur Anstey and Neil Sutherland, *British Columbia: A Short History* (Toronto: W.J. Gage, 1957), 24.
p. 136 *By the mid-1800s, Americans and Europeans: Canadian Encyclopedia*, s.v. "British Columbia," thecanadianencyclopedia.ca/en/article/british-columbia.
p. 137 *Sḵwx̱wú7mesh women took part:* Kirsten Baker-Williams, "Na Mi K'anatsut ta Sḵwx̱wú7mesh Sníchim Chet: Squamish Language Revitalization: From the Hearts and the Minds of the Language Speakers" (master's thesis, University of British Columbia, 2006), 22, open.library.ubc.ca/soa/cIRcle/collections/ubctheses/831/items/1.0092805.
p. 138 *There had been smaller outbreaks:* "The Fur Trade Era, 1770s–1849," Great Bear Rainforest Trust, 11, greatbearrainforesttrust.org/wp-content/uploads/2018/08/5-Fur-Trade-Era-1770-1849.pdf.
p. 138 *That means about 95 percent:* "The Fur Trade Era."
p. 138 *According to one estimate:* Baker-Williams, "Na Mi K'anatsut ta Sḵwx̱wú7mesh Sníchim Chet."
p. 138 *The Royal Proclamation of 1763:* "Royal Proclamation, 1763," Indigenous Foundations, First Nations & Indigenous Studies, University of British Columbia, indigenousfoundations.arts.ubc.ca/royal_proclamation_1763.
p. 139 *In 1863, the first sawmill:* R.A. McDonald, *Making Vancouver: Class, Status, and Social Boundaries, 1863–1913* (Vancouver: UBC Press, 1996), 7.

10. Sts'its'áp iy Sḵ'aw: Work and Payment

p. 141 *"White man food change everything":* J.S. Matthews, *Conversations with Khahtsahlano: 1932–1954* (Vancouver: self-published, 1955), 10.
p. 141 *X̱áts'alánexw Siỷám̓ described how:* Matthews, *Conversations with Khahtsahlano*, 11; sea otter garments, 168.
p. 142 *"Shall we allow a few vagrants:* "British Columbia Colonization," *Canada: A People's History*, CBC, cbc.ca/history/EPCONTENTSE1EP9CH3PA1LE.html.
p. 142 *Indigenous people were paid less:* William Bauer, "Sudsy Sovereignty: Indigenous Workers and the Hops Industry of the Pacific Slope," *Labor: Studies in Working Class History* 12, nos. 1–2 (2015): 78, doi.org/10.1215/15476715-2837508.
p. 142 *Immigration increased in the 1800s:* "History of Wrongs Towards BC's Chinese Canadians," Government of British Columbia (website), www2.gov.bc.ca/gov/content/governments/multiculturalism-anti-racism/chinese-legacy-bc/history; "Early Chinese Canadian Experiences in British Columbia," Royal BC Museum Learning Portal, learning.royalbcmuseum.bc.ca/pathways/chinese-canadian-experiences.

p. 142 *European settlers were offered 160 acres:* Mathias et al. v. Canada (2001) FCT 480 (CanLII), 40.

p. 142 *This meant First Nations in British Columbia:* Chris Roine, "The Squamish Aboriginal Economy, 1860–1940" (master's thesis, Simon Fraser University, 1996), 47, core.ac.uk/download/pdf/56371285.pdf.

p. 143 *In an 1859 letter:* J.S. Matthews, *Early Vancouver*, vol. 2, rev. ed. (1933; repr., Vancouver: City of Vancouver, 2011), 53, archives.vancouver.ca/projects/EarlyVan/SearchEarlyVan/Vol2pdf/MatthewsEarlyVancouverVol2_TheNameCapilano.pdf; Kirsten Baker-Williams, "Na Mi K'anatsut ta Sḵwx̱wú7mesh Sníchim Chet: Squamish Language Revitalization: From the Hearts and the Minds of the Language Speakers" (master's thesis, University of British Columbia, 2006), 20, open.library.ubc.ca/soa/cIRcle/collections/ubctheses/831/items/1.0092805.

p. 143 *In her master's thesis:* Baker-Williams, "Na Mi K'anatsut ta Sḵwx̱wú7mesh Sníchim Chet," 20.

p. 144 *"The mothers of them:* Charles Hill-Tout, *The Squamish and the Lillooet*, vol. 2 of *The Salish People: The Local Contribution of Charles Hill-Tout*, ed. Ralph Maud (Vancouver: Talonbooks, 1978), 50.

p. 145 *Around the turn of the century:* Roine, "The Squamish Aboriginal Economy."

p. 145 *Simon Baker of the Sḵwx̱wú7mesh Úxwumixw:* Bauer, "Sudsy Sovereignty," 78.

p. 145 *After they were dried:* Upland Agricultural Consulting, "Squamish Valley Agricultural Plan: Background Report: Biophysical, Agricultural, and Policy Context," Squamish-Lillooet Regional District and District of Squamish, October 2019, slrd.bc.ca/sites/default/files/SVAP%20-%20Background%20Summary%20Report.pdf.

p. 145 *Indigenous labour was integral:* "18 Historic Milestones and Incredible Women in BC Labour," BC Labour Heritage Centre, March 5, 2019, labourheritagecentre.ca/18-historic-milestones-and-incredible-women-in-bc-labour.

p. 145 *Sḵwx̱wú7mesh people paddled across the water:* Randy Bouchard and Dorothy Kennedy, *Squamish Indian Land Use and Occupancy*, report submitted to the Squamish Nation Chiefs and Council (Victoria, BC: BC Indian Language Project, 1986), chap. 3, 55; Matthews, *Conversations with Khahtsahlano*, 401.

p. 146 *The city was less than a year old:* "Vancouver," Hudson's Bay Company History Foundation, hbcheritage.ca/places/places-other-institutions/Vancouver.

p. 147 *But the Canadian federal government's Department of Indian Affairs:* Roine.

p. 147 *They had their first meeting:* Lani Russwurm, "Vancouver Was Awesome: Bows and Arrows," Vancouver Is Awesome, October 17, 2012, vancouverisawesome.com/history/vancouver-was-awesome-bows-and-arrows-1925756.

p. 148 *William "Bill" Nahanee spent fifty-two years:* Bailey Garden, "Don Garcia: Indigenous and Hawaiian Roots in BC's Longshore Unions," BC Labour Heritage Centre, June 22, 2020, labourheritagecentre.ca/don-garcia.

p. 148 *"'I had to find work:* Gavin Hainsworth, "'Bows and Arrows' Lesson Plan," *Working People: A History of Labour in British Columbia*, Labour History Project of Labour Heritage Centre and British Columbia Teachers' Foundation, February 28, 2022.

p. 150 *Xwechtáal himself played a central role:* Andrew Parnaby, *Citizen Docker: Making a New Deal on the Vancouver Waterfront 1919–1939* (Toronto: University of Toronto Press, 2008), 92.

p. 150 *These same veterans pushed:* Garden, "Don Garcia."

p. 150 *The woolly dogs were usually white:* Russel L. Barsh, Joan Megan Jones, and Wayne Suttles, "History, Ethnography, and Archaeology of the Coast Salish Woolly-Dog," in *Dogs and People in Social, Working, Economic, or Symbolic Interaction*, ed. Lynn M. Snyder and Elizabeth A. Moore (Oxford: Oxbow Books, 2016), 2; Virginia Morell, "The Dogs That Grew Wool and the People Who Love Them," *Hakai Magazine*, February 23, 2021, hakaimagazine.com/features/the-dogs-that-grew-wool-and-the-people-who-love-them.

p. 150 *These dogs were associated:* Morell, "The Dogs That Grew Wool."

p. 150 *The Sḵwx̱wú7mesh would keep:* Hannah M. Edmunds, "More Than Food: An Exploration of the Social Significance of Faunal Remains at St'á7mes (DkRs 6)" (master's thesis, Simon Fraser University, 2017), 82, summit.sfu.ca/item/17198.

p. 151 *"They were also a beloved pet:* "Whatever Happened to the Salish Woolly Dog?" CBC News, July 21, 2021, cbc.ca/news/canada/british-columbia/salish-dog-history-1.6111629.

p. 151 *Researchers estimate woolly dogs:* Barsh et al., "History, Ethnography, and Archaeology of the Coast Salish Woolly-Dog," 4; "Whatever Happened to the Salish Woolly Dog?" CBC News.

p. 151 *According to one study, excavation at St'á7mes:* Edmunds, "More Than Food," 27–28, 52, 79.

p. 152 *The dogs in various communities:* Barsh et al., 2, 9.

p. 152 *With the arrival of Europeans: Canadian Encyclopedia*, s.v. "Salish Woolly Dog," by Regan Shrumm, thecanadianencyclopedia.ca/en/article/salish-woolly-dog.

p. 152 *As well, in her research:* "Whatever Happened to the Salish Woolly Dog?" CBC News.

p. 152 *"There were mussels, sea eggs:* Olga Ruskin, "Memories of Vancouver," *Vancouver Sun*, July 16, 1971.

p. 153 *"My grand mom [sic] swam with a seal:* Shellene Paull to Ministry of Environment Water Protection and Sustainability Branch, Government of British Columbia, regarding Water Sustainability Act, 2013, 1, engage.gov.bc.ca/app/uploads/sites/71/2013/11/Waters-of-Ut7slawn.pdf.

p. 153 *A less healthy forest impacts:* Roine.

11. Chilh Siỷám̓ Shísiḵli: Religion

p. 155 *For wider context, in 1455:* The Bull *Romanus Pontifex* (Nicholas V), January 8, 1455, 3, caid.ca/Bull_Romanus_Pontifex_1455.pdf.

p. 155 *Another papal bull:* "Background," The Bull *Inter Caetera* (Alexander VI), May 4, 1493, nativeweb.org/pages/legal/indig-inter-caetera.html.

p. 156 *"The adoption of Christianity:* Truth and Reconciliation Commission of Canada, *Honouring the Truth, Reconciling for the Future: Summary of the Final Report of the Truth and Reconciliation Commission of Canada*, 2015, 46, ehprnh2mwo3.exactdn.com/wp-content/uploads/2021/01/Executive_Summary_English_Web.pdf.

p. 156 *In New Westminster, the first mission was established:* Thomas A. Lascelles, *Mission on the Inlet: St. Paul's Indian Catholic Church, North Vancouver, BC, 1863–1984* (Vancouver: St. Paul's Province, Order of the Oblates of Mary Immaculate, 1984), 6.

p. 156 *In 1868, the first St. Paul's Church:* "Preserving Our Heritage," St. Paul's Indian Church Preservation Trust, stpaulsindianchurch.com/preserving-our-heritage.html.

p. 156 *"Your ancestors came here:* Canada, Parliament, SJC (1946), *Minutes*, no. 9, 423.

p. 156 *The Truth and Reconciliation Commission reached:* Truth and Reconciliation Commission of Canada, *Honouring the Truth, Reconciling for the Future*, 48.

p. 156 *In an unpublished article:* Sean Wilkinson, "Missionization and Sḵwx̱wú7mesh Political Economy, 1864–1923" (master's thesis, Simon Fraser University, 2013), 47, summit.sfu.ca/_flysystem/fedora/sfu_migrate/12683/etd7664_swilkinson.pdf.

p. 157 *After ground-penetrating radar suggested:* Courtney Dickson and Bridgette Watson, "Remains of 215 Children Found Buried at Former B.C. Residential School, First Nation Says," CBC News, May 27, 2021, cbc.ca/news/canada/british-columbia/tk-emlúps-te-secwépemc-215-children-former-kamloops-indian-residential-school-1.6043778.

p. 158 *"The Doctrine is built upon:* Robert J. Miller, Jacinta Ruru, Larissa Behrendt, and Tracy Lindenberg, *Discovering Indigenous Lands: The Doctrine of Discovery in the English Colonies* (Oxford: Oxford University Press, 2010).

p. 158 *Canada replaced "papal imperialism":* Wilkinson, "Missionization and Sḵwx̱wú7mesh Political Economy," 93, 95.

p. 158 *When Europeans arrived in Indigenous territories:* Truth and Reconciliation Commission, 46.
p. 159 *The earliest missionary visited:* Lascelles, *Mission on the Inlet*, 4.
p. 159 *X̱áts'alánexw Siy̓ám̓ (Chief August Jack Khatsahlano) said:* J.S. Matthews, *Conversations with Khahtsahlano: 1932–1954* (Vancouver: self-published, 1955), 65.
p. 160 *"[It] was a little box of a place:* Matthews, *Conversations with Khahtsahlano*, 156.
p. 160 *More people began to live:* Matthews, 65–66.
p. 160 *He spoke to anthropologist Oliver Wells about religion:* Oliver Wells, *The Chilliwacks and Their Neighbors* (Vancouver: Talonbooks, 1987), 141.
p. 162 *In 1890, Father Leon Fouquet:* Lascelles, 10.
p. 162 *The church and St. Paul's Indian Residential School:* "Saint Paul's Roman Catholic Church," Canada's Historic Places, historicplaces.ca/en/rep-reg/place-lieu.aspx?id=12683&pid=0.
p. 162 *The Missionary Oblates of Mary Immaculate led the way:* "Missionary Oblates of Mary Immaculate," Indian Residential School History and Dialogue Centre, collections.irshdc .ubc.ca/index.php/Detail/entities/1211.
p. 162 *"All have embraced with joy:* Wilkinson, 36.
p. 162 SIR,—I have the honour to report: *British Columbia Papers Connected with the Indian Land Question, 1850–1875* (Victoria, BC: Government Printing Office, 1875), 78.
p. 163 *According to records, the American:* Lascelles, 10; *British Columbia Papers Connected with the Indian Land Question*, 79.
p. 163 *Those who "wished to reject their evil ways:* Kay Cronin, *Cross in the Wilderness* (Toronto: Toronto Mission Press, 1959), 123–24, cited in Wilkinson, 42.
p. 163 *"Father Fouquet went over:* Sx̱áaltxw Siy̓ám̓ (Chief Louis Miranda), 1979 Interview, Tape 4356:14, British Columbia Archives, quoted in Wilkinson, 43, 45.
p. 163 *Xwechtáal told a similar history:* Xwechtáal (Andrew Paull), "Indians Fight for Rights of Reserve," *Vancouver Sun*, April 25, 1936; Andrew Paull, "History of St. Paul's Church," ARC.CULM.0116b, Squamish Nation Archives and Cultural Collections, North Vancouver, BC.
p. 164 *The church was renovated in 1884:* "Preserving Our Heritage," St. Paul's Indian Church Preservation Trust; Layne Christensen, "St. Paul's Restoration: Stately Landmark Returned to Glory," *North Shore News*, November 30, 2014, nsnews.com/local-news/ st-pauls-restoration-stately-landmark-returned-to-glory-2990056.
p. 164 The Roman Catholic priests instructed: Matthews, *Conversations with Khahtsahlano*, 148–50.
p. 167 *When Matthews asked him why:* Matthews, 40.
p. 168 *Davin said children were still too influenced:* Nicholas Flood Davin, "Report on Industrial Schools for Indians and Half-Breeds [Davin Report]," March 14, 1879, 16, dev.nctr.ca/ wp-content/uploads/2021/01/Davin-Report.pdf.
p. 169 *"I left there not knowing:* Jane Seyd, "Squamish Nation Survivor of Kamloops Residential School Shares Her Story," *Squamish Chief*, June 1, 2021, squamishchief.com/local-news/ squamish-nation-survivor-of-kamloops-residential-school-shares-her-story-3835730.
p. 169 *As Indian Affairs official Andsell Macrae:* Truth and Reconciliation Commission, 117.
p. 169 *"There [at residential school]:* Squamish Historical Society, "Squamish Nation Stories from the Heart Part 2," April 20, 2012, 5:56, youtube.com/watch?v=nx5bTAdi3yo.
p. 169 *"It wasn't a school:* Elisia Seeber, "'It Wasn't a School. It Was a Place to Kill the Indian in Us': Survivor of BC Residential School Shares His Story," CTV News Vancouver, July 19, 2021, bc.ctvnews.ca/it-wasn-t-a-school-it-was-a-place-to-kill-the-indian-in-us-survivor-of-b-c-residential-school-shares-his-story-1.5514874. See also Sam George et al., *The Fire Still Burns: Life In and After Residential School* (Vancouver: Purich Books, 2023).
p. 169 *In 1933, the Indian Commissioner:* "Backgrounder: Squamish, Musqueam, and Tsleil-Waututh Nations Announce Investigation at Former St. Paul's Indian Residential School Site,"

Sḵwx̱wú7mesh Úxwumixw, 2021, squamish.net/wp-content/uploads/2021/09/2021-08-09_Backgrounder-1-ABOUT-ST.-PAULS-RESIDENTIAL-SCHOOL-FINAL.pdf.

p. 170 *"I am deaf in my right ear:* Seeber, "'It Wasn't a School.'"

p. 170 *"You got to wonder how these people:* Squamish Public Library, "Honouring Residential School Survivors," September 29, 2021, 1:18:21, youtube.com/watch?v=vpDku8XKDFU.

p. 171 *"We were strangers in a way:* Squamish Public Library, "Honouring Residential School Survivors."

p. 172 *"It's your identity:* Kirsten Baker-Williams, "Na Mi K'anatsut ta Sḵwx̱wú7mesh Sníchim Chet: Squamish Language Revitalization: From the Hearts and the Minds of the Language Speakers" (master's thesis, University of British Columbia, 2006), 97, open.library.ubc.ca/soa/cIRcle/collections/ubctheses/831/items/1.0092805.

p. 172 *"I feel the language is so important:* Baker-Williams, "Na Mi K'anatsut ta Sḵwx̱wú7mesh Sníchim Chet," 100, 111.

p. 173 *The commission spent six years:* "About the Truth and Reconciliation Commission," Crown-Indigenous Relations and Northern Affairs Canada, rcaanc-cirnac.gc.ca/eng/1450124405592/1529106060525#chp1.

p. 174 *But as of December 2022, only eleven:* Eva Jewell and Ian Mosby, eds., "Calls to Action Accountability: A 2022 Status Update on Reconciliation," Yellowhead Institute, December 2022, yellowheadinstitute.org/trc.

p. 174 *The investigation aims to find:* "Squamish, Musqueam, and Tsleil-Waututh Nations Announce Investigation at Former St. Paul's Indian Residential School Site," Sḵwx̱wú7mesh Úxwumixw, August 10, 2021, squamish.net/wp-content/uploads/2022/08/Squamish-Musqueam-and-Tsleil-Waututh-Nations-Announce-Investigation-at-Former-St.-Pauls-Indian-Residential-School-Site.pdf.

p. 175 *In July 2022, the Nation oversaw:* "Yúusnew̓as," Sḵwx̱wú7mesh Úxwumixw, squamish.net/yuusnewas.

p. 176 *He told the CBC that he anticipated:* Ka'nhehsí:io Deer, "Why It's Difficult to Put a Number on How Many Children Died at Residential Schools," CBC News, September 29, 2021, cbc.ca/news/indigenous/residential-school-children-deaths-numbers-1.6182456.

p. 176 *One of the Truth and Reconciliation Commission's:* "Church Apologies and Reconciliation," Crown-Indigenous Relations and Northern Affairs Canada, rcaanc-cirnac.gc.ca/eng/1524504325663/1557513116819.

p. 176 *"I was thinking of my parents:* Jane Seyd, "Witnessing Pope's Apology a 'Once-in-a-Lifetime Experience,' Says Indigenous Church Deacon," *North Shore News*, July 29, 2022, nsnews.com/local-news/witnessing-popes-apology-once-in-a-lifetime-experience-says-indigenous-church-deacon-5638107.

p. 177 *"It was the duty of the more responsible:* J.S. Matthews, *Early Vancouver*, vol. 2, rev. ed. (1933; repr., Vancouver: City of Vancouver, 2011), 56, archives.vancouver.ca/projects/EarlyVan/SearchEarlyVan/Vol2pdf/MatthewsEarlyVancouverVol2_ArrivalOfCaptainVancouver.pdf.

p. 177 *"We still carried on our potlatches:* Sx̱áaltxw Siy̓ám̓ (Chief Louis Miranda), "The Life Cycle of the Squamish People: Say̓xw Sx̱áaltxw t Siy̓ám̓—The Words of the Late Chief Louis Miranda," unpublished, n.d., 46, Squamish Nation Archives and Cultural Collections, North Vancouver, BC.

p. 177 *In 2014, in the* Tsilhqot'in Nation v. British Columbia *case:* "The Doctrine of Discovery," Christian Aboriginal Infrastructure Developments, caid.ca/doc_dom.html.

p. 177 *In 2021, under Justin Trudeau's:* Teresa Wright, "How Canada's UNDRIP Bill Was Strengthened to Reject 'Racist' Doctrine of Discovery," CTV News, June 19, 2021, ctvnews.ca/canada/how-canada-s-undrip-bill-was-strengthened-to-reject-racist-doctrine-of-discovery-1.5477403.

Part Four. Sḵwx̱wú7mesh iy Ḵánata: The Squamish and Canada

p. 181 *After first contact in 1792:* Randy Bouchard and Dorothy Kennedy, *Squamish Indian Land Use and Occupancy*, report submitted to the Squamish Nation Chiefs and Council (Victoria, BC: BC Indian Language Project, 1986), chap. 3, 11, 18, 22.

p. 181 *The province began fixing Indian reserve boundaries:* "The Royal BC Museum Digitizes an Historic Ledger Documenting Decisions by the Indian Reserve Commission," Royal BC Museum, June 5, 2020, royalbcmuseum.bc.ca/about/our-work/publications-news/latest-news/royal-bc-museum-digitizes-historic-ledger-documenting; "Home Page," Federal and Provincial Collections of Minutes of Decision, Correspondence, and Sketches: Materials Produced by the Joint Indian Reserve Commission and Indian Reserve Commission, 1876–1910, jirc.ubcic.bc.ca; Erin Hanson, "The Indian Act," Indigenous Foundations, First Nations & Indigenous Studies, University of British Columbia, indigenousfoundations .arts.ubc.ca/the_indian_act.

p. 182 *Amateur anthropologist Charles Hill-Tout:* Charles Hill-Tout, *The Squamish and the Lillooet*, vol. 2 of *The Salish People: The Local Contribution of Charles Hill-Tout*, ed. Ralph Maud (Vancouver: Talonbooks, 1978), 24.

p. 183 *While other Indigenous Peoples:* Douglas C. Harris, "Property and Sovereignty: An Indian Reserve and a Canadian City," *UBC Law Review* 20, no. 2 (2017): 321–92, 334, commons.allard.ubc.ca/cgi/viewcontent.cgi?article=1393&context=fac_pubs.

p. 183 *Today, Indian reserves represent only 0.4 percent:* The total land base in BC is 96,646,000 hectares; the total area of reserves is 360,000 hectares as of 2010. See Province of British Columbia, *Crown Land: Indicators & Statistics Report 2010*, www2.gov.bc.ca/assets/gov/farming-natural-resources-and-industry/natural-resource-use/land-water-use/crown-land/crown_land_indicators__statistics_report.pdf.

12. Í7x̱wix̱wat Stélmexw: All of Us "Indians"

p. 185 *Correspondence suggests that:* Kenneth Brealey, "Travels from Point Ellice: Peter O'Reilly and the Indian Reserve System in British Columbia," *BC Studies* 115/116 (1997–98): 185, ojs.library.ubc.ca/index.php/bcstudies/article/view/1731/1776.

p. 185 *Douglas was instructed to negotiate treaties:* Randy Bouchard and Dorothy Kennedy, *Squamish Indian Land Use and Occupancy*, report submitted to the Squamish Nation Chiefs and Council (Victoria, BC: BC Indian Language Project, 1986), chap. 3, 18.

p. 185 *The reserves created under Douglas:* "Background: Indian Reserve Creation in Colonial British Columbia," Our Homes Are Bleeding Digital Collection, Union of BC Indian Chiefs, ourhomesarebleeding.ubcic.bc.ca/narratives/Background_2.htm.

p. 186 *Apparently, some were escorted:* Bouchard and Kennedy, *Squamish Indian Land Use and Occupancy*, chap. 3, 19, 20.

p. 186 *It turns out those men:* Bouchard and Kennedy, chap. 3, 20.

p. 186 *Use like agriculture and extraction:* G.V.F. Akrigg and Helen Akrigg, *British Columbia Chronicle 1847–1871: Gold and Colonists* (Vancouver: Discovery Press, 1977), 208–9, cited in Bouchard and Kennedy, chap. 3, 23.

p. 187 *As such, the act was in conflict:* "Royal Proclamation, 1763," Indigenous Foundations, First Nations & Indigenous Studies, University of British Columbia, indigenousfoundations .arts.ubc.ca/royal_proclamation_1763.

p. 187 *As early as 1865:* Bouchard and Kennedy, chap. 3, 24.

p. 187 *Missionary Louis-Joseph D'Herbomez:* Bouchard and Kennedy, chap. 3, 27.

p. 188 *The* Fort Langley Journals *describes:* Morag Maclachlan, ed., *The Fort Langley Journals, 1827–30* (Vancouver: UBC Press, 1999), 129.

p. 188 *Missionaries also selected chiefs:* Kirsten Baker-Williams, "Na Mi K'anatsut ta Skwxwú7mesh Snichim Chet: Squamish Language Revitalization: From the Hearts and the Minds of the Language Speakers" (master's thesis, University of British Columbia, 2006), 23, open.library.ubc.ca/soa/cIRcle/collections/ubctheses/831/items/1.0092805.

p. 188 *Some accounts say Skwatatwámkin:* Thomas A. Lascelles, *Mission on the Inlet: St. Paul's Indian Catholic Church, North Vancouver, BC, 1863–1984* (Vancouver: St. Paul's Province, Order of the Oblates of Mary Immaculate, 1984), 9.

p. 188 *In one letter, he wrote:* Bouchard and Kennedy, chap. 3, 30.

p. 188 *He said each tribe's:* Bouchard and Kennedy, chap. 3, 30.

p. 188 *Moody directed missionaries to stop:* Bouchard and Kennedy, chap. 3, 31.

p. 188 *Reserve allocations began in the 1850s:* Brealey, "Travels from Point Ellice."

p. 189 *He saw British Columbia as:* Bouchard and Kennedy, chap. 3, 33.

p. 189 *When land conflicts arose:* Brealey.

p. 189 *"These presents were, as I understand:* "British Columbia Colonization," *Canada: A People's History*, CBC, cbc.ca/history/EPCONTENTSE1EP9CH3PA1LE.html.

p. 189 *The province refused to discuss:* Douglas C. Harris, "Property and Sovereignty: An Indian Reserve and a Canadian City," *UBC Law Review* 20, no. 2 (2017): 321–92, commons.allard.ubc.ca/cgi/viewcontent.cgi?article=1393&context=fac_pubs.

p. 189 *The Dominion of Canada:* "1871—BC Joins Confederation," Legislative Assembly of British Columbia, leg.bc.ca/dyl/Pages/1871-BC-Joins-Confederation.aspx; Bill Dunn and Linda West, "British Columbia Joins Confederation: Introduction," *Canada: A Country by Consent* (website), canadahistoryproject.ca/1871.

p. 189 *Indigenous people outnumbered settlers:* Bouchard and Kennedy, chap. 3, 45.

p. 189 *The Government of Canada:* Bouchard and Kennedy, chap. 3, 45; Mathias et al. v. Canada (2001) FCT 480 (CanLII), 151.

p. 189 *Unceded Indigenous lands were viewed:* Mathias et al. v. Canada, 151.

p. 190 *British Columbia and Canada agreed:* Leslie Anthony, "A Crucial Piece: BC Joined Confederation 150 Years Ago Today," *Canadian Geographic*, July 19, 2021, canadiangeographic.ca/articles/a-crucial-piece-b-c-joined-confederation-150-years-ago-today.

p. 190 *They also agreed that Indian land:* Jean Barman, *The West Beyond the West: A History of British Columbia*, rev. ed. (Toronto: University of Toronto Press, 1996), 153–54, 158–59.

p. 191 *"The white man have taken our land:* Bouchard and Kennedy, chap. 3, 46.

p. 191 *The federal government was expected:* Mathias et al. v. Canada, 152.

p. 191 *This meant the province claimed:* "Confederation Onward: Dominion/Provincial Disputes," Our Homes Are Bleeding Digital Collection, Union of BC Indian Chiefs, ourhomesarebleeding.ubcic.bc.ca/narratives/Background_3.htm.

p. 191 *Author Bob Joseph, hereditary chief:* Bob Joseph, *21 Things You May Not Know about the Indian Act: Helping Canadians Make Reconciliation with Indigenous Peoples a Reality* (Vancouver: Page Two, 2018), loc. 1, ebook.

13. Ta Xwelítn Kwelkwálwn: The Xwelítn Way of Thinking

p. 193 *Indigenous Peoples were banned:* Union of BC Indian Chiefs, *Stolen Lands, Broken Promises: Researching the Indian Land Question in British Columbia*, 2nd ed. (Vancouver: Union of British Columbia Indian Chiefs, 2005), ubcic.bc.ca/stolenlands_brokenpromises; Khelsilem (Dustin Rivers), "A People United: How the Squamish People Founded the Squamish Nation," Coast Salish History Project, July 2021.

p. 193 *Obviously, Indigenous people did not want: Canadian Encyclopedia*, s.v. "Indian Act," thecanadianencyclopedia.ca/en/article/indian-act; Royal Commission on Aboriginal

Peoples, *Report of the Royal Commission on Aboriginal Peoples: Looking Forward, Looking Back*, vol. 1 (Ottawa: Royal Commission on Aboriginal Peoples, 1996), 250, cited in Erin Hanson, "The Indian Act," Indigenous Foundations, First Nations & Indigenous Studies, University of British Columbia, indigenousfoundations.arts.ubc.ca/the_indian_act.

p. 194 *No Indigenous person could live on reserve: Canadian Encyclopedia*, s.v. "Gradual Enfranchisement Act," by John Boileau, thecanadianencyclopedia.ca/en/article/gradual-enfranchisement-act.

p. 194 *The many diverse forms:* Bob Joseph, *21 Things You May Not Know about the Indian Act: Helping Canadians Make Reconciliation with Indigenous Peoples a Reality* (Vancouver: Page Two, 2018); Jean Barman, *The West Beyond the West: A History of British Columbia*, rev. ed. (Toronto: University of Toronto Press, 1996), 159.

p. 195 *In 1900, the pass system: Canadian Encyclopedia*, s.v. "Indian Act."

p. 195 *Other people from around the world:* Barman, *The West Beyond the West*, 99–100.

p. 195 *In 1884, about nine hundred settlers:* Barman, 108; Randy Bouchard and Dorothy Kennedy, *Squamish Indian Land Use and Occupancy*, report submitted to the Squamish Nation Chiefs and Council (Victoria, BC: BC Indian Language Project, 1986), chap. 3, 54.

p. 195 *At the same time:* Barman, 129.

p. 195 *In 1891, Vancouver established: Encyclopedia Britannica Online*, s.v. "History of British Columbia," britannica.com/place/British-Columbia/History.

p. 195 *The two levels of colonial government:* Bouchard and Kennedy, *Squamish Indian Land Use and Occupancy*, chap. 3, 48.

p. 195 *This is a stark contrast:* Barman, 158.

p. 196 *With this shift to reserves:* "Background: Indian Reserve Creation in Colonial British Columbia," Our Homes Are Bleeding Digital Collection, Union of BC Indian Chiefs, ourhomesarebleeding.ubcic.bc.ca/narratives/Background_2.htm.

p. 196 *The JIRC immediately turned down:* Bouchard and Kennedy, chap. 3, 50.

p. 196 *Committee member A.C. Anderson:* Bouchard and Kennedy, chap. 3, 51–52.

p. 196 *Overall, however, the JIRC left Indigenous communities:* Kenneth Brealey, "Travels from Point Ellice: Peter O'Reilly and the Indian Reserve System in British Columbia," *BC Studies* 115/116 (1997–98): 118–236, ojs.library.ubc.ca/index.php/bcstudies/article/view/1731/1776.

p. 196 *"It is no wonder, then:* Bouchard and Kennedy, chap. 3, 52.

p. 196 *As one geography professor put it:* Brealey, "Travels from Point Ellice."

p. 199 *Chepx̱ím Siýám passed away in 1907:* Khelsilem, "A People United."

p. 200 *In early 1904, when discussions:* Mathias et al. v. Canada et al. (2001) 207 FTR 1 (TD), 100.

p. 200 *Indian Agent Frank Devlin said:* Bouchard and Kennedy, chap. 3, 55–56.

p. 200 *Indigenous groups and critics called the act:* "Indian Act Amendment," Gladue Rights Research Database, University of Saskatchewan gladue.usask.ca/node/2366; Joseph, *21 Things You May Not Know about the Indian Act*, chap. 2.

p. 200 *In 1913, British Columbia:* Mathias et al. v. Canada.

p. 200 *"The remains of those buried:* J.S. Matthews, *Conversations with Khahtsahlano: 1932–1954* (Vancouver: self-published, 1955), 6.

p. 202 *But slowly, over time:* Mathias et al. v. Canada, 26.

p. 202 *"These chiefs fully realize:* Khelsilem.

p. 202 *The government was supposed to manage:* Mathias et al. v. Canada, 26, 27.

p. 203 *"We was inside this house:* Matthews, *Conversations with Khahtsahlano*, 26.

p. 203 *"George Tom objects to move it any more:* Bouchard and Kennedy, chap. 3, 56.

p. 204 *A year later when the railway:* Bouchard and Kennedy, chap. 3, 57.

p. 204 *"In the past few years white men:* Lesh Siegel, "The 1906 London Delegation," British Columbia: An Untold History, bcanuntoldhistory.knowledge.ca/1900/the-1906-london-delegation.

p. 205 *The king advised the chiefs:* Union of BC Indian Chiefs, *Stolen Lands, Broken Promises.*

p. 205 *BC Premier Richard McBride:* Union of BC Indian Chiefs.

p. 205 *By 1914, with the onset:* Barman, 129; *Encyclopedia Britannica Online*, s.v. "British Columbia: The Early 20th Century," britannica.com/place/British-Columbia/The-early-20th-century.

p. 205 *"They weren't being treated as equal:* Elisia Seeber, "Squamish Nation Veterans Knowledge Keeper Ensures Indigenous Sacrifice Never Forgotten," *Toronto Star*, November 11, 2020, thestar.com/news/canada/2020/11/11/squamish-nation-veterans-knowledge-keeper-ensures-indigenous-sacrifice-never-forgotten.html.

14. Sḵwx̱wú7mesh Úxwumixw: The Squamish Nation

p. 207 *In 1901, reserve land:* Randy Bouchard and Dorothy Kennedy, *Squamish Indian Land Use and Occupancy*, report submitted to the Squamish Nation Chiefs and Council (Victoria, BC: BC Indian Language Project, 1986), chap. 3, 59.

p. 207 *The federal government treated each Sḵwx̱wú7mesh community:* Kirsten Baker-Williams, "Na Mi K'anatsut ta Sḵwx̱wú7mesh Sníchim Chet: Squamish Language Revitalization: From the Hearts and the Minds of the Language Speakers" (master's thesis, University of British Columbia, 2006), 28, open.library.ubc.ca/soa/cIRcle/collections/ubctheses/831/items/1.0092805.

p. 208 *So, while Indigenous land:* "The McKenna McBride Agreement," Our Homes Are Bleeding Digital Collection, Union of BC Indian Chiefs, ourhomesarebleeding.ubcic.bc.ca/narratives/Background_4.htm.

p. 208 *Notably, the Commission refused:* "Work of the McKenna McBride Royal Commission," Our Homes Are Bleeding Digital Collection, Union of BC Indian Chiefs, ourhomesarebleeding.ubcic.bc.ca/narratives/Background_5.htm.

p. 208 *The chiefs pushed for title:* Bouchard and Kennedy, *Squamish Indian Land Use and Occupancy*, chap. 3, 62.

p. 208 *Chief Jimmy Harry asked:* Bouchard and Kennedy, chap. 3, 63–64.

p. 208 *On the other hand, they implied:* Royal Commission on Indian Affairs for the Province of British Columbia, "Meeting with the Indians at Mission," June 17, 1913, New Westminster Agency collection, Union of BC Indian Chiefs. This and several interim and final reports can be found in the following archive: gsdl.ubcic.bc.ca/cgi-bin/library.cgi.

p. 209 *Xwechtáal (Andy Paull), one of the leaders:* Royal Commission on Indian Affairs for the Province of British Columbia, "Meeting with the Indians at Mission."

p. 210 *The St'á7mes Reserve was reduced:* New Westminster Agency collection, Union of BC Indian Chiefs, gsdl.ubcic.bc.ca/cgi-bin/library.cgi.

p. 210 *The McKenna-McBride Commission shaved:* Bouchard and Kennedy, chap. 3, 65.

p. 211 *If the court decided they had no title:* Bouchard and Kennedy, chap. 3, 66.

p. 211 *The Sḵwx̱wú7mesh were encouraged to use the land:* Bouchard and Kennedy, chap. 3, 64.

p. 212 *By the 1940s, roughly half:* Reports of W. Graham Allen for Sḵwx̱wú7mesh Úxwumixw, 1977–1978. Documents held by the Sḵwx̱wú7mesh Úxwumixw.

p. 212 *According to one historian:* Jean Barman, *The West Beyond the West: A History of British Columbia*, rev. ed. (Toronto: University of Toronto Press, 1996), 159; "The McKenna McBride Agreement," Our Homes Are Bleeding Digital Collection.

p. 212 *By the Commission's end:* Barman, *The West Beyond the West*, 159.

p. 212 *The Sḵwx̱wú7mesh have ownership over 0.423 percent:* Baker-Williams, "Na Mi K'anatsut ta Sḵwx̱wú7mesh Sníchim Chet," 28.

p. 212 *Only 45 percent of land applications:* Dana McFarland, "Indian Reserve Cut-Offs in British Columbia, 1912–1924: An Examination of Federal-Provincial Negotiations and Consultation with Indians" (master's thesis, University of British Columbia, 1990), 77, open.library.ubc.ca/media/stream/pdf/831/1.0302324/1.

p. 212 *Commission minutes show:* "McKenna-McBride Royal Commission: Minutes of Decision 1913–1916," Union of BC Indian Chiefs, ubcic.bc.ca/mckenna_mcbride_royal_commission; Royal Commission on Indian Affairs, "New Westminster Agency: Additional Lands Applications 2" and "New Westminster Agency: Additional Lands Applications 3," New Westminster Agency collection, Union of BC Indian Chiefs, gsdl.ubcic.bc.ca/cgi-bin/library.cgi.

p. 212 *He wanted to "strengthen the hand":* E. Palmer Patterson II, "Andrew Paull and Canadian Indian Resurgence" (PhD dissertation, University of Washington, 1962), proquest.com/openview/3912f43318ce33da9cb5be009dc531e6.

p. 213 *But since the Sḵwx̱wú7mesh saw themselves:* Xwechtáal (Andy Paull) letter to Deputy Superintendent General Duncan Campbell Scott, November 1921, cited in Khelsilem (Dustin Rivers), "A People United: How the Squamish People Founded the Squamish Nation," Coast Salish History Project, July 2021.

p. 213 *It stipulated that the profits:* Khelsilem, "A People United."

p. 213 *He would raise the issue of:* Khelsilem.

p. 213 *Xwechtáal wrote, "It is now the prayers:* Khelsilem.

p. 214 *In 1922, he told Inspector William Ditchburn:* Khelsilem; spellings as in source.

p. 214 *People were concerned about the sales:* Bouchard and Kennedy, chap. 3, 68; Royal Commission on Indian Affairs for the Province of British Columbia, "Meeting with the Indians at Mission"; Khelsilem.

p. 214 *Kwenáx̱tn Siỷám̓ (Chief Andrew) of Sen̓áḵw said:* Khelsilem.

p. 215 *According to a handwritten note:* Khelsilem.

p. 216 *The letter expressed concern:* Khelsilem.

p. 217 *The document reads:* Bouchard and Kennedy, chap. 3, 69.

p. 221 *After a council member died:* Khelsilem.

p. 221 *In 2020, the Nation reported $102 million: syétsem tl'a syelánm: Annual Report 2020/2021*, Sḵwx̱wú7mesh Úxwumixw, 7, squamish.net/wp-content/uploads/2021/09/Squamish-Nation-Annual-Report-2020-2021-Digital_FINAL.pdf.

p. 221 *The McKenna-McBride Commission's recommendations:* "Implementation of the Commission Recommendations," Our Homes Are Bleeding Digital Collection, Union of BC Indian Chiefs, ourhomesarebleeding.ubcic.bc.ca/narratives/Background_8.htm.

p. 221 *First Nations challenged the Commission's authority:* "Implementation of the Commission Recommendations," Union of BC Indian Chiefs; McFarland, "Indian Reserve Cut-Offs in British Columbia, 1912–1924."

p. 221 *The Allied Tribes of British Columbia, the organization:* E. Palmer Patterson II, "Andrew Paull and the Early History of British Columbia Indian Organizations," ARC.CULM.0116a, Squamish Nation Archives and Cultural Collections, North Vancouver, BC, 1.

p. 221 *That same year, Canada followed:* Barman, 173; *Indian Residential Schools & Reconciliation: Teacher Resource Guide 11/12*, book 1 (West Vancouver: First Nations Education Steering Committee and First Nations Schools Association, 2015), 18; *Canadian Encyclopedia*, s.v. "Indian Act," thecanadianencyclopedia.ca/en/article/indian-act.

p. 221 *The amendment was "aimed directly at:* Paul Tennant, "Native Indian Political Organization in British Columbia, 1900–1969: A Response to Internal Colonialism," *BC Studies* 55 (1982): 3–49, 16, cited in Barman, 173.

15. Swat melh ta New: Now Who Are You?

p. 223 *When British Columbia joined Confederation:* Donald Myles Smith, "Title to Indian Reserves in British Columbia: A Critical Analysis of Order in Council 1036" (master's thesis, University of British Columbia, 1988), 8, open.library.ubc.ca/media/stream/

pdf/831/1.0077705/1; Union of BC Indian Chiefs, *Stolen Lands, Broken Promises: Researching the Indian Land Question in British Columbia*, 2nd ed. (Vancouver: Union of British Columbia Indian Chiefs, 2005), ubcic.bc.ca/stolenlands_brokenpromises.

p. 223 *Author Bob Joseph connected the shift in public views:* Bob Joseph, *21 Things You May Not Know about the Indian Act: Helping Canadians Make Reconciliation with Indigenous Peoples a Reality* (Vancouver: Page Two, 2018).

p. 223 *A special committee between:* Standing Committee on Aboriginal Affairs, Northern Development and Natural Resources, Meeting 43, *Committee Evidence*, 37th Parliament, 1st Session, March 12, 2002, ourcommons.ca/DocumentViewer/en/37-1/AANR/meeting-43/evidence.

p. 224 *"By the time 1951 came:* Elisia Seeber, "Squamish Nation Veterans Knowledge Keeper Ensures Indigenous Sacrifice Never Forgotten," *Toronto Star*, November 11, 2020, thestar.com/news/canada/2020/11/11/squamish-nation-veterans-knowledge-keeper-ensures-indigenous-sacrifice-never-forgotten.html.

p. 224 *He had "imagination and vision":* E. Palmer Patterson II, "Andrew Paull and the Early History of British Columbia Indian Organizations," ARC.CULM.0116a, Squamish Nation Archives and Cultural Collections, North Vancouver, BC, 3.

p. 224 *"The Indians were so talented:* Andy Prest, "Legendary Lacrosse Coach Headed to North Shore Sports Hall of Fame," *North Shore News*, February 20, 2019, nsnews.com/local-sports/legendary-lacrosse-coach-headed-to-north-shore-sports-hall-of-fame-3094009.

p. 226 *Finally, Canada consulted with First Nations: Canadian Encyclopedia*, s.v. "Indian Act," thecanadianencyclopedia.ca/en/article/indian-act.

p. 227 *But people with Indian status:* "Indigenous Alcohol Intolerance," Indigenous Corporate Training Inc., May 28, 2014, ictinc.ca/blog/indigenous-alcohol-intolerance.

p. 227 *The concept of Indian blood: Canadian Encyclopedia*, s.v. "Women and the Indian Act," thecanadianencyclopedia.ca/en/article/women-and-the-indian-act.

p. 227 *A year later, the compulsory enfranchisement clause: Canadian Encyclopedia*, s.v. "Indian Act"; Karrmen Crey, "Enfranchisement," Indigenous Foundations, First Nations & Indigenous Studies, University of British Columbia, indigenousfoundations.arts.ubc.ca/enfranchisement.

p. 227 *And the number would only get higher:* "Children and Youth in Care (CYIC)," Ministry of Children and Family Development Portal, Government of British Columbia, mcfd.gov.bc.ca/reporting/services/child-protection/permanency-for-children-and-youth/performance-indicators/children-in-care.

p. 227 *S<u>x</u>áaltxw Siỷám̓ (Chief Louis Miranda) talked about:* S<u>x</u>áaltxw Siỷám̓ (Chief Louis Miranda), "The Life Cycle of the Squamish People: Saỷxw S<u>x</u>áaltxw t Siỷám̓—The Words of the Late Chief Louis Miranda," unpublished, n.d., 47, Squamish Nation Archives and Cultural Collections, North Vancouver, BC.

p. 228 *Despite a special committee review: Canadian Encyclopedia*, s.v. "Indian Act."

p. 228 *The 1951 amendments introduced: Canadian Encyclopedia*, s.v. "Women and the Indian Act."

p. 228 *The fight was not easy: Canadian Encyclopedia*, s.v. "Indian Act."

p. 229 *"For well over one hundred years:* Aboriginal Women's Council of BC, "Traditional Self-Government, Economic Development and Aboriginal Women," Submission to the Royal Commission on Aboriginal Peoples, February 1992, Ref. 8200-50A2, Item No. 540, Library and Archives Canada, 36–37, 18, recherche-collection-search.bac-lac.gc.ca/eng/home/record?app=rcap&IdNumber=540.

p. 231 *"It is under Indian Act governments:* Judith F. Sayers et al., *First Nations Women, Governance and the Indian Act: A Collection of Policy Research Reports* (Ottawa: Status of Women Canada, 2001), 142, fngovernance.org/wp-content/uploads/2020/07/First_Nation_Women_and_Governance.pdf.

p. 231 *Across British Columbia, more than ten thousand:* Stewart Bell, "Problems Seen in Reserve Boom," *Vancouver Sun*, January 7, 1991.

p. 232 *Bill C-31 did allow bands: Canadian Encyclopedia*, s.v. "Indian Act."

p. 232 *In 1987, the Sḵwx̱wú7mesh Úxwumixw:* "Squamish Nation Membership Code," 1987, Sḵwx̱wú7mesh Úxwumixw, squamish.net/wp-content/uploads/2021/09/1987_membership_code.pdf.

p. 232 *Bill C-3 did not completely rid:* "What Is Bill C-31 and Bill C-3?" Assembly of First Nations, 2020, afn.ca/wp-content/uploads/2020/01/16-19-02-06-AFN-Fact-Sheet-Bill-C-31-Bill-C-3-final-revised.pdf.

p. 232 *In 2017, Bill S-3 was introduced:* "Bill S-3: Eliminating Known Sex-Based Inequities in Registration," Indigenous Services Canada, September 13, 2022, sac-isc.gc.ca/eng/1467214955663/15724603115.

p. 232 *In 2019, further amendments to Bill S-3:* "Removal of the 1951 Cut-Off," Crown-Indigenous Relations and Northern Affairs Canada, November 11, 2018, rcaanc-cirnac.gc.ca/eng/1540403451139/1568898699984.

p. 232 *The journey to eliminate gender discrimination:* "Canada Introduces Bill C-38 to Further Address Inequities in the Registration and Band Membership Provisions of the Indian Act," Indigenous Services Canada, December 14, 2022, canada.ca/en/indigenous-services-canada/news/2022/12/canada-introduces-bill-c-38-to-further-address-inequities-in-the-registration-and-band-membership-provisions-of-the-indian-act.html.

p. 232 *In 1981, the Nation elected:* Khelsilem (Dustin Rivers), "A People United: How the Squamish People Founded the Squamish Nation," Coast Salish History Project, July 2021.

p. 233 *"How do you destroy a people?:* "Capilano Longhouse Public Meeting 1990," Temixw Planning Limited (YouTube), April 19, 2017, 23:30, youtu.be/Ldc2TMSmu8I.

p. 233 *"They did not object to parks:* "British Columbia—Squamish Band," R1044, RG33-115, Library and Archives Canada, 33, 44, recherche-collection-search.bac-lac.gc.ca/eng/home/record?app=fonandcol&IdNumber=5095363.

Part Five. Sḵwx̱wú7mesh Stitúyntsam̓: Squamish Inheritance

p. 236 *"Ottawa needs to hear:* Laura Kane, "Squamish Nation Files Court Case against NEB Approval of Kinder Morgan Expansion," *Canada's National Observer*, June 17, 2016, nationalobserver.com/2016/06/17/news/squamish-nation-files-court-case-against-neb-approval-kinder-morgan-expansion.

p. 237 *From 1927 until 1951:* Erin Hanson, "The Indian Act," Indigenous Foundations, First Nations & Indigenous Studies, University of British Columbia, indigenousfoundations.arts.ubc.ca/the_indian_act.

p. 237 *The federal ban had been lifted:* Hanson, "The Indian Act."

p. 237 *They told Mr. Reecke about being forced off Seṅáḵw:* "Our Firm," Ratcliff & Company LLP (website), ratcliff.com/our-firm.

16. Haw ḵ'at Máynexw Seṅáḵw: We Never Forgot Seṅáḵw

p. 241 *As a guest on the CBC podcast* Land Back: Angela Sterritt (host) and Chepx̱ímiya Siỷám̓ (Chief Janice George), "Episode 5: A Village Burned," *Land Back* (podcast), December 5, 2022, 39:01, cbc.ca/listen/cbc-podcasts/1341-landback/episode/15952788-e5-a-village-burned.

p. 242 *More than sixty years after Squamish people:* "Sḵwx̱wú7mesh Úxwumixw Trust," Sḵwx̱wú7mesh Úxwumixw, squamish.net/squamish-nation-trust; Robert Matas, "Squamish Band Settles Claim for $92.5 Million," *Globe and Mail*, July 25, 2000, theglobeandmail.com/news/national/squamish-band-settles-claim-for-925-million/article1041312.

p. 242 *A total of 1,488:* Matas, "Squamish Band Settles Claim for $92.5 Million."
p. 243 *The federal government had breached its fiduciary duty:* Mathias et al. v. Canada, 2001 FCT 480 (CanLII), "Final Reasons for Judgment," 1.
p. 244 *The Squamish Action:* Mathias et al. v. Canada, 29, 30.
p. 244 *The Selílwitulh argued that the Crown:* Mathias et al. v. Canada, 29.
p. 245 *The court acknowledged the importance:* Mathias et al. v. Canada, 13.
p. 247 *Everyone in court agreed:* Mathias et al. v. Canada et al. (2001) 207 FTR 1 (TD), 263, 265, 298, 300, 306.
p. 248 *In the 1980s, the Sḵwx̱wú7mesh, Xwmétskwiyam, and Selílwitulh:* Mathias v. Canadian Pacific Ltd., [1991] B.C.T.C. Uned. 357 (SC), bccourts.ca/jdb-txt/sc/91/03/s91-0322.htm.
p. 249 *In 2000, the Supreme Court:* Canada (Attorney General) v. Canadian Pacific Ltd., 2000 BCSC 933 (CanLII), canlii.ca/t/53fz: "The benefit of whichever Indian Band, Squamish, Musqueam or Burrard, which, in other proceedings, may be found to be entitled to it."
p. 249 *Both Canadian Pacific and Canada:* Canada (Attorney General) v. Canadian Pacific Ltd., 2002 BCCA 478 (CanLII), canlii.ca/t/5jsf.
p. 251 *On September 6, 2022, the Nation:* Kenneth Chan, "Prime Minister Justin Trudeau Commits $1.4 Billion in Construction Financing for Seṅáḵw Rental Housing," *Daily Hive*, September 6, 2022, dailyhive.com/vancouver/senakw-vancouver-construction-start-squamish-nation-federal-justin-trudeau.
p. 251 *That same day, council Chairperson Khelsilem (Dustin Rivers) said:* Kier Junos, "Squamish Nation Signs Deal with Vancouver for Seṅáḵw Development," *CityNews Vancouver*, May 26, 2022, vancouver.citynews.ca/2022/05/26/squamish-nation-vancouver-senakw-deal.

17. I7x̱w Sts'úḵw'i7: All Salmon

p. 253 *At the centre of many:* Squamish First Nation v. Canada (Fisheries and Oceans), 2019 FCA 216 (CanLII), canlii.ca/t/j1vd2.
p. 254 *Bones must always be thrown back:* Sx̱áaltxw Siy̓áṁ (Chief Louis Miranda), "The Life Cycle of the Squamish People: Say̓xw Sx̱áaltxw t Siy̓áṁ—The Words of the Late Chief Louis Miranda," unpublished, n.d., 20–21, Squamish Nation Archives and Cultural Collections, North Vancouver, BC.
p. 254 *The Fraser River estuary alone:* Kwetásel'wet (Steph Wood), "Scientists Make Final Bid to Stop Port of Vancouver's Terminal Expansion: 'They Can't Mitigate the Consequences,'" *The Narwhal*, February 10, 2022, thenarwhal.ca/port-of-vancouver-roberts-bank-scientists.
p. 254 *In 2020, only 291,000 returned:* "Record Low Fraser River Sockeye Returns," Pacific Salmon Commission, November 2020, psc.org/about-us/history-purpose/our-history.
p. 254 *Syetáx̱tn (Chris Lewis) spoke about the importance:* National Energy Board, "Trans Mountain Pipeline ULC, Trans Mountain Expansion Project: National Energy Board Reconsideration of Aspects of Its Recommendation Report as Directed by Order in Council P.C. 2018-1177, Hearing Order MH-052-2018," vol. 7, November 29, 2018, Canada Energy Regulator, 21–23, docs2.cer-rec.gc.ca/ll-eng/llisapi.dll/fetch/2000/90464/90552/548311/956726/2392873/3614457/3689831/3716786/A96243-1_18-11-29_-_Volume_7_-_A6L2F4.pdf?nodeid=3716347&vernum=-2.
p. 255 We would go to a village: Denise Cook, "Pattullo Bridge Replacement Project: Historical Heritage Study," British Columbia Ministry of Transportation and Infrastructure, April 2018, projects.eao.gov.bc.ca/api/document/5b73439a5bc7e60024dc108b/fetch/Appendix__18.13_Historical_Heritage_Study.pdf.
p. 256 *At the time, the Nation:* Mathias et al. v. Canada et al. (2001) 207 FTR 1 (TD), 3: 1,927 members.
p. 256 *By 2011, we had about 3,500 members:* Squamish First Nation v. Canada (Fisheries and Oceans), 3–4, 18.

p. 259 *According to Xwechtáal (Andy Paull):* Shellene Paull, to National Energy Board, Letter of Comment regarding Hearing Order OH-001-2014, Trans Mountain Pipeline Expansion Project, August 18, 2015, Canada Energy Regulator, 18, apps.cer-rec.gc.ca/REGDOCS/Item/View/2811357.

p. 259 *At that time,* sts'úḵw'i7 *were plentiful:* National Energy Board, "Trans Mountain Pipeline ULC, 2.

p. 259 *The Nation sought a judicial review:* Squamish First Nation v. Canada (Fisheries and Oceans).

p. 259 *The idea of a "spectrum" of consultation:* Haida Nation v. British Columbia (Minister of Forests), 2004 SCC 73, scc-csc.lexum.com/scc-csc/scc-csc/en/item/2189/index.do.

p. 259 *The Sḵwx̱wú7mesh appealed the decision:* Kate Gunn and Jesse Donovan, "Squamish v. Canada: Case Comment," First Peoples Law, September 9, 2019, firstpeopleslaw.com/public-education/blog/squamish-v-canada-case-comment.

p. 259 *The court decided that the Sḵwx̱wú7mesh Úxwumixw:* Squamish First Nation v. Canada (Fisheries and Oceans), 5, 12–14, 18, 27, 22.

p. 261 *The court called for a fresh round of consultation:* Keili Bartlett, "Squamish Nation Not Properly Consulted on Fish Allowance: Court," *Pique Newsmagazine*, August 22, 2019, piquenewsmagazine.com/bc-news/squamish-nation-not-properly-consulted-on-fish-allowance-court-2507949; Bridget Gilbride and Sarah Noble, "First Nation's Request for an Increased Allocation of Sockeye Triggers the Duty to Consult," Indigenous Law Bulletin, Fasken Martineau DuMoulin LLP (website), August 15, 2019, fasken.com/en/knowledge/2019/08/van-squamish-first-nations-request; Lisa C. Fong, "The Duty to Consult about Inadequate Fishing Allocations: Squamish Nation v. Canada, 2019 FCA 216," Ng Ariss Fong Lawyers (website), August 19, 2019, ngariss.com/our-in-dispute-posts/the-duty-to-consult-about-inadequate-fishing-allocations; Anita Boscariol, "Federal Court Decision in Squamish Fishing Case Overturned," *Lawyer's Daily*, September 26, 2019, watsongoepel.com/wp-content/uploads/2019/10/Federal-Court-decision-in-Squamish-fishing-case-overturned-The-Lawyers-Daily.pdf; Gunn and Donovan, "Squamish v. Canada."

18. S7ulh Chiỷáxw: Our Protocol

p. 263 *The pipeline runs from Edmonton:* "Pipeline Profiles: Trans Mountain," Canada Energy Regulator, updated March 2023, rec-cer.gc.ca/en/data-analysis/facilities-we-regulate/pipeline-profiles/oil-and-liquids/pipeline-profiles-trans-mountain.html.

p. 264 *A number of biologists, climate scientists:* "Trans Mountain: Tar Sands Oil to and from Our Coast," Raincoast Conservation Foundation, raincoast.org/trans-mountain-pipeline; Carol Linnitt, "27 B.C. Climate Experts Rejected from Kinder Morgan Trans Mountain Pipeline Hearings," *The Narwhal*, April 11, 2014, thenarwhal.ca/27-b-c-climate-experts-rejected-kinder-morgan-trans-mountain-pipeline-hearings; Natasha Bulowski, "Trans Mountain Pipeline Insurers Dropping Like Flies," *Canada's National Observer*, April 25, 2022, nationalobserver.com/2022/04/25/news/trans-mountain-pipeline-insurers-dropping-flies; "BC Physician Sentenced to Jail for Fighting to Protect Public Health from Trans Mountain's Impacts," June 15, 2022, STAND.earth, stand.earth/press-releases/b-c-physician-sentenced-to-jail-for-fighting-to-protect-public-health-from-trans-mountains-impacts; "Statement in Support of Health Workers Acting to Stop the Trans Mountain Expansion," Canadian Association of Physicians for the Environment, July 28, 2021, cape.ca/press_release/statement-in-support-of-health-workers-acting-to-stop-the-trans-mountain-expansion; "The Dilbit Dilemma," Concerned Professional Engineers, concernedengineers.org/the-dilbit-dilemma; "Trans Mountain," Concerned Professional Engineers, concernedengineers.org/about-kinder-morgans-proposal; Romilly

Cavanaugh, "Former Kinder Morgan Engineer Speaks Out against Trans Mountain Pipeline," Real News Network, March 27, 2018, therealnews.com/former-kinder-morgan-engineer-speaks-out-against-trans-mountain-pipeline; Chantelle Bellrichard, "Hundreds of Landowners Still Haven't Signed Agreements with Trans Mountain for Pipeline Expansion," CBC News, July 22, 2019, cbc.ca/news/indigenous/hundreds-of-landowners-still-haven-t-signed-agreements-with-trans-mountain-for-pipeline-expansion-1.5213478.

p. 264 *The Squamish Nation fought:* Aaron S. Bruce and Michelle L. Bradley to Squamish Nation Chiefs and Council, Memorandum re. Filing an Application for Leave for Judicial Review of the Governor in Council Decision for the Trans Mountain Expansion Project, November 29, 2016, Ratcliff & Company LLP.

p. 265 *When the original proponent, Kinder Morgan:* Alex Ballingall, Bruce Campion-Smith, and Tonda MacCharles, "Justin Trudeau's $4.5 Billion Trans Mountain Pipeline Purchase Met with a Storm of Criticism," *Toronto Star*, May 29, 2018, thestar.com/news/canada/2018/05/29/justin-trudeaus-45-billion-trans-mountain-pipeline-purchase-met-with-a-storm-of-criticism.html.

p. 265 *All the while, the cost:* Josh Aldrich, "Cost of Government-Owned Trans Mountain Pipeline Expansion Soars to $21.4 Billion," *Calgary Herald*, February 18, 2022, calgaryherald.com/business/energy/price-for-trans-mountain-pipeline-expansion-soars-to-21-4-billion.

p. 265 *This is a stark contrast:* Trans Mountain, "Proposed Expansion," Internet Archive, April 23, 2016, web.archive.org/web/20160423093813/https://www.transmountain.com/proposed-expansion.

p. 265 *As of 2022, Canada's parliamentary budget officer:* Rod Nickel and Ismail Shakil, "Canada-Owned Trans Mountain Oil Pipeline Not Profitable—Budget Officer," Reuters, June 22, 2022, reuters.com/business/energy/trans-mountain-oil-pipeline-no-longer-profitable-canada-budget-officer-2022-06-22.

p. 265 *In 2012, the Sḵwx̱wú7mesh Úxwumixw chiefs:* Bruce and Bradley, Memorandum, 1.

p. 266 *The Sḵwx̱wú7mesh would travel by canoe:* "Trans Mountain Expansion Project: Final Argument of Squamish Nation," January 12, 2016, Canada Energy Regulator, 17, docs2.cer-rec.gc.ca/ll-eng/llisapi.dll/fetch/2000/90464/90552/548311/956726/2392873/2449925/2451054/2905662/C319-40-2_-_Final_Argument_of_the_Squamish_Nation_%2801164829%29_-_A4X5E7.pdf?nodeid=2905007&vernum=-2.

p. 266 *The Sḵwx̱wú7mesh described how travel:* "Trans Mountain Expansion Project," 18–19.

p. 266 *Elder Paítsmuḵ (David Jacobs) described:* "Trans Mountain Expansion Project," 20–21.

p. 267 *"Squamish have long occupied:* "Trans Mountain Expansion Project," 2.

p. 269 *Instead, the governor-in-council approval:* "Project Background, Trans Mountain Pipeline ULC—Trans Mountain Expansion," Canada Energy Regulator, cer-rec.gc.ca/en/applications-hearings/view-applications-projects/trans-mountain-expansion/project-background.html?=undefined&wbdisable=true#s2.

p. 269 *Council only had fifteen days:* Bruce and Bradley, 3.

p. 269 *That same year, the Federal Court of Appeal:* "Gitxaala Nation v. Canada, 2016 FCA 187—Case Summary," Mandell Pinder LLP (website), July 5, 2016, mandellpinder.com/gitxaala-nation-v-canada-2016-fca-187-case-summary; Bruce and Bradley, 4.

p. 269 *But they warned our council:* Bruce and Bradley, 4.

p. 269 *The legal counsel knew:* Bruce and Bradley, 5.

p. 269 *Bitumen itself is a heavy crude oil:* "Diluted Bitumen Information," Trans Mountain (website), transmountain.com/diluted-bitumen-information; "Diluted Bitumen," American Petroleum Institute, api.org/oil-and-natural-gas/wells-to-consumer/exploration-and-production/oil-sands/diluted-bitumen.

p. 269 *Trans Mountain continues to argue:* "Diluted Bitumen Information," Trans Mountain; "Lessons from the Kalamazoo River Tar Sands Oil Spill," Wilderness Committee, wildernesscommittee.org/kalamazoo; Mitchell Anderson, "Spill from Hell: Diluted Bitumen," *The Tyee*, March 5, 2012, thetyee.ca/News/2012/03/05/Diluted-Bitumen; "Wildlife in Kalamazoo River 5 Years After Enbridge Oil Spill," Inside Climate News, July 26, 2015, insideclimatenews.org/infographics/wildlife-kalamazoo-river-5-years-after-enbridge-oil-spill.

p. 269 *Other reports have shown:* Carol Linnitt, "It's Official: Federal Report Confirms Diluted Bitumen Sinks," *The Narwhal*, January 14, 2014, thenarwhal.ca/it-s-official-federal-report-confirms-diluted-bitumen-sinks; Jeffrey Cederwall and Sawyer Stoyanovich, "We Found Half of Spilled Oilsands Bitumen Sinks in Freshwater after Heavy Rain," *The Narwhal*, August 12, 2020, thenarwhal.ca/we-found-half-of-spilled-oilsands-bitumen-sinks-in-freshwater-after-heavy-rain; Lisa Song, "Dilbit Sinks in Enbridge Oil Spill, but Floats in Its Lab Study," Inside Climate News, March 14, 2013, insideclimatenews.org/news/14032013/tar-sands-dilbit-sinks-enbridge-oil-spill-floats-its-lab-study.

p. 270 *In early 2018, facing such widespread opposition:* David Ljunggren, Liz Hampton, and Gary McWilliams, "How Kinder Morgan Won a Billion-Dollar Bailout on Canada Pipeline," Reuters, May 30, 2018, reuters.com/article/us-kinder-morgan-cn-strategy-insight-idUSKCN1IV1B5.

p. 270 *So, Trudeau's government did:* Ljunggren et al., "How Kinder Morgan Won a Billion-Dollar Bailout on Canada Pipeline."

p. 270 *On August 30, 2018, the Federal Court of Appeal:* Tsleil-Waututh Nation v. Canada (Attorney General), 2018 FCA 153, decisions.fca-caf.gc.ca/fca-caf/decisions/en/item/343511/index.do#_Remedy.

p. 271 *Just thirty minutes after the decision:* John Gibson, "With Project in Doubt, Kinder Morgan Shareholders Vote to Sell Trans Mountain Pipeline to Ottawa," CBC News, August 30, 2018, cbc.ca/news/canada/calgary/kinder-morgan-canada-shareholders-vote-sale-trans-mountain-pipeline-1.4804503.

p. 271 *"How can Canada go back to the First Nations:* Judith Lavoie, "The Death of Trans Mountain Pipeline Signals Future of Indigenous Rights: Chiefs," *The Narwhal*, August 30, 2018, thenarwhal.ca/death-trans-mountain-pipeline-signals-future-indigenous-rights-chiefs.

p. 272 *The court's decision was largely based:* "Supreme Court Dismisses First Nations' Challenge against Trans Mountain Pipeline," CBC News, July 2, 2020, cbc.ca/news/canada/british-columbia/trans-mountain-pipeline-challenge-bc-first-nations-supreme-court-of-canada-1.5634232.

p. 272 *"To let the federal government:* "Supreme Court Dismisses First Nations' Challenge against Trans Mountain Pipeline," CBC News.

p. 272 *In July 2020, the Supreme Court of Canada:* Brent Richter, "Supreme Court Ends Squamish and Tsleil-Waututh Pipeline Appeal," *North Shore News*, July 2, 2020, nsnews.com/local-news/supreme-court-ends-squamish-and-tsleil-waututh-pipeline-appeal-3124530; Coldwater et al. v. Canada (Attorney General) et al., 2020 FCA 34; Coldwater Indian Band, et al. v. Attorney General of Canada, et al., 2020, scc-csc.lexum.com/scc-csc/scc-l-csc-a/en/item/18411/index.do?q=tsleil-waututh; "Judgments in Leave Applications," Supreme Court of Canada, July 2, 2020, decisions.scc-csc.ca/scc-csc/news/en/item/6899/index.do; "Supreme Court Dismisses First Nations' Challenge against Trans Mountain Pipeline."

p. 273 *The province wound up:* Justine Hunter, "Trans Mountain Clears Legal Hurdle as B.C. Supreme Court Dismisses Environmental Certificate Challenges," *Globe and Mail*, May 24, 2018, theglobeandmail.com/canada/british-columbia/article-trans-mountain-clears-legal-hurdle-as-bc-supreme-court-dismisses.

p. 273 *The conditions require consulting:* "Changes to Environmental Assessment Certificate for Trans Mountain," Environment and Climate Change Strategy, BC Gov News, February 24, 2022, news.gov.bc.ca/releases/2022ENV0004-000218.

19. Steta7áteltway Chet: We're on Even Ground

p. 275 *While Whistler had undertaken consultation:* Squamish Nation v. British Columbia (Community, Sport and Cultural Development), 2014 BCSC 991, bccourts.ca/jdb-txt/sc/14/09/2014BCSC0991.htm.

p. 277 *In 2011, both the Squamish and Lil'wat Nations:* Squamish Nation v. British Columbia (Community, Sport and Cultural Development), paras. 32, 59, 60.

p. 277 *The Nations reiterated:* Squamish Nation v. British Columbia (Community, Sport and Cultural Development), paras. 67, 68.

p. 279 *The province would only review:* Squamish Nation v. British Columbia (Community, Sport and Cultural Development), para. 90.

p. 281 *The BC Supreme Court found:* Squamish Nation v. British Columbia (Community, Sport and Cultural Development), para. 93.

p. 281 *In fact, the duty to consult:* Squamish Nation v. British Columbia (Community, Sport and Cultural Development), para. 137.

p. 281 *The court said it was no surprise:* Isabelle Brideau, *The Duty to Consult Indigenous Peoples* (Ottawa: Library of Parliament, 2019), 2, lop.parl.ca/sites/PublicWebsite/default/en_CA/ResearchPublications/201917E.

p. 281 *In 2017, the province, Whistler:* Memorandum of Understanding between the Squamish Nation, the Lil'wat Nation, the Government of British Columbia, Resort Municipality of Whistler, and Whistler Blackcomb, February 24, 2017, whistler.ca/sites/default/files/2021/Aug/related/27564/final_signed_mou_amended.pdf; Protocol Agreement between Lil'Wat Nation, Squamish Nation, and Resort Municipality of Whistler, July 16, 2018, whistler.ca/sites/default/files/2020/Jul/current-projects/pdf/24515/2018-07-16-protocol_agreement-signed.pdf.

p. 281 *A revised official community plan:* Official Community Plan, 28, whistler.ca/ocp/.

p. 281 *Referencing this court challenge:* Braden Dupuis, "Whistler's Official Community Plan Adopted at Long Last," *Pique Newsmagazine*, June 25, 2020, piquenewsmagazine.com/whistler-news/whistlers-official-community-plan-adopted-2516930.

p. 282 *"I really believe there is:* Dupuis, "Whistler's Official Community Plan Adopted at Long Last."

p. 282 *Shortly after the community plan was approved:* Framework Agreement between the Queen, the Squamish Nation, the Lil'wat Nation, Resort Municipality of Whistler, and Whistler Blackcomb, 2020, whistler.ca/sites/default/files/2020/Jul/current-projects/pdf/24515/framework-agreement-01824707.pdf.

p. 282 *But the court case confirmed:* Whistler is 600,000 acres/2,428 square kilometres. Greater Vancouver is 2,883 square kilometres.

p. 282 *This case came hot on the heels:* Aaron Bruce, case summary of Squamish Indian Band v. British Columbia (Minister of Sustainable Resource Management), [2004] B.C.J. No. 2143.

p. 283 *"Judge (Marvyn) Koenigsberg's decision:* James Tate to Chief Gibby Jacob, Squamish Nation, Memorandum re. Garibaldi Ski Hill—03/0076, in Squamish Nation et al. v. Minister of Sustainable Resource Management et al., 2004 BCSC 1320, October 26, 2004, Ratcliff & Company LLP.

p. 283 *In another case:* Aaron Bruce, case summary of R. v. Lewis, [1996] S.C.J. No. 46.

p. 283 *They lost in the Supreme Court:* Aaron Bruce, communication with author, February 2023.

Part Six. Sḵwx̱wú7mesh Temíxwcht: Our Squamish Lands

p. 286 *"We look at the maps:* "Trans Mountain Expansion Project: Final Argument of Squamish Nation," January 12, 2016, Canada Energy Regulator, 11, docs2.cer-rec.gc.ca/ll-eng/llisapi.dll/fetch/2000/90464/90552/548311/956726/2392873/2449925/2451054/2905662/C319-40-2_-_Final_Argument_of_the_Squamish_Nation_%2801164829%29_-_A4X5E7.pdf?nodeid=2905007&vernum=-2.

p. 287 *The Squamish Nation had closely watched:* Minutes of the Squamish Indian Band Council Meeting, October 26, 1971, ARC.CPJI.0004b, Squamish Nation Archives and Cultural Collections, North Vancouver, BC, 16.

p. 287 *The federal government decided:* "Chronology of Events Leading to the Final Agreement with the Nisga'a Tribal Council," Crown-Indigenous Relations and Northern Affairs Canada, September 15, 2010, rcaanc-cirnac.gc.ca/eng/1100100031295/1543409973702.

20. Ch'xwitas Chet kwi Úxwumixwcht: We're Adding On to Our Communities

p. 289 *In a 1992 profile:* Scott Simpson, "Joe Mathias Possesses the Inner Strength of a True, Traditional Leader," *Vancouver Sun*, September 21, 1992.

p. 290 *He worked with the First Nations Summit:* "First Nations Summit Mourns the Loss of Chief Joe Mathias," First Nations Summit, March 10, 2000, fns.bc.ca/wp-content/uploads/1969/12/joe-mathias031000.pdf.

p. 290 *They fought for further clauses:* "Constitution Act, 1982 Section 35," Indigenous Foundations, First Nations & Indigenous Studies, University of British Columbia, indigenousfoundations.arts.ubc.ca/constitution_act_1982_section_35.

p. 290 *"It's a logical follow-through:* Glenn Bohn, "Chief a Life-Long Rights Advocate," *Vancouver Sun*, March 11, 2000.

p. 290 *"Chief Joe Mathias" became synonymous:* Karen Gram, "Squamish People Run Their Band Like a Business," *Vancouver Sun*, July 26, 1989.

p. 290 *"Our band councils and our people:* "British Columbia—Squamish Band," R1044, RG33-115, 1969–1974, Library and Archives Canada, 5–6, 11–12, 22–23, 34, recherche-collection-search.bac-lac.gc.ca/eng/home/record?app=fonandcol&IdNumber=5095363.

p. 291 *"We're not in a position:* Larry Pynn, "We'll Take the Money, Chief Says of Claims," *Vancouver Sun*, 1985.

p. 291 *But the Ambleside land was valued at:* Pynn, "We'll Take the Money."

p. 291 *Again, T'echux̱ánm Siýám̓ was quick to call out:* Ron Rose, "'Band Won't Be Exploited': Chief Questions Roadblocks When Indians Act on Own," *Vancouver Sun*, July 31, 1971.

p. 292 *"Chief Mathias came to the conclusion:* "A Community Development Plan," Sḵwx̱wú7mesh Úxwumixw, 2010, 12.

p. 292 *"We learned in the first two years:* Jennifer M. Sankey, "Using Indigenous Legal Processes to Strengthen Indigenous Jurisdiction: Squamish Nation Land Use Planning and the Squamish Nation Assessment of the Woodfibre Liquefied Natural Gas Projects" (PhD thesis, University of British Columbia, 2021), 108, open.library.ubc.ca/media/stream/pdf/24/1.0402462/4.

p. 293 *In a* Vancouver Sun *article:* Mary Lynn Young, "Native Awareness Urged," *Vancouver Sun*, August 3, 1990.

p. 293 *As Saskatchewan Premier Tommy Douglas put it:* "A Look at First Nations Prohibition of Alcohol," Indigenous Corporate Training Inc., October 20, 2016, ictinc.ca/blog/first-nations-prohibition-of-alcohol.

p. 293 *Going ahead without treaty:* "BC and Squamish First Nation Sign Sea-to-Sky Agreement," Ministry Transportation and Infrastructure, Government of British Columbia, September 12, 2008, archive.news.gov.bc.ca/releases/news_releases_2005-2009/2008TRAN0072-001387.pdf.

p. 294 *These additions may expand:* "What Is an Addition to Reserve?" Indigenous Services Canada, March 17, 2023, sac-isc.gc.ca/eng/1332267668918/1611930372477#chp1.

p. 294 *An improved process was updated:* "Overview of the Reserve Creation Process," Links to Learning, Indigenous and Northern Affairs Canada, December 2017, links-to-learning.ca/files/additions-to-reserve-inac-pdf.pdf.

p. 294 *The province also agreed:* "British Columbia—Squamish Nation Umbrella Agreement," June 2006; "A Community Development Plan," Sḵwx̱wú7mesh Úxwumixw, 2010.

p. 294 *This included adding the Mortenson property:* "A Community Development Plan."

p. 295 *The Cheekye development is meant:* MNP, "Economic Impact Analysis of the Cheekye Fan Development," prepared for Sḵwx̱wú7mesh Úxwumixw, October 2011.

p. 295 *The plan includes building:* "Economic Impact Analysis of the Cheekye Fan Development"; Steven Chua, "Cheekye Fan Debris Barrier Application Inches Forward," *Squamish Chief*, October 7, 2022, squamishchief.com/local-news/cheeky-fan-debris-barrier-application-inches-forward-5929496.

p. 295 *The Sḵwx̱wú7mesh have pursued:* Lori Culbert, "Squamish Nation Plans to Develop 350 Acres, Most of It in North Vancouver and West Vancouver," *Vancouver Sun*, March 29, 2023, vancouversun.com/business/real-estate/squamish-nation-plans-to-develop-350-acres-most-of-it-in-north-vancouver-and-west-vancouver.

p. 295 *Back in 1968, Simon Baker wrote:* "A Community Development Plan," 16.

p. 297 *In 2011, the Sḵwx̱wú7mesh Úxwumixw announced:* Jennifer Thuncher, "Housing beyond Quest Uni Part of Long-Term Squamish Nation Plan," *Squamish Chief*, July 19, 2017, squamishchief.com/local-news/housing-beyond-quest-uni-part-of-long-term-squamish-nation-plan-3346949; Culbert, "Squamish Nation Plans to Develop 350 Acres."

p. 297 *"This is an historic day:* Jesse Ferreras, "Squamish Nation Purchases New Land for Reserves in Squamish Valley," *Pique Newsmagazine*, November 2, 2011, piquenewsmagazine.com/sea-to-sky/squamish-nation-purchases-new-land-for-reserves-in-squamish-valley-2489682; "Squamish Nation Buys Crown Land for Future Housing," BC Gov News (news release), November 2, 2011, news.gov.bc.ca/01086.

p. 297 *In combination with a contribution:* Alison Taylor, "A Cornerstone of Indigenous Culture," *Empire-Advance*, July 17, 2018, empireadvance.ca/local-news/a-cornerstone-of-indigenous-culture-4290033; Partners Creating Shared Legacies from the 2010 Olympic and Paralympic Winter Games (Shared Legacies Agreement) between the Squamish and Lil'wat Nations, the Vancouver 2010 Bid Corporation, and the Province of British Columbia, November 22, 2002.

p. 297 *The Shared Legacies Agreement also included:* Shared Legacies Agreement.

p. 297 *Decades later, in 2021:* Steven Chua, "First Nation Reclaims Land in Squamish," *Squamish Chief*, August 13, 2021, squamishchief.com/local-news/squamish-nation-reclaims-lands-near-stawamus-ir-24-reserve-4221001.

21. Swiy̓át: Woodfibre

p. 299 *In a document written for:* Kelts'tkínem (Aaron Bruce) and Emma Hume, "The Squamish Nation Assessment Process: Getting to Consent," Ratcliff & Company LLP (website), November 2015, ratcliff.com/wp-content/uploads/2020/10/The-Squamish-Nation-Assessment-Process-Getting-To-Consent-Ratcliff.pdf.

p. 300 *Woodfibre LNG first sought:* Jennifer M. Sankey, "Using Indigenous Legal Processes to Strengthen Indigenous Jurisdiction: Squamish Nation Land Use Planning and the Squamish Nation Assessment of the Woodfibre Liquefied Natural Gas Projects" (PhD thesis, University of British Columbia, 2021), 212–22, open.library.ubc.ca/media/stream/pdf/24/1.0402462/4.

p. 300 We were involved in many other EA processes: in Sankey, "Using Indigenous Legal Processes to Strengthen Indigenous Jurisdiction," 226.

p. 302 *The Nation built strict confidentiality:* Sankey, 232–33, 236.

p. 302 *Syetáx̱tn spoke to this:* Sankey, 257.

p. 303 *The team prepared an assessment report:* Sankey, 266–67.

p. 303 *Council voted in favour of proceeding:* Sankey, 269–70, 272.

p. 303 *The province promised several parcels:* Clare Hennig, "Crown Land to Be Returned to Squamish Nation, Including World-Class Rock Climbing Area," CBC News, October 28, 2019, cbc.ca/news/canada/british-columbia/land-transfer-murrin-park-climbing-1.5337627.

p. 304 *"In order to get to consent:* Kelts'tkínem and Hume, "The Squamish Nation Assessment Process,"12, 15, 17, 19.

22. Seṅáḵw: Inside the Head of the Bay

p. 308 *In 2019, 87 percent:* "Squamish Nation Members Approve Seṅáḵw Development Project and Partnership through Referendum Vote," Sḵwx̱wú7mesh Úxwumixw, December 10, 2019; see also the project website at senakw.com/vision.

p. 310 *On May 25, 2022:* "Services Agreement Signed for Seṅáḵw Development," Sḵwx̱wú7mesh Úxwumixw, May 25, 2022, squamish.net/senakw-services-agreement/.

p. 311 *Construction began in September 2022:* Nch'ḵaỷ Keynote Presentation, Nch'ḵaỷ Development Corporation, February 2023.

p. 311 *"Today's announcement not only:* "Historic Partnership between Sḵwx̱wú7mesh Úxwumixw and Canada to Create Nearly 3,000 Homes in Vancouver," Sḵwx̱wú7mesh Úxwumixw, September 6, 2022, squamish.net/senakw-funding/.

23. Chet wa Nséyx̱nitas wa lhtiṁácht: We Are Protecting Our Ways of Life

p. 313 *"In my wildest dreams:* "Trans Mountain Expansion Project: Final Argument of Squamish Nation," January 12, 2016, Canada Energy Regulator, 20–21, docs2.cer-rec.gc.ca/ll-eng/llisapi.dll/fetch/2000/90464/90552/548311/956726/2392873/2449925/2451054/2905662/C319-40-2_-_Final_Argument_of_the_Squamish_Nation_%2801164829%29_-_A4X5E7.pdf?nodeid=2905007&vernum=-2.

p. 314 *"There was nothing else to do:* Nancy Bleck, Katherine Dodds, and Telálsemḵin Siỷáṁ (Chief Bill Williams), *Picturing Transformation: Nexw-Áyantsut* (Vancouver: Figure 1 Publishing, 2013), 87.

p. 316 *In 2001, the Sḵwx̱wú7mesh Úxwumixw created:* Land and Resources Committee, *X̱ay Temíxw Land Use Plan*, first draft, Sḵwx̱wú7mesh Úxwumixw, May 2001, static1.squarespace.com/static/58c0c358ebbd1a9d3cd1ecf0/t/5ee52954ac46160bd52a731e/1592076630541/Squamish+Nation+Sacred+Land+Use+Plan.pdf; "A Community Development Plan," Sḵwx̱wú7mesh Úxwumixw, 2010, 12.

p. 316 *For our people, the creation of this plan:* Land and Resources Committee, *X̱ay Temíxw Land Use Plan*, 6.

p. 316 *"It is harder for our carvers:* Land and Resources Committee.

p. 316 *"It's important to show:* Land and Resources Committee.

p. 317 *"Without this land:* Land and Resources Committee, 7.

p. 317 *This X̱ay Temíxw Land Use Plan:* Land and Resources Committee, 18.

p. 317 *The agreement further protects:* "A Community Development Plan," Sḵwx̱wú7mesh Úxwumixw, 12.

p. 317 *The agreement added over 11,000 hectares:* "Province and Squamish Nation Reach Land-Use Agreement," Ministry of Agriculture and Lands, Government of British Columbia, July 26, 2007, archive.news.gov.bc.ca/releases/news_releases_2005-2009/2007AL0036-000961.pdf.

p. 318 *According to Fisheries and Oceans Canada:* "Preliminary Impact Assessments of Proposed Port Development in the Mamquam Channel and Rail Yard Expansion in the Squamish Estuary," Department of the Environment, December 1972, waves-vagues.dfo-mpo.gc.ca/Library/40591517.pdf.

p. 318 *By the 1980s, they counted:* "Squamish River Watershed Salmon Recovery Plan," Golder Associates Ltd., May 2005, waves-vagues.dfo-mpo.gc.ca/Library/332825.pdf.

p. 319 *Removing the spit:* Kwetásel'wet (Steph Wood), "Inside a 50-Year Journey to Reopen the 'Lungs' of the Squamish River," *The Narwhal*, September 17, 2022, thenarwhal.ca/squamish-nation-estuary-restoration.

p. 319 *The Sḵwx̱wú7mesh Úxwumixw also funded:* "Natural Capital Assets: The Squamish Estuary," Squamish River Watershed Society, squamishwatershed.com/uploads/1/1/2/1/11216935/squamish_estuary_natural_capital_assets_report_srws.pdf.

p. 319 *"As our lands heal:* Patricia Heintzman and Joyce Williams, "Let's Bring Back the Health of the Squamish Estuary through Restoration and Reconciliation," *Squamish Reporter*, October 29, 2021, squamishreporter.com/2021/10/29/lets-bring-back-the-health-of-the-squamish-estuary-through-restoration-and-reconciliation.

p. 319 *As of 2022, the two First Nations:* Kwetásel'wet (Steph Wood), "Meet the Cheakamus, the Only Community Forest to Develop Carbon Offsets in B.C.," *The Narwhal*, August 14, 2021, thenarwhal.ca/bc-forests-carbon-offsets-cheakamus/.

p. 320 *The Nation also asserted:* "Squamish Nation Demands Moratorium of Old-Growth Logging," Sḵwx̱wú7mesh Úxwumixw, June 10, 2021, squamish.net/old-growth; Sḵwx̱wú7mesh Úxwumixw to Premier John Horgan, letter re. Old Growth Strategic Review Recommendations and Immediate Referrals, June 10, 2021, squamish.net/wp-content/uploads/2021/09/Letter-re-Old-Growth-Strategic-Review-Recommendations-Immediate-Deferrals-in-SN-Territory_Signed.pdf.

p. 320 *In 2021, the Nation also protected:* "Information Notice: Dakota Bowl—BC Timber Sales Licence A87126 in Sḵwx̱wú7mesh (Squamish Nation) Territory," agreement between Sḵwx̱wú7mesh Úxwumixw and the Province of British Columbia, February 4, 2021, www2.gov.bc.ca/assets/gov/farming-natural-resources-and-industry/forestry/bc-timber-sales/updates-information-releases/bcts_tch_dakota_bowl_infonote_a87126_final.pdf.

p. 320 *The preserved forest is important:* Keili Bartlett, "Dakota Bowl Protected under Deal with Squamish Nation," *Coast Reporter*, March 1, 2021, coastreporter.net/local-news/dakota-bowl-protected-under-deal-with-squamish-nation-3469610.

p. 320 *According to X̱áts'alánexw Siýám̓:* X̱áts'alánexw Siýám̓ (Chief August Jack Khatsahlano) and Syex̱wáltn (Dominic Charlie), *Squamish Legends*, ed. Oliver Wells (Vancouver: C. Chamberlain and F.T. Coan, 1967).

p. 320 *Here is the story as told by:* Sx̱áaltxw Siýám̓ (Chief Louis Miranda), "Say-noth-kay: The Two-Headed Serpent," ARC.CULM.0055, Squamish Nation Archives and Cultural Collections, North Vancouver, BC.

p. 323 *Sesémiya (Tracy Williams) explained:* Land and Resources Committee, 40.

Wanáxwsw̓it Chat eḵ' tkwi aw̓t Stélmexwcht: We Honour Our Future Generations

p. 326 *While there were only a handful:* Suzanne Gessner, Tracey Herbert, and Aliana Parker, *Report on the Status of BC First Nations Languages*, 4th ed. (Brentwood Bay, BC: First Peoples' Cultural Council, 2022), fpcc.ca/wp-content/uploads/2023/02/FPCC-LanguageReport-23.02.14-FINAL.pdf.

p. 326 *Sḵwx̱wú7mesh Sníchim classes:* "Sḵwx̱wú7mesh Sníchim: Learn More," "Language and Cultural Affairs," Sḵwx̱wú7mesh Úxwumixw, squamish.net/language-cultural-affairs.

p. 327 *"It's my language:* Kirsten Baker-Williams, "Na Mi K'anatsut ta Sḵwx̱wú7mesh Sníchim Chet: Squamish Language Revitalization: From the Hearts and the Minds of the Language Speakers" (master's thesis, University of British Columbia, 2006), 66, open.library.ubc.ca/soa/cIRcle/collections/ubctheses/831/items/1.0092805.

p. 327 *Canoe journeys have taken off:* "Written Evidence of the Squamish Nation: Westridge Delivery Line Relocation, Hearing Order MH-048-2018, File No. OF-Fac-Oil-T260-2017-10 01," July 27, 2018, Canada Energy Regulator, docs2.cer-rec.gc.ca/ll-eng/llisapi.dll/fetch/2000/90464/90552/548311/3173243/3412396/3563432/3575539/3595843/A93274-2_Written_Evidence_of_the_Squamish_Nation_-_A6G4F8.pdf?nodeid=3593638&vernum=-2.

p. 327 *They co-founded the Lheṅt Aw̓txw:* Clare Hennig, "Two Weavers Stop Salish Tradition from 'Slipping into History,'" CBC News, August 28, 2017, cbc.ca/news/canada/british-columbia/salish-wool-weaving-teachings-1.4264028.

p. 328 *The Nation has said:* "Developing Úxwumixw 2050: Sḵwx̱wú7mesh Generational Plan," Sḵwx̱wú7mesh Úxwumixw, July 15, 2022, 1; see also the plan's website at squamish2050.net.

p. 329 *A consultant hired by the Nation:* Rebecca Wortzman, Big River Analytics, to Ruby Carrico, email re planning with Sḵwx̱wú7mesh Úxwumixw, March 24, 2023.

p. 329 *Hiy̓áṁ Housing wrote a strategic plan: The Squamish Nation Strategic Plan 2022–2026*, Sḵwx̱wú7mesh Úxwumixw, 2022, reports.squamish.net/wp-content/uploads/2022/08/Strategic-Plan-2022-2026_web-1.pdf.

p. 331 *In addition to Hiy̓áṁ Housing, the Sḵwx̱wú7mesh:* Dan Fumano and Lori Culbert, "'This Is Just the Beginning': First Nations' Real Estate Megaprojects Game-Changing for Metro Vancouver," *Vancouver Sun*, July 15, 2022, vancouversun.com/business/real-estate/indigenous-developers-to-create-25000-new-homes-in-metro-vancouver.

p. 331 *In 2022, the MST Corporation:* "Vanmag's 2022 Power 50 List," *Vancouver Magazine*, January 20, 2022, vanmag.com/city/power-50/vanmags-2022-power-50-list.

p. 332 *According to Sx̱áaltxw Siy̓áṁ:* Randy Bouchard and Dorothy Kennedy, "Utilization of Fish, Beach Foods, and Marine Mammals by the Squamish Indian People of British Columbia," 1976, ARC.CULM.06.01, Squamish Nation Archives and Cultural Collections, North Vancouver, BC, 111.

p. 334 *"In our world, where we come from:* Squamish Lil'wat Cultural Centre, *Where Rivers, Mountains and People Meet* (Whistler, BC: Spo7ez Cultural Centre & Community Society, 2010), 162.

p. 335 I am telling the story of a seal: Kwítelut (Lena Jacobs), *Sealiya* (Victoria, BC: Trafford Publishing, 2010).

ACKNOWLEDGEMENTS

MANY HANDS were involved in and essential to creating this book. Kelts'tkínem (Aaron Bruce), Iyál̓ (Vanessa Campbell), Paítsmuk̲ (David Jacobs), Yumk̲s (Dr. Rudy Reimer), Khelsilem (Dustin Rivers), and Ts'elsáwanexw (Aaron Williams) provided invaluable consultation on Squamish Language, history, and culture.

For their tremendous research support, we acknowledge James Bradshaw, Kelts'tkínem (Aaron Bruce), Calvin Dawson, Andrew Latimer, Arthur Macapagal, Alexis Mellish, Alyssa Mulat, Yumk̲s (Dr. Rudy Reimer), Leslhá7lhamaat (Elizabeth Ross), Lilian Shams-Amiri, Nick Weber, Genevieve Wick, Louise Williams, and Sit'ax̲el (Peter Yelton).

For their vital administrative support in coordinating the logistics of this project, we thank Peter Baker, Arthur Macapagal, Ts'uxalwet (Danielle Mellish), Alyssa Mulat, Karen Ng, Jill Peters, Grace Strachan, and Nick Weber.

Finally, we are grateful to Kwetásel'wet (Stephanie Wood), without whom there would be no words in this book.

Huy chexw a! (Thank you!)

IMAGE CREDITS

Cover (L–R, top to bottom)

Courtesy of the Squamish Lil'wat Cultural Centre (Squamish River); Flowmarq Creative, 2017 (basket); Museum of North Vancouver, "Chief Joe Capilano," NVMA 2849; Simon Hayter, "Welcome Figure," 2017; Museum of North Vancouver, "First Nations men in the canoe *Capilano Warrior*," NVMA 955; Ben Nelms, with permission from Chepx̱ímiya Siỷám̓ (Chief Janice George); Courtesy of the Squamish Lil'wat Cultural Centre (cedar harvest); Courtesy of the Squamish Lil'wat Cultural Centre (child); Albert Law, courtesy of X̱álek̲'/Sek̲'yú Siỷám̓ (Chief Ian Campbell) (painting); Museum of North Vancouver, "Louis Miranda in his home on the Mission Reserve, December 1983," NVMA 6214; Renderings courtesy of the Squamish Nation, Design Architect: Revery Architecture, Architect of Record: Kasian Architecture, Interior Design and Planning, Renderings: Tandem Studios; Alana Paterson, with permission from Styawat (Leigh Joseph)

Interior (by page number)

ii Andrew Darlington/Unsplash; **xii** Alana Paterson; **2** Alana Paterson; **5** Alana Paterson, with permission from Styawat (Leigh Joseph) and Myia Antone; **6** Anastase Maragos/Unsplash; **11** Albert Law, courtesy of X̱álek̲'/Sek̲'yú Siỷám̓ (Chief Ian Campbell); **12** Albert Law, courtesy of X̱álek̲'/Sek̲'yú Siỷám̓ (Chief Ian Campbell); **14** Courtesy of the Squamish Lil'wat Cultural Centre; **18** Courtesy of X̱álek̲'/Sek̲'yú Siỷám̓ (Chief Ian Campbell); **23** Museum of North Vancouver, "Sk̲wx̱wú7mesh (Squamish) Welcome Figure," NVMA 1310; **24** Dave Alan/iStock; **28** Courtesy of Yumk̲s (Dr. Rudy Reimer); **32** With the permission of artist Tyee (Floyd Joseph); **35** Museum of North Vancouver, "Watching the weather—Dominic Charlie, 14 July 1972," NVMA 16013; **38** Courtesy of X̱álek̲'/Sek̲'yú Siỷám̓ (Chief Ian Campbell); **43** Isaac Borrego; **46** City of Vancouver Archives, "Siwash Rock, English Bay," AM1376-: CVA 1376-375.13; **49** Tom Wheatly/Unsplash; **50** Courtesy of the Squamish Lil'wat Cultural Centre; **55** Courtesy of the Squamish Lil'wat Cultural Centre; **58** Alana Paterson; **61** Courtesy of the Squamish Lil'wat Cultural Centre; **64** City of Vancouver Archives, "Mrs. Chief George (Ce-qual-lia/Se-quail-yah) cooking salmon over open fire at No. 3 Reserve," AM54-S4-: In P114; **68** Courtesy of the Squamish Lil'wat Cultural Centre; **71** City of Vancouver Archives, "Squamish dwellings on the shore of Coal Harbour," AM54-S4-: St Pk N4; **72** Courtesy of the Squamish Lil'wat Cultural Centre; **75** Courtesy of the Royal BC Museum, Image 18294 A, B; **77** Courtesy of the Squamish Lil'wat Cultural Centre; **78** Isaac Borrego; **81** Courtesy of Yumk̲s (Dr. Rudy Reimer), DjRt-12 Archaeological Site Inventory Form by Dave Hall; **84** Courtesy of Yumk̲s (Dr. Rudy Reimer); **87** Courtesy of Yumk̲s (Dr. Rudy Reimer); **88** Alana Paterson; **93** City of Vancouver Archives, "View of Kitsilano Indian Reserve looking east," AM1376-: CVA 1376-203; **94** Overflightstock Ltd./iStock;

101 Courtesy of the Squamish Lil'wat Cultural Centre; **105** Stockstudiox/iStock; **110** Jason Mrachina/Flickr; **112** Overflightstock Ltd./iStock; **118** City of Vancouver Archives, "*Supplejack's Grave* [detail], Chaythoos, First Narrows, circa 1888," from J.S. Matthews, *Conversations with Khahtsahlano: 1932–1954* (Vancouver: self-published, 1955), 136D; **122** The High Fin Sperm Whale/Wikimedia Commons, "Model of HMS *Discovery* (1789) at the Vancouver Maritime Museum"; **124** Museum of North Vancouver, "Louis Miranda in his home on the Mission Reserve, December 1983," NVMA 6214; **129** Museum of North Vancouver, "Basket weaver and relatives, 1930s," NVMA 7120; **132** R_Koopmans/iStock; **135** Library and Archives Canada, "Royal Proclamation, King George III of England, Issued October 7, 1763, Broadside," e010778430, AMICUS no. 7468714; **136–37** City of Vancouver Archives, "Hastings Sawmill, 1872," AM54-S4-: CVA 371-3178; **140** With permission from the Squamish Public Library History Archives; **144** City of Vancouver Archives, "William Nahanee with a group of longshoremen on the dock of Moodyville Sawmill," AM54-S4-: Mi P2; **146** City of Vancouver Archives, "The Great Vancouver Fire," AM1562-: 75-54; **149** With permission from the Squamish Public Library History Archives; **151** City of Vancouver Archives, "Indians making canoe from tree trunk at mission, opposite Vancouver, B.C.," AM54-S4-: SGN 437; **154** © Vatican Media; **159** Museum of North Vancouver, "St. Paul's Indian School," NVMA 4838; **161** City of Vancouver Archives, "St. Paul's Catholic Church, North Vancouver," AM1376-F14-: CVA 312-24; **165** City of Vancouver Archives, "*Supplejack's Grave*, Chaythoos, First Narrows, circa 1888," from J.S. Matthews, *Conversations with Khahtsahlano: 1932–1954* (Vancouver: self-published, 1955), 136D; **166** Museum of North Vancouver, "Primary pupils outside St. Paul's Indian Residential School, 541 W. Keith Rd.," NVMA 4839; **171** Courtesy of the *North Shore News*; **175** Adrian Wyld/The Canadian Press; **178** Museum of North Vancouver, "Canoeing on Capilano River at the Salmon Pool, 1900," NVMA 1470; **182–83** Museum of North Vancouver, "Chief Joe Capilano and delegation of First Nations leaders, May 1908," NVMA 957; **184** City of Vancouver Archives, "Head and shoulders portrait of August Jack Khahtsahlano," AM54-S4-: LP 3; **190** City of Vancouver Archives, "Dominion Day Indian canoe races near the foot of Carrall Street," AM54-S4-: In P4; **192** City of Vancouver Archives, "August Jack Khahtsahlano and others at the Re-dedication of Stanley Park," AM54-S4-2-: CVA 371-2406; **194** City of Vancouver Archives, "Indian Teepees at Mission," AM54-S4-: In P12; **197** City of Vancouver Archives, "Plan showing parcels 'A', 'B' & 'C': Kitsilano Indian Reserve, No. 6 of the Squamish Band, Vancouver, B.C.," COV-S365-: MAP 859; **198** City of Vancouver Archives, "Indian Canoes [at] foot of Richards [Street]," AM54-S4-: In P29; **201** Courtesy of the Royal BC Museum, Image PN08924; **204** Provided by the Squamish Nation; **206** Alana Paterson; **211** City of Vancouver Archives, "Mission Indian Village, opposite Vancouver," AM54-S4-: SGN 1460; **215** Museum of North Vancouver, "North Vancouver Squamish Reserve Indian Band outside Dept. of Indian Affairs building, Vancouver, all identified, 1921," NVMA 4834; **218** Museum of North Vancouver, "Commemorating Squamish Amalgamation," NVMA 4835; **222** *The Native Voice* 2, no. 7 (July 1914): 4; **225** Museum of North Vancouver, "Baseball team, 1929," NVMA 4843; **226** Museum of North Vancouver, "Lacrosse team outside St. Paul's Church, all identified," NVMA 4799; **229** City of Vancouver Archives, "Mrs. August Jack (Swanania or Marion) Khahtsahlano holding a baby," AM54-S4-: Port P469; **230** City of Vancouver Archives, "Sko-Mish-Oath: The territory of the Squamish Indian Peoples: Indian villages and landmarks: Burrard Inlet and Howe Sound before the whitemans came," AM54-S13-: MAP 351b; **234** Renderings courtesy of the Squamish Nation, Design Architect: Revery Architecture, Architect of

Record: Kasian Architecture, Interior Design and Planning, Renderings: Tandem Studios; **238** Michael Wheatley/Alamy; **240** Alana Paterson, with permission from Khelsilem (Dustin Rivers) and Sxwíxwtn (Wilson Williams); **243** City of Vancouver Archives, "Group near Jericho Charlie's home on Kitsilano Indian Reserve (Snauq)," AM54-S4-: In P1.1; **245** City of Vancouver Archives, "Plate 83: Grandview, Victoria Drive–Napier Street–False Creek–Fifth/Railway Avenue," AM1594-: MAP 342b-: MAP 342b.19; **246** City of Vancouver Archives, "Fairview looking west across False Creek," AM54-S4-: Dist P81; **249** Ts'uxalwet (Danielle Mellish); **250** Alana Paterson; **252** Courtesy of Downtown Vancouver BIA; **257** Courtesy of the Squamish Lil'wat Cultural Centre; **258** Courtesy of the Squamish Lil'wat Cultural Centre; **262** Michael Wheatley/ Alamy; **267** Darryl Dyck/The Canadian Press; **268** Jonathan Hayward/The Canadian Press; **271** Darryl Dyck/The Canadian Press; **274** Isaac Borrego; **279** Courtesy of the Squamish Lil'wat Cultural Centre; **280** Courtesy of the Squamish Lil'wat Cultural Centre; **284** Renderings courtesy of the Squamish Nation, Design Architect: Revery Architecture, Architect of Record: Kasian Architecture, Interior Design and Planning, Renderings: Tandem Studios; **288** David Neel/Collection, National Gallery of Canada, Ottawa; **295** Sean Kilpatrick/ The Canadian Press; **296** Courtesy of Postmedia Network Inc., *Vancouver Sun*, March 11, 2000; **298** Courtesy of Woodfibre LNG; **301** Courtesy of Woodfibre LNG; **304** SEASTOCK/iStock; **306** Renderings courtesy of the Squamish Nation, Design Architect: Revery Architecture, Architect of Record: Kasian Architecture, Interior Design and Planning, Renderings: Tandem Studios; **309** Ben Nelms, with permission from Chepx̱ímiya Siỷám̓ (Chief Janice George); **310** Provided by the Squamish Nation; **312** Jasper Garratt/Unsplash; **315** Alana Paterson; **318** Isaac Borrego; **323** Alana Paterson; **327** Courtesy of Ta na wa Ns7éyx̱nitm ta Snew̓íyelh (Squamish Nation Language & Cultural Affairs); **328** Courtesy of the Squamish Nation; **330** Alana Paterson, with permission from Styawat (Leigh Joseph); **333** Alana Paterson; **334** Courtesy of the Squamish Nation Education Department, Kwítelut (Lena Jacobs), *Sealiya* (Victoria, BC: Trafford Publishing, 2010)

INDEX

Note: Page references in italics refer to photographs and illustrations

Black Tusk (T'ak't'ak'muy̓íṅ tl'a iṅinyáx̱a7n), 22
blackberries (*sk̲w'élemxw*), 65
blankets, x, 70, 73–74, 75, 152
blueberries, 26; *iyálk̲p* (Alaska blueberries), 65
Boas, Franz, 38, 143
Bouchard, Randy: on kin-groups, 53; on moral code, 52; on seasonal activities, 65; on settlers, 187, 196; on Sk̲wx̱wú7mesh relations with neighbours, 19, 98, 99, 100, 103, 113, 114; *Squamish Indian Land Use and Occupancy* report (with Kennedy), 37, 53, 90, 91, 99, 104, 106, 116; on summer spots in Burrard Inlet, 20; on Trutch, 189
boxing, 224
Brackendale, 203–4
Brevner, Lauren: *snékwem* mural (with Xwalacktun (James Harry)), *252*
Britannia Beach (Shishay̓u7áy), 104, *105*
British Columbia: colonial development, 137–39, 146–47, 181–83; Douglas treaties, 185; European settlement and encroachment, 186–87, 187–89; joins Confederation, 189–91, 223; modern treaty negotiations, 287, 290, 292; reserves and, 183, 185, 188–89, 195–96, 205, 207, 208–12, 223; Trans Mountain Expansion Project and, 273
broadleaf maple (*k̲'emel̓áy̓*), 69
Brown, Orene, 180
Bruce, Aaron (Kelts'tkínem), 299–300, 304–5
Buck Mountain rock shelter (Nepítl'), 86
Buckskin Gloves (boxing program), 224
bullrushes, 74
burial practices, 66–67, 87, 167
Burnaby, Robert, 186
Burnaby Mountain (Lhek̲w'lhúk̲w'ay̓tn), 25, 265–66
Burrard Inlet: clam beds, 26, 65; ecological impacts from colonialism, 152–53, 266, 313; first church in, 159–60; first colonial survey, 186; first Europeans in, 125–27, 128–30, 130–31; lithics (stone tools) found in, 81; settler attempts to determine Indigenous "ownership," 196; as traditional Sk̲wx̱wú7mesh territory, 10–11, 15, 16–17, 20, 25, 92, 265–66
Bushby, Arthur, 162–63
calendar (months), 27
Campbell, Chief Ian. *See* X̱álek̲'/Sek̲'yú Siy̓áṁ
Canada (federal government): Aboriginal title and, 210–11, 248–49; establishment, 139, 189; land claims and, 287, 292; modern treaty negotiations, 287; relations with Indigenous Peoples, 239; reserves and, 189–91, 195–96, 199–200, 202, 205, 223; Seńák̲w development by Sk̲wx̱wú7mesh and, 251, 311; Trans Mountain Expansion Project and, 265, 272. *See also* Indian Act (1876)
Canada v. Canadian Pacific Ltd. (2002), 248–49
Canadian Charter of Rights and Freedoms, 228–29
Canadian Pacific Railway, 195, 248–49
canoes: cedar dugout canoes, 76–77, *77*, *151*; Dominion Day canoe races, *190*; at foot of Richard Street, *198*; revitalization, 327
Capilano, Chief Joe (S7ápelek̲ Siy̓áṁ), 19, 97, 117, 131, *182–83*, 204–5, 290
Capilano, Chief Mathias Joe, 220
Capilano River (Xwmélch'stn), 259, 283. *See also* Xwmélch'stn (Capilano Reserve)
Catholic Church. *See* Roman Catholic Church
cattail, 74
cedar. See *x̱áp'ay̓ay*
census, by the Sk̲wx̱wú7mesh Úxwumixw (Squamish Nation) (2021), 329
ceremony, 70–71
Ch'átatult (Florence, Lena Jacobs's sister), 77
Ch'ax̱áy̓ (Horseshoe Bay), 125
Ch'ék̲ch'ek̲ts (village), 20, 199
Ch'ích'elxwi7k̲w (Seymour Creek, Seymour Reserve), viii, 65, 190, 208, 214, 295, 330
Ch'ich'iyúy (Two Sisters/Lions), 13, 108–9, *110*, 111
Ch'iyák̲mesh (Cheakamus Reserve), 36, 37–38, 47, 130, 214, 215–16, 283
Ch'k̲w'élhp (Scheńk̲, Gibsons Landing), 44–47, 113, 295
Charley, Basil, 219
Charley, Chief, 220
Charley, Dominic, 220
Charley, Louis, 219
Charley, Squamish, 199, 220
Charlie, Dominic (Syex̱wáltn), 26, 34, 35, 36, 37–38, 113, 152–53, 325

Charlie, Frank, 19
Charlie, Jericho (Chinalset), 97, 166, *243*
Cheakamus Community Forest, 319–20, *323*, *330*
Cheakamus Reserve (Ch'iyáḵmesh), 36, 37–38, 47, 130, 214, 215–16, 283
Cheakamus River, 79, 93
Cheekye Fan development, 295
Chepx̱íṁ Siỷáṁ (Chief William George), 199, 200
Chepx̱ímiya Siỷáṁ (Chief Janice George), 73–74, 152, 241, *309*, 316, 327, 332
Chief Mountain (Stawamus Chief, Siỷáṁ Smánit), 13, 48, *49*, *58*, 83
Chilcotin (Sx̱íx̱nam) raid, 106–8
childhood, 59–60
Chinalset (Jericho Charlie), 97, 166, *243*
Chinese people, 142, 195
Chinook Jargon, 44, 133
Chiyálhiya (Lila Johnston), 172
Christianity: attempts to erase traditional culture and spirituality, 164, 166–67; beginnings of Catholic mission, 162–63; Catholic assistance with land claims, 187–88, 190; colonialism and, 155–57, 177; first church in Burrard Inlet, 159–60; oral tradition and, 42; Sḵwx̱wú7mesh engagement with, 114, 156–57, 162; St. Paul's Church (Eslha7áṅ), 153, 156, 157, 160, *161*, 162, 164, *171*. *See also* residential schools; Roman Catholic Church
clams, 25, 26, 65, 99, 152, 266
climate change, 153, 261, 264
clothing, 69, 74–75
Coal Harbour, *71*, 96, 186
Coast Salish Peoples, 19–20, 65–66, 71, 73
Coldwater First Nation v. Canada (Attorney General) (2020), 263. *See also* Trans Mountain Expansion Project
colonialism: Burrard Inlet dispossession, 199–200, 202–4; Christianity and, 155–57, 177; Confederation and, 189–91; disease, 121–22, 138; Doctrine of Discovery, 158, 177; "dying Indian" trope, 123; ecological impacts on Burrard Inlet, 152–53, 266, 313; enfranchisement, 193, 227; Eurocentric view of Indigenous Peoples, 122–23; first contact with explorers, 125–27, 128–30; first survey of Burrard Inlet, 186; Fraser Canyon Gold Rush, 137, 185–86; impacts of, 123, 138, 139, 141–42, 155, 181–82; Indigenous activism against, 183, 187, 207, 221, 224, 289–91; Indigenous labour, 137–38, 145, 146–47, *149*; Indigenous petition to King Edward VII, 117, 204–5; land encroachment, 134, 136, 138–39, 186–87; legislation against Indigenous Peoples, 193–95; predatory treatment of Indigenous Peoples, 142–45; Royal Proclamation, *135*, 136, 138–39, 187, 221; Salish woolly dogs and, 150–52; Sixties Scoop, 227; Sḵwx̱wú7mesh attempts to secure land, 187–89; *terra nullius*, 123, 158, 177; trade and traders, 131, 133–34, 139; treaties, 185, 287, 290, 292. *See also* Indian Act (1876); reserves; residential schools
consent, 208–9, 221, 260, 299, 304–5. *See also* Aboriginal title; consult, duty to
Constitution Act (1982), 260, 290
consult, duty to, 253, 259–61, 265, 269, 270–72, 275–76, 281. *See also* Aboriginal title; consent
Coquitlam (Kw'ikw'tl'ám, Kwikwetlem), 95, 115, 116
Cosmos, Amor de, 142
cottonwood, 26
cranberries, 115
Cronie, 220
culturally modified trees (CMTs), *61*, 79–80, 85, 86
currants, 26

D'Herbomez, Louis-Joseph, 187–88
Dakota Bowl, 320
dance and music, 70–71
David, Chief Basil, 117, 204–5
Davin Report (1879), 168
debitage, 81
Declaration on the Rights of Indigenous Peoples, 299
deer, 57, 86
Defence Islands (Ḵw'émḵw'em), 86–87
Deighton, "Gassy Jack," 163, 187
Delgamuukw v. British Columbia (1997), 276, 245
devil's club, 26–27

Macdonald, John A., 168
Mack, A., 219
Mack, Charlie, 100
Mack, Denny, 219
Mack, Payton, *333*
Macrae, Andsell, 169
"Many People, One Canoe" (2012 gathering), *238*, *262*
maples: *k̲'emel̓áy̓* (broadleaf maple), 69; *t'ek̲t'k̲áy̓* (vine maple), 69
marriage: intermarriage, 19, 92, 97, 114, 115–16, 196; peace through with Stek'ín (Haida), 108–9, 111; Sk̲wx̱wú7mesh practices, 52, 53, 62, 90; women's status and, 228–32
Mary (Yamschloot), *243*
mat shelters, 20
Mathias, Buffalo, 19, 37, 97, 103
Mathias, Chief Joe. *See* T'echux̱ánm Siy̓ám̓
Mathias et al. v. Canada (2001) (Mathias Litigation), viii, 237, 239, 242–43, 243–48, 307
Matthews, J.S.: conversation with Charles Tate, 159–60; conversation with Háx̱sten (Harriet George), 104–6; conversations with X̱ats'alánexw Siy̓ám̓ (Chief August Jack Khatsahlano), 57, 66, 93, 102–3, 113, 125–26, 141, 200, 203; on X̱ats'alánexw Siy̓ám̓, 114, 164–67
McBride, Richard, 205, 208
McDonald, Archibald, 102
McKenna, Joseph, 208
McKenna-McBride Commission, 208–12, 221, 297
medicine man (ritualist, *kwtsi7ts*), 39, 40–42, 59, 60, 66, 67
medicines, traditional, 26–27
Melk̲ws, 29–34, 121, 122
milkweed, 74
Miranda, B., 219
Miranda, Chief Louis. *See* Sx̱áaltxw Siy̓ám̓
Mission Reserve. *See* Eslha7áń
Missionary Oblates of Mary Immaculate, 162
Moberly, Walter, 186
months (calendar), 27
Moody, Emily, 37
Moody, Gabriel, 219
Moody, George, 37, 38, 104
Moody, Harry, 219
Moody, Napoleon, 219
Moody, Richard Clement, 163, 188
Moody, Sewell "Sue," 139
Moody, Tim, 16–17, 19, 66, 106
Moodyville Sawmill, 139, *144*
moral code, 52
Moses, Tommy, 220
Mosquito Creek Marina, 153
Mount Baker (Xwsa7k̲), 42, 47
Mount Garibaldi (Nch'k̲ay̓), 13, *38*, 41, *43*, 47, 79, 80, 115, 282–83
mountain goats, 26, 59, 74, 85
MST Development Corporation, 331
music and dance, 70–71
Musqueam (Xwmétskwiyam), 95, 96, 98, 116, 170, 243–48, 331

Nahanee, Ed, 37, 99, 146
Nahanee, Jason, 174
Nahanee, Jo-Ann, 169, 176
Nahanee, Rennie, 176
Nahanee, Robert, 205, 224
Nahanee, Teressa, 231
Nahanee, Theresa Anne, 228
Nahanee, William, Jr., 219
Nahanee, William "Bill," *144*, 148
names: ancestral names, 71, 138; English (colonial) names, 339–40; place names, viii, 22, 93
Narváez, José María, 125
National Energy Board, 265–66, 268–69, 270, 272, 273
Natrall, Andrew, 220
Natrall, Andy, 26, 37, 104
Nch'áy̓uw̓am (descendants of one head/headman), 52
Nch'k̲ay̓ (Mount Garibaldi), 13, *38*, 41, *43*, 47, 79, 80, 115, 282–83
Nch'k̲ay̓ Development Corporation, 307
neighbouring Peoples: about, 91–92, 96–99, 117; Chilcotin (Sx̱íx̱nam) raid, 106–8; intermarriage with, 19, 92, 97, 114, 115–16, 196; Lúx̱wels (Lil'wat), 99–100, 102; Shishá7lh (Sechelt), 113–14; Stek'ín (Haida), 106, 108–9, 111; Téytk̲in (Stó:lō)-speaking people, 115, 116–17; Yík̲wilhtax̱ (Lekwiltok), 87, 102–4, 106. *See also* Sel̓íl̓witulh (Tsleil-Waututh)
Nekwsáliya (Margaret Locke), 173

ABOUT THE NATION

THE SḴWX̱WÚ7MESH ÚXWUMIXW (Squamish Nation), as a government, has existed since 1923. Prior to 1923, Sḵwx̱wú7meshulh (Squamish's People) were socially, economically, and politically organized into several physical communities, each called an *úxwumixw* ("village; people") in the territory of the Squamish people.

The Sḵwx̱wú7mesh Sníchim (Squamish Language) is spoken today by over three hundred Squamish people as a second language. It has been learned from our Elders who held on to the knowledge after a significant decline in the population of first-language speakers. The Sḵwx̱wú7mesh Sníchim is unique from the language of neighbouring Indigenous Peoples, but considered part of the Coast Salish language family, and part of the wider Salishan language family.

Our people's history spans many millennia of living in and governing our territory. The oldest archaeological site in the territory of the Squamish people is 8,600 years old, at Porteau Cove in Howe Sound. Our oral literature speaks to our origins as a people in our lands through the stories of the first ancestors of the Squamish people. Our people consider ourselves descendants of those first Squamish ancestors who were made or appeared in different parts of Squamish territory.

Squamish culture has been created from our lands, waters, and people over generations. Our people continue to practise many of the traditions, customs, and ways of our ancestors and pass them on to future generations.

Cataloguing in publication information is
available from Library and Archives Canada.
ISBN 978-1-77458-392-0 (paperback)
ISBN 978-1-77458-439-2 (ebook)

Page Two
pagetwo.com

Copyedited by Steph VanderMeulen, Kendra Ward, and Jenny Govier
Proofread by Alison Strobel
Cover design by Khelsilem (Dustin Rivers) and Peter Cocking
Interior design by Peter Cocking
Photo research and permissions by Nadine Bachan
Indexed by Stephen Ullstrom
Printed and bound in Canada by Friesens
Distributed in Canada by Raincoast Books
Distributed in the US and internationally by Macmillan

24 25 26 27 28 5 4 3 2 1

squamish.net